JACQUELINE KAHANOFF

PERSPECTIVES ON ISRAEL STUDIES
S. ILAN TROEN, NATAN ARIDAN, DONNA DIVINE,
DAVID ELLENSON, ARIEH SAPOSNIK, AND
JONATHAN SARNA, EDITORS

Sponsored by the Ben-Gurion Research Institute for the
Study of Israel and Zionism of the Ben-Gurion University of
the Negev and the Schusterman Center for
Israel Studies of Brandeis University

JACQUELINE KAHANOFF

A LEVANTINE WOMAN

—⁂—

DAVID OHANA

INDIANA UNIVERSITY PRESS

This book is a publication of

Indiana University Press
Office of Scholarly Publishing
Herman B Wells Library 350
1320 East 10th Street
Bloomington, Indiana 47405 USA

iupress.org

© 2023 by David Ohana

All rights reserved

No part of this book may be reproduced or utilized in any form or by any means, electronic or mechanical, including photocopying and recording, or by any information storage and retrieval system, without permission in writing from the publisher. The paper used in this publication meets the minimum requirements of the American National Standard for Information Sciences—Permanence of Paper for Printed Library Materials, ANSI Z39.48-1992.

Manufactured in the United States of America

First printing 2023

Library of Congress Cataloging-in-Publication Data

Names: Ohana, David, author.
Title: Jacqueline Kahanoff : a Levantine woman / David Ohana.
Description: Bloomington, Indiana : Indiana University Press, [2023] |
    Series: Perspectives on Israel Studies | Includes bibliographical
    references and index.
Identifiers: LCCN 2023018012 (print) | LCCN 2023018013 (ebook) | ISBN
    9780253066879 (hardback) | ISBN 9780253066886 (paperback) | ISBN
    9780253066893 (ebook)
Subjects: LCSH: Kahanof, Jacqueline. | Jewish women—Egypt—Alexandria—
    Biography. | Jews, Egyptian—Israel—Biography. | BISAC: BIOGRAPHY &
    AUTOBIOGRAPHY / Jewish | BIOGRAPHY & AUTOBIOGRAPHY /
    Women
Classification: LCC DS135.E43 K2986 2023 (print) | LCC DS135.E43 (ebook)
    | DDC 305.892/4062092 [B]—dc23/eng/20230421
LC record available at https://lccn.loc.gov/2023018012
LC ebook record available at https://lccn.loc.gov/2023018013

CONTENTS

Preface   *vii*

Introduction: Levantinism—*Ex oriente lux*   *1*

1. A Tale of Four Cities: Cairo: 1917–1941   *9*
2. Levantinism: A Cultural Theory   *124*
3. Kahanoff's Poetic Journey   *161*
4. "Where Can I Feel at Home?"   *189*
5. Being a Modern Woman   *212*
6. Beyond the Levant   *237*
7. Life at the Edge of the Line   *270*

   Epilogue: Kahanoff and the Humanist
   Mediterranean Heritage   *282*

Notes   *299*
Bibliography   *327*
Index   *347*

PREFACE

THE ESSAYS AND WRITINGS OF Jacqueline Shohet Kahanoff (1917–1979) have made a long journey from their initial appearance, in the 1950s in the United States and in Israel, to the renaissance they currently enjoy in the academic and literary world. Kahanoff now has a secure place in the intellectual pantheon as a herald of Levantine culture. This place has been secured by the publication of *Mongrels or Marvels* (2011), a collection of her essays published by Stanford University Press; three books of her essays (1978, 2005, 2022); and her novel *Jacob's Ladder* (1951) and by academic conferences and extensive research devoted to her legacy.[1] Egyptian-born Kahanoff has thus gained ever-increasing recognition as an esteemed Levantine essayist, as a Mediterranean intellectual, and as one of the central figures of east-west dialogue.

Kahanoff was born in Cairo in 1917. She grew up in a Jewish community embedded in the cosmopolitan society of British-ruled Egypt; she attended a French high school, conversed with her governesses in English, and spoke with the servants in Arabic.[2] Her cosmopolitan sensibilities were later inflected by her experience of French culture and by the pluralistic immigrant culture of the United States and of Israel in its early days.

At the age of twenty-four, Kahanoff immigrated to the United States, where she studied journalism and literature at Columbia University in New York. Concurrently, she attended courses at the New School for Social Research in Greenwich Village. During the Second World War, the New School welcomed many professors and intellectuals, especially Jews, who fled Nazi Europe, inter alia Hannah Arendt, Hans Jonas, Leo Strauss, and Erich Fromm.[3] In New York she befriended French émigré intellectuals such as Raymond Aron, Claude Vigée, and, especially, the anthropologist Claude Lévi-Strauss, with whom she had bonded both romantically and intellectually. Lévi-Strauss's anthropological structuralism became a dominant influence in her own cultural and anthropological essays.[4]

During this period, she published her first novel, *Jacob's Ladder* (for which she won a Houghton Mifflin Literary Fellowship Award), and short autobiographical novellas that earned several prizes, including one given by *The Atlantic Monthly* (the story "Such Is Rachel" was awarded second place in the Atlantic First competition in 1946).[5] From her stories, which record her reflections on her travels in the New World, it is clear that she felt alien to the cultural homogeneity engendered by consumer capitalism; hence, she sought in her stories to introduce some color into what she perceived to be a one-dimensional cultural and human landscape.

In the first story she wrote after leaving Egypt, "Cairo Wedding," she crossed all the boundaries between generations, between social classes, between sexes, and between western and eastern traditions.[6] In 1946, newly divorced, she returned to Egypt, but three years later she traveled with her sister to Paris. She remarried and lived in Paris from 1951 to 1954. Thereafter she immigrated to Israel. She now addressed the "provinciality" and "ethnic nationalism" she had first encountered in her earlier visit to Palestine in 1937.[7] She soon published essays in various Hebrew journals, especially in *Keshet* under the editorship of

Aharon Amir. Amir was one of the leading intellectual figures of the "Canaanite group," which was founded in 1939 in Mandatory Palestine and propounded nativist principles to the Israeli public. The "Canaanites" called for supporters to reject the Diaspora and Jewish religious civilization and to reestablish the ancient Hebrew entity together with the other Levantine peoples. Amir also translated Kahanoff's English writings into Hebrew and edited her only Hebrew collection of essays, *From East the Sun* (1978). Kahanoff passed away a year after this volume was published.

Her works are studied in universities; articles are written about her in academic journals in Israel and elsewhere; her essays are included in Israeli school curricula; and excerpts from her books appeared in a Levantine anthology published by Yale University Press.[8] In Israel, a school and a street have been named after her, and a Hebrew children's book presents her literary portrait. There have been radio programs about her and a film in the documentary series *The Hebrews*; in addition, the Eretz-Israel Museum in Tel Aviv devoted an exhibit to Kahanoff's life and work.

All of these assure her place as a writer and an essayist who was hailed as the princess of the Levant and the herald of Israel's integration in the Mediterranean culture of the Levant.[9] A photomontage of Y. H. Brenner, a pioneer of Modern Hebrew literature, and Kahanoff adorns the covers of a series of books published by the Open University about the secularization of the Jewish culture. This adds an interesting secular interpretative commentary on various movements and ideologies—the Canaanites, the Mizrahim, and feminists—that have embraced her warmly (perhaps too warmly) and claimed her as one of their own. The significance of her impact on the cultural life of Israel may be further measured by the voluminous collection of her correspondence and unpublished essays in the Gnazim archives of the Hebrew Writers' Association and the Heksherim Institute in Ben-Gurion University. To mark the hundredth anniversary of her birth, Ben-Gurion University held an international conference on her ramified intellectual legacy.

The articles for which she is best known are of a personal, reflective genre, presenting people and places from her distinctive cosmopolitan perspective. As noted earlier, Kahanoff did not grow up in Israel, and Hebrew literature was not her natural point of reference. Rather, that point of reference was the intellectual circles she frequented, journals she read, and libraries and museums she visited during winters in New York and autumns in Paris. The principal literary influence on her work was the American "new journalism" in the 1940s, when she lived in the United States, and French writings such as Montaigne's *Essays* (1580).

Susan Sontag (1933–2004) was also a great source of inspiration for her. Sontag is known above all for her essays on photography, cancer and AIDS, the Vietnam and Yugoslav wars, human rights, literature, and the media. Manifestly inspired by this American Jewish female intellectual, Kahanoff thus duly lauded her: "There is a side that is both elevating and refreshing about Susan Sontag, a successful young lady who is quoted a great deal and whose articles are published in a great variety of American journals. She is a product of New York culture, highly intelligent, knowledgeable about literature, familiar with the languages, literatures and intellectual tendencies of Europe, self-assured, a bit presumptuous, and—of course—Jewish." With a few alterations, one might have thought that Kahanoff was writing about herself. Despite the great differences in their backgrounds and personal situations, there are points of similarity between the two. Both were born to Jewish families and were known for their literary talents, their feminist consciousness, and their intellectual achievements. As young students, they fell in love with famous lecturers. Columbia University and the city of Paris left their mark on both of them in their formative years; they wrote about subjects that interested them and their contemporaries from a personal viewpoint, and, as Kahanoff said about Sontag, "She used the word 'I' quite easily as someone sufficiently self-confident to express her subjective, though educated, reaction to whatever she was talking about, with great pleasure." Yoram Bronowski, a friend of Kahanoff's, remarked that "she said that Susan Sontag represented something new and important for her, and she wanted a little to be like her."

Apart from writing articles, which was her main vocation, Kahanoff had great interest in theater, cinema, television, architecture, and other forms of art and culture. In Israel, she worked for a living as a self-employed contributor to the *WIZO-Hadassah* journal, and in 1965 she began to serve on the executive committee of the Israel Broadcasting Authority. Even when ill with cancer, she regularly attended the theater and the cinema. She was generally disappointed with the Israeli films she saw, and she told producers that "they were insufficiently *avant-garde* and should rather return to classicism and reinterpret it in a modern way." She was impressed, however, with films that showed an original side of young Israel. At an early stage, she perceived the revolutionary potential of television; she showed an interest in art collectors, interviewed writers visiting Israel, analyzed various Israeli customs, described revolutions in architecture, and wrote book reviews in the Israeli newspapers. Yet she not only reported on artistic and cultural developments in Israel but also tried her hand at writing poems, painting, and drawing. She also especially liked reporting on her periodic visits to the cultural centers of Europe.

The essays, for which she is best known, are a form of in-depth personal theoretical writing based on an original vision, a genre that has played a decisive role in the history of Hebrew literature. From the end of the 1950s to the 1970s, Kahanoff commanded critical attention with a series of essays that presented the Levantine world to the Israeli public, who were unfamiliar with the cultural life of Cairo, Alexandria, Beirut, or Istanbul. The subjects she wrote about were manifold: Levantinism as an idea and as a cultural concept; the status of women at the geographical periphery of the land of Israel; the dialogue between Paris and Tel Aviv; the ideas of artists and writers and cultural critics such as Emmanuel Lvinas [Levinas], Claude Vigée, and Edmond Jabès; contemporary cultural life of Africa and Japan; the dialectical ambiguities of the technological era; matters pertaining to health and old age; political leadership from Gandhi to de Gaulle; and much else.

The aim of this book is, among other things, to describe the place of Kahanoff in the Levantine network through an examination of her relationships or affinities with Levantine writers and poets, some of whom were native-born and some of whom were immigrants. Their immigration and their affinity with the place they had left or the place they came to was not objective or hierarchical but was governed by the network. By means of a methodological distinction between "influence" and "affinity," I distinguish between Kahanoff's influence on thinkers, writers, and poets such as Aharon Amir, Edmond Jabès, and Albert Memmi and her affinity with thinkers and writers such as Charles Corm, Amin Maalouf, and Taha Hussein. Their inclusion in the study reveals the Levantine intellectual and cultural network to which Kahanoff was exposed and to which she belonged.

Kahanoff did not use the concept of "network" like historians from Fernand Braudel to Nicholas Purcell, Peregrine Horden, and Irad Malkin do in their works on the Mediterranean region. A network implies an affinity for exchange, mutuality, intersection, and ramification, resulting in a common discourse through language and dialogue, meetings, literary salons, translations, conferences, and so forth. The network is not only a territorial concept but also a *spacial* one, a blanket term for complex systems and internal relationships centered on man. What matters is not things in themselves but the relationships between them. Man creates this Levantine sphere of relationships by his use of it, by the "practice of space."

PREFACE   xiii

Kahanoff had a historical and comprehensive view of the Levant. The Levant was "the cradle of civilization"; from the midst of Egypt, Mesopotamia, Persia, and ancient Israel emerged the formative elements of western culture.[10] Judaism and Christianity were born in the Levant, and the Roman, Byzantine, and Islamic empires all left their mark on the area. In drawing on this distinctive heritage, Levantinism is, for Kahanoff, a geocultural hybrid identity that crystallized in the eastern Mediterranean during the twentieth century when the colonial presence of the French and the English brought about a dialectical fusion of cultures, rich combinations of language, and unique literary encounters. Already at the start of the modern era, the Levant began to be defined as a distinct geographical area where the European west was involved commercially, militarily, and culturally, such as in Egypt and Lebanon.

Kahanoff conceived of Levantinism as a uniquely multilayered cultural matrix, facilitating Israel's modus vivendi with its Mediterranean neighbors. Her gaze was directed toward the Braudelian *longue durée*: she thought that in the long run, it might help Israel to integrate in the Levant.[11] The Levantine option is thus not only a cultural possibility but also a concrete political proposal. In place of pan-Arabism on the one hand and Zionism on the European-Ashkenazi model on the other, Kahanoff proposed a political culture of the Levant, the essence of which was "live and let live." The reconstruction of the Levant could help to redefine the Israelis' relationship to the political and cultural space in which they reside.[12]

A modern and critical Levantinism was from her point of view a cultural possibility of that kind, an option for a comprehensive solution for the Mediterranean region above and beyond the interests of the great powers. One finds it extraordinary to see how much her analysis, which proposed a "mosaic of the Levant" made up of different local narratives and not an all-embracing ideology, anticipated the contemporary Mediterranean theses of Peregrine

Horden and Nicholas Purcell in their book *The Corrupting Sea: A Study of Mediterranean History.* They attempted to "postmodernize Braudel"—that is, to transform "the Braudelian Mediterranean meta-narrative" into "local and varied narratives."[13] What Horden and Purcell attempted to do with Mediterraneanism, Kahanoff anticipated with her theory of Levantinism.

Kahanoff described the historical connotations of the concept "Levantinism," its cultural ramifications, and its yet to be fully realized sociopolitical potential. She proposed examining the deeply rooted local subcultures and the multilayered identities of the people of the Levant. For her, it is not exclusively western or eastern, Christian, Jewish, or Muslim. In all her articles, stories, and interviews, Kahanoff stressed the variety, the multiplicity, and the continuity of the Levant. In so doing, she anticipated the concept of "multiple modernities."[14] This anticipation of the multicultural outlook and early recognition of many-sidedness did not come to Kahanoff from a postmodernist climate of opinion or a zeitgeist emanating from the academic world. As she herself underscored, her vision of an integrative Levantine culture was grounded in her biography as a cosmopolitan Egyptian Jew: "When I was a child, it seemed natural that people understood each other although they spoke different languages, and were called names of Greek, Muslim, Syrian, Jewish, Christian, Arab, Italian, Tunisian and Armenian traditions."[15] The cultural heterogeneity of the Levant reflects, more than anything else, its cosmopolitan character. In the words of Aharon Amir, Kahanoff's principal translator into Hebrew, describing the Levant, it is the "cosmopolitanism of the Mediterranean, a colorful hybrid."[16] Levantinism as Kahanoff's spiritual landscape became the basis of a systematic, well-formulated, and deeply inspiring world outlook. She wished to cure the colonialist sickness by reclaiming "Levantinism," transforming this concept, which had previously signified a lack of authenticity and cultural stability, into a positive cultural force with therapeutic power.

Kahanoff was not a philosopher or a political thinker but a theoretician of culture, a seismographer of the modern developments she encountered in the course of her life. Many critics relegate her to a theoretical ghetto concerned with the Levant alone. Her articles and essays, however, range far beyond the Levant and engage in a general critique of the modern world.

—∿∿—

This present study seeks to analyze and explain Kahanoff's writings in a biographical context and thus view her as embodying the vision she sought to promote: a vision as borne by her intellectual peregrinations—a spiritual and cultural journey that crisscrossed Egypt, the United States, France, and Israel—that has increasingly commanded critical attention. It examines the world of Kahanoff's childhood, her family situation, her education, her youth in the Cairo immigrant community celebrated as "the Europe of the East," and the social, cultural, and political environment in Egypt in the 1920s and 1930s.[17]

Kahanoff's family history illustrates the long and circuitous path taken by the Jewish communities in the Levant and was the cradle of her outlook. She was surrounded by the children of the Levantine minorities: Jewish, Greek, Muslim, and Armenian. Indeed, Cairo was a metropolis in which "something exciting was happening all the time."[18] Kahanoff's descriptions of the city of her youth were picturesque and colorful. The teaching of English in the government schools; the excellent educational establishments of the British, Greeks, and Italians; the French culture disseminated by the schools, religious orders, and colleges of the Jesuits; and the American University all contributed to giving Cairo its international flavor. Kahanoff witnessed the transition from the British colonial rule to the national and Islamic regime, and the hardships the transition brought with it to the Jewish community in Egypt.[19] Upon marrying Izzy Margoliash, at the age of twenty-four, she left Egypt for the United States in 1941 at the beginning of the Second World War. She soon divorced Margoliash and settled in New York City, where she attended courses at the famous "New School" in Greenwich Village. She would subsequently study journalism and literature at Columbia University. The capitalist order of the United States, however, disturbed Kahanoff's peace of mind. She described the country's bureaucracy, which made people into regimented masses, as the capitalist golem turning on its maker: "One felt that something new and frightening which is inescapable and out of control was happening in our century."[20] However, despite her criticism, Kahanoff praised not only the educational achievements of the United States but also its spiritual values, which she attributed to the pioneering tradition, "which in building a new world, rebuilds the world."[21]

In a series of articles, Kahanoff described the Promethean passion of America, as reflected in the American Megalopolis. She perceived at an early stage the dual nature of the technological era at a time when many people related to its discoveries in an uncritical manner. She discerned the Promethean possibilities represented by America: "This acknowledgment released a tremendous energy like that of Prometheus, who took fire from the gods in order to give it to mankind."[22] At the same time, Kahanoff, following some members of the Frankfurt school, warned of the technological golem lying at humanity's door.

After her long sojourn in the United States, Kahanoff returned to Cairo for a short time but did not feel at home there. She soon returned to Paris, where she lived from 1951 to 1954, a period in which the city nursed its wounds after the war.[23] The cultural ferment and philosophical fashions like existentialism, personalism, and structuralism; the birth of the "new novel"; and an influx of writers and intellectuals from all over the world left a strong impression on her. Kahanoff introduced readers to political and religious groups, the figures involved in the Algerian War of Independence (1954–1962), and especially de Gaulle; interviewed

PREFACE xvii

publishers and the editors of journals; reviewed novels and philosophical works; and gave her impressions of some of the leading writers and thinkers of her time.

Kahanoff's impressions of French intellectual and literary life are especially indebted to Jean-Paul Sartre and to Simone de Beauvoir, whose "road to liberty" signified for her the path of a woman fighting for her freedom in a patriarchal world.[24] In a series of essays on French literature and culture, she discussed the novels of Jules Romains, John Dos Passos, André Malraux, and others. Although Kahanoff's Parisian episode was central to her life, it must be pointed out that she acquired the knowledge of French culture and language earlier, in her youth in Cairo, and increased her acquaintance with them in her time in New York in the company of French émigré intellectuals. When she lived in Israel, she would periodically visit the "city of lights," which continued to be integral to her cultural landscape.

Kahanoff's romance with Israel, the country she chose as her homeland after all her wanderings, began with her first visit to Palestine-Eretz-Israel in 1937, when she went from Cairo to Palestine with her friend Sylvie to see the pioneering society. Her immigration to Israel in 1954 signified the end of her spiritual peregrinations. Anwar Sadat's visit to Israel in 1978 (and later the conclusion of a peace treaty between Israel and Egypt) took place during the period of her fatal illness, a year before her death.[25] The visit of the president of Egypt, the land where she was born, to the State of Israel, the place where she chose to live and end her days, shed a meaningful light on the story of a life with a beginning and an end: a private exodus from Egypt that ended peacefully.

Kahanoff lived in Israel for a quarter of a century, most of the time in Tel Aviv, but in her first two years in the country, from 1954 to 1956, she lived with her second husband, Alexander Kahanoff, in Beersheba, a major city in the south of Israel. She taught French to the local schoolchildren.[26] As already noted, Aharon

Amir began to translate her essays and publish them in *Keshet*, Kahanoff's initial forum, the journal that broke away from the European orientation regnant in Israel and opened a window on the Levantine world.[27] Her series of articles titled The Levantine Generation made her name known throughout Israel.

In 1960, the hundredth anniversary of the birth of Henrietta Szold, Kahanoff published *Ramat-Hadassah-Szold: Youth Aliyah Screening and Classification Centre*, describing the reception of immigrant children into Israeli social institutions.[28] The nature of Kahanoff's heroes, such as the humanist philosopher Martin Buber and the peace activist Abie Nathan, showed that she had a nonpolitical type of idealism.

Kahanoff's visits to Gaza, the Golan, and East Jerusalem and her direct encounters with Palestinians and Druze attest to the fact that despite her goodwill and desire for rapprochement, she shared in the nationalist exuberance of the majority of Israelis of the period after the Six-Day War (1967). She was given to a self-confident political conservatism based on military might and national pride—a conservatism that brought to an end the hopes for a reconciliation with the Arab world that had been quickened by Anwar Sadat's visit to Jerusalem after the Yom Kippur War (1973).

Levantinism as Kahanoff's home landscape became the basis of a systematic, well-formulated, and deeply inspiring world outlook.[29] She represented the Levantine culture as having the right to a full, authentic, independent existence. Kahanoff contributed to the discourse on Levantinism taking place in Israel. In what respect was the Levantinism of the mid-twentieth century similar to or different from the Levantinism of the second decade of the twenty-first century? Which writers and cultural critics in Israel were influenced by Kahanoff's Levantinism, and in what way? Is it possible to formulate a systematic theory of a Kahanoff-type Levantinism?

Kahanoff belongs to the intellectual current of writers, thinkers, and cultural critics who are characterized by what has been called the Mediterranean idea. The purveyors of this idea, which that I would rather call "Mediterranean humanism," did not refer to themselves as an aesthetic or intellectual "school." These authors, including Albert Camus, Albert Memmi, Tahar Ben-Jelloun, Jorge Semprún, Najib Mahfouz, and Edmond Jabès, were opposed to all kinds of racism, violence, colonialism, and political radicalism.[30] Their unyielding campaign against racism reflected their Levantine-cosmopolitan affirmation of the cultural other. Theirs was a multicultural outlook that affirms dialogue as a form of human activity. Kahanoff, like these other writers, rebelled against the western tradition that wanted to create a new man; instead, she emphasized the concrete problems of the Mediterranean societies, using Israel as a case study. Kahanoff reached the conclusion that this Mediterranean outlook stood a chance only if one was firmly planted in the soil of one's own country.

As a promoter of the Mediterranean idea, Kahanoff abandoned the prevalent Israeli confrontational ethos in favor of a broad, rich, and polyphonic mesh of geopolitical cultural elements. Her observation of Israel together with her life outside the country and her widespread interests made Kahanoff the herald and initiator of a different cultural possibility, more extensive than that offered in her time, and also, perhaps, more extensive than what is offered today.

Kahanoff also had a great interest in poetry and conducted a dialogue with the Israeli poet Dahlia Ravikovitch and the French poets Charles Péguy, Edmond Jabès, and Claude Vigée. She also wrote poetry herself. Ravikovitch could be rescued from the provincial Israel of her time only through imaginary journeys to the Bible and the world of mysticism, to Canaanism and the Crusades, Hannibal, and Saladin—but even more decisively by a cosmopolitan sensibility nurtured by peregrinations in the streets of Cairo and the pavements of Alexandria, the cafés of Paris, the jazz clubs of Chicago, and the intellectual atmosphere of New York City.

Kahanoff held the French poet Charles Péguy (1873–1914) in special regard, one might say, a *spiritus rector*. She viewed him as an original thinker, an individualist, a wandering French pilgrim who was before his time. As a returning Catholic, his intellectual faculties were unharmed, and he criticized the politics of both the Church and the socialist party. Kahanoff astutely described him as "the controversialist who wrestled in the arena of concrete reality while the poet expressed his vision in another world, but the two were always linked."[31] She explained his support of Alfred Dreyfus, for example, by the fact that he thought that the latter was excluded from the national society because he was Jewish and because he believed that the honor of France took precedence over the honor of its army.

Yet another example of religious poetry was that written by Edmond Jabès (1912–1991), whom Kahanoff considered to be the best of the Jewish writers from Egypt. The theme of Jabès's works is religious existentialism, which he expressed as "Judaism after God." According to Kahanoff, a reading of Jabès reveals the code connecting the Mediterranean world and the Jewish world.[32] Another Franco-Jewish poet, Claude Vigée (1921–2020), an Alsatian Jew who went to Brandeis University, settled in Israel, and until his recent death, lived in France, is also characterized by religious existentialism. Kahanoff wrote essays on his works, befriended him, and interviewed him. She regarded him as "the most outstanding of the Jewish poets in France" who struck roots in Israel.[33] Through him, she examined the nihilistic and narcissistic roots of the modern sensibility as reflected in the poets, writers, and philosophers of her time. Kahanoff always sought a place that would be a home, a place where her polyphonic identity would find rest, where east and west would have a fruitful meeting.

The literature of social mutation, said Kahanoff, represents a cultural and social trend to which insufficient attention has been paid and which is not limited to the Levantine phenomenon but is a worldwide tendency. The writing of these hybrids is characterized by a "search for identity" and a refusal to accept an alien definition of themselves.[34] In their personalities and writings, its creators blend the different elements that formed them, while allowing no element to be relinquished. Kahanoff welcomed these "cultural hybrids" and "the challenges of the new combinations"; without their vitality and surprising mutations, culture, she thought, could petrify.

The writers of the "literature of social mutation," such as Emmanuel Lvinas, Claude Vigée, and Albert Memmi, did not submit to what Kahanoff called the "hegemony" of the western model, despite its great influence, but instead produced multicultural and multinational compounds.

Kahanoff would acknowledge that "I have sometimes used book reviews as a pretext to write about women in that society."[35] And indeed, in a series of book reviews, she refined her own special feminist approach, a moderate comparative approach, in various social contexts. She spoke not only of the theoretical aspects of feminism or the intellectual consequences of distinguishing between sexual freedom and the female gender but also of women of flesh and blood, who interested her as much as the heroines of novels. She examined the situation of the modern woman and possible solutions to the lack of gender equality. Her feminism excelled at eliminating class and racial divisions. It was a universal feminism that was balanced, not at all confrontational, and far from provincialism or political or national considerations.[36] I shall examine Kahanoff's feminism and its limits by taking into account the critiques of feminist scholars. Kahanoff foresaw that the right to free abortion and the possibilities of lesbianism may anticipate the day when women's biological functions will no longer be needed. It may be that their traditional roles as companions and mothers will be completely unnecessary. Kahanoff had gone a long way before she could arrive at a radical idea like this.

As noted, Kahanoff's intellectual horizons were not limited to the Levant and the countries of the Mediterranean. She also took a passionate interest in the world at large, from Japan to Africa. She edited an anthology in Hebrew called *African Stories*, which included poetry, folklore, and tales from countries south of the Sahara and also from the islands of the Caribbean.[37] She wrote detailed introductions to all the writers and presented each writer's biography and cultural world. In addition to her work on the anthology of African writers, she wrote a series of essays and critiques of modern Japanese literature, such as that of the writer Yukio Mishima. She also wrote movingly on the Indo-Caribbean writer V. S. Naipaul and the Indo-American writer Santha Rama Rau.

Kahanoff saw the prolongation of the life expectancy of the elderly as a metaphor for the technological possibilities of the modern age, and at the same time as a symptom of the chimerical quest for eternal youth. In keeping with her discussion in her youth of the illusions of progress furthered by technology, she came to the conclusion in her maturity—following her father's confinement to an old-age home and the anguish that he and his family suffered as his health rapidly declined in his final years—that advanced technology does not necessarily bring happiness and comfort but often brings unnecessary pain and suffering to the old, their families, and those around them. Her essay "To Die a Modern Death," published in two parts in two issues of *Keshet*, describes that tragic, vulnerable, and degenerate stage of her father's life, which was extended by the delusory hope that technology would spare him from the indignities of senescence.[38]

In April 1976, three years before her own death, Kahanoff began to keep a diary in which she described her sufferings from the cancer that afflicted her.[39] As in her description of the suffering and loneliness of her father in his old-age home, a meticulous portrayal of the last stage of his life, in this diary she held back nothing in describing her experiences in a hospital during her operation there and afterward.[40]

The honesty and candor with which Kahanoff wrote about her illness is characteristic of her biography, from her birth in Cairo to her death in Tel Aviv. Her experiences in different periods of her life resulted in a cultural theory based on the Mediterranean idea, in which the personal and the general, the biographical and the theoretical, all played a part. The following chapter about the cities in which Kahanoff lived—Cairo, New York, Paris, and Tel Aviv—is meant to give the reader a comprehensive account of Kahanoff's experiences in these places. At times these memories and reflections are offered outside of their chronological order, for the sake of maintaining thematic unity.

JACQUELINE
KAHANOFF

INTRODUCTION
Levantinism—*Ex oriente lux*

JACQUELINE KAHANOFF BELONGS TO AN extensive circle of intellectuals, writers, and cultural critics who understood Levantinism as a concept denoting eminently more than a geographical region. Indeed, they consistently distinguish between the Levant and Levantinism. The Levant is "the area of the lands on the shores of the eastern Mediterranean"[1] or "the eastern Mediterranean littoral between Anatolia and Egypt."[2] Levantinism, on the other hand, is an idea, a state of mind, a geocultural concept whose historical roots derive from a certain region and also from a metaphorical sphere whose special feature is the mutual attraction and influence of the eastern Mediterranean and the European west (as was manifest, for instance, in the Crusades, in the Ottoman Empire, and in British and French colonialism). The concept of the Levant thus embraces the Levantine as a meeting place of diverse cultures, often as an ideal, a utopian vision that also serves as a critique of contemporary realities.

Accordingly, the historian Philip Mansel begins his book *Levant: Splendour and Catastrophe on the Mediterranean* with the following words: "The Levant is an area, a dialogue and a quest."[3] The word *orient* derives from the Latin word *oriens*, which means "sunrise." *Ex oriente lux*. Likewise, the word *Levant*, which first appeared at the end of the fifteenth century, derives from the French word *levant* (from *lever*, which derives from the Latin *levare*), meaning "point of sunrise." In the sixteenth century, the word began to be applied specifically to the areas under Ottoman rule in the eastern Mediterranean, including Greece and the coasts of Asia Minor. The term *Levantine* was applied to Italians, to French, and to the peoples of the Mediterranean. The official title of the French mandate in Syria and Lebanon after the First World War was *Le Mandat aux États du Levant* (The Mandate for the States of the Levant).[4]

The Arabic term corresponding to the western term for the eastern region is *Mashrak* ("where the sun rises"). For western Europeans, *Le Levant* was a synonym for the eastern Mediterranean, where dawn begins, an area that includes Greece, Turkey, Syria, Lebanon, Israel, and Egypt, which were part of the Ottoman Empire from the sixteenth century to the twentieth. The historical Levant included Turkish Asia Minor, Iraq, Cyrenaica in Libya, the Sinai Desert in Egypt, Greece, and Cyprus. The Levantine region was also identified with what is known in Arabic as *Ash-Shams*, "the Sun" (one of the terms for Damascus in Arabic), an area under the suzerainty of Damascus.

The Levant is not necessarily an Islamic or Arabic concept, however. A crusader who came to Jerusalem from Chartres in France gave a description of the formation of Levantine society: "How God in our time has brought the West to the East, for we who were westerners have become easterners."[5] He related how a Roman became a Galilean and how a man from Rheims became an inhabitant of Tyre. Many people, he said, forgot their place of birth, and some married Syrian or Armenian women. Various languages came together, and people of different religions who had been separate in the past began to have a common faith. "Foreigners have become natives and residents have become settlers [from Christian Europe]."[6]

INTRODUCTION

But this utopian description of the east, in which Europeans blended into the Levant and its cultural landscape utterly free of contradictions, was far from the historical reality. For the most part, the native population regarded the Europeans as hostile intruders, and the western Christian settlers looked askance at both the native Islamic and eastern Christian populations. Indicatively, there was even a rumor that the eastern Christians had asked Saladin (*Salah-ed-Din*) to conquer Jerusalem and liberate it from the Europeans. The crusaders were hardly a bridge between east and west. As the historian of the Crusades, Joshua Prawer succinctly noted, "The [Levant's] Orientalization, or, if you will, their Levantinization . . . was deliberately arrested by the crusaders."[7] In consonance with their belief in their religious and cultural superiority, the crusaders viewed the Levantine region and its inhabitants with contempt. The partial Orientalization of the crusaders in the Levant did not bring them closer to the Muslims, while it did distance them from their relatives and coreligionists in Europe. The crusaders continued to believe that they were the lawful heirs to the Holy Land, and the Muslim *fellahin* (peasants) felt humiliated at being conquered by infidels. The crusaders in effect created in the Levant—Syria, Lebanon, and the area of today's Israel—a "Europe overseas." Historians have, therefore, tended to trace to the Crusades the origins of the "Eastern Question," adversarial confrontation between east and west. The Crusades hardly inaugurated an era of cultural harmony or integration, but rather one of perpetual confrontation on the battlefield and of unrelenting religious antagonism. The harsh reality of the medieval Christians in the Levant persisted in modern times.

The sad cultural and political legacy of the Crusades as emblematic of the Eastern Question is perhaps best represented by the king of France Louis IX (1214–1270), the *roi très chrétien, le fils ainé de l'église* (the firstborn son of the Church). Louis led the Seventh and Eighth Crusades against the Muslims—Ayyubids,

Bahriyya Mamluks, and the Hafsid dynasty. In recognition of his bravery as incarnating exemplary religious devotion, he was canonized in 1297.[8]

There was also a positive side to the historical record, however. In the wake of the First Crusade, ever-increasing masses of European pilgrims settled in the Holy Land not to liberate the Church of the Holy Sepulchre from the infidels but to realize their religious ideals in hundreds of villages. They thereby created the foundations of a Levantine space.[9] The pilgrims brought with them a developed system of rural administration, improved the roads, built new ones, developed irrigation, and grew crops that they brought from Europe. All of this redounded to the benefit of the indigenous population and facilitated amiable relations. Eventually, European Christians settled throughout the eastern Mediterranean, the birthplace of Christianity.

The Ottoman Turks also had a role in creating the Levant as a distinct geographic and culture space. After the fall of the Latin Levant at the end of the thirteenth century, the area consisted of six countries joining the Ottoman and Mameluke domains. That Ottoman Levant would be characterized by political pragmatism, with lines of defense by mountain ranges at its eastern frontier fending off the Mongols and Armenians. For hundreds of years, the Ottoman Levant was threatened or invaded from all sides, and sometimes from several sides simultaneously. Nonetheless, until the seventeenth century, under Ottoman rule, the Levant served as a commercial conduit between the Indian Ocean and the Mediterranean. Two centuries later, the global rivalry of the European powers made the Levant into a strategic axis involving the British, the French, and the Russians. The economic efflorescence of Acre and Beirut in the eighteenth and nineteenth centuries was a headache for the Ottomans because they were gateways to Europe. The immigration of Jews to the land of Israel at the end of the nineteenth century and the waves of Jewish immigration at the beginning of the twentieth century made the situation in the Levant even more complex and politically unstable. At the same time, the "initial globalization" that was a consequence of the importation of European technology enabled the Ottomans to impose their rule on the vast Levantine region in an unprecedented way. On the eve of the First World War, it seemed that the Levant would remain under Ottoman rule for the foreseeable future.[10]

The Ottoman Empire existed for more than six hundred years, from the end of the thirteenth century to the beginning of the twentieth. In 1512, Sultan Selim the First, who conquered many regions, annexed these regions, including the whole of Asia Minor, to the eastern Mediterranean part of the empire. After the Mameluke-Ottoman war, he conquered the Levant, the land of Israel-Palestine, Mecca and Medina, and Egypt. As a result of his control of all the Muslim holy places, there was a demand that the sultan, the secular ruler, should replace the *sharif*, the supreme religious authority. Jihad, or Muslim holy war, was a central feature of the Ottoman Empire. The Ottoman sultans were regarded as holy warriors. As they saw it, war, like the Arab conquest of the Levant in the seventh century, was a "holy enterprise," and the fallen were considered martyrs. After the conquest of Mecca and Medina in the sixteenth century, the sultans were called "servants of the two holy places," and they were caliphs—successors of Muhammad as temporal and spiritual heads of Islam. Many Muslims thought it was God's will that this was to be the final empire, just as Muhammad was the final prophet.[11]

Later on, the Ottomans were troubled by the lack of security in Greater Syria, the European influence on the coast, and the challenge posed by the French and by the British in Egypt. The political and commercial power of Western Europe not only enhanced the importance of the Levant but also furthered the relationship between Europe and Asia. If the Crusades marked the confrontation between East and West, between Christianity and Islam, the European Levant led to a meeting of cultures, the cross-fertilization of East and West that was to give rise to what would be celebrated as Levantinism.

The emergence of the Levant as a distinct cultural space was due in large measure to a confluence of shared political interests between Paris and Constantinople. Political realism prevailed over religious difference as a source of conflict. Alliances with Christian power, in fact, had characterized the realpolitik of the Ottoman Empire since its forces first crossed into Europe in 1350 as allies of Genoa. Jihad was interpreted not only as war in the name of Islam but also as an act of spiritual elevation, which allowed for this-worldly pragmatic consideration. Muslim caliphs thus occasionally made alliances with the "most Christian" kings. Despite frequent disputes and pronounced religious differences, Mecca and Medina were drawn into the European diplomatic system. As a result of the alliance, the French ambassador said in 1672 that France was "the oldest and most faithful friend of the Ottoman government."[12]

The success of the Franco-Ottoman alliance came to the fore with crystallization of Levant as a coherent geopolitical region. The concessions that the Ottoman sultan granted to the king of France became the legal basis for the European presence in the Levant and decisively served to promote the growth of international trade. If strategic considerations were the initial motivation for the alliance, it was the flourishing commercial trade that sustained the political alliance and allowed for a large measure of legal and cultural autonomy of French citizens within the bounds of the Ottoman Empire. Crimes committed by French citizens, apart from murder, were subject to French law administered by French juridical procedures administered at the consulates of the Republic of France. Similarly, there was freedom of worship and exemption from Ottoman taxation.

From the nineteenth century onward, this arrangement enabled the cities of the Levant to become a laboratory of coexistence between different ethnic communities and religions, a rare

INTRODUCTION 7

phenomenon in the world of that time. The cities of the Levant were, indeed, cosmopolitan in character, places where individuals of diverse cultural backgrounds would intermingle and socialize freely. In this respect, the urban landscape of the Levant was at the time unique. For the sake of comparison, one may note, for example, that in nineteenth-century Baghdad and in twentieth-century Belfast, the ethnic and religious communities lived apart in quasi-enclosed residential enclaves.[13]

The Ottoman authorities allowed the inhabitants of the Levant to travel freely throughout the region. The journey from Jerusalem to Beirut overland along the coast, two hundred miles in all, shortened the way for travelers, who no longer had to take a more circuitous route to reach Jerusalem. Hence, under Ottoman rule, the Levant was a bastion of international trade and finance, in which individuals of various European provenances met and created the basis of a flourishing cosmopolitan Ottoman subculture. Contemporary Europe had yet to fully emerge from its legacy of religious intolerance. The ban on Jewish religious life in Spain was lifted only in 1968; from the mid-sixteenth century to the mid-nineteenth, Catholics in London were allowed to hold mass only in the chapels of foreign embassies. It was only toward the end of the eighteenth century that Protestants were permitted to hold public prayer in Paris. And it was only a hundred years later that Muslims were allowed to conduct religious service ceremonies in Paris or Marseilles as the French Catholics had throughout the Levant. The first mosque was built in Paris only in 1926, not as an expression of religious tolerance but for patriotic reasons, to honor Muslims killed as French soldiers in the First World War. Even in Amsterdam, the most tolerant city in the seventeenth century, the Catholics were obliged to hold their services in churches not visible from the street.

In stark contrast to the way it was viewed in Europe on the cusp of the modern age, the Levant under the Ottomans emerged not only as a distinct geographical and commercial region. One may thus speak of Levantinism.

—◊—

In the course of her life and writings, Kahanoff personified the spirit and cultural sensibilities of Levantinism. She was born in May 1917 and raised in Cairo, the metropolitan hub of the Mashrak. In her early twenties, she embarked on a cosmopolitan journey that took her to the United States and France, back to the eastern Mediterranean to Egypt, and then to Israel, where she lived for the last two decades of her life.

ONE

A TALE OF FOUR CITIES
Cairo: 1917–1941

JACQUELINE KAHANOFF'S (NÉE SHOHET) FAMILY history demonstrates the long and circuitous path taken by the Jewish communities in the Levant, which was the cradle of her intellectual and cultural vision. Her family on her father's side was part of the Jewish community of Iraq for hundreds of years, one that was her father's pride: "the greatest exilic community, having produced the Babylonian Talmud and Rabbi Saadia Gaon."[1] Her paternal grandfather, Jacob Shohet, was engaged in the export of goods from the east to the west and in the financing of the transport by caravans. The onrush of modernity, however, prompted many members of the Iraqi Jewish community to immigrate to Egypt and to Britain, as the development of modern transportation routes such as the Suez Canal, which opened in November 1869, put an end to the traditional trade routes.

Three years previously, western modern values had made their mark on Jewish education in Iraq with the opening of an *Alliance française* Jewish school, which began to accept girls as students and to provide vocational training and instruction in European languages.[2] Jacob Shohet decided to send his daughters to this school, much to the displeasure of the more traditional Jews of his family and circle. The Jewish merchants who imported cotton fabrics from Britain, agents of the British colonial economy that had spread throughout the Levant, would also send their children to *Alliance* schools.

When Kahanoff asked her father Joseph Shohet why he had immigrated to Egypt, he answered, "It was only reasonable to choose the order, justice and security provided by Great Britain rather than to continue a miserable existence under the corrupt and autocratic rule of the Ottoman Turkish governors of Iraq."[3] The Iraqi Jewish community spread out in all directions: to Palestine, Britain, the United States, and Egypt. Like many members of the Jewish community in Egypt, Kahanoff's family gradually adjusted to life in Cairo, slowly adapting themselves to European modernity, western technology, and British colonial rule. Western education offered new professional horizons, studies in universities, and opportunities abroad.

The family of Kahanoff's mother, Yvonne Chemla, came from Tunisia. The Chemla family was proud of its origin in the town of Monastir. In the early stages of French colonialism, her grandfather and elder brother immigrated to Turkey, where they were poor and uneducated although they spoke four languages: Italian, Arabic, French, and basic Hebrew. Starting out as petty traders, they became entrepreneurs and set up department stores in which the whole family, which in the meantime had arrived from Tunisia, was employed. The Chemlas immigrated to Egypt at the encouragement of a member of the family, a teacher in the *Alliance* school in Egypt, who spoke enthusiastically about the "land of plenty" on the banks of the Nile.

Kahanoff, who spoke French and English, acknowledged that there was no common language between her father's and mother's families, and when her parents spoke together in Arabic, she could scarcely grasp what they were saying.[4] As she recalled, "I had no words with which to express what I was thinking. I had long been an immigrant, but I nevertheless felt that in none of the languages we knew could we express our thoughts, for none of them were ours. We were people without a language, and we could only speak with signs."[5] Later, when speaking of the lack of words with which to express her Levantine experience, she said, "No language and no book in any language described us to ourselves and what happened to us in our own words. We ourselves had to find the words."[6] Nonetheless, she was assured that a mixed family like hers inevitably produced talented children. Their linguistic and cultural hybridity was characteristic of the Mizrahi Jewish community of Egypt. Although the Ashkenazic community was generally less cosmopolitan, their children studied in the same schools, and occasionally there were marriages between the two communities. The Egyptian Jewish community was thus not solely Mizrahi. The young peoples' desire to abandon the conservative ways of their parents was reflected in their choice of a western lifestyle and in the emergence of "an extended, flourishing community whose spirit remained close to Sephardic [and Oriental] Judaism but which gained vitality from the currents coming from Europe."[7] Westernization and Iraqi Jewish origins were thus the basis of the new community. The original local Egyptian communities were too small and weak to run schools, hospitals, and charitable institutions on their own, so this expansion benefited them as well.

The new Jewish community in Egypt in the 1920s and 1930s was somewhat isolated economically, socially, and culturally; the new bourgeois families wished to obtain marriages that would make European social connections for their sons and daughters. They sought to make these connections via two kinds of marriages: that of couples originating from the same place who had immigrated to Egypt and that of individuals from different communities of origin. These latter, mixed marriages were the basis of the new community, and in the next stage, marriages between Christians and Jews were accepted. These transitional generations with their mixed culture reflected the changes that were taking place among the Jewish immigrants from North Africa who had a pronounced western-French cultural and economic orientation. This sociocultural development suddenly came to an end and caused a crisis in the Sephardic-Mizrahi Jewish community from North Africa and Iraq. Ultimately, the old Mizrahi communities of Egypt ceased to exist as such for various reasons, most notably a lack of security and the pressures of the Egyptian masses borne by a proud Arab nationalism. There was nationalism in the air in Egypt from the 1920s onward. The death of Egyptian prime minister Saad Zaghloul (1859–1927), leader of the Wafd Party and the premier who headed the national struggle against British colonialism, in Kahanoff's opinion marked the end of an era.

These circumstances constituted the childhood and adolescence of Kahanoff in Cairo. Her parents, Joseph and Yvonne, who knew each other from the *Alliance* school in Cairo, married and made their home in the heart of the city. Soon, when her father became established as a merchant, they went to live in the suburbs in the area known as the "Garden City" along the banks of the Nile, which was also where the British high commissioner had his residence. The affluent Jewish inhabitants of this neighborhood mixed with bourgeois Arab youth and British officers in the "Gezira" sports club. Her father, who read the Arabic newspapers and the French bulletins of the *Alliance*, feared that his daughters would break away from their Jewish roots, and so he sought to bring them back to tradition. He feared that the pull of western culture would destroy the Jewish community in Egypt.[8] Her mother, however, was of a different opinion, and drew Jacqueline and her sister toward European culture, art, and fashion. The French author Marcel Proust, who exercised a great influence on educated Jews, represented for Yvonne the ideal of bourgeois society as well as its decadence. Before little Jacqueline knew how to read and write, she was able to recite whole chapters of *À la recherche du temps perdu* (In Search of Lost Time), which her mother read to her.

Jacqueline and other children of her age were educated at home and in French, English, and Italian schools, either secular schools or schools run by Christian missions. In the schools she attended—the Lycée Français and the secular schools—there were no Muslims. The Muslim boys went to British or Arab schools. Instead of education bringing the different religious communities together, it increased the social gap between the Jews, Christians, and Muslims. There was also a clear ethnic and tribal protocol: in the clubs, it was forbidden for Jewish girls to dance with Muslims, whatever their social status. Jacqueline met Muslims of her age only at the charity balls at the large hotels.

Religion did not play a central role in Jacqueline's childhood and youth, but she had a certain affinity with Christianity and Christians. Sometimes on Sundays, old Maria her Italian governess would take her to mass in St. Joseph's Cathedral, "in whose blue dome small, fat angels fluttered between pink-painted clouds."[9] Her father understood that God was everywhere, so he allowed her to go to mass, providing she abstained from touching the holy water and the cross that were offered to her. But Jacqueline dipped her finger in the water: "I was aware it was the precious blood of Jesus, but I didn't make the sign of the cross."[10] She liked it when a monk in a brown robe and sandals smiled at her in the street: "It seemed to me natural that the one who was crucified and resurrected would meet you face to face and smile at a child." Her father thought that every people had its own religion, "just as every kind of bird has its own song," Kahanoff added naively. Her father believed that the Jewish religion was "to await the coming of the Messiah," and Jacqueline hoped that "the Messiah would come quickly so that everyone could enjoy everything about other people's religions, as well as their own."[11] She said, "My own religious figure was my father," whom she described as returning from synagogue on the Sabbath carrying a bouquet of sweet-smelling flowers and saying in Arabic *santak hijira*: "Blessed is he who made the greenery." Her own religion was primarily expressed in the Hebrew language and in the blessing given by her grandfather when she visited him: "I felt that his blessing was something very ancient and special— a treasure—that the grandfathers of our grandfathers received from God." She understood that it was through this blessing that she belonged to the Jewish community whose history was written in the prayer books.[12]

As a child Jacqueline played in Cairo's Azbakeya Gardens, in the protected park set aside for children and the British nurses, who told her not to behave like "one of the other children," and indeed, she and her friends refused to be like "the ugly, dirty little children"[13] who were there. British soldiers flirted with the nurses, and little Jacqueline knew the soldiers were the colonialists whom the Egyptian students demonstrated against (she felt sympathy for the students as she felt that part of her was "native"). In her childhood, she was annoyed by the fact that no Egyptians came to her home. She no doubt thought that the majority of Egyptian Jews of her generation felt "a painful ambivalence at belonging and not belonging." When she was asked about her identity, she did not know what to answer: "I knew I was not Egyptian like the Arabs, and that it was shameful not to know what one was."[14] Finally, she said she was Persian, believing Baghdad was "in the country from which all beautiful rugs came."[15] The English women ridiculed this answer. Her mother also disliked it and told her that in the future she should say she was European. But Jacqueline felt that this was an even greater lie. Her parents, not the Europeans, were the foundation of her identity, or, as she put it, "the pillars that supported the frail bridge which tied me to my past, and without which there could no future."[16]

Her parents were pro-British "as a matter of business and security,"[17] and she and the people of her age were theoretically pronationalist, although in fact she knew few Muslims.[18] The young people wondered if the masses should be educated through social work, or whether they themselves should go to Europe and become Europeans. She decided against the Europeans and in favor of the Levantines: "We Jews, Greeks, Syrians, Copts, the studious minorities, the truly civilized, we would take their place, if we could but learn the secret of their power without allowing ourselves to be poisoned by it. From us would come the shape and color of tomorrow, and it would not be stained with blood if only we remembered the commandment 'Thou shalt not kill.'"[19] She admitted that among the Levantines there was a curious mixture of "desperate sincerity and of pretense, a tremendous thirst for truth and knowledge, coupled with an obscure desire for vindication, from both arrogant domination of Europe and the [Muslim] majority which, we did not quite forget, despised its minorities."[20]

In her childhood, it seemed natural to Jacqueline "that people understood each other although they spoke different languages, and were called by different names."[21] She was surrounded by the children of the Levantine minorities: Jewish, Greek, Muslim, and Armenian little girls who learned the slogan *patrie, liberté, égalité, fraternité* of the French Revolution even though these words had no bearing on their lives. The women who taught them thought it would be "right" for these girls to wish to be French, although "actually, we were nobody at all."[22] The question of her identity weighed on her, as it weighed on the other Levantine children, who were both here and there and neither here nor there: "What were we supposed to be when we grew up if we could be neither Europeans nor natives, nor even pious Jews, [Muslims], or Christians, as our grandparents had been?"[23] It never entered their heads to ask their parents or teachers these bothersome questions, because they themselves believed that "the world in which we grew up was genuine and good." Perhaps the parents and teachers were also pretending, because they knew they were standing on the edge of a volcano about to erupt and destroy the remains of their Levantine world, a world they looked upon as their home, whether in reality or only in appearance.

Even if their teachers and parents were no longer around, these Levantine children thought that perhaps they would live to see the fall of Europe and return to their countries of origin, "just as the Greeks, who were also Levantines, and who, like us, were scattered among the nations, returned and regained their ancient land." In her youth, it seemed natural to Jacqueline that the people of Cairo understood one another. Although they spoke different languages and came from different cities—Baghdad, Tunis, Aleppo, Beirut, Damascus, Istanbul, Salonika, Casablanca, Jerusalem—they were alike, because people, especially relatives, intermingled as if in the rooms of a large house.[24]

Indeed, Cairo was a metropolis in which "something exciting was happening all the time."[25] The adult Kahanoff's descriptions of the city of her youth were picturesque and colorful. Crowds filled the streets and wore festive costumes at the end of Ramadan, and "hawkers sold wonderful sugar dolls in paper dresses for a trifling sum, with little bells that tinkled on their heads."[26] On the return of the "holy carpet" from Mecca or the opening of parliament by the king, there were processions "in streets strewn with golden sand and decorated with flags and a multitude of lights." At Easter, the Greeks would sell purple-, orange-, and red-colored eggs, and on the feast of Sham-el-nessim, the sun festival, everyone went for a picnic on the banks of the Nile to celebrate the coming of spring. The teaching of English in the government schools; the excellent educational establishments of the British, Greeks, and Italians; French culture disseminated by the schools, religious orders, and colleges of the Jesuits; and the American University—all contributed to giving Cairo its international flavor. Cosmopolitan Cairo also hosted the best theaters and orchestras from all over the world: the "Old Vic" from London, the "Comédie française" from Paris, operas from Italy, and the Philharmonic from Palestine-Eretz-Israel conducted by Arturo Toscanini. The lower levels of society and the mixed groups in Cairo had the Kish-Kish Bey Theater, which performed in Arabic.

Together with this cultural abundance, Kahanoff also described the beggars in the streets, "surrounded by swarms of flies. They picked about in the dustbins looking for food." Her grandfather drove them away, and at night they slept on street corners. "Did they feel hunger, cold, heat, pain? How could kindhearted people like Nono and my parents regard them with indifference?"[27]

In the Cairo of that era, there was no practical purpose for educating girls.[28] Hence, in "that wretched society," Kahanoff attended, in a dilettantish fashion, courses in drawing, sculpture, philosophy, dancing, and yoga. She did not finish anything, and she looked down on people who were self-satisfied and made money. But for as long as she could remember, she had wanted to write. She began to examine the possibilities of publishing the first things she came out with: "oddly unreal because all reference to any social context was carefully omitted."[29] Without telling her parents, she met secretly with the Lebanese Christian editor of the French-language journal *Egypte nouvelle* and gave him sections from her diary to publish in the first issue. In them she described the frustrations of a young girl in Egypt. When her parents saw that first issue, they were outraged and told her she had treated them with contempt. "I felt that any spark of creativity was stifled within me."[30] She said that she wanted "to act in the way that women did in Europe," to be a doctor or "a writer who would find words, our own words, to describe our past time and our recovery of it through progress, not only within its framework but beyond it."[31] Did this ambitious girl wish to be the Marcel Proust of the Jews in Egypt?

Whatever the case may be, she wanted to define in her own words the meaning of *progress*. "What was this 'progress' that everyone talked about?"[32] Its meaning did not necessarily signify being good, loving, and generous, for she saw the Europeans as cold, hard, and repellent. "Progress" conjured up two different images: on the one hand, the *fellah* (peasant) on the banks of the Nile who waters his field of *ful* (brown beans) with a pail and, on the other, luxurious villas, new cars, steamships, and airplanes. These represent progress, "and one cannot pretend that all this never existed." And, to turn to another matter, why did mothers leave their children in the care of embittered nurses? "Why? Because of progress. Our mothers wanted us to be better than they were. They wanted progress, and progress changed the world more than they expected."[33] Progress was reflected not only in new products but also, above all, in a feeling of loss of direction, to which the mothers replied, "And don't you want progress?" Jacqueline wanted to study women's rights and free love. These were matters distasteful to her mother, "who attempted to draw me back although she drove me beyond 'progress' at a time when I was not particularly attracted to it."[34]

In opposition to the linear, teleological conception of progress, Jacqueline placed mythical time. When asked the meaning of Proust's title *À la Recherche du temps perdu*, her mother answered, "This is not time one loses when one is idle, but another kind of time which is inside a person," an inner time, deep, like the time of her childhood in Tunis. "That time no longer exists and will never return."[35] That kind of time, Jacqueline thought, was like digging a well on the seashore. "Now" is the top level and "the past" goes deeper and deeper until one reaches water, and the sides of the well cave in and one cannot go any further. Nevertheless, can a certain event belong to different times simultaneously? For example, if, according to Jacqueline's father, the Jews were slaves in Egypt before leaving for the Promised Land, could one say that the Jews and Egyptians constituted a single people? This question connected her to mythical time when she looked out of the window of her new home near the Nile at the pyramids, "which spoke in a secret language about the time when what is called 'history' happened." That was long before the European civilization embodied by the English nurses who taught her to read *Alice in Wonderland* and by the French teachers who taught her to "memorize all kinds of nonsense about our ancestors the

A TALE OF FOUR CITIES   19

Gauls." The Gauls! Those savages, adds Kahanoff, wore the furs of the beasts whose flesh they devoured raw, at a time when her actual ancestors created what are called "ancient cultures."[36]

Mythical time is also time that embraces the future, as happened when Jacqueline crossed the Qasr el Nil Bridge, when it seemed to her that the distant desert contained the past: "This was the treasure I must find when I would be grown up and free, so that the past could come alive and become the future."[37] The bridge was constructed so that *feluccas* (boats) would pass "to or from the mysterious place where the river and the world began."[38] She thought she would fall into a *felucca* that would bring her "to that beginning or to that end, where the river flowed into God." The meaning of mythical time was also revealed when the remote past infiltrated the present—for example, when she played as a little girl next to the Nile, "where Pharaoh's daughter had found Moses, and where He, who would be the Messiah, was perhaps already born, a little child sleeping amidst the reeds."[39] (In another article, the story of Pharaoh's daughter finding Moses appeared again, but without the idea of Moses as a future Messiah.[40])

Apart from linear time and mythical time, she wanted to do something useful in the present time—"something useful for the Egyptian people"—and she fulfilled this desire by engaging in voluntary work in the Mohammed Ali clinic in the Muslim Quarter.[41] Sick people turned up there with various illnesses from flu to trachoma, but above all there were babies who had contracted illnesses incurred by the sex-lives of their prostitute-mothers. Long afterward, she wrote the following trenchant words: "Years later, in America, when I saw pictures of the faintly living corpses in Auschwitz, they reminded me of the tiny, still faintly breathing skeletons on the dispensary's table."[42] The doctor, a relative who attended to his patients conscientiously, urged them angrily and with desperation to "go to Palestine, where the Zionists are building a society that makes sense."[43] Realizing that their efforts were no more than a drop in the ocean, Jacqueline and her friends went to work in the Jewish Quarter, the *Harat al-yahud*, where they set up a clinic. Although she thought it was "an offense against the masses," she succeeded in convincing herself that there was more value in working for the Jewish poor than in the Muslim Quarter, where Muslim women social workers treated their sisters. The Jewish clinic enlisted young Jewish doctors to look after the patients, some of whom they sent to be treated at the local WIZO (Women's International Zionist Organization). The girls collected shoes and socks from their homes for the children and also dealt with the children's malnutrition. The clinic was finally closed down due to the jealousy of the sheikh, the head of the neighborhood, who felt his authority was infringed upon by the activities of the girls, whom he called "godless communists."

Only the Levantine minorities were close to western culture. Looking back with a critical eye, Kahanoff was surprised at the way the teachers wasted their pupils' time having them study Darwin: "We seemed to progress backwards from Jesus Christ's 'Love one another' to [Darwin's] barbaric nonsense."[44] Side by side with the European brilliance in philosophy, "a brute lust for blood was always there." In her opinion, Darwin and Nietzsche led to the *swastika*: "And it wasn't the Jews alone who would be crucified on it, but Christian Europe itself . . . the twilight of the Gods."[45] She believed that the Levantines who would succeed the Europeans would reject this intellectual poison, as they were truly people of culture.

At the same time, it was right to study what Europe had to offer. And so the Levantines discussed socialism and communism, the Léon Blum government in France and the Spanish civil war, materialism and feminism: "The only language we could think in was the language of Europe, and our deeper selves were submerged under this crust of European dialectics, a word we love to use."[46] Levantinism had no meaning or value without the continent of enlightenment and colonialism: "Europe, although far away, was inseparably part of us, because it had so much to offer."[47] Although she felt sympathy for Egyptian national aspirations, "as Levantines, we instinctively searched for fruitful compromises," and they felt that the end of colonialism would not change anything unless they learned from Europe, and only then could they be free.[48] The Muslims in Egypt, for their part, adopted only the external and superficial manifestations of Europe. The wealthy flaunted their luxurious cars, and the officials swatted flies in the government offices. The Levantines wanted to break out of the "minority status" into which they were born and the pressures of the "Arab masses" to arrive at "something universal."

The special quality of the Levantines, according to Kahanoff, is bound up with the idea that "a person, however worthless, counts more than principles, however sacred."[49] And she asks, "What then of patriotism, heroism, honor, the courage of those who gave their lives? Of course, there was an essential difference between a martyr and a soldier, but still weren't they justified in saying that we were the crafty, cowardly Levantines?"[50] Ruminating on this subject, Kahanoff suggests that "it was perhaps our destiny to learn to think anew, the Greeks with their clarity, the Jews with their passion, the Phoenicians with their adroitness, to pass on what we learned and to grow."[51] The Jewish Levantine minority was especially educated, and thus, "no Arab country that wished to be modern could do without them—without the cultured Levantine element with a western education."[52]

Jacqueline the Jew used to play with her friends Hadria the Muslim and Marie the Christian at "class" on the banks of the Nile, and they sometimes conceived of a change in time and imagined that history returned and entered their lives directly. The wicked priest who hardened Pharaoh's heart against Moses suddenly resembled the head of the British police, but when the priest hatched his evil schemes, Pharaoh sent him back to his own country. With her sensitive instincts, Jacqueline knew that she should not involve her friends in the story of the ten plagues: "I couldn't tell [them] about the Ten Plagues that had devastated Egypt; I was too ashamed. Then I thought perhaps it would be bad for the Jews if the Egyptians knew about the Ten Plagues (they seemed to have forgotten), even if they were [Muslims] now."[53] Her Muslim friend Hadria regretted that God was not "a bit of a woman"; Kahanoff often envisioned Hadria as a silent ally in Egypt.[54] The remote past penetrated the present, and myth mingled times and places. Pharaoh found Moses at the place where Jacqueline and her friends were now playing, "and perhaps the man who would be the Messiah was already born." It was a mix-up of religions, races, and classes. When her friend Marie claimed that "Jesus the Messiah has already come," Jacqueline could not bear the thought that the Messiah had failed and there would not be a second opportunity to redeem the world.[55]

Jacqueline's and other people's somewhat naive statements about the Messiah were an admission of a feeling of distress or of great expectations. She had little traditional knowledge, and, according to her, what she did have was mainly gleaned from things she had read about in books, from the English Haggadah that her father gave her, and from the stories he told her. The coming of many "near-Messiahs" was a story in itself. While the Jews were patiently waiting for the Messiah to come, she said to herself, the Christians claimed to be with him and said that the Jews had killed him. The messianic myth became part of her life: "The Messiah who would come would most certainly forgive even the British soldiers and the English Misses, so ... perhaps I should forgive them myself."[56]

Kahanoff, ruminating long afterward on Jacqueline the little girl, perceived the paradox of messianism, the obstacle or snare implicit in the realization of messianic expectations: "The Messiah who is to come will fail again, as Moses failed, and nothing will change, and if nothing changes, there is no point in being Jewish and waiting for the Messiah to come."[57] From the Passover Haggadah she learned that the Jews are the chosen people who have been promised the Promised Land, but the members of that people were unfaithful to their mission and preferred the golden calf (which she thought resembled Tutankhamun's coffin in Cairo's Museum of Egyptian Antiquities) and therefore cannot enter the Promised Land. The punishment was exile. Only when the Jews "learned to know what [they] had been chosen *for*" would they be able to return to the Promised Land.[58]

"We had a religious approach to the problems of our day, transposed to the secular world."[59] Of the Jewish holidays, she was acquainted only with the feast of Passover, when her family gluttonously celebrated the memory of events that meant nothing to the youngsters.[60] But her thoughts, which strayed again and again to different times, returned to the past that invaded the present: "I felt great pride that my people should be God's chosen people; after all, it wasn't for everybody that He opened a dry passage through the sea. I didn't think, for instance, that He would accomplish such a miracle for the British, when they would leave Egypt."[61] From the first Passover Seder she attended, she feared that the events related in the Haggadah would reoccur. Her father had told her that the events of the past in the Passover Seder "were liable to happen again to us and to them in our own time."[62] She imagined the waters of the Nile turning into blood and sowing ruin and destruction: "Was that how we were going to leave Egypt?" While many people remembered the exodus from Egypt on Passover, she personally bore this collective memory every day.

But she did not think about the past of only her own people: "Why should innocent *fellahin* [peasants] have to pay such a heavy price for the Hebrews to be set free?"[63] She also feared the possibility that if the people of Israel were attacked by the Egyptians and were on the verge of despair, something like the ten plagues would happen to the Egyptians; for instance, the dams would burst and cause the flooding of large parts of Egypt. In Egypt, she replaced Moses with Joseph: "My hero was Joseph, for he was judicious, good-hearted, and intelligent, and although devoted like Moses he was not hot-tempered and harsh. I was proud of Joseph, who saved Egypt from starvation."[64]

These thoughts were, to be sure, not formulated systematically as a political theology, but they contained hints of a modern theory of that kind. Her preoccupation in childhood with the matter of the Messiah had consequences for her attitude to all the ideological and political manifestations she was to encounter, such as communism, nationalism, and Zionism.

Kahanoff associated with members of antifascist groups and members of the leagues for democratic action: "unmarriageable, fascinatingly disquieting young men."[65] Their political discussions were about fashionable topics such as Stalinism and Trotskyism. Most of them were Levantine intellectuals, and they included Henri and Raoul Curiel, Albert Mosseri, Georges Henein, and Lotfallah Soliman. The best-known communist was Henri Curiel (1914–1978), a left-wing Egyptian Jewish activist who headed the Democratic Movement for National Liberation. Kahanoff described him as "tall, thin, ascetic-looking, the son of a Jewish banker, educated by the Jesuits."[66] He was arrested many times in Egypt, and in 1950 was forced by King Farouk to emigrate from the country. In France he was active in the National Front for the Liberation of Algeria. He was finally murdered in Paris in 1978.

But more important was the death of Zaghloul: "The beloved national leader who was twice exiled by the British symbolized liberal Egyptian nationalism."[67] Kahanoff observed Zaghloul's funeral from her uncle's balcony, and on every side saw the Egyptian masses taking part in the funeral procession. Looking down from the balcony, she observed the stream of politicians, diplomats, and clerics, including the chief rabbi Nahum Effendi who strode between the bishops and patriarchs of the eastern churches. She was also struck by the young children in the procession, the pupils of the Greek school in their green uniforms and the children of the Jewish orphanage in blue uniforms.

The death of Zaghloul was a turning point not only in the history of Egyptian nationalism but also, as Kahanoff argued, for the Jews: "The more westernized we became, the less were we able to prevent our growing isolation in Egypt." The liberal Egyptian nationalism soon turned into pan-Islamic and pan-Arab nationalism, with its hostile attitude toward the minorities in Egypt. Modernization, industrialization, and capitalism did not make things easier for the *fellahin* (peasants) and workers in the country. The fundamentalist extremism of the "Muslim Brotherhood" attracted both the frustrated masses and the members of the lower middle class. A resurgence of anti-Semitism was shared by Christians, Syrians, and Lebanese Muslims who added a hatred of Jews to their hatred of foreigners. The Jewish communities found themselves between a rampant nationalism on the one hand and Zionism and the emergence of the State of Israel on the other. The Islamic nationalist propaganda, conveyed mainly through the newspapers, directed its fury against the Jews on the grounds that they were allies of the liberal colonialists and a tool of international imperialism. Hitler's *Mein Kampf*, translated into Arabic, was widely disseminated. Thus, the Hitlerian expulsion of the Jews from the commercial sphere was of primary importance to them, although it was generally acknowledged that no modern Arab country could dispense with "the educated Levantine class with its western education," as Kahanoff maintained.[68] The prospect of the Muslim fundamentalists coming to power frightened the Jews, who correctly understood that they would be the first to be expelled, followed by the Christians.

Kahanoff's Jewish contemporaries in Egypt felt that they lacked roots, and so they sought a faith or an ideology that would give meaning to their lives. The first generation that came to Egypt, she wrote, gained a profession, worked in commerce, and set themselves up economically. The second generation adopted the values of the west, and the members of the third generation, her own, experienced the rise of the totalitarian movements in Europe. This third generation was naturally drawn to the liberal and democratic forces. She drew attention to an interesting aspect of the attitude of the Jews of Egypt to the Jewish national question. It was impossible to ignore the tremendous impression made by the Zionist *halutzim* (pioneers) in their settlement project in Palestine. Most of the Egyptian Jews of Ashkenazi origin thought that Zionism was the only solution to Jewish survival, but many Sephardic and Oriental Jews feared that to express sympathy for the Zionist cause would only provoke an angry reaction from the Arabs. Someone who did not feel this way was Kahanoff's grandfather, who was delighted with the Balfour Declaration, which was hanging on the wall of his apartment next to the Ten Commandments. (He apparently thought there was no contradiction between them.) "On the day we accompanied grandpa Jacob to the railway station (he wanted to end his days in Jerusalem), we met a group of young pioneers on their way to kibbutzim. They sang *Hatikvah* [the Zionist national anthem] in a loud voice."[69]

Kahanoff candidly noted that neither she nor her Jewish friends were Zionists, because they aspired to attend university, and this was apparently contradictory. Yet they did "discuss Zionism almost as ardently as Marxism."[70] They thought that before they made a decision about Zionism, they should acquire a knowledge of secular European culture, and "that one shouldn't go from the [Jewish Quarter in Cairo] to a kibbutz without preparation." Already on her first visit to Eretz-Israel, she noted, "I was tempted by the kibbutz. One did not need money there, so I could do without my parents' consent." Having reached the age of twenty-one, she could escape from her constricting life in Egypt.[71]

Many of her generation left Egypt already in the 1920s and 1930s. "All we had gained in Egypt we gave to other societies and countries. Perhaps it was our good fortune that we were able to adapt to new conditions and find a place in Israel, Europe or the

United States."[72] Kahanoff gave some hints of things to come: Once, when she was visiting friends with her parents, young demonstrators surrounded the vehicle in which they were traveling, handed her a green flag with the crescent moon, and asked her to join them in shouting, "Egypt for the Egyptians!" On another occasion, she was trapped in an alleyway and excited nationalist students closed in on her. She escaped by a miracle. To these two incidents she added another, in which her uncle found himself in a side street after an explosion had occurred. Because of his western appearance, beggars nearby suspected him of being a Zionist agent. They accused him of having concealed the explosives, and they began to beat him severely. Fortunately, a friend turned up who knew him from the fencing club; the friend identified himself as a policeman and released him from the clutches of the mob.[73]

The situation of the Jews in Egypt, which was inextricably bound up with the Arab-Israeli conflict, worsened over the years. In 1948, communists and Zionists were arrested. The "Free Officers" who came to power after the defeat by Israel ordered the Jews who were communists or Zionists to leave Egypt. In the wake of the Suez Canal crisis of 1956, the Jews of Egypt were summarily expelled on the grounds that they either were stateless or were hostile British or French subjects. The few who remained were harassed or imprisoned after Egypt's defeat in the Six-Day War of 1967. Kahanoff's description of these events is sad and painful. For her, the end of Egyptian Judaism was represented by the fate of the chief rabbi Nahum Effendi, who decided to remain in Egypt as long as a single Jew was to be found there. As she said, "He stayed there until he was unable to prevent the death of the community."[74]

In the course of her life, Kahanoff met, in various times and places, Levantine acquaintances—Greeks, Muslims, Syrians, Copts, and Jews—who were scattered all over the world. What they all had in common was that in the past they were "culturally displaced and dispossessed, without yet being able to fully define our predicament."[75] But, finally, each one turned to his or her own political camp: Arab nationalism or Zionism, Marxism or Trotskyism, the priesthood or teaching. They were all nostalgic, wounded, astonished to find how alike they were to one another in their lives' experience: "Our youth ... when our souls were torn and we were so divided within ourselves that we had feared we could never recover."[76] From the time she left Egypt, she knew that "history is our childish fantasies come true, and ... they sometimes turn into nightmares."[77]

NEW YORK: 1941–1946

First Steps

When the young couple Jacqueline Shohet and Izzy Margoliash reached the Eastern shore of the American Promised Land at the outbreak of the Second World War, Mrs. Shohet (who divorced Margoliash later in United States and became Kahanoff upon her second marriage in Paris) said she had "a feeling that I had come to a world completely different from anything that I had known before, different not only in scale but also in its lifestyle and ways of doing things which, if they were difficult to define, I discerned immediately, and in my eyes at that time—the eyes of a very young woman—they seemed somewhat deranged, laughable and frightening."[78] That is how Jacqueline Kahanoff began the only essay she wrote about her life in America. In 1941, she made her first exodus from Egypt and set out on her American adventure with an Egyptian Russian-Jewish doctor born in the United States, where his parents lived. Jacqueline and Izzy settled in Chicago. When she crossed the Atlantic Ocean at the age of twenty-four, she encountered a freezing cold, but this was not only to do with climate. What she saw in the land of liberty did not correspond to her expectations, and she was confronted with a "new world of ice and steel."

She initially wanted to settle in Palestine but thought she ought first to gain an independent knowledge of the western world. Yet when she reached the United States, it was "a different, frightening world."[79] Apart from her marriage and her desire for freedom, the journey had another explanation. After reading a book in which the heroine became a famous author, she believed that in the land of boundless opportunity, in contrast to her conservative homeland, "it was possible to be a normal woman and at the same time a writer."[80]

Disembarking at the port of New York, she already had her first lesson, seeing the difference between the porters in Alexandria—who, despite their shouting and quarreling, took care that the luggage would reach its destination—and the American conveyor belt, a mechanism that seemed to work efficiently but required everyone to wait for ages to get through customs. "At least," she remarked to her husband, who had no sense of humor, "the injustice is democratic." Like many people who came to New York City for the first time, she felt "small, trampled underfoot, anonymous." The couple traveled for three days to California, where her sister-in-law lived. Not only did the people seem to her all alike, but so did the buildings in the cities: "How big America was, how monotonous and ugly!" The advertising posters were always the same and the fields were flat, but what did one expect of fields of agricultural crops? And even the small towns resembled one another. "And what ugliness! . . . Huge oilfields, unfinished frontier-towns like San Diego, and the people also looked unfinished—robots." In the Arizona desert, there were petrol stations that everyone said to themselves were "the last stop." There were fields of peaches and apricots that were mass-production enterprises: "The same thing applied to people: they were also mass-produced." People went from place to place in search of a livelihood, but because the places were all alike, there was not the excitement and sense of adventure that usually accompanies the discovery of the unknown.

Kahanoff drew attention to the paradox that, despite America's wealth, its citizens were not happy. The forced smiles and laconic speech were loosened only under the effect of alcohol. "Although America was known as 'God's own country,' it was a country lacking in charm."[81] A visit to a poultry farm shocked her with its inhuman industrial "efficiency." In this cruel treatment of animals, efficiency prevailed over conscience and progress profaned religion. Some have said that the analogy she drew between this poultry farm and the Nazis' attempt to exterminate the races they considered superfluous was highly exaggerated, but others say that in this she anticipated the present discourse on vegetarianism, veganism, and the treatment of animals. She admitted that ignorance prevailed in many places in the Levant, but she never expected that in the progressive west lethal practices would be encouraged in the name of progress. Kahanoff should have known at the time that the idea was mistaken. It was precisely in the west that the most lethal economic and ideological forces in the history of humankind were produced.

Her American experience also touched on the matter of official racial segregation that still prevailed at that time. In her travels, she saw Blacks lying around in groups, passing the time in idleness, "waiting for life to go by." White women generally felt uncomfortable in their presence in restaurants: "How can one sit at the counter with Blacks?"[82] The couple had to eat their hamburgers outside the restaurant, and the Blacks remained sitting silently at the counter.

In her essay "My America," she described a poor white woman, on a bus with a small child, "who related how, in Steinbeck's *Grapes of Wrath*, which she had just read," a woman abandoned her child on the way to Virginia. Steinbeck-like situations like this, characteristic of the 1920s and 1930s, the years of the Great Depression, were also a common phenomenon in the 1940s. In her article "The Nobel Prize 1962—Why John Steinbeck?" Kahanoff expressed surprise that he received the prize.[83] Although

Steinbeck did not, in her opinion, have the stature of William Faulkner (1897–1968), the sense of period of F. Scott Fitzgerald (1896–1940), the style of Ernest Hemingway (1899–1961), or the brooding pessimism of John Dos Passos (1896–1970), she recognized the great merit of *The Grapes of Wrath*, a work of social protest that shook America. But unlike the "aggressive literature of despair" of that period, the book did not proclaim revolutionary slogans or issue calls for violence.

> Steinbeck's epic novel describes tenant farmers who could not pay their debts to the banks and had to see their homes demolished and their fields destroyed.[84] As a result, they began to seek their luck in California. The Joad family had to wander westward through camps of refugees and accept humiliating and exploitative occupations. As Kahanoff expressed it, "It was a pitiful version of the great American legend of the conquest of the West." In the situation depicted by Frederick Jackson Turner in his book *The Significance of the Frontier in American History* (1893), the American character was described as the product of the initiative and pioneering spirit of those who went to conquer new territories in the western United States.[85] In contrast to Turner's thesis, for Steinbeck the destitute and dispirited westward emigrants he depicted were certainly not robust pioneers. They were bankrupt refugees, not pioneers and daring entrepreneurs. According to Kahanoff, however, Steinbeck's common sense and manifest compassion failed to capture the depth of the horror she witnessed: "This was not Steinbeck's fault, but while we have the capacity to reach the moon and blow up the planet, it is doubtful if we have the humility to live in harmony with nature." Thus, *The Grapes of Wrath* was in her opinion a warning to save the planet with its forests and other natural resources. It would seem that here, too, Kahanoff anticipated a contemporary discourse: the concern with the quality of the environment. She asked an important question: How can one renew what we destroy so easily? Trees require years to grow, and it needs a very long time for them to reach maturity.[86]
>
> But this was before the period of the exploitation of national resources by profiteers, before the uncontrolled use of chemical

pesticides, before the nuclear terror. We still rely on the goodwill of humanity and believe that nature and the world will continue forever, and that we shall be here forever, despite all that is being done around us.

In Chicago, she managed with great difficulty because the war made it hard for funds to be transferred from her family in Cairo. Her student husband lived in a boarding school, and she rented a small flat in one of the suburbs next door to a hospital. The Polish workers in the neighborhood used to drink until drunk, especially after they received their wages, and many of them beat their wives. Kahanoff began to learn secretarial work at the inexpensive college of the YMCA, where there was not a quota as in other colleges. It was very hard for young people to be accepted into institutions of higher learning, because they did not have the means to pay. Most of the graduates of the YMCA were from the minorities—Blacks, Asians, and Jews—but "It was a pleasant world of companionship among people who really wanted education and who worked very hard [studying] all sorts of subjects in order to get it."[87] However, there were quotas for acceptance after one passed the entrance examination, and Kahanoff knew that her future depended on acceptance.

At the college, she made friends with a girl called Louise, whose father, a coal miner from Siberia, had come to America as a young man. Kahanoff understood from Louise that "Apparently, the best part of America was founded by people like her and me. This was a new way of looking at my situation and at America."[88] Louise, a Protestant and something of a mystic, who followed the anthroposophical teachings of Rudolf Steiner, showed Kahanoff the Chicago neighborhoods and said that a new tradition was coming into being in America and that the two of them were preparing it. Kahanoff was constantly surprised at the way in which white America suppressed peoples, minorities, and children from other continents; her friend said that it was the mission of the new country to receive those people, and the country had to atone for this discrimination by showing solidarity with Blacks and native Americans.

On Sundays, the home of the Langstrom family was thrown open to her. This was Kahanoff's family in America, and she liked its members very much. The hostess's grandfather had fought with Lincoln in the American Civil War, and Mrs. Langstrom always had stories to tell about the slaves who escaped to the north. Slavery was a sin that had to be atoned for, and one was therefore obliged to fight for equal rights for citizens of all races. Kahanoff learned a lesson from her, a lesson in the education that this American mother gave to her children in the time of the Great Depression. Her education imparted a sense of discipline, responsibility, and freedom. This was also the freedom to decide when to be proud, a freedom of which women in the east were deprived, while in Europe there was the contrary phenomenon of "women contemptuous of their femininity or who sacrificed it." On these Sundays, there were arguments between supporters of Roosevelt and isolationists about America entering the war. Through this family Kahanoff discovered what is generally called "the American way of life," which in her case meant being both a housewife and a student. Inspired by Max Weber, who associated the Protestant spirit with capitalism, Kahanoff liked the American ethos of hard work, starting with nothing and developing the potentiality of each person. Her experience of life gave her an appreciation of "farming and bourgeois America in which the family was preserved, but without throttling independence and enterprise."[89] There is no doubt that with the Langstrom family in Chicago, where she learned important things about American life and life in general, Kahanoff's intellectual and political sensibilities developed rapidly.

Her economic outlook was also formed during that period, and she ironically described saleswomen in the large stores in Chicago who went on strike in protest of starvation wages, but who went to the hairdresser's first: "But they are not poor if they

34 JACQUELINE KAHANOFF

can go to the hairdresser's!"[90] Although there were people who enjoyed concerts, went to exhibitions, and bought books, workers were not able to afford these "luxuries." Nonetheless, at the YMCA, everyone described themselves as middle class, although many of them were unemployed: "And can a man be unemployed and bourgeois at the same time?"[91] She was told that in America, unlike in Europe, most of the citizens viewed themselves as middle class. In that case, she asked, why were they so frightened of communism in America? She recognized that these were her first steps in becoming acquainted with the American experience. She soon reached the metropolis on the Hudson River, where she began to develop her intellectual profile and to write her first works.

The Challenge of Modernity

After Kahanoff had settled in New York, she began to attend courses at the New School for Social Research in Greenwich Village. During the Second World War, the New School welcomed many professors and intellectuals, especially Jews, who fled Europe. Among these were Hannah Arendt, Hans Jonas, Leo Strauss, Erich Fromm, Raymond Aron, and Claude Lévi-Strauss.[92] Lévi-Strauss (1908–2009), a French Jewish intellectual, had taught law and philosophy in Paris, where he was close to Jean-Paul Sartre's intellectual circle. In the early 1930s, he was a professor of sociology in the University of São Paulo and made field studies of the Brazilian Indians.[93] When the Germans occupied France, he immigrated to New York and from 1941 to 1945 was a visiting professor at the New School. There he befriended Roman Jakobson (1896–1982), the Russian-Jewish pioneer of structural linguistics, who upon fleeing Nazi Europe in 1941 assumed a professorship at the New School. Jakobson exercised a seminal influence on Lévi-Strauss's adaptation of structuralism to anthropology. Kahanoff attended Lévi-Strauss's lectures, where he developed his view on the structural linguistic structure

A TALE OF FOUR CITIES

common to all myths. The anthropological inspiration she received from his lectures decisively informed her writing, and gave her essays a special quality combining personal stories, meditative reflections, and deep insights.

When strolling with Lévi-Strauss, as she recalled, in Central Park, "a soft light came over the ironic face of the Jewish intellectual."[94] When a squirrel gathered some nuts, he said to her, "The miracle of America is to find these squirrels in the heart of New York and to see that they are not afraid of people's malevolence. America is so rich that it can allow them absolute freedom. We European intellectuals are a bit like these squirrels." And Kahanoff answered him with a biblical analogy with which she was familiar: "America is a bit like Noah's ark that continued to float when the whole world was immersed in the waters of the flood. And the European scholars are like the animals in the ark—they will leave it in the end and fill the earth."[95]

Kahanoff was not one of these European scholars, but as a young intellectual she left the ark and began to record her impressions of the New World. In a series of articles that she later wrote in Israel, she tried to internalize her American experience and scrutinize America's modernity.

Kahanoff thought that the film *L'Amérique insolite*, directed by François Reichenbach (1921–1993), depicted America as a Prometheus unleashed from his chains: "In America in the atomic age, man is totally dominated by the very forces he released."[96] Reichenbach was a songwriter before he became a director of documentaries and a leader of the Cinéma vérité movement, which focused on aspects of American life. In *L'Amérique insolite*, observed Kahanoff, the Americans accelerate the economy to increase wealth, but this affluent society does not achieve satisfaction. She said it seemed that in the New World the golem had risen against its creator, resulting in "the tragic irony of this surrealistic vision of a world that is upside-down: people toil to satisfy a machine." The automobile industry, for example, produces an ever-increasing number of useless cars, which end up in large "cemeteries." In a mechanistic society of this kind, "where most people can be replaced [by] a conveyor belt and where the work is boring and monotonous," there is anger and alienation, especially among the youth, whose human image seems to have been taken from them. Among the youth, this form of life often gives rise to gangs. There is a scene in the film that Kahanoff describes caustically: A youth imprisoned behind bars receives his daily ration of food from a robot-like guard. The guard is also a prisoner of this mechanism. The imprisoned youth and the guard are both bound up in this regimented institution.

Kahanoff discerned similar sentiments in a book by Paul Goodman (1911–1972), *Growing Up Absurd* (1960).[97] Goodman, an American author, playwright, poet, and literary and social critic, portrayed with the hands of an artist the degeneration of the traditional American social institutions. This was the damaged fruit of a repressive industrial world dominated by huge companies, a world that had lost all meaning for its inhabitants. Kahanoff compared this book to *Eros and Civilization* (1955) by Herbert Marcuse, a work that sought an understanding of the modern reality through a blend of Marxist social-historical analysis and Freudian psychoanalysis.[98]

After reading Goodman's book, Kahanoff saw its conclusions to be similar to those of Reichenbach. The American consumer society had a boundless appetite for technological innovation, which included a surfeit of products for which there was no palpable need whatsoever. To increase the demand for its products (an artificial demand, according to Marcuse),[99] the society created an advertising apparatus. This apparatus gave rise to feelings of dissatisfaction and insufficiency among the people at not being able to acquire all the advertised products, an insatiable hunger driven by a psychological need—"a false consciousness"—rather than a genuine need. One had a high standard of living, material abundance, luxury, and comfort based on a maximum acquisition of products, but these things did not necessarily bring satisfaction and happiness.

Kahanoff described the Promethean passion of America that was expressed in *Megalopolis: The Urbanized Northeastern Seaboard of the United States* (1961)[100] by Jean Gottmann (1915–1994). Gottmann was a French geographer invited by Fernand Braudel and Claude Lévi-Strauss to teach in the Higher School for Social Sciences in Paris, and afterward at Oxford. He maintained that the whole northeastern seaboard from New Hampshire to Virginia had become a "mega"-city, an urban space made up of a succession of towns, the largest urban unit of its time and a nucleus of world power.[101] Dimensions of growth and development such as these were becoming accepted in the world—including in Israel, where Kahanoff saw the coastal strip from Ashkelon to Rosh Hanikra as a single urban area. Lewis Mumford and Patrick Geddes had used the term *megalopolis* before Gottmann, but the documentation and analysis of thirty-seven million inhabitants—the size of the population in the northeastern United States at the time the book was written—are to be accredited to the French geographer. Gottmann created a new and challenging concept—with the help of various means: population registers; 225 maps, including traffic maps; data concerning occupations; and economic analyses—to prove that this was a single space distinct from others.

There seem to be some personal similarities between Kahanoff and Gottmann, which could partly explain Kahanoff's interest in him. Both of them were migrant intellectuals who lived in France and the United States, with deep roots in French culture and special relationships to Zionism and Israel. Gottmann, wrote Ilan Troen, "applied his scientific skills on behalf of the Zionist position."[102] The American scholar was imbued in the well-developed tradition of French humanities at that time, which focused on the study of people and culture in their physical context. Braudel developed this into a large enterprise that included the Levant.

In accordance with the French tradition, Gottmann is concerned with "human geography," a field of inquiry that examines behavior, culture, and national psychology as related to a defined space and what transpires in it.

In her review of Gottmann's book, with reference to its subheading, "Prometheus Unbound," Kahanoff surveyed what she called "the dynamics of urbanization," a phenomenon that began with the first Puritan settlers, who, imbued with a sense of mission, rebelled against the great European feudal tradition. The Dutch and the Quakers in Pennsylvania, for example, thought they had made an alliance with God and they were destined to create a new society, a difficult mission also for the immigrants who came after them. Although Kahanoff did not mention Max Weber by name, the Protestant-capitalist correlation, the result of his celebrated analyses, is seen in her assertion that the settlers regarded success in this world as a reward for hard work. They viewed success in their enterprises as "a sign that the Ruler of the Universe had blessed their mission." The Promethean passion—the change from the Ruler of the Universe to the independent modern man—was expressed by Kahanoff as follows: "This acknowledgment released a tremendous energy like that of Prometheus, who took fire from the gods in order to give it to mankind."[103] The American city-state had a precedent in the Peloponnese peninsula, which the Greeks called "Megapolis," and Gottmann used this term to describe the new metropolitan phenomenon on the eastern seaboard of the United States.

The American Prometheans read the Bible and believed in it and also believed in education. The drive for settlement found expression among the middle class in industrialization and technology. Kahanoff described their Promethean release from their chains: "They were no longer subject to traditions and customs but devoted themselves to exploitation of technology for the purpose of subduing the chosen but undeveloped land."[104] The immigrants acquired education that they saw as essential to the construction of cities. Kahanoff mentioned Gottmann's assertion that the new settler was not a product of his environment. Although the population density of the American Indians was less than one person per square mile, later (at the time Kahanoff was writing) the population of the United States was 180 million, and in certain areas of the megapolis, the density reached at least a thousand people per square mile. The new settlements were a completely new human entity: it was not the environment that formed the settlers; rather, it was the new Prometheans who created the environment through rationalism, hard work, and industrialization.

The Promethean ethos of America is expressed on the Great Seal of the United States: "Novus ordo seclorum" (New order of the ages). This motto, derived from Virgil, depicts the American approach to life and symbolizes the "start of the new American era."[105] The new Promethean order was reflected in skyscrapers and bridges, banks, commercial organizations, mass production and consumption, and, of course, technology.

The fact that Gottmann was a European gave depth to his vision, in which America was "the cradle of a new order in the organization of inhabited space."[106] The American megapolis impressed the French scholar, as it had Kahanoff, as rich in spirit and matter, in earnings and in consumption. India also had densely populated areas with more than a thousand people per square mile, but it was one of the poorest places on earth compared to the American megapolis, which was considered one of the richest places. America was also an area rich in cultural values. While in Britain there were six libraries (at the time Kahanoff was writing), each of which contained more than a million books, and in France there were eight such libraries, in the United States there were forty-four, and in the megapolis alone there were eighteen libraries of that size. Education—the "white-collar revolution"—and an effective educational system were, in Gottmann's opinion, which Kahanoff shared, the source of American wealth, and not its natural resources.

The contemporary parallel with the northeastern American megapolis may be Silicon Valley in California.[107] In the megapolis, the wealth and standard of living of workers in the services, trade, research, and management surpasses that of people engaged in agriculture, although agriculture too is more dependent on research and on machines than on manual labor. For the sake of comparison, in poor countries about half the population subsists by working in agriculture, while in rich countries only a fifth of the population does so. Kahanoff agreed with Gottmann that the fact that the European immigrants to America did not find gold was actually nothing but a blessing, for as a result they had to work with determination and devotion, by virtue of which the United States became the "land of opportunity."

Gottmann, like Alexis de Tocqueville, presented America from a new perspective that affected people's idea of its civilization and its role in human history.[108] And indeed, both Tocqueville and Gottman had a fascinating view of America because they were foreign observers looking at the New World with curiosity. Jacqueline Kahanoff was also an outsider fascinated by the Promethean dimension of American life.

In her article "The Migration of Peoples in the West," Kahanoff again discussed the American megapolis, considering its effects on Israel.[109] Under the subheading "How can one save the towns after the well-to-do people leave them?" she reflected on the issues raised by Gottmann regarding the urban space between Boston and Washington. Between these two cities was a "vague" structure of towns surrounded by vast affluent suburbs, a "multi-nuclear" structure in which large towns and their suburbs were interconnected by transport, the media, and trade. A large part of the population lived in the suburbs, although most of them worked in the large towns and were dependent on them for hospitalization, entertainment, and education. The distance from the town created a social division—one that did not exist in the past to such a degree—between those with large incomes and those with small ones, who previously had often lived on the same street. The difference became extreme, and thus society became more stratified with regard to income. People of means who went to live in the suburbs ceased to pay their taxes in the town, and thus the gap between the inhabitants of the suburbs and the inhabitants of the towns increased.

Gottmann's book raised a problem for Kahanoff: Were the kibbutzim in Israel really "villages," or did their members, like the inhabitants of the American suburbs, receive more from the nearby towns than they contributed to them? The towns supplied the kibbutzim with cheap labor, purchased their agricultural and industrial products, and provided them with services. Here, Kahanoff may have been inspired by reading Tocqueville's work on American democracy. The French aristocrat was less concerned with studying the New World than with drawing practical conclusions for his own country.[110]

Kahanoff continued to discuss urban problems and the Promethean question in connection with the vision of Buckminster Fuller (1895–1983).[111] Fuller, who called himself a "comprehensive anticipatory design scientist," was an American futuristic architect and he suggested solutions to the environmental problems of the planet.[112] The "geodesic dome," which was first shown at the World's Fair in Montreal in 1967, was a light structure intended to provide a roofing for large surfaces, and especially for cities and protected areas. Kahanoff saw Fuller as "a very practical man, although in a way suited to the expanding dimensions of our world." He believed that instead of thinking of the world as fixed and static, one must think of it as a space in which forces move in relation to one another. Concerning the Promethean passion that motivated him, Kahanoff wrote that modern man, who "has already given himself wings, has found sources of energy which impel him to explore outer space." But she recognized the dangers of the unbound Prometheus, and, as she put it, "What matters, finally, is how and to what purpose we use the new sources of energy, and how we apply the scientific and technological knowledge of which we have so much."[113]

Fuller claimed that power comes not from political leaders but from the discoveries whose application changes the way we live. He believed that a revolution in education was needed that would create, among other things, "comprehensive designers," enterprising people with great multidisciplinary knowledge in science, technology, and philosophy. He said that up to the current day, science had been used for war, but the time had now come to move from "the production of weapons" to "the production of means of living." Promethean desire must be increased: instead of changing man, one must change the human environment. Kahanoff thought that Fuller's proposals tended to be practical and concrete, based on changing the conditions of human existence and not on revolutionary abstract theories. She saw him as "an American through and through" who had broken away completely from his former country and therefore had difficulty in understanding the difficulties of traditional societies, which had not yet embraced science, technology, and industrialization. To the question "To what degree can new ideas and ways of thinking be absorbed by minds that do not belong to the western cultural tradition?"[114] she answered that one must distinguish between the "closed" dimension of the white Christian world, characterized by a scientific, technological culture, and its "open" dimension, which can be universally applied.

Kahanoff thought that Fuller's basic outlook was essentially American: a naive faith in the rationality of the modern ethos, a belief that gave rise to the idea that the efficient use of technology and industrialization would solve the distress of non-American societies. But in her opinion, the "have-nots" prevented change by their conservatism. Technology is worthless if people do not apply it to their needs. Here, too, Kahanoff drew an analogy with the Middle East. The Israelis are more technologically advanced than most Arabs and Palestinians, and could—should—thus

A TALE OF FOUR CITIES   43

help them to attain a higher standard of living, but the hostility between them overcomes reason.

The Promethean Golem

Kahanoff's view of the Promethean golem was furthered by her reading of Norbert Wiener's (1894–1964) book entitled *The Human Use of Human Beings: Cybernetics and Society* (1950).[115] The American Jewish mathematician is known as the founder of cybernetics, "the new science of communications and information," which includes a study of accidental forces. For instance, the preparation of soil and the sowing of seeds unintentionally created agriculture, and the discovery of electricity led to the invention of the telephone and the media. It is obvious, said Kahanoff, that anything can be used destructively, like a golem rising against its maker or like Prometheus threatening to cast off his chains and act without restraint. Kahanoff was frightened of people "who give themselves up to a technological madness and forget that the sciences can be used for evil purposes if one disregards moral values."[116]

Indeed, at the end of his widely acclaimed book *God & Golem* (1964), Wiener declared, "The machine is the modern counterpart of the Golem of the Rabbi of Prague. Since I have insisted upon discussing creative activity under one heading, and in not parceling it out into separate pieces belonging to God, to man, and to the machine, I do not consider that I have taken more than an author's normal liberty in calling this book *God and Golem*."[117] Wiener discussed the "Golem syndrome," seeing it in the genie in *One Thousand and One Nights*; in Karel Čapek, who was the first to use the word *robot*, in his 1922 play *R.U.R.* (Rossum's Universal Robots); in Goethe's poem about a sorcerer's apprentice who cast a spell on a broomstick that went out of control; and in the story by W. Jacobs about a talisman that granted wishes—wishes that turned against those who made them. The common denominator of all these was the danger inherent in the use of magic. There is a resemblance between cybernetics and the rabbi of Prague, both of which create artificial beings with lethal potentialities like a mechanical man.[118] This is an age, said Kahanoff, in which machines "can remember, think, record, calculate, act, and also destroy on their own initiative."

Kahanoff had mixed feelings of attraction and fear with regard to scientific research and the extension of the limits of the universe, but she understood that one could not return to the days before electricity, electronics, atomic energy, and satellites (today she would undoubtedly add computers). It was humans who created them: "No bomb explodes, and no satellite goes into space without someone setting them off."[119] Some say that only tradition is of value, and some believe that science must be subject to morality. In this respect, Kahanoff explained the concept of "human use" in Wiener's cybernetic teachings. Human information is liable to be misleading, and modern humans are able to tell untruths with the use of the laws and symbols they have made. For example, the wrong use of the waving of a white flag to indicate a cease-fire can cause confusion. Efficacity requires systematic order, not *anthropia* (disorder) or anarchy (the absence of control). "The world and living things were created in a state of chaos and tend to return to it."[120] The world, said Kahanoff, need not be afraid of anthropia—although various religions predict that anthropia will be the situation at the end of the world and is a punishment for sin—because it periodically creates a new order.

The capitalist order, however, deeply troubled Kahanoff. At the beginning of her article on the books of the social-democratic theoretician Michael Harrington (1928–1989), *The Other America: Poverty in the United States* (1962) and *The Accidental Century* (1965), she continued to discuss the self-destructiveness of power in America and the poverty that results from it.[121] *The Other America* influenced the policies of President John F. Kennedy and the formation of President Lyndon Johnson's "War on

Poverty." Harrington, the most eminent American socialist of his day, revealed that a quarter of the population of the United States lived in poverty. The rapid development of technology made millions of farmers poor because of their inability to compete with the economic methods of the large corporations. Many of the workers—about a third of the population—depended on welfare allowances and lived in slums.

Already in 1959, Harrington sought in his article "Our Fifty Million Poor" to disprove the common idea that the United States had become a middle-class society. Taking the sum of $3,000 a year for the annual income of a family of four as the poverty line, he claimed that a third of the population lived below this norm. This American poverty "created a separate culture, another nation, with its own view of life."[122] The poor American lacked education, had poor health, and was mentally depressed. He was badly housed, had a low level of expectation, and had few hopes for the future. Not only was the poor person neglected and forgotten, he was not even visible—because the middle classes were not exposed to the ghettos of the masses. It is not difficult to discern Kahanoff's identification with the findings of this American intellectual, who discussed his findings again in *The Accidental Century*, where he dwelt on the connection between technological development and social degeneration.

Kahanoff saw *The Accidental Century* as a book about degeneration in the mid-twentieth century, but the book's message gave grounds for hope. The world of yesterday, in which a cyclical economy was an accepted fact and poverty was regarded as a stroke of fate, was on the way out. The technological revolution had unintentionally created the means for eliminating poverty. The heyday of capitalism had passed, in view of the fact that a planned economy had been created in place of free enterprise. American business had become "the most effective anti-capitalist system in the western world" because the processes of production did not require individual initiative but a concentration of capital, knowledge, and machines. At the same time, socialism was also in crisis because it had no solution to the problem of poverty and the new class distribution, which was no longer between the capitalist and the worker but between the skilled worker and the unskilled worker.[123]

Kahanoff described bureaucracy, which made people into regimented masses, as the capitalist golem turning on its maker: "The recognition that something new and frightening which is inescapable and out of control is happening in our century."[124] In the past, it was believed that poverty was a stroke of fate, but Kahanoff said that man's fate depended on himself and not on powers beyond him: "Technology is made by man, and he is learning to use it." The paradoxical consequence of technology was the invisible poverty of many Blacks, old people living on meager pensions, and young people who did not complete their studies. She identified with Harrington's criticism of the liberal rhetoric of "equal opportunity," which had no basis in reality. The dividing line remained social status and ethnic origin.

Kahanoff said that it was therefore surprising that, despite the ill effects of capitalism and technology, there had arisen a new generation of Americans, young people who were critical of the existing situation and who worked to change it. The "new radicals," to which Harrington, Saul David Alinsky, Nat Hentoff, Bayard Rustin, and others belonged, were intellectuals who believed in social change and practicality rather than in theories, and favored personal fulfillment, action against war and poverty, and the struggle for civil rights.[125] Kahanoff, who called them "the aristocrats of America," was of course on their side. Their critical sense made them call for technology to be used to eliminate poverty. Although the global expansion of the technological revolution inevitably gave rise to many problems, its revolutionary content—freedom, democracy, and socialism—gained a practical significance from the "new radicals" and made them the catalysts of change in the new technological society.

"One cannot deny that the United States has progressed a great deal in the technological sphere, not only in connection with space exploration but also in daily life," said Kahanoff in her article "The Revolution in Education," whose subtitle was "Education and Study Are Now Undergoing Revolutionary Developments and Changes, Especially in the United States."[126] She took as an example the fact that only 8 percent of Americans work in agriculture, but the United States produces about half the world's food. The number of schools, libraries, and books per person in the United States is also the largest in the world. In Lyndon Johnson's "Great Society" program, America was to export its intellectual and educational achievements as well as its technology. Kahanoff wrote this after she had met Dr. Ralph Flint, the American government representative dealing with the international programs of the Department of Health, Education, and Welfare (HEW). This uncritical hymn of praise was the reverse side of her criticism of the extent of poverty in the United States.

The globalization of the technology produced in the United States, said Kahanoff, also permits the dissemination of a number of programs of foreign aid and a greater participation of Americans in international organizations. "In order to survive in a technological world," she said, "people and scientists can and must use technology to solve some of the most pressing problems, and first of all the problems of poverty, illiteracy and want." One could not, in her opinion, differentiate between the educational challenge and technological capabilities. The aid was mainly given to countries that lacked scientific and technological resources, and it was intended to bring them closer to more advanced societies. She did not, of course, speak of the American interests behind these programs, such as curbing communism, but uncritically echoed the idea of the American president that if the world could not find a way to extend the rule of light, the forces of darkness would probably engulf everything.

To achieve these goals, it was necessary, in her opinion, to reduce the gap between the United States and the of the world [?]—a gap resulting from the former's great material progress—and this was possible, for example, through the export of medical knowledge and education in the same way as food. The United States had to increase its aid to other parts of the world, like its aid to Europe after the Second World War: "The main idea is that, thanks to technology, poverty can be wiped out for the first time in history, and the efficient methods which created the flourishing economy of the United States can also be applied in other places." The revolution in the United States in the 1950s released the Americans from the isolationism that characterized them in the past, and they continued their pioneering tradition in their belief that their educational revolution can be exported to the world. Kahanoff called not only for the educational achievements of the United States to be studied but also for its spiritual values to be drawn on, the result of a pioneering tradition "which in building a new world, rebuilds the world."[127] That, she said, was the reason for her support of the programs of American aid to the world and also to Israel in the spheres of culture, education, health, social welfare, and the teaching of English. Israel, she noted, is a miniature model of American society that still has the characteristics of an immigrant society. She said that this idea does not correspond to the idealistic Israeli self-image of a return to one's historical homeland.

In her article "Television as a Springboard: To Swim or to Sink," Kahanoff continued her discussion of the Promethean possibilities of modern technology.[128] In her opinion, pioneering in our time is a social and intellectual phenomenon rather than a physical one, and an intelligent use of television to spread knowledge and facilitate an exchange of opinions can therefore be an effective means of achieving social change. A commentary on the book *Television: A World View* (1966) by Wilson Dizard served her as a pretext to express her views about the consequences of

A TALE OF FOUR CITIES

this modern apparatus.[129] In the questions she asked, she anticipated the discussion that has taken place since the 1970s on the influence of American television in the world, the setting up of local networks, the proper balance between culture and advertising, television as a political and educational tool, and the development of a critical attitude to the media. Leaders' powers of persuasion are tested on this mechanism, for "it is no easier for politicians to be convincing in the arena of this apparatus than it is for an animal tamer to be convincing in a circus. Both of them have to be first-rate actors."

Dizard was a former journalist and an official of the United States Information Agency, tasks which Kahanoff believed made him an expert on this modern medium of communication, but also tied him to the American view that the rest of the world was America's backyard. She thought he was right in his prescient belief that the world after the advent of television would be a different world, in his idea about the revolutionary impact this instrument would have as a medium of mass communication, and in foreseeing, like Marshall McLuhan, the increasing power of television in the world. But *Television: A World View* was at best incomplete and at worst propagandist. The critic Herbert Schiller claimed that in this book Dizard showed himself to be an American agent in the Cold War and a propagandist of the generation of the rivalry between the power blocs. The American official, who failed to mention that American television was dominated by advertising and the promotion of sales, was naive in thinking that the solution to the bad quality of programs lay in the will of the industrial societies to improve their level.[130] Indeed, the idea that the market could be a guarantor of good programs was enough to raise a smile.

Unlike Dizard, who deemed television to be a modern means of spreading the American "new order" throughout the world, Kahanoff saw television as an effective means for small countries to preserve their cultural independence. She urged other countries not to copy American television, which was chiefly concerned with selling consumer goods. Dizard wrote, "The public interest and the morality of American broadcasting see the development of television as a mechanism that creates a healthy balance between commercial and public requirements."[131] He added that the new medium not only reflected the desires of the middle class but appealed to it through its capacity to represent it in an attractive manner. In response to Dizard, Kahanoff called on small countries not to exclude American goods from their programs but to produce goods of quality worthy of export. Rather than complain of "the boring monotony of the world-order," she took a positive view of different national authorities that set up regional bodies such as Eurovision for the exchange of news and programs.[132]

Kahanoff, in her articles and insights on America, perceived early the dual nature of the technological era at a time when many people related to its discoveries in an uncritical manner. In her extensive and ramified analysis of the Promethean possibilities represented by America, she warned of the technological golem lying at the entire world's door.

PARIS: 1951–1954

After her long sojourn in the United States, Kahanoff returned to Cairo for a short time, but she no longer felt at home there. She soon settled in Paris, where she lived from 1951 to 1954, a period in which the city dressed its wounds after the war. These were years of cultural ferment and the crystallization of new philosophical schools like existentialism and structuralism, a flourishing bohemianism, Left Bank cafés, the birth of the "new novel," and an influx of writers and intellectuals from all over the world. Before she settled in *la ville lumière*, she had stayed there from time to time, both before her marriage and afterward. When she was living in New York, the French writers already engaged her interest: "I recall that when I was depressed by the wild, overpowering, steel and concrete wasteland of New York, when both distance and the war cut me off from the world in which I grew up, whenever I had longings and needed spiritual support, I always turned to my old French paperbacks."[133]

> During those New York years, in her diary, articles, and letters Kahanoff gave us written portraits of Parisian figures who commanded her attention. She wandered about in the various quarters and parks of the city, introducing readers to political and religious groups, the characters involved in the Algerian War, and especially Charles de Gaulle. She interviewed publishers and the editors of journals, reviewed novels and philosophical works, and recorded her impressions of some of the leading writers and thinkers of her time. Hence, when she first arrived in Paris in June 1951, she was full of enthusiasm about the city: How beautiful Paris is in the summer! I am almost ready to forgive the brooding, harsh, angry Paris of my winter visit, and I'm a bit sorry that the masses of tourists inundate its heavenly charm in June, a sort of shared experience between myself and Paris. I conceal from these foreigners what I know about its other aspects. They only think of it as beautiful, elegant, a great lady that welcomes them, the unkempt mass of tourists in sandals, with their binoculars and cameras, dressed in the ridiculous way they imagine is Parisian *chic*.[134]

But Kahanoff learned to keep to herself the hidden secrets of the dark side of the city, the bitter-souled metropolis, when even the Place de la Concorde looks neglected in the rain. "Lady Paris is a great actress, and she forces me against my will to know the secrets of her alleyways, her sick and lame secrets, dangerous ones, wrapped in old and torn materials, just as I know her beauty, her stealthy, hesitant, delicate charm."[135]

Large families ran about excitedly in the city, the mothers in black suits with starched white blouses. Happy sunburnt girls filled the buses. Kahanoff wanted to capture each day, to forget the gray skies, the dark mornings, the cold. She wished to escape to warm countries, to blue skies. She felt that winter was a kind of death: "I was born in a land of blazing sun. It always seems to me that in winter I'm not going to survive." And then the miracle of spring returns.

Although France was a familiar country to her, the French seemed to her to be strangers. Kahanoff could see the historical and literary associations of places, streets, and landscapes, but she found it difficult to make friends. Her friends were all foreigners, and apart from bus drivers, bus conductors, and post office clerks, she met only "the servile woman door-keeper at the hotel, the waiters in the restaurants and the attendants in the theaters, all of whom wanted tips."[136] They were irritable, grumpy, and full of complaints in those years after the war, in which France was ambiguously felt to be both defeated and victorious. The French wanted to be human only to the extent that would make them satisfied with their unhappiness. Perhaps they had reason to complain, but Kahanoff could not understand the bitterness of the bourgeoisie, who only recently had had such admiration for Pétain. Someone who, like her, had read the medieval tales of a sweet and chivalrous France and who knew the generous France of Rousseau and the French Revolution, was inevitably disappointed with the petty, depressing age in which she found herself. At the same time, her descriptions of Paris are full of charm.

Each time she looked at the parts of Paris next to the River Seine, the picture changed. The trees changed from one season to the next; the skies changed from hour to hour—bright blue, or misty, or filled with feathery clouds, or dotted with a pearly tint of rose, or heavy with great, majestic clouds like statues on monuments to the glory of Rome. The waters also changed: they sometimes reflected things directly, with sharp, clear lines, like a seventeenth-century print of those monuments, and sometimes, when the wind passed over them, they were like bubbles that dissipated and were shattered like the spots of color in an impressionist painting.[137]

A TALE OF FOUR CITIES

Her picture of Paris was painted with a discerning eye, sometimes critically and sometimes sympathetically. She was unable to make contact with people except in chance conversations at the Café de Flore or at the bar of Hotel Ritz. Despite her anthropological knowledge, she admitted that she was unable to hold a conversation with a fisherman or a *clochard* (tramp), to sip the bottles of wine she was offered or discover how the *concierge*, the worker in the hotel, or the bus driver really lived. Mademoiselle Joséphine, first Kahanoff's dressmaker and soon a close confidante, was the first individual Kahanoff knew in France as a person, not as a representative of something or a subject to write about. While she stuck pins in Kahanoff's dress, Joséphine would prattle about this and that, including the question of what the French would do if the Russians conquered France. She answered simply and to the point: "We would do exactly what we did when the Germans came down upon us. Half the country fled to America, and the other half welcomed the invaders with open arms."[138] Underlying this statement by the girl measuring Kahanoff's dress was a shrewdness also shown in her view of the American soldiers, Black and white alike: "All the soldiers, there's no difference between them.... Why do human beings want wars when so little is needed in order to be happy? A little sunshine, a few flowers, a good book, a glass of wine, and war does not provide any of these things."[139]

In Joséphine's room, there were roughly the same books that Kahanoff took with her to America, including books by Jacques Prévert. Prévert reminded Kahanoff of François Villon (1431–1463), a medieval French poet who was a student of arts at the University of Paris, an unruly young man who got into fights, in one of which he killed a priest, a deed for which he was expelled. He led a band of robbers, associated with thieves, stole from a church, and was sentenced to hanging, a punishment that was finally commuted to banishment. His major poetic work, *Le grand testament* (The Great Testament), written in 1461,[140] is distinguished by its poetic linguistic innovation and its contempt for the morals of the priesthood and nobility. Kahanoff thought that Prévert and Villon had the same "sensual, independent and anarchic tendencies." Villon was a medieval poet of Christian inspiration; Prévert was a Villon in reverse, "religious in his anti-religiosity."[141] He was an outstanding example of what might be called "heretical religiosity."[142] Joséphine laughingly responded to Kahanoff's comparison of the two: "If that is so, then you love Villon as well!" Unfortunately, she had lost her copy of his book. Kahanoff declared that "books interested me more than dresses,"[143] and the similarity of their tastes deepened their friendship.

Joséphine was a slender girl, not tall, whose grayish-yellow hair was well arranged. Kahanoff's description of her was a literary composition: "She was opinionated and funny, a mixture of cruel humor with a pleasing poetic quality, and her movements were graceful, deliberate and at the same time sweet, like a ballet dancer's, and there was something about them that was proud, free, full of life, like a goat scampering about in the hills. Her face and her eyes with their green make-up, were not specially beautiful, but were so expressive that a slightly raised eyebrow, a twitch of her lips or a touch on her nostrils indicating disdain gave everything she said a sort of incomparably entertaining buffoonery."[144] Joséphine made fun of the behavior of the French during the war, noting that they had allowed the Germans to take masses of them prisoner without firing a shot, "as afraid as rabbits." On the other hand, the women wore themselves out with hard work to feed their families and sent food parcels to the "heroes" in the labor camps. "They didn't even try to escape from their imprisonment."

Her confessions were made while she fitted dresses, and Kahanoff added with empathy, "One could say that she did the talking, and I listened." Joséphine learned the fashion trade with Madame Germaine, who sent her to gain inspiration for her work from the sculptures in Notre Dame cathedral or to study Roman costumes

A TALE OF FOUR CITIES

in the Librairie Nationale. Working-class girls like her were "a group of shy, dirty working-girls who went up to the National Library without knowing how to take out a book." Joséphine did not know what was worse: girls of the neighborhood who had never been to church or village girls who appealed to the saints to learn how to make dresses. Madame Germaine taught her "to recognize and appreciate beauty and enjoy it, which is the best protection against the degrading influence of poverty."[145]

Joséphine gave an amusing description of how her boss, Madame Germaine, would take everything she could lay hands on in department stores and "empty out the booty on the great working tables."[146] Joséphine would also threaten the management with magic spells, threats that prevented her dismissal again and again. She also mentioned that she knew the actress Cécile Sorel, who, the first time she saw her, appeared on the stage "as naked as a mother giving birth in a maternity hospital (apart from a large hat decorated with plumes and a long cigarette-holder in her hand), and her fingers were full of rings." To educate the girls in the workshop, Joséphine decided to let them hear Jean-Louis Barrault reading Molière instead of the "usual rubbish" on the radio. She asked only a small payment from Kahanoff, because her profits came from removing the skin of the wives of Black marketeers whose husbands charged ordinary people exorbitant prices. This young woman may in her foibles have embodied the city of Paris: "The city had a face like Joséphine's, a youthful, ironic, embittered and delicate face, a bit like those one sees in portraits by sixteenth-century painters." Kahanoff was wrong, however, to think there was a parallel between that wonderful city and its inhabitants, because her images of France were often derived from her readings of French authors in her youth: "Nowhere could one find characters like those one meets in the pages of Proust or Jules Romains."[147]

But Joséphine might easily have been the heroine of one of the books by Jules Romains (1885–1972). Paris, wrote Kahanoff in her article "Jules Romains, on his Seventy-fifth Birthday," was the French author's center of creativity. "The city lives in the hearts of many inhabitants, and each person reacts in his own way to the changes that take place there."[148] Romains was close to the utopian circle that included Georges Duhamel, editor of the journal *Mercure de France*, and the painter and theoretician Albert Gleizes, who in the opinion of many people was the father of cubism. Romains supported pacifism and a European union against fascism, and in 1927, he joined Jean-Paul Sartre and Raymond Aron in signing a petition against a law for a general mobilization in time of war that rescinded freedom of expression and other liberties. Romains, a member of the Académie Française and president of PEN, the International Association of Writers, is best known for his work *Les hommes de bonne volonté* (Men of Goodwill), a series of twenty-seven volumes, the last of which appeared in 1946. Many critics called the series "the greatest modern novel," referring to its size and not to its quality. Kahanoff wrote that "Each volume of Jules Romains's great epic was eagerly awaited and earnestly debated."[149]

The novel is a huge fresco depicting about a quarter of a century of the friendship of Jallez, sensitive and refined, and Jerphanion, the life-loving son of a farming family. Both of them had attended the *École normale supérieur*, as had Romains himself. This odyssey of Parisian life in the time of the Third Republic reflects the intellectual lives of young people with their hopes and ideas and introduces literary figures of that generation. In the series, the friends became major political figures, and according to Kahanoff demonstrated "the attitudes of 'men of goodwill' with regard to common sense, progress, and the changes in society after the Russian Revolution."[150] She saw that like John Dos Passos (1896–1970),[151] "a writer of the 'lost generation'" who also described similar types engaged in the improvement of society, Romains lost faith in the humanism and utopianism of his youth.[152] Dos Passos abandoned his communist ideas and joined the political right, and Romains began to write for *L'Aurore,* a newspaper of the far right in France.

The joy had dissipated in Romains's postwar Paris, and this was reflected in the feelings and statements of the two literary friends, who went around together seeking out the city's secrets. Jallez guided his provincial friend in the byways of the capital, but the difference in their personalities gave rise to many disputes concerning literature, politics, and life. In the course of their wanderings in Paris, they revealed to each other their hidden feelings, their dreams and their hopes for the future, and their thoughts about women and love. Kahanoff, like these characters, went along the banks of the Seine looking in the old stores for valuable books at bargain prices, but literature was one thing and life another: "In the green-painted bookstalls on whose shutters there were entertaining old prints, I never found a book of poetry with a dark cover or witty or scholarly works—anything that was not bored to death at lying there beneath the heavens in sunshine and rain under the eyes of the tourists."[153]

Kahanoff lauded Romains's Parisian figures as distinguished by the vitality and intensity of their actions. The writer not only expressed the uneasiness of his generation but was able, in that context, to point to its weaknesses and penetrate the human heart. In the aristocratic quarters people talked about cars and carriages, the *nouveaux riches* were preoccupied with their wealth, the bistro on the street corner was crowded with workers and artisans, the unfortunate continued to populate the old, decaying quarters, and "we are silent witnesses of the intrigues of the politicians, the churchmen, the businessmen, the Freemasons and the fiery young revolutionaries."[154] The reader can only raise a smile on reading about the actresses, the directors, the theater managers, and the gossip-column writers. Each one lived in a different Paris. The life-beat of the quarter was seen in people's movements, in the tensions between them, and in their interconnections. This view of things gave rise to a movement that Romains called "unanism," a French literary current based on the idea of a collective consciousness, when the members of a group feel or act in the same way. Finally, said Kahanoff, since Romains, as a theoretician and writer, had presented his detailed description of Paris, the city of light and darkness, its streets and its people, not much had changed.

Take, for instance, the lives of the workers. On visiting the working-class family of Monsieur Touchy, the foreman of husband Simon, Kahanoff did not judge matters like a bourgeois visitor or analyze things like a researcher. The Kahanoffs were invited to the Touchy home for a Sunday lunch, but because Kahanoff had no knowledge of working-class families, she had no idea of how to address her hosts. Jacqueline and Simon traveled to the lower-class suburb in an old Citroën, and on the front of the building of the city council a huge picture of Stalin stared out at them. This suburb was part of Paris's "red belt," many of whose inhabitants voted for the Communist Party. In a small square, there was a bistro and an old church that bore witness to the place's rural past. Touchy and his children waited for their guests in their two-roomed flat, and the whole neighborhood observed their welcome with curiosity. Madame Touchy was in the meantime worried that the food was burnt, and Kahanoff told herself that [?]was no doubt how a foreman's wife receives the wife of an engineer.

The guest's attention was drawn to things that were considered important. One could have a folding table, and in that way save space, but that, she was told, "would be a disgrace for any self-respecting woman."[155] She saw piles of salary slips, and she deduced from that [?]the mistress of the house was responsible for household expenses. The Touchy girls, who wore gold chains around their necks, were "as beautiful as Raphael's virgins." Touchy was a socialist of the old school. His daughters were silent, but his communist sons quarreled as they always did about colonial politics: "You, dirty rag that you are, at your father's table, shut your

A TALE OF FOUR CITIES

trap, do you hear?"[156] Kahanoff was reserved in her behavior, very conscious of her actions, and concerned that too great a closeness might spoil things. She observed the family's social attitudes. The mother said, "I regard my daughters as my equals. They work as secretaries in banks and do not dirty their hands."[157] The married daughter, who lived nearby, had her own refrigerator and television, but the shower and toilet outside the flat were used by others as well. Kahanoff's account of her visit, which was like a scene from a neorealist film of the 1950s or 1960s, was devoid of any feelings of superiority. Despite her unfamiliarity with the proletarian way of life of the family, she showed sympathy, and behaved in a way that was reserved but not detached.

Madame Touchy was responsible for the order and cleanliness of the flat that the Kahanoff couple rented in the Malakoff Quarter in southwest Paris in 1954, during their last two years in France before their immigration to Israel. In their three years in Paris, they were not in a position to buy a flat and went from one rented apartment to another. Unluckily for them, their former landlord suddenly broke off his contract with them when he was called up for military service in Indochina. In the intervals between Madame Touchy' housecleaning jobs, when Kahanoff invited her for a drink at a nearby bistro, she would take off her apron, wash her face, and put on her shoes. Madame Touchy, however, was content to just wear her slippers. This difference between bourgeois behavior and proletarian simplicity was also reflected in a remark of Madame Touchy's: "You know, we workers don't make such a fuss!"[158] The silk shawl Madame Touchy wore seemed familiar to Kahanoff. Indeed, one winter when a bundle of clothes Kahanoff gave to the poor was collected by Madame Touchy, the latter said, "There are things here that are much too good to give to the poor!"

At first, the Malakoff Quarter struck her as a poor area and as an abandoned and neglected suburb: "Weak and skinny children play in the empty open spaces, their checkered pinafores come down to their shriveled legs, the legs of children who don't sleep and who don't eat enough, except for wine, which they drink with every meal."

Kahanoff looked out of the window and saw children "playing their age-old games, marking with chalk mysterious, incomprehensible signs, the wondrous keys to childhood." She compared their quiet and gentle games to those in the noisy streets of New York, and thought that "even when they squabble, it's not with the violence of the American children."

One sees Kahanoff's humanity and social sensitivity in her description of the wretched lives of people in the poorer suburbs:

> In the market next to the cemetery, I see women whose appearance has been ruined by hard work and bad fat. Their legs have streaks of red and blue, as even in winter most of them do not wear socks. In their distress, they recover from these afflictions, aggravated by a lack of vitamins, until the following winter. Cripples come limping on a cane attached to their knee which replaces an amputated leg. In the cemetery where there are flowers, many of the graves are only marked by a pile of dust with a miserable wooden cross made from the remains of boxes, without a date and with careless and hurried inscriptions—a sign that a poor man's death is worse than that of other people, and it takes place much more quickly.[159]

Kahanoff thought she knew Paris, but only in Malakoff did she see how different this suburb was from the glittering city known to the tourists. "Did I want to know France better from within? If so, my request was granted." Every time she left her home, the neighbors peered at her out of their windows. She was sure that the neighboring taxi driver's wife listened in at their adjoining wall. Apart from looking out of the windows, the women of the suburb spent their days polishing up their homes and were knowledgeable about recipes and minor handicrafts. "These little people in France, whom I observed with curiosity, how well they know how to live despite their frightful difficulties! They overcome them with determination . . . , nerve-wracking though they are, and I gradually came to sympathize with these people . . . who asked no more than to keep on living."[160]

In the suburb, there was a certain degree of order—unlike the situation in the alleyways outside the center, where one found a Paris of great squalor. In the long summer evenings, she liked to go to the park in Vanves, and she would sit on a bench under the trees next to a stream and watch the swans. Sometimes an old woman would come and chat with her, "like all lonely old people longing for company." One of these old women told her about her employer who had had to dismiss her, and who now traveled around the world and sent postcards from every place. Owing to a postal strike, she received seven postcards from different places at the same time, and this confused her, "because I don't know about all these places. It spoiled all the fun!"

Kahanoff related all this without sarcasm but with a touch of irony and continued to listen to the old woman's stories about her excursions every two weeks to the Tuileries, to the Orangerie, and to the Place de la Concorde. She lived in a small room in an attic, and in the mornings looked after a lady's children, an occupation that provided her with a livelihood. Kahanoff wrote in her diary, "How little one needs, sometimes, in order to be happy! I have never seen such resignation and such humility of spirit, a deep humility of spirit and acceptance of one's lot."[161]

Petronia, an Italian housemaid, who had a particularly difficult life, supported her sick and idle husband. She was once a dressmaker by profession, but she now had to do housework. "Much though she wanted children to love, she was like an orphan. God didn't agree." Was Kahanoff hinting at her own fate here, or perhaps even referring to it? The Ministry of National Insurance told Petronia that she had to pay all her fines for the last ten years to receive the pension to which she was entitled. She had not saved enough, and therefore turned to the women for whom she had worked to let her work extra hours. They all refused, with the exception of one Jewish lady. "The Jews have more compassion for the poor, yet, believe it or not, the French always say bad things about them. You know, during the war the French didn't behave well towards the Jews."[162] Kahanoff warned Petronia not to become too attached to her, because she intended to leave France soon. "I couldn't tell her that we were seriously considering settling in Israel, and I hoped we would soon leave behind all the cold, the grayness, the rain, and live under blue Mediterranean skies."[163]

> Kahanoff nevertheless felt that France was an inseparable part of her, but the country that gave her its language and culture could not be her homeland, and to her surprise she did not even want it. The French people were not close to her, and it even seemed to her that French culture, which she loved so much, had become a kind of illusion. For someone like her, an educated Jewess from the Middle East, culture was primarily a matter of ideas; for most of the French, however, culture was "a certain approach to things, one of intimacy and solitude, not with the materials themselves but with the people who made them. Culture, for them, was not abstract but concrete, rooted in the land and in history."[164] Perhaps only later did she succeed in unraveling the secret of French culture: From the beginning of our childhood we imbibed, to the point of intoxication, the delicate scent of the flower of French civilization without realizing that it had very deep roots and that, for the French, culture is not a matter of ideas, books, museums, or theaters and cinemas, but has to do with everything. It is bread and wine and two hundred and fifty kinds of cheese, and felt slippers by the door, and the dish cooking on the stove, trees and vines and handicrafts, and some places known intimately from within.[165]

In August 1952, she wrote in her diary, "The Frenchman has reached such a level of civilization that he loves himself and his weaknesses."[166] Life was "tension, struggle, elevation," and what interest is there in indifference or passivity, or in abandoning a fight to the finish? Paris seemed to be stricken with death, and the French were the only people in the world who knew that it is useless to struggle against a predetermined fate, and because "all things are doomed to extinction, nothing or anyone is of any importance." The French meditated in cemeteries a great deal, but, immediately afterward, the taste for life returned. "There's nothing like a visit to a cemetery to give you that taste." Generally speaking (though that was far from the reality), Kahanoff described the Frenchman as a person who was indifferent to his fate. He did nothing to end the war in Indochina, which he considered a matter for the government; he was not disturbed by the static economy, and he wanted to live well and to work less. He was also indifferent to "the hegemony of America," and was unwilling to sacrifice anything to end it. Many French believed that, in any case, in another ten years the communists would be victorious, so one should enjoy oneself in the meantime. Kahanoff thought it was a decadent pleasure: the French compared their situation to the end of ancient Greece. Paris had chosen to die the death of a swan with all its beauty and melancholy. "It is wholly preoccupied with beauty, with enjoying oneself before one dies."[167] To this lament, she added, "Paris is a boring city. Nobody desires anything beyond everyday concerns, nobody takes an interest in his neighbor."

On her return visit to Paris eight years after she left it for Israel, one has the impression, from what she said, that France, including Paris, had changed considerably. She had "a feeling of discomfort, of weariness, of airlessness, almost suffocation. The working-class districts over which the railway passed seemed more oppressive, ugly and dirty than ever."[168] The grayness of the city was depressing, unlike the city in Naomi Shemer's song (in Hebrew) "A City in Grey," in which there were doves flying and there were piles of leaves that the wind blew away. It was very cold in Paris, everything seemed too big, and Kahanoff lost the capacity to estimate distances. "Paris is not a city that smiles at you like Rome." It was forbidding and awesome, but, at the same time, many of the buildings had been freshened up and stone walls had regained their original color. "Paris is a whirlpool of emotions, feelings, people, desolation, and a wasteland of streams of traffic. Everything is in a rush, is silent, and everywhere policemen pass in pairs. One sometimes sees iron bars next to police posts, and one feels the tension in the air."

Despite her desire to live in the Latin Quarter, she understood that the deafening noise in its streets made living there impossible. People of all races and colors filled the pavements, cafés, gambling parlors, and restaurants: "It's like America taking over a place that isn't suitable."[169] The medley of languages and accents made her dizzy: male and female students, Indo-Chinese and Africans, Europeans and Asiatics, Mizrahi Jews and pure French, "all the races and peoples in the world come together in this capital of the West." This perhaps was the sign of "the birth of a new race," a new culture. An ethnic mixture had invaded the French capital "as though it were its turn to be colonized." She was amazed at this demonstration of the extraordinary racial tolerance of France, which made it particularly attractive to the different, the stranger, the other.

France was preoccupied with the problem of the "foreigner." People from various countries immigrating to France, the homeland of the rights of man, silently thronged the Métro stations carrying little notes directing them to some destination under the guidance of some girl, elderly worker, or housewife. Many restaurants offered "foreign" foods such as couscous or Indo-Chinese fare. "Without any fear of Levantinization, France adopts couscous just as it adopted Picasso and Chagall. It makes the particular the possession of the generality, and thus she herself is enriched both materially and spiritually."[170] France is a great and strong culture able to absorb many foreigners, but in fact, continues Kahanoff, in the early 1960s, it succeeded in assimilating only a small number. For instance, in the area of Belleville inhabited by workers and immigrants, there live several hundred

Jews from Tunisia. In that noisy quarter, there are many cafés in which the men lean on the counter surrounded by the clamor of children. In the streets, frequented by many Jews from the Maghreb and Poland, there are kosher stores with many foods, particularly couscous, but also "golden honey-cakes, shortcakes stuffed with dates, almonds and walnuts, and displays of large trays with white paper coverings."[171]

Belleville is a Middle Eastern enclave in the heart of Paris. Monsieur Frage, an inhabitant, told Kahanoff that many people come to the quarter to make purchases, including Levantines from their countries of origin: "They are full of nostalgia," he said. She saw how easily the North African (mainly Tunisian) community resettled in Paris. But the courtyards were dirty, the plaster on the buildings was peeling, and cats overturned the dustbins. "Yet, nevertheless, I feel drawn when I go back there and see the gaiety, the good-naturedness, the *joie de vivre*! In Paris, and also in the South of France, a whole community has reassembled, and it still throbs with the living warmth it had in the past." In her description of Belleville, Kahanoff anticipated Romain Gary (1914–1980), known for his 1975 book *La vie devant soi* (The Life before Us), which he wrote under the pen name Émile Ajar.[172] Gary made Belleville universally famous when he described it picturesquely as an area of the poor who despite their wretched condition displayed human solidarity.

"Belleville is also a microcosm of a hybrid culture," said Kahanoff. Old cultures that have outlived their vitality sometimes give birth to dialectical phenomena containing different social elements that come together, creating new human relationships. She looked beyond France, and for instance examined the "Ashkenazi Levantinization" of Israel, which has "signs" of the aging culture of the Jews of Central and Eastern Europe and of the aging culture of the "ancient Mizrahi communities." In her opinion, there should be new words (she anticipated the discourse on "symbolization" and "signs") to indicate the changes taking place in contemporary culture. She felt we should abandon the use of the failed concept of "Levantinazion," seeing it as a crude simplification that also has fearful emotional implications.[173] This old symbolization obscures the fact that Israel has achievements that it can be proud of in the world at-large. To have "roots" may be a positive concept, but there is no point in shutting oneself up in a spiritual ghetto. A culture, whether hegemonic or not, that has difficulty perpetuating itself is "a negative, coercive fidelity, almost a neurosis."[174]

Like the "hybrid literature," the ethnic composition of France has broadened out, and new ethnologists do not have to go off in search of "authentic" countries; they can find "little worlds hidden in the great city of Paris." These worlds not only have a past but also are visible in daily life, in customs, and in ways of thinking. The French social groups are studied much as primitive communities were formerly studied by Claude Lévi-Strauss.[175] There is no doubt that the very fact of her being in Paris, the capital of structuralism and ethnography, like Kahanoff's personal association with Lévi-Strauss in the past, influenced her writings on the subject. She foresaw that also in Tel Aviv there would be ethnological studies of human differences. But she thought that instead of limiting the studies' subjects to Jews from Morocco, Kurdistan, and Yemen, it would be interesting to extend the field and study, for instance, the roots of the folklore and mentality of the Old Yishuv.

"It seems that I am more interested in people's actions than in their experiences," wrote Kahanoff after visiting the Musée de l'Homme in Paris. She was interested in everything that humans had done from prehistory onward. People had built houses and worked on the land, increased and multiplied, married and had children, learned to live together and come to terms with death, to understand their place in the world and be concerned with more than their basic needs. She was impressed by the children's visits to the museum in the company of their parents. "It would be hard to find anything as universal as that museum,"[176] she said. She then went from her description of the ethnological museum to the real ethnology of people's lives in Paris. From the Palais de Chaillot where the Musée de l'Homme is situated, she went down into the street where Algerian workers toiled on the sides of the boulevards with *gendarmes* (policemen) watching over them. She noticed the ambiguous switches from Arabic to French and back in the workers' conversations. When she spoke to one of the workers, a *gendarme* immediately understood what she was saying. She thought it would be a long time before there would be real human solidarity as was symbolized by the Musée de l'Homme. She recalled the words of an Algerian poet who, before leaving France to join the FLN (*Front de libération nationale*, or National Liberation Front), wrote, "I did not talk to Verlaine this evening."[177]

The Algerian Problem

The problem of Algeria and its repercussions on society and politics in France were the central political experience of the French in the 1950s and early 1960s, a period during which Kahanoff partly lived in France and made frequent visits to the country. The Kahanoff couple left France and immigrated to Israel in 1954, the year the Algerian War of Independence began. In her diary for May of that year, she expressed surprise that only a few of the French, who generally spoke a great deal about politics, were interested in the Algerian problem. That winter was terrible because of the plastic bombs of the OAS (*Organisation armée secrète*). Many of the intellectuals avoided one another because some supported the FLN and others supported *Algérie française* (French Algeria). Kahanoff's friends, including the Franco-Jewish intellectuals she knew in the United States during the Second World War, quarreled among themselves. A few of them had children who had deserted from the army, helped the FLN, and were imprisoned.

JACQUELINE KAHANOFF

Others, among them pupils in *lycées* (secondary schools), including the famous *Lycée Louis le Grand*, were arrested on account of their activities on behalf of the OAS. Kahanoff's conclusion concerning "these hotheads" who supported the throwers of bombs was that "prosperity is not enough for young people. They have a need for faith and action. As they are not able to build a better world, they destroy the existing one."[178] In France, she saw the members of the younger generation as confused, each one rebelling in his own way. "These boys do not accept the society of the past."

In writing about the "Algerian problem," she was particularly concerned with the immigration and uprooting of more than a hundred thousand French Jews who lived in Algeria. These, like the other European settlers, most of whom were French, were called *pieds noirs* (black feet). In their former homeland, the *pieds noirs* were trapped between the terror of the OAS and fear of the violent Muslim vengeance of the FLN. They went from their North African homeland to the security provided by France, despite their feeling that France had betrayed and abandoned them. Many families left their homes and belongings behind. The OAS warned them not to leave without OAS permission, accompanying the warning with a threat that, if they did leave, the OAS would throw plastic bombs on their homes. During that war, the slogan *la valise ou le cerceuil* (the suitcase or the grave) was constantly heard. The thousands of French Algerians who arrived every day in the seaports and airports of France were described by Kahanoff as panic-stricken, embittered, and frightened. They refused to remain in an Algeria that was no longer French, even though there had been a history of 130 years of coexistence between European and Muslim communities. A life together no longer seemed possible.[179]

After the signing of the "Évian Accords" on March 18, 1962, which brought an end to the war, and the granting of independence to Algeria, about a million and four hundred thousand *pieds noirs* left Algeria for France. Although many *pieds noirs* declared that they preferred to die rather than return to France, the great majority understood that there was no alternative. Before they left, they were assembled in camps protected by French soldiers and waited a long time before being taken to France by plane or ship. In June 1962, 350,000 men and women left Algeria. Kahanoff saw them in Paris standing in queues waiting for assistance from the relocation centers. She was touched by one scene in particular: a little girl was crying because her pet canary had been taken away from her. The little songbird had been put in a cage. Seeing the long queues, Kahanoff wrote, "In these queues, a hundred and thirty years of French colonialism came to an end."[180]

The Jewish community in Algeria also came to an end in 1962. By July of that year, 70,000 or 80,000 out of the 130,000 Jews there had left for France. Kahanoff had estimated that not more than 15,000 Jews would leave Algeria under Muslim rule (in fact, contrary to her prediction, only a very small number remained). There had been Jews living in Algeria already at the time of the First Temple, and there is archaeological evidence that they were living there already in the time of Roman rule. Kahanoff briefly touched on the history of the Jewish community—from Al-Kahina, the Berber Jewess who led the struggle of the Berber tribes, many of whom converted to Judaism, against the Arab-Muslim invaders, to Adolphe Crémieux (1796–1880), a liberal politician and cofounder of the Alliance Israélite (the international Jewish organization) and Minister of Justice in the Second Republic. In 1870 he enacted the "Crémieux Decree," confirmed by the French parliament, granting French citizenship to all Algerian Jews who desired it.

Most of the Jews in Algeria were of French citizenship and culture, and a third of the students in the University of Algiers were Jews. The Jews conversed in the French language and not in Arabic. This identification with France gradually made the Algerian Jews feel part of the European population. Kahanoff said that "no other Sephardic community could boast of a development that prepared it so well for the modern western world."[181] The FLN's declarations that the Jews would enjoy full civil rights in free Algeria were less convincing than its threats that were finally realized in murders, arson, and attacks on Jewish neighborhoods. To survive, the Jews had to join one side or the other. Jews were expelled from places and the OAS took over. Kahanoff claimed that some Jews, whose number has been exaggerated, joined the OAS due to the despair and hysteria prevalent in Algeria. It seems strange that Jews would support an extreme right-wing racist movement, but in her opinion strange things could happen in the Algerian situation at that time.

The French government, said Kahanoff, paid the travel costs of those returning, and the transportation and storage of their household goods, and provided every family with a monthly allowance. Despite the drastic situation, they were not refugees and did not look like refugees. Social insurance payments and old-age pensions were increased, and many organizations and volunteers helped the needy with loans and lodging. All those who returned were given the right as French citizens to work and live in France. Kahanoff quoted the words of a greengrocer, a Jew with a dilemma: "Every summer, war or no war, our trucks go south to collect the crops we have bought from the farmers. The whole of the south is in the hands of the F.L.N., but how else can we earn our living? My grandfather created this business and I can't abandon it."[182] The pattern of Jewish return was different from that of the others. Before May 1962, about 40 percent of those who returned were Jews, but after that, the number declined to 8 percent. The Jewish population, which felt most exposed to attack, left Algeria before the European population did. Like most of those who returned, the Jews tended to settle in the south of France (apart from those who settled in Paris), where the climate and the Mediterranean lifestyle resembled that to which they were accustomed. The Jewish refugees from Egypt and the

Maghreb, who preceded the Jews who returned from Algeria, also tended to settle in the south of France, where there were relatives and friends as well as synagogues and kosher butchers.

Despite the special characteristics of the end of the Jewish community in Algeria, it was also part of the general exodus of the Jews from the Arab countries in the wake of the establishment of the State of Israel. In the 1960s, all the Jewish communities in the Middle East and the Maghreb had come to an end. Without specifying the reasons for it—the refusal of the new Arab states to recognize the Jews as citizens with equal rights, the Jews' dissatisfaction as a result, the conflict between Israel and the Arab countries—Kahanoff said that the emigration, whether voluntary or by coercion, became an established fact. The Jews left the Arab countries, and France came to have the second largest Mizrahi Jewish community after Israel. At the time of this writing, there are about half a million Jews in France, and three hundred thousand of them belong to communities mainly consisting of Mizrahi Jews.

The Algerian Jews generally settled in neighborhoods in which Eastern European Jews had lived for several decades. "The kosher food stores simply replaced their gefilte fish with couscous and poppy-seed cakes,"[183] wrote Kahanoff. Old synagogues in southern French towns like Nice, Toulouse, and Montpellier, which had been neglected for many years, were frequented once again. Ancient Jewish communities had disappeared because many Jews in France had assimilated and broken their ties with the formal organized framework of Jewish life. The French Jewish community did not allow itself to be deterred by anxious considerations like "the more Jews, the more antisemitism" (researchers have shown that anti-Semitism occasionally exists in places without Jews).[184] Kahanoff said that one has to appreciate the great respect that the French and the French Jews have for the rights of man and the citizen. She quoted the report of the United Jewish Appeal, which declared that "Aliyah to Israel, as desirable as it is, will not come about as a result of our failures."[185] A social worker in one of the absorption centers of the United Jewish Appeal in Paris said to Kahanoff that when many immigrants came from Tunisia in 1961 after the troubles in Bizerte, some of them contacted the Jewish organizations for assistance, and the French authorities gave most of them permission to settle in France. The situation was more difficult for the Jews of Morocco, who had to present a signed work contract, in view of the fact that many of them lacked professional training. Another social worker related that despite the good living conditions and employment prospects in the industrial north, people could not be persuaded to live there. Unlike the Algerians, said Kahanoff, who "think that everything is due to them," and were therefore very selective, the Tunisians adapted very quickly because they decided that they did not wish to live in an Arab-Muslim country and were consequently ready to make sacrifices and do whatever was required of them.

Kahanoff broached the question of why many of the Algerian Jews could not be persuaded to settle in Israel. There were several reasons for this. A hundred years of French education in the schools of the *Alliance* and French *Lycées* had created a cultural and emotional attachment to France, which for many Mizrahi Jews was the one and only country: in fact, home. Zionism was remote for people who had not known violent persecution; their Jewish consciousness was predominantly religious and community-centered, not national. Zionism did not, in their opinion, provide a solution to these communities' greatest need, which was the adaptation of the young people to the modern world. The idea of a common Jewish mission for which Israel would be a suitable basis required careful scrutiny. The fact that Israel was surrounded by hostile Arab countries was not reassuring. "We're through with the Arabs. Israel is too close to them for our liking,"[186] and there were also practical considerations: the thriving French economy, employment for most of the newcomers, free education in high school and university. The potential immigrants to Israel knew that they were likely to be sent to development towns.

Kahanoff thought that the Jewish organizations that provided immigrants with cultural and communal services to strengthen their Jewish identity contributed to Israel in the long run, for Jews who were conscious of their Jewishness could adapt to the country more easily than others. A Jew who was active in the founding of Jewish centers told her, "The loss of a sense of identity destroys society." Social organizations in France think that people have to be connected to their communities because of the importance of identity. Moreover, in view of the anonymous character of modern mass culture, membership in a group is significant for those who have been uprooted. In Kahanoff's opinion, a visit to an absorption center of the United Jewish Appeal confirmed this idea in practice. A large board with the addresses of Jewish and vocational schools and the names of synagogues with their style of prayer convinced her that "someone who feels lost in Paris knows where to go to find people with whom he can have a heart-to-heart talk with someone who speaks the same language."[187] In the final analysis, the integration of the Algerian Jews in France has been a success, as can be seen in the large number of writers and philosophers, poets and politicians—members of the first and second generations—who have had great celebrity from the beginning of the 1960s and into today.

De Gaulle: Between Machiavelli and Charles Péguy

The failure of the leaders of the Fourth Republic to find a solution to the Algerian problem led to the formation of the Fifth Republic under Charles de Gaulle, who it was at first believed would strengthen French rule in Algeria. However, his realization that he was unable to suppress the revolt there convinced him that the only solution was to grant full national independence to the rebels. He reinforced his political decisions by holding frequent referendums, while eluding attempts on his life, and he finally succeeded in giving his country political stability. In two articles, Kahanoff briefly described the secret of the fascination of "this king chosen by grace of the people," as she put it.

Kahanoff referred to the book *I, General de Gaulle* (1964) by the French journalist Eugene Mannoni, who described the great French statesman as a combination of the political theoretician and diplomat Nicolo Machiavelli, author of *The Prince* (1532), and the French poet Charles Péguy, who regarded France as "a princess."

Machiavelli, whom de Gaulle read with great interest, taught him what Kahanoff called "forceful realism," which meant the duty of a great leader to harden his heart in pursuit of lofty objectives. Renaissance churchmen and twentieth-century politicians saw Machiavelli as a cynical thinker, but finally, wrote Kahanoff, after reading Mannoni's book, it appeared that the prince depended on the people, represented the people's aspirations, and refused to gain legitimacy from respected figures in the past or political organizations in the present. That is how de Gaulle behaved with "respected figures" in Paris and Algiers, and he arrived at the presidency by appealing directly to the people, who wished to put an end to the Algerian War. He even represented the aspirations of the Algerian Muslims by honoring the desire for respect expressed in their revolt. De Gaulle came to power legally, without a coup d'état. Although he was somewhat Machiavellian in the game he played with his rivals, this Machiavellianism saved France from a civil war. Kahanoff quoted *The Prince*: "A ruler must be cautious in his beliefs and measured in his actions. He should not refrain from acting forcefully but at the same time must take care to have a measured human approach. He should have all this in order that an excessive self-confidence will not cause him to do something rash and develop an intolerant, judgmental attitude."[188]

De Gaulle and Charles Péguy, a Catholic mystic and socialist killed in the First World War, were alike, according to Kahanoff, in giving France a lofty mystical role. In the speeches of de Gaulle, one very often finds echoes of the long sentences of the Catholic poet. In his great work *Le mystère de la charité de Jeanne d'Arc* (1910), Péguy extolled the greatness of France, as his admirer de Gaulle was to do forty years later. Kahanoff wrote in her essay on Péguy, "People laughed at Charles Péguy as they were to laugh at another Charles, who not only in June 1940 adopted the cross of Lorraine, symbol of the 'maid of Lorraine' (Joan of Arc) as his own, but identified with her in declaring that he would fight for France."[189] Péguy's and de Gaulle's ornate patriotic writings were similar in style. Whole sentences of Péguy's last poem, "Eve," were echoed in the general's speeches.

Conscious of his place in history and his mythical status, de Gaulle referred to himself partly in the first person and partly in circumlocutions, as if he were something between an ordinary mortal and someone placed above the people: "The person speaking to you is greatly encouraged by your demonstration on his behalf."[190] The first time the French heard the words "I, General de Gaulle," was in June 1940 on the BBC. He said, "France is not abandoned. I, General de Gaulle, now in London, call on officers and soldiers, armed or unarmed, engineers and workers, to join us. The French resistance must continue."[191] As the Undersecretary of State for National Defense, he also called on his superiors, both military and civil, to join him in the resistance movement. When his call was not answered, he grew suspicious of the leaders who preferred to stay in France, and he decided to bypass the leaders and turn directly to the people.

Before the war, de Gaulle saw the futility of making aggressive declarations like "France guarantees the frontiers of Poland" while at the same time continuing to pursue the static military policies reflected in the Maginot Line. In his books *Vers l'armée du métier* (Towards a Professional Army) and *Le fil de l'épée* (The

Edge of the Sword), he advocated a motorized and mobile army, and events proved him right. His attempts to convince Léon Blum to adopt a different military policy were unsuccessful. Kahanoff thought that de Gaulle's singularity was due to the fact that he was neither left nor right. He did not identify with the left with its idealization of the people or with the fanatical right that opposed communism while adopting anti-Semitism. "De Gaulle was not a dreamy idealist, nor an adventurer without a conscience, nor a scheming politician."[192] He was a combination of idealism and realism and embodied the ideal of France from which he gained his inspiration. He tried the patience of Roosevelt and Churchill, but he succeeded in preserving France's place among the nations.

After the war, de Gaulle was in political exile for about twelve years, during which he wrote his memoirs. Kahanoff summed up those years in a way that did not conceal her admiration for him: "When De Gaulle was no longer involved in history, he wrote about it, and when he stopped writing about it, it was in order to begin a new page in the great book he loved, called *The History of France*." She gave a remarkable description of the magical power of the words with which the "savior of France" turned to his audience of millions over the heads of the elected representatives and senior officials. With the magic of his voice, he turned failures into successes. "He was a great actor who expounded his personal vision of the history of peoples and the greatness of France, and at the same time never lacked a strong sense of realism. Perhaps he was able to create illusions because he himself was almost completely devoid of illusions."[193]

Few answered his dramatic call from London in 1940 to create a movement of resistance, but among those who did there were Jews, intellectuals, and communists. The people did not arise in their masses to confront the Nazi invaders. Nevertheless, said Kahanoff, at the end of the war de Gaulle—through a mixture of strength of will, stubbornness, outbursts of anger, and a great sense of political strategy—did succeed in giving France a place among the "great four" in the deliberations of the statesmen of the winning side. By these means, he created the image of a strong, radiant, defiant France both in the eyes of the world and in the eyes of his own people.

"The French themselves had little to do with this magical image."[194] Like many people of the right, de Gaulle was permeated with a belief in an "eternal France" personified in famous kings and, above all, in Joan of Arc, who represented the fighting spirit of France in a time of crisis. It was "France arising from the ashes, feminine and vulnerable but also vital and courageous." He managed to act within the framework of the French legal system despite the fact that he himself appeared to be above the law. He was helped in this by his belief in the continuous historical greatness of the country, his nonadherence to any particular political party, and his declared intention of saving the country from an anticipated civil war. De Gaulle was not a dictator or a seeker of power in the usual sense, but he also was not a democrat as normally accepted.

France shed blood in her wars to perpetuate colonialism, the legacy of the nineteenth century. Most of these wars were lost. De Gaulle's bitter opponents, especially where his Algerian policies were concerned, accused him of making false promises, but in fact he did not lie but maneuvered between different courses of action, none of which were entirely feasible or accepted by all. He wanted to prevent a civil war and at the same time to strengthen the cultural, political, and economic standing of his country without the settlements overseas. In the case of Algeria, he intended to preserve its closeness to France even if it was not officially under French rule. He acted in this way not only in connection with Algeria but also with regard to other colonial possessions in Africa. Kahanoff saw him as the most successful "neo-colonialist" among the statesmen of his time. With relatively few resources, he succeeded in his projects, more than the

United States did in Vietnam. De Gaulle was accused of opening up the Mediterranean Sea to the Soviets, but people forget, she added, that he was not the one responsible for the failure of the Suez campaign in 1956.

After the Algerian episode, there was a cooling in the hitherto warm relationship between France and Israel. Kahanoff reacted to de Gaulle's embargo on Israel and support of the Arab countries after 1967 as follows: "Perhaps if we had more carefully considered all that De Gaulle had written, we would have known how ready he was to be opportunistic in France's interests, but we in Israel do not distinguish sufficiently between interests and feelings."[195] But de Gaulle was far from confusing the two; rather, he acted largely in accordance with the principles laid down by Machiavelli. Already in 1920, when he served as an army officer in Lebanon, he declared the east (the "Levant") to be "a French continent," as if nothing had happened since the Crusades, in which French knights played a major role. De Gaulle was not an anti-Semite, but it was inevitable that he would be resentful of Israel, a country that, according to Kahanoff, lives in a dual dimension, historical and mystical simultaneously. Little Israel embodied the spirit of rebellion against slavery, and the young Israeli commanders reminded de Gaulle of the promoters and defenders of France's greatness in the past. She offered a personal explanation for de Gaulle's behavior. It is possible that in the depths of his being his pride was hurt more than he dared to admit by the fact that, in his lifetime, the French had not succeeded in being "the salt of the earth" and a "chosen people" as he desired, but that this role had fallen to the Israelis. His famous assertion that the Jews are "an elite, dominant and sure of itself" reveals a certain jealousy, and paradoxically betrays an admiration for the Jewish people, shared by his master, Péguy. Underlying these words of praise there are "hidden resonances," as in the idea that there is a certain parallel between "eternal France" and "the eternity of Israel."[196]

On the Intellectual Circuit

On a visit to the Éditions du Seuil publishing house, Kahanoff spoke to one of the editors about the Algerian-French writer of Berber origin Kateb Yacine (1929–1989).[197] Yacine was an example of the writers for whom French was the language of their culture but not their mother tongue. The editor saw Yacine as a gifted writer who combined Arabic poetry and legend with the "new novel" and the French surrealist tradition. As a student in Algeria, Yacine participated in demonstrations against the French; one of these demonstrations ended in the massacre of Sétif in May 1945, in which six thousand to seven thousand Algerians were killed. Imprisoned for two months, he became a political activist in the service of the Algerian national movement. His first collection of poems was published in 1946, and a year later he began living in Paris, which he called a "lions' den." As a journalist working with the Communist Party, he made friends with Bertolt Brecht and Jean-Paul Sartre and wrote a play about Nelson Mandela. During the Algerian War, he had to leave his country and live in other places, including the Soviet Union and Vietnam. His books were successfully adapted for the theater. He saw French-speaking culture as a colonialist tool that strengthened differences, but he embraced it because the use of the French language did not, in his opinion, obligate the speaker to regard it as the tool of a foreign power. Yacine claimed that his writing in French was intended to convey to the French that his writing in their language did not mean that he regarded himself as a Frenchman. Kahanoff thought that he exemplified the story of her generation. At first, the "liberated" people were mainly young Jews and, later, Muslims, particularly women. She said that they found it difficult to break free of the past: one has to give up attachments and habits. And, finally, "One goes back to one's old home that is destroyed, or what is left of it."[198]

The Éditions du Seuil publishing house and the journal *L'Esprit* were inspired by the socialist Catholicism of Emmanuel Mounier (1905–1950).[199] Kahanoff saw Mounier as a Christian existentialist who believed that a Christian should not be detached from the world around him but should be involved in the reality of his time. The son of peasants and a brilliant scholar in the Sorbonne, he was greatly influenced by Charles Péguy, to whom he ascribed the spirit of the personalist movement. Mounier situated himself between the temporal and spiritual spheres, believing that despite the fact that human aspirations transcended the temporal order and human history, one must testify to eternal truths through a commitment to the affairs of this world and pursue one's objectives through the dynamic of history. Unlike the comprehensive ideologies of the nineteenth century, personalism made man the center of philosophical, theological, and humanistic inquiry. Before the Second World War, Mounier attacked liberal democracy for fostering a depersonalization of the individual and a culture of the masses. The historian of ideas Tony Judt accused him of failing to condemn Stalinism after the war.[200] Mounier thought there had to be a revolution that would produce a new humanism in which the consumer would be confronted with Christian values, which require a partnership with others. Kahanoff thought that in advocating a "radical personalism," Mounier intended to create a form of social organization that would favor the development of the personality. His outlook was based on his respect for the human personality and was a reaction to the industrial age and the age of parties in which human beings had become a mass. A new community with a personalist spirit in dealing with other communities could provide a solution to the alienation of modern man. Kahanoff appreciated the fact that in France there was an elite group of clergy and secular people who were concerned with questions of faith and modernity.[201]

One of the communities founded under the inspiration of Mounier's personalism was "Vie Nouvelle." Kahanoff visited the community's main office, where there was a joyful atmosphere among the workers. They were setting up a reception committee to provide people returning from Algeria with assistance in finding accommodation and employment and to protest against the torture of Algerians in their own country—and all this without adopting a political position on the question of Algerian independence, which was tearing France apart. The editor of the journal *Vie Nouvelle* explained to Kahanoff Mounier's ideas on personalism, the believing individual, and the Christian who lives according to his faith and is active in society.[202] The personalist community was not attached to the Catholic hierarchy or a party, and it was financially independent. The members, who were opposed to egotism, materialism, and permissiveness, were characterized by their modest lifestyle, their conviction of the necessity for things of the intellect no less than for food, and their belief that excessive wealth is as degrading as poverty. The communities in urban districts and provincial towns acted as pressure groups on the city authorities and government ministries for things like setting up children's homes, repairing pavements, and guiding the people returning from Algeria through the complexities of the French bureaucracy. From the point of view of the personalist community, comprising about fifteen thousand members from all sections of society, what the people returning from Algeria have in common is a combination of "human problems, moral values, and techniques."[203] A member of the community in Paris said he felt that he lived both in his own quarter and in the world at large. The editor told Kahanoff that his community, for example, stressed physical health in reaction to the Catholic separation of the spirit from the body. If one despises the creation, one despises the creator as well.

There were other personalist communities in France, and in Kahanoff's opinion they showed that "behind France's facade of egotism there are new cells of social organization."[204] "Vie ouvrière" (the worker's life) was a proletarian group inspired by

Mounier that represented a labor personalism as against that of the intellectuals and academics, and it enabled workers to see beyond their work, to perceive new horizons, to link technology to the humanistic tradition, and to view their work in the larger context of production, economics, and society. Another labor group was "The Movement for the Liberation of the Worker," which operated outside the context of Catholicism. Yet another group, "Economics and Humanism," run by Dominican monks, encouraged experts to work in Africa with the view that technology is not the primary concern but should be subordinated to humanistic values. These personalist communities were independent of party politics in France and sought to persuade the worker and the ordinary citizen to deepen their perceptions and to see themselves in a broader human context. Kahanoff commented: "There is a need for a bridge of this kind in Israel as well."[205]

On her visit to the office of *L'Esprit*, Kahanoff talked to Jean-Marie Domenach, who edited the journal from 1957 to 1976. Founded by Mounier in 1932, *L'Esprit* was an outlet for independent-minded, cosmopolitan intellectuals committed to social and political justice, and was the organ of a group of specialists who gave its readers their views on contemporary problems and the question of democracy. In Kahanoff's time, the journal had about twenty thousand readers, and it had great influence on left-wing circles and among Catholic believers.[206] Domenach was on the "blacklist" of the 123 intellectuals who protested against the tortures and infringement of human rights in Algeria. Kahanoff, who said she had long been a reader of journals, thought it was one of the most influential in France. In her conversation with the editor, he said that he considered Israel a progressive country, but that at the same time it was very reactionary in its racist treatment of the Arabs living there. In his opinion, they were kept in a kind of ghetto (at that time, they were under military supervision). Unlike these Muslims, in his country the Jews from the Maghreb and regular Frenchmen lived together.

One cannot describe Kahanoff's impressions of French intellectual and literary life without considering her attitude to Jean-Paul Sartre, the outstanding intellectual in the time of her stay in Paris. Sartre, "who was not particularly handsome, and whose eyes protruded from behind his spectacles,"[207] was not one of her favorite authors, but she thought that without him something very important would be missing from our lives. He was worthy of respect because, as a writer who struggled against conformism, as a fighting political figure, and as a symbol of conscience, he refused to accept the Nobel Prize. Sartre needed no prizes to prove his worth: "It's the writers who give honor to the prizes, not the prizes that honor the writers." His refusal to accept honors and his vigorous defense of his values preserved the reputation of writers and intellectuals. Kahanoff liked Sartre because he continued the critical tradition in French literature and because he was in the line of the most distinguished Frenchmen, such as Rousseau and Molière who were not members of the national academy. It would not have enhanced their status if they were.

Kahanoff said that Sartre, the prophet of *engagement,* never committed himself to something he had not deliberately chosen, but what he did choose to fight for, he fought for without compromise.[208] It is possible that his values were somewhat dated in relation to the values of the period regarding ideology, technology, and efficiency, she noted, but they were like "a summation of the vision of the prophets of Israel in ancient times who did not care if they were a voice crying in the wilderness or if they stirred up hostility among their people." Sartre wrote a play called *Les mains sales* (Dirty Hands), but his hands were cleaner than those of most of his generation. Although his dry, abstract, and philosophical style was not to her taste, she liked his plays, such as *Les séquestrés d'Altona* (The Condemned of Altona) and *Huis clos* (No Exit), and admired his dramatic talents, but she disapproved of "the mixture of strange desires, hopeless despair and tortured intellectualism, essential characteristics of his figures—figures forever trapped in situations without a solution."[209] The waverings and perpetual searchings of the characters in his novel *L'âge de raison*, the first volume of the trilogy *Les chemins de la liberté* (The Roads to Freedom), were remote from her, but with time she came to understand him better when she saw how human actions can end in absurdity, a concept central to his thinking. She tended to agree with Sartre that people have to be uncompromisingly faithful to their path. An example of this was his refusal to join the Communist Party because it did not subscribe to the important value of intellectual freedom. Other examples are his support in principle of the FLN and of Castro's Cuba and his opposition to the war in Vietnam. But Kahanoff thought that it may also have been because, like many intellectuals, he did not know enough about "the ordinary people who support the leaders, who always betray them."[210]

Claude Lévi-Strauss was another French intellectual who had great influence on Kahanoff. The painful end of their love affair in New York did not prevent her from relating to his writings and admitting that in her youth she was under the influence of his universal and humanistic approach, called "social structuralism." The conclusions he drew from his anthropological journeys around the world in search of an internal human grammar also influenced her. This can be seen, for example, in her discussion of the culture of food, a discussion that exemplified his imaginative interpretation of the role of myth in human culture.[211] In his 1964 book *Le cru et le cuit* (The Raw and the Cooked), Lévi-Strauss wrote that of all the creatures in nature who eat to live, only humans change the things that nature provides by subjecting them to fire—or, in other words, by cooking.[212] Humans also create stories about cooking, and cooking becomes an important stage in the change from the natural state to the state of culture. This change is brought about by the creation of human-made laws, which are different from the laws of nature. The analogy to this is in the behavior of different species. Every species reproduces, each one according to its special laws, but only the human species has made complex social laws forbidding certain forms of union and permitting or enforcing others. The prohibition of incest, for example, is universal among humans, but in the world of nature it is meaningless. It is a prohibition of culture, not of nature. Similarly, said Kahanoff following Lévi-Strauss, there are rules in every society concerning permitted and forbidden foods. Food has an important role in culture, and it has a symbolic or mystical value. Thus, fasting represents penitence for sins and atonement is accompanied by festive foods.

Raw food is associated with a primitive state of existence. We visualize savages tearing apart the animals they have killed in a hunt and devouring their raw flesh. Modern culture depicts these savages as clothed in animal skins, living in caves, and the men dragging women by their hair. There is also a parallel idea that denies the achievements of civilization from its beginnings, which were in the state of nature. In this interpretation, humans in the state of nature are represented as living solely on fruit growing on trees and as being dressed in leaves and flowers—men and women naturally drawn to each other in a green and fertile garden of Eden without any feelings of guilt. One sees here a similarity between the story of Adam and Eve before their expulsion from the garden of Eden and the Hollywoodian depiction of the inhabitants of the South Seas before the white man came and corrupted the natives with alcohol and money. These noble savages did not hunt and did not eat meat, either cooked or uncooked. At the most, they engaged in fishing.[213] From this Kahanoff deduced that both ancient myths and modern ones reveal humanity's ambivalent feelings toward nature and culture, both of which are seen as good and bad at the same time. In Kahanoff's opinion, the importance of food is also seen in the biblical struggle between Jacob and Esau. Jacob won the wager over the lentil pottage, the symbol of cultural inheritance, because he was shrewder and more intelligent according to the cultural codes of that time, codes that made him fit to inherit. The symbols of that early culture—the pottage, the food, the birthright—are beautifully interwoven in that story. Esau wastes the inheritance provided for him while Jacob preserves and increases it.

Kahanoff also explained some other ideas of Lévi-Strauss. She addressed ideas concerning the killing of animals and the consumption of their flesh, when these actions are accompanied by pangs of conscience and feelings of guilt and people try to rid themselves of those responses by engaging in expulsion ceremonies. Another idea is that cooking and clothing are connected in that the first is excused by not cooking and the second is excused by nakedness. By cooking and dressing, humans also give the laws of nature another dimension, a key to culture, like music, which creates a melodic whole from the sounds and rhythms of nature. Few societies eat raw meat, let alone the flesh and blood of human beings, and when their members do so, it has a very loaded symbolic significance. In a few primitive societies, the members of the tribe eat the flesh of enemies killed in battle, or of a father who has died, hoping to imbibe his qualities. As soon as a culture defines the metaphysical values that guide it, the definition is made in terms of its particular system of laws and also includes an aesthetic description of its eating habits. There are societies that have made their way of cooking into an art of cookery, an art relating to the preparation, appearance, and aesthetic consumption of food. These are refined and coherent criteria, like the laws of grammar and the syntax of a language. A dinner, for example, is a ritual in which the composition of the meal, the laying of the table, table manners, the subjects of conversation, the way of dressing, and the order of seating all have a complex interconnection, like the parts of a musical work. Only a combination of different notes will create a musical style. Kahanoff concluded her account of the findings of Lévi-Strauss by saying that eating, cooking, and table manners are part of the culture that humans have made.

A TALE OF FOUR CITIES   87

But Kahanoff was not interested only in famous French intellectuals. She admitted to a certain uneasiness with regard to French culture, agreeing with a critic in the newspaper *Le Monde* who wrote in his article "Have We All Become Idiots?" that "all the French journals lament the rarity of first-class writers. André Malraux, Henry de Montherlant and Louis Aragon are still living among us, but the youngest of them, Sartre, is sixty-six years old, and the others are well over seventy. They are the remnants of a past era, and no member of the younger generation in France has taken their place."[214] The French lived comfortably with indifference and perpetual discontent. The plays Kahanoff saw in Paris that winter were translated from English or were revivals. There was not a single French film of the standard of those by Jean Renoir or Jean-Luc Goddard. She also felt a decline in journalism—and a sign of it was *Le Monde*, which had become heavy and stale. Many newspapers no longer had a literary supplement because their number of readers had diminished. There had never been so many students in France, but mostly they read professional publications. A correspondent of *L'Express* wrote about "the smell of the decaying establishment coming out of the dustbins."[215] The quality of life had deteriorated to such an extent that there was nothing the French were ready to fight for and there were no values to defend.

Kahanoff believed that this decline in creativity was a temporary phenomenon in the history of French culture, and that such decline requires an explanation. Some place the blame on modern life, which does not provide tranquility; some ascribe the decline to the apocalyptic character of the age. Others claim that de Gaulle destroyed the spirit of France with his subtle form of dictatorship and say that Pompidou, his successor, lacked the greatness of his predecessor. Although the riots of May 1968 were unsuccessful, they revived the discourse on various aspects of modern life: youth, pollution, the environment, changes in lifestyle. One also heard the explanation that the young are interested only in the present, only in things that can be evaluated in the future. Kahanoff thought that this explanation was unfounded, as the works of great artists and writers have generally evoked immediate reactions. For instance, Malraux's book *La Condition humaine* and each volume of Jules Romains's epic aroused enthusiasm as soon as they appeared.[216]

Two books, in her opinion, reflected this temporary decline of French culture. The first, Françoise Sagan's *Des bleus à l'âme* (Scars on the Soul), followed up on the characters of her famous play *Château en Suède* (Castle in Sweden) and described the gloom that prevailed in Paris and the exasperating mediocrity.[217] The second, Romain Gary's *Europa*, was about a French ambassador to Italy who in his youth had loved an Austro-Hungarian lady but abandoned her because she was an invalid, and who now fell in love with her daughter. His world was now dominated by fear.[218] Kahanoff asked, Was Gary's novel a metaphor for Europe? The ambassador was sad on account of Europe, a continent of great thinkers and artists that had betrayed its mission and human values and was no longer able to live in accordance with them. Europe and its crowning glory, France, were like a store of works of art whose splendor had departed. And the students who in May 1968 wanted to begin a revolution against the bourgeois way of life had also failed in their mission.[219]

Kahanoff also reviewed Laine Pascal's *L'irrévolution* (Nonrevolution), which made the extraordinary claim that the "revolution" of 1968 never took place.[220] The students were enthusiastic about this revolution, by means of which they could be reborn, but the fact is that they failed. And the working-class youths kept their distance from the disturbances that endangered the relative prosperity they had achieved; these young people wanted to gain middle-class status. The book spoke of a young philosopher, the son of middle-class parents, who taught in a *lycée* in an industrial town in northern France. He longed to discuss the disturbances with his pupils, to befriend them and imbue them with class consciousness, but his pupils, the children of workers and clerks, were content to obtain well-paid managerial positions. Those learning to operate machines hoped to become skilled workers and nothing more. They accepted the existing social order, whereas their teacher wished to do away with classes. He urged his pupils to speak of the problems that were on their minds, and they finally agreed and put out a school journal. In the journal was an article containing strong criticism of the management and the industrialists who financed the school. The pupil who wrote the article was dismissed from the school, and the teacher fled to Paris.

As a result of reading Pascal's book, Kahanoff suggested that educated youth in France should be employed for a time in industrial factories so that they could be acquainted with workers of their own age. But the educated youth are sent to distant countries in the framework of "co-operative programs," and the working-class youths, who remain at home in army camps throughout their period of military service, lose faith in declarations of love between the classes. The working-class youths hardly know how to read and are therefore unable to enjoy the treasures of French culture. Each side goes its own way, and the cultural gulf between them only grows deeper.

Although Kahanoff's Parisian episode was central to her life, it must be pointed out that she had acquired the treasures of the French culture and language earlier, in her youth in Cairo, and increased her knowledge of them in her time in New York in the company of French intellectuals, political exiles who stayed there during the Second World War. When she lived in Israel, she also made short visits to the "city of lights." These periods made her French experience a significant part of her Levantine cultural landscape.

TEL AVIV: 1954–1979

Where should one begin to give an account of Kahanoff's romance with Israel, the country she chose as her homeland after all her wanderings? Should it be with her first visit to Palestine-Eretz-Israel in 1937, when she went from Cairo to the Yishuv with her friend Sylvie to see the pioneering society of Israel-on-the-way?[221] Or should it perhaps be ten years later, on November 29, 1947, when, moved and tense, she, together with many American Jews, listened in a hall in Chicago to a broadcast of the vote in the United Nations in favor of the partition of Palestine into a Jewish state and Arab states?[222] Or should it perhaps be with her immigration to Israel in 1954 at the end of her travels between Cairo, New York, and Paris? If there is any question about the starting point, it is not difficult to decide in the end. It was Anwar Sadat's visit to Israel (and later the conclusion of a peace treaty between the Egypt and Israel), which took place during her final illness, a year before her death. The visit of the president of Egypt, the land where she was born, to the State of Israel, the place where she chose to live and end her days, shed a meaningful light on the story of a life with a beginning and an end: a private exodus from Egypt that concluded in a public way.[223]

In 1937, to mark her graduation from the French *lycée* in Cairo, the parents of her friend Sylvie invited her to visit Palestine with them to celebrate the feast of Passover. After a night's journey by train, young Jacqueline was awakened in the morning "by the marvelous and intoxicating scent of orange-blossoms. . . . The air was crystal-clear, and the dew glistened on the blossoms which glowed like precious stones, and on the shining leaves."[224] The romanticism of the land of Israel filled her heart, and it seemed to her that she would never see "a brighter and happier morning." She was filled with a joy that she had never known before. Every few minutes, crates of oranges were loaded onto the train, and the fruit was so close that one could put one's hand out of the window and touch it. She imbibed "the scent of Eretz-Israel." She was very excited when, near Lod or Rehovot, Jewish workers in the orchards waved to them as they passed by. When she recalled this journey long afterward, she felt that the apartment blocks and industrial buildings that replaced the orchards had "destroyed the rural innocence of the Jewish settlements."

Jacqueline was overcome with biblical romanticism, which she evoked in the language of the Song of Songs in the Judean hills she saw from the train: "The flowers appear on the earth: the time of the singing of the birds is come, and the voice of the turtle is heard in our land." Arabs in their traditional costumes sat by "a fig-tree, and the vines gave out a scent."

This "biblical charm," as she described it, which went together with "a simple faith," has disappeared since Jacqueline's romantic visit of 1937. The Arab coffeehouses with their vine-covered arches have also disappeared. Her "Orientalism" viewpoint, to use Edward Said's expression, was demonstrated by her description of how "the Jewish settlers would contrast the cleanliness and order of their settlements with the dirt and untidiness of the Arab villages, the Jewish eucalyptus with the Arab cactus, the energy and initiative with the lassitude."[225] At the same time, she criticized the colonialist attitude that was shown in "a way of speaking that recalled the British colonialist attitude to 'natives.'"

Jacqueline perceived a political theology among the Jewish settlers of the 1930s. Although this concept from the sphere of political thought was not yet current in the local discourse of that time, in describing her first impressions of Eretz-Israel she wrote, "For them it's like a gospel: they believe it's forbidden to miss an opportunity."[226] As mentioned, she criticized the colonialist manner of speaking about the Arabs of Palestine; she was shocked by the prejudices of Zionist settlers. She later admitted that she too was prone to judge things in a simplistic colonialist way due to her education and status in Egypt: "We were unable to decide in what category to put Zionism—whether it was white, native, or Jewish."[227]

> She admired the desire of the settlers in Palestine "to labor for their redemption and perhaps ours as well." She appreciated their socialist vision and egalitarian spirit. She was therefore surprised

at their alienation from the Arabs, "their brothers of the Semitic race." Although the Arabs were Ishmaelites, this meant little to the Zionists, who "were not at all religious." Perhaps she thought that their secularism might prevent them from harboring feelings of hostility toward gentiles, "as might perhaps be expected of religious believers who were brought up on the myth of Cain and Abel." But the Zionists, she said, "disregard this common origin and do not settle these ever-changing and recurring disputes." The secular settlers saw everyone outside their camp as a gentile or an Ishmaelite. The Mizrahi Jews like Jacqueline also forbade any relations with the Ishmaelites, their separated brothers. Although Jacqueline and Sylvie never stopped discussing whether the Zionists they met in Palestine were "reactionaries" or "socialists," they agreed on one important point concerning the people of the Yishuv. Jacqueline said, "The boastfulness of the guides and most of the people who showed us their kibbutzim, their inability to believe that their achievements spoke for themselves, the tone of superiority in which they always spoke of themselves in comparison with other peoples—all this aroused ridicule and was also annoying." And Sylvie added, "They have a distorted vision and a narrow-mindedness. They all say exactly the same thing. How boring it is![228]

Years later, Kahanoff understood that talk of this kind revealed scars that hid old wounds. She envied the Zionist settlers above all for their feminist outlook, which made no distinction between male and female, and for their work in reviving the language and the nation. But, more than anything else, the visits to the kibbutzim revealed the chasm that existed between the aristocratic tourists from Cairo and the pioneers. The visits highlighted the differences in the order of priorities of the banker, Sylvie's father, and the kibbutzniks who were mainly interested in growing fruit and producing eggs. The impression the kibbutzniks made on Jacqueline was expressed in a few words: "Everything seemed too rigid to be real."[229] She felt that the kibbutzniks, with whom she did not exchange a word, in the way they looked at the stylish clothes of the honored guests from Egypt, were comparing their pioneering enterprise and the national revival of the Jewish people with what they regarded as the parasitic preoccupation with banking and commerce of exilic Jews.

The guide at the Wailing Wall made a similar distinction between "Jews" and "Israelis." His comparison of the "proud and erect bearing" of the khaki-clad youths and the religious Jews, "hunchbacked peddlers and idlers," stressed those who were active versus those who were sedentary, the erect versus the bent, the secular versus the religious. As Kahanoff later recalled, "We were ashamed of our Judaism." Jacqueline was torn between her attraction to Judaism and its ugly manifestation at the Wailing Wall—a Judaism mainly represented by religious Sephardic and Mizrahi Jews. She tried not to react on hearing the guide's rhetorical question: "They have prayed so long for the Messiah to come, and what have they got so far?"[230] The Jews kissing the stones of the Wall, "torn and tattered, with diseased eyes and deformities," weeping in the squalor by the Wall, reminded her of the squalor of the *Harat-al-yahud*, the Jewish Quarter in Cairo. Her hands caressed the stones of the Wall, but she felt that this was a low point of the Jewish people, a state of humiliation. Her feelings were confused, but she felt a certain happiness at not being separated from her people. Simultaneously, she let out the biting words "Look, Mister, that's quite enough!"

About ten years later, Kahanoff, together with a huge crowd, celebrated the founding of the State of Israel at the Chicago Stadium. As "thousands and thousands of people were filled with emotion when the blue-and-white flag with the star of David in its center was slowly hoisted to the strains of 'Hatikvah,'" Kahanoff wrote,

> In my mind's eye I saw Jerusalem as I remembered it on my visit on Passover 1937. The Wailing Wall at that time symbolized for me the hopelessness of the Jewish fate when the shadow of Hitler hung over Europe. There was only a narrow way to the Wall, an

alley in the Jewish Quarter: British soldiers guarded the entrance to it. Arabs jeered at us in the area of the Dome of the Rock above and the Jews crowded in the narrow passageway below. Old Jews prayed and made blessings close to the Wall, which seemed to exude the sadness of hundreds of years.[231]

A hint of her future views may be seen in her brief visit to Hebron. On the steps of the Cave of the Patriarchs, Jacqueline was warned not to go beyond the seventh step, which was as far as anyone was allowed to go. She thought it "disgraceful that we, precisely, are not allowed to go to the grave of our father Abraham. Acting on an impulse, I went one step further."[232] There were shouts and the firing of a shot. The tumult that ensued prompted her and Sylvie's family to immediately leave, accompanied by the hostile glances of the local Arabs.

Her secularism did not cease to trouble her: "Why should I care about all this?" On their way back to Jerusalem, they stopped to visit the tomb traditionally believed to be that of "Our Mother Rachel." In her childhood, she said, Rachel was "my favorite Hebrew woman . . . , the mother of the Jewish people," a charming girl who resembled one of the beautiful Bedouin women. Jacqueline's amorphous Judaism, which was undefined and not based on a traditional education or the ritual precepts of the Torah, surprisingly betrayed a primordial Jewish identity. The immediate feelings she had on her visit to the Wall, to the Cave of the Patriarchs, and to Rachel's tomb were undoubtedly authentic, feelings that did not necessarily depend on a knowledge of the Torah, or the observance of its commandments.

On her last day in Eretz-Israel, she visited the Hebrew University on Mount Scopus, which overlooked in the distance the Dead Sea and the Judean Desert. The visit made a great impression on her, the complete opposite from the one she had from the holy sites. She was excited by the fact that here "scholars would pave the way to the revival of the Jews." The guide in the library, with a thick German accent, boasted that it was "the best and largest library in the entire Middle East," and that the university had the best scholars of Jewish studies in the world, who were German Jews. Sylvie was annoyed that nearly all the lecturers and students were from Germany. She teased the guide by pointing out the achievements of French and British scholars, and she ridiculed "this mixture of German arrogance and Yiddish chauvinism, with the addition of the Hebrew language. No, that's just too much!"[233]

On the return journey to Cairo by train, the two friends had a discussion on the nationalism that had arisen in Europe in the 1930s. Sylvie optimistically claimed that nationalism would give way to internationalism, and Jacqueline wondered why, if this was so, Egypt and India were striving for national independence. And she also asked, revealing the first indications of a Zionist outlook, "why the Jews have to be the only people without a country."[234] The best thing, she said, would be if the Jews first settled their country and only after that made revolutions. Sylvie answered that the fact that the Jews were not a colonial people showed that they could skip the anticolonial stage. Jacqueline also feared that the founding of a Jewish state could endanger the lives of the Jews in the Arab countries. "If the thing is so necessary to other Jews," she said, "our security becomes a thing of lesser importance. But, even then, we can go to Eretz-Israel if we have to." She added that in a future Jewish state, their status in relation to that of the Jews of Eastern Europe was likely to be adversely affected.

> Sylvie: "We will never feel secure among these people in Palestine, and don't pretend you like these Polish and German Jews any more than I do."
>
> Jacqueline: "The Jews of Eastern Europe are not to be blamed for having lived in different conditions from us. Their great sufferings, much greater than our own, inevitably made them more extreme and narrow-minded, and, apart from that, they are just as enthusiastic about German culture as we are about French culture."[235]

Jacqueline nevertheless thought that there had to be a balance to the rigid German-Yiddish culture she encountered in Palestine, but at the same time she was able to eschew feelings that could degenerate into hostility to the "other." For example, she said that French professors and students had to make their mark at the Hebrew University. Already at this early stage, she recognized that it was her duty, and the duty of those like her, "as Sephardi Jews with a French education, to help Zionism find its place in a new, modern, progressive Middle East." Although she would have preferred to have studied in the Sorbonne after she finished high school, she held that "I will have—it seems to me—to live and work in Palestine."

From Paris to Beersheba

Kahanoff was in Israel for a quarter of a century, most of the time in Tel Aviv, but in her first two years in the country, from 1954 to 1956, she lived with her husband Alexander Kahanoff in the southern city of Beersheba. Relatives, friends, and acquaintances thought them a bit crazy when they said they wanted to go down to the Negev desert: "As immigrants from western countries with university diplomas, both of us could find opportunities in Tel Aviv, as we were promised."[236] A friend asked her to try to persuade Alexander, an acoustic engineer, not to settle in the Negev: "First of all, you have come here at your own expense, and it can't be said that you don't have any relatives in the country. Your husband's family knew all the old Zionists: Ussishkin." "Ussi—what? I've never heard of him," she answered. "We're new immigrants and not even Zionists. And because we're beginning our life here from nothing, it's best we should do it the hard way. Moreover, Eilat and Beersheba are undoubtedly more attractive than Tel-Aviv."

Jacqueline thought that Tel Aviv did not have much to offer compared to Paris or New York. In addition, the Kahanoff couple did not know Hebrew, and Tel Aviv's cultural life was therefore closed to them. They wanted to begin in a new place where Hebrew did not matter too much. Some of her friends called them pioneers or Zionists, adding that "there are still some around," but others told them that "the time of idealism was over, and said we were simply foolish." Alexander began to work as an engineer for Solel Boneh (a construction company) and Jacqueline attended an *ulpan* (a center for learning Hebrew). They lived in a dilapidated Arab house with a courtyard and a trailing vine, and for them "it was an ideal home, and we were sorry we had to leave it." The couple moved to permanent accommodation in the HIAS (Hebrew Immigrant Aid Society) building, which was intended for foreign experts, engineers, and technicians. She felt that everything was fresh and new there, and she was especially impressed by "the sight of the sun shining on the hills of the desert." On Thursdays, she went shopping in the market and liked to see the Bedouins with their camels. One should remember, she said, that in 1955 Beersheba was far from being the "little Switzerland" envisaged by the first settlers. When she closed the windows, the heat was suffocating, and if she opened the windows, she had to sit in the shade. When friends came to visit, the couple had everyone sit on the balcony in the shade, and it was hard to carry on a conversation as they were busy swatting away mosquitoes.

A few days after they settled in the HIAS building, they were visited by the headmistress of the city's high school, who immediately turned to Jacqueline: "I heard that you are from Paris and have finished university. I need someone to teach French. Could you start tomorrow morning?" When Jacqueline protested that she was not a teacher by profession and was a graduate of an American university, not a French one, the headmistress answered with Zionist rhetoric: that Israel would not exist if the first Israelis had waited until they had all they needed. Jacqueline felt that this reply contained the essence of everything she liked about Israel: the drive, the urge to forge ahead, to achieve, and at the same time the willingness to take risks and make mistakes.[237]

The next day, the pupils were excited about their first French lesson. The parents of about half the children in the class, who had emigrated from Romania, were survivors of the concentration camps. She was touched by their idea of normality: they "saw learning French as a step towards normal life." In Beersheba at that time, education was considered a great and expensive luxury. Although the classrooms were scattered throughout the city, Kahanoff thought it the most wonderful school she had ever known, perhaps because of the effort made by the headmistress and teachers and native-born people from outside to help the pupils overcome their difficulties and to persuade them to continue their studies despite the trouble their families had in making a living. She related that one day a boy came to the school and said that he wanted to learn. He used to work until late at night selling peanuts in the local cinema because his father was an invalid and blind: "He not only wanted to help himself but also wanted to do his duty to others. He was far from mature, but the little fellow had a desire for self-improvement, a touch of greatness that I found in many people in Beersheba and which I see as the true wealth of Israel."[238]

In the early 1950s, she thought Beersheba was like an armed camp. To do the research for a series of articles she planned to write about the schools in the new moshavim (cooperative settlements), she needed to go to dangerous areas of the Negev.[239] In one instance, she went to the remote desert town of Dimona to meet with parents and teachers and an educational inspector. At the end of the meeting, she waited alone on an empty road in the middle of the night, and every gust of wind made her shiver. She was finally given a lift by an army patrol. When she sat down in the vehicle, the driver put his weapon on the alert and wanted to give her a rifle as well. She declined and replied, "All I can say is, if something happens, I won't use it."

In retrospect, Beersheba and many settlements in the Negev seemed to her to have been populated by people in a wretched condition:

> Angry, disappointed, lonely and often frightened, each one bore in his own way the scars of the history of mankind and of his own particular history. The confrontation between the "Mizrahis" and the westerners was very pronounced and sometimes dreadful and even cruel, but despite this, although they had all known times of despair, the majority, with all their limitations, tried to overcome the difficulties. . . . They were people who chose in their distress to be Israelis in Israel, although they were hardly aware of it. . . . This effort to subsist was my experience and that of others in Beersheba.[240]

Finally, the Kahanoff couple settled in Tel Aviv, because work in Alexander's field was readily found there. "Leaving Beersheba was one of the great heartbreaks of my life." As a farewell present the children of the school gave her an album of photographs of themselves, and each one added something in his own hand. She was very proud of the fact that after only a few months many of them could write good French. "The Negev and its capital [Beersheba], which at that time was quite miserable, have been part of my inner landscape ever since."

Aharon Amir, *Keshet*, and Kahanoff

In 1958, two years after she moved from Beersheba to Tel Aviv, the "Orientalist" and publicist Nissim Rejwan (1924–2017) drew Aharon Amir's attention to Kahanoff after reading her article "Reflections of a Levantine" in the American Jewish journal *Jewish Frontier*. A Hebrew poet, Amir (1923–2008) was the editor of the Hebrew literary journal *Keshet*. Rejwan himself was the editor of *Al-yom*, the Arabic newspaper of the Histadrut (the Federation of Labor). He was an Israeli intellectual of Iraqi origin and an Anglophile who had published books with American publishing houses on the Jews in Iraq, modern Islam, and Israeli identity. He saw in Kahanoff a typical Levantine, since according to him, "To be a Levantine is to live in two worlds, or more, without belonging to either of them."[241]

In 1958, Amir began to translate her essays and to publish them in *Keshet*, the journal he founded that same year. *Keshet* was Kahanoff's main Hebrew outlet, although she also published in the literary sections of Israeli newspapers and a bit in other journals. It was the readers of *Keshet* who began to develop Kahanoff's literary "aura," and her personal, expressive writing was a great novelty. Amir saw in her writing style something Mizrahi and ultrarefined, expressed in a western intellectual idiom yet better than that of the "westerners" who came out of the European shtetls. Kahanoff possessed sensitivity, cultural broadmindedness, and human tenderness. She had a yearning to identify with the Israeli experience and at the same time to retain her eastern identity.[242]

A. B. Yehoshua, who was on the staff of *Keshet*, wrote that Kahanoff's openness to the region complemented Amir's Western European outlook. Amir himself believed that the journal aimed at breaking away from the European orientation that prevailed in Israel and opening a window on the Levantine world. He accomplished this departure by giving writers from Arab countries— such as Nissim Rejwan, Sasson Somekh, and Kahanoff—an opportunity that was in keeping with his own desire to acquaint the Israeli public with the cultural and intellectual sensibilities of the Levantine world, marked by a combination of rootedness and a cosmopolitan openness. Amir spoke of this combination in his last interview: "When the first years of *Keshet* came to an end, I summarized them by saying that the principles that guided me were rootedness together with openness. The rootedness complemented the openness and the openness complemented the rootedness. As Nietzsche once said, 'If one doesn't listen to many voices, one's own voice will never be heard.'"[243]

Amir's work as a translator from English and French into Hebrew gave Yehoshua the idea that "the Levantine connection that later became one of the distinguishing features of *Keshet*'s ideology, especially through Jacqueline Kahanoff's contributions, was not a sign of weakness and want but a sign of a wealth and plenitude which it is worth bringing into our culture."[244] This is what Amir wrote in his short introduction to the selection of Kahanoff's articles, *From East the Sun*, which he assembled and published a year before his death:

> Jacqueline Kahanoff, essayist, novelist and critic, stands out in the cultural backdrop of our country as the brilliant quintessential representative of the "Levantine generation" at its best—that colorful, cosmopolitan stratum of the Mediterranean intelligentsia which perhaps began more than two and a half millennia ago—in Canaan, over the sea, and in Greece, over the sea,—and which we are perhaps returning to in our time. This stratum is one of which pluralism is the heart and soul, for which openness and tolerance are the elixir of life, for whom the bridging of cultures, adaptation and fertilization are perhaps a mission, a decree of fate or an existential command.[245]

About two decades later, at the inauguration of the "Forum for Mediterranean Cultures" at the Van Leer Jerusalem Institute, Amir delivered a lecture in Kahanoff's memory, published under the title "A Promise Rising on the Nile with Dawn." In his opinion, she was a woman with a highly developed sense of criticism, self-criticism, and irony. "As someone who had known her for most of the time she was in the country, when I try to grasp her image with my eyes and visualize her with the eyes of the spirit, she seems to me to be hiding—with that restraint that was one of her outstanding characteristics—a smile of forgiveness and disbelief."[246] He went on to make some remarks about "the promise represented by Kahanoff and the extent to which that promise was fulfilled. It was the promise of a dawn rising in the Nile which later spread rose-colored fingers over the Atlantic Ocean, and which then perhaps took the form of strong sunshine on the eastern coast of the Mediterranean in the country to which she linked her fate and to which she hoped to link her soul."[247]

One should remember that Kahanoff and Amir did not have the same ideological positions. Whereas she advocated Levantinism, he persisted in adhering to the Canaanite outlook. Like his teacher and mentor Yonatan Ratosh, he believed there was a basic incompatibility between the Hebrew people, whose origins reach back to prebiblical Canaan, and the Jewish religion (in his translations of Kahanoff's articles, he omitted sentences dealing with Judaism). After the Six-Day War, he outlined an ideal state, supporting both the neo-Canaanite principle of a large "Hebrew" nation with "a political-institutional structure that would embrace everything west of the Jordan"[248] and include and Hebraicize the Palestinians within it, and the secularist neo-Canaanite principle of the equality of all citizens, "for it is important to me that everyone should be a citizen, and everyone should be considered a native of the land."[249] It is interesting, in this connection, that Rabbi Zvi Yehuda Kook, a revered leader of religious Zionism and an advocate of a Greater Israel in the wake of the Six-Day War of 1967, was the first to make a financial contribution to Amir when he sought to revive the Canaanite movement with Israel's conquest of the West Bank. The esteemed rabbi was reported to have noted that "Amir's involvement in the establishment of the movement for a Greater Israel was joined shortly afterwards by Kahanoff."[250] There is no substance to the statement about Kahanoff, and Amir refused to accept Rabbi Kook's signature on the manifesto of the movement for fear that it would identify the rabbi's religious views with Amir's Canaanite vision.

The affinity that developed between Amir and Kahanoff was due to his belief that there was a fundamental compatibility between her Levantine outlook and his Canaanite ideology. One could thus say that Amir wished to "Canaanite" Kahanoff.

Yet Amir did acknowledge that one should distinguish between Levantinism and the discourse on the Mediterranean identity as upheld by Canaanism, for Levantinism and Mediterraneanism are not the same. In Amir's opinion, Levantinism was purely eastern, whereas the Mediterranean included both East and West. The Mediterranean, not the Levant, gave birth to European and western culture. The culture of the Mediterranean Basin was a phenomenon of the greatest importance and produced many generations of Canaanite Hebrew speakers and speakers of Greek and other languages. Among these peoples there was a terrible war that could be compared to the world wars of the twentieth century, although finally there was a unity of opposites, a productive and impressive unity in diversity. But the Levant was something else, in Amir's opinion. As he saw it, when Kahanoff presented the Levantine generation to the Israeli reader, she was speaking of a small group of minorities in the Middle East who were the cosmopolitans of the area. It was a variegated cultural interweave of Copts and Maronites, Jews, Greeks, and Italians represented by the Alexandrian Greek poet Constantine P. Cavafy (1863–1933) and by the *Alexandria Quartet* of Lawrence Durrell, who worked in Egypt at the time of British rule there.[251]

Amir saw in Kahanoff's language and way of thinking the influence of French culture, which had taken hold in Egypt when Napoleon conquered the country with the aim of controlling the eastern Mediterranean Basin. When the British became a major influence in Egypt, those who had been reared on French culture were also instructed by English and Irish teachers. Amir thought that this was how Kahanoff came to consider a career in the United States (which ended with only partial success), an idea supported by her sister Josette d'Amade. Amir also mentioned her Russian-Jewish surname and her two marriages to Ashkenazi Jews who were guests in Egypt. He thought that she perhaps sought a more extensive and solid existence than that of the

"Levantine generation"—one that to no small degree depended on a mastery of language—in New York, Paris, and finally Beer-sheba and Tel Aviv.

In April 1979, Amir wrote a poem, "Two Sisters," that described the final meeting of Jacqueline Kahanoff and her sister Josette d'Amade "in the twilight hour of atonement and grace." Unlike Jacqueline who went to New York, Josette preferred to live in Paris. There she married a French nobleman, and they had one child: a daughter, Laura. Jacqueline and Josette met from time to time in Tel Aviv and Paris, and their last meeting was in hospital during the months when Jacqueline was dying. Josette arrived from Paris to say her final goodbye to her sister. Amir's poem concisely expresses the love between the two sisters and describes how they embraced one another while remembering with longing their happy childhood in Cairo.[252]

Kahanoff also wanted to participate in the life of the Hebrew-speaking inhabitants of the land who were building a new country. Like Amir, who spoke of "the parallel between the historical experience of the new American nation and the nation-building process in this country [Israel]"[253] she duly, as he approvingly underscored, compared the Israeli experience to that of America:

> The points of resemblance—if not exaggerated—between [America] and Israel are unmistakable. Here, too, there was a nation with a sense of mission which imposed a new society, better educated and more technologically advanced, on an older, more primitive agricultural society, and the new society was made up of people who came from overseas and were not originally native to the country. Just as America drew the poor of Europe, who settled there, Israel drew the poor Jews, who improved their situation. Both the first Zionists and those who came after them had a profound feeling that they were creating a new reality here and were turning their backs on the European past.[254]

In her home in the Tel Aviv neighborhood of Yad Eliyahu, from time to time Kahanoff held a literary salon where people met

A TALE OF FOUR CITIES

and discussed literary matters, politics, and subjects pertaining to the Middle East, which they called *ha-merhav* (the "region"). This literary salon was frequented by Professor Sasson Somekh, Professor Ezra Zohar, Haim Be'er, Yitzhak Livni, Dahlia Ravikovitch, Aharon Amir, and others. Kahanoff was happy to publish in Amir's journal *Keshet*, which aimed to give expression to nonconformism and pluralism, and, according to Amir, *Keshet* "was glad to have her, just as its readers enjoyed her articles and reactions. With us at *Keshet*, she found receptiveness and a willingness to serve her, to translate her, to build her up, to provide her with access to the Israeli intelligentsia."[255] The promise she brought with her was fulfilled—partly, in his opinion—in the articles collected in *From the East the Sun* and in the inaugural evening of the Forum for Mediterranean Cultures devoted to her, and which was "the realization of her pent-up but intense aspiration to a cultural, social, human roof over her head in this country."

Israeli Society

Two years after her immigration to Israel, Kahanoff published four short articles under the heading "A Bridge towards the 'Olim' of the East." With the titles "They Need an Attentive Ear," "Why They Did Not Understand Regina," "In Gilat 'All Problems Are Solved,'" and "They Do Not Absorb Children," they were published in the left-wing newspaper *Al-Hamishmar* in August and September 1956. It was the beginning of a journalistic, publicistic, freelancing kind of writing that helped provide her with a livelihood. Her articles were published in several Israeli daily papers, of various ideological orientations. One found in them the social sentiments of an immigrant writer concerning her fellow immigrants from the Levantine countries and their children, in whom she began to take an interest, "not so much because of what was done to the immigrant children twenty-two years ago, but because of what should be done for them right now: to help the children from Iraq, Yemen, Morocco and Egypt to find a common language with the children from Poland, Hungary and Romania."

Kahanoff wrote that after the processes of separation that the immigrants from the Mizrahi countries experienced in Israel, many of them felt a loss of direction. Although in her opinion eastern Judaism survived only in Israel, the main problems were their hurried immigration, which happened before a cultural change had taken place, and the pressure to westernize the masses of Jews in the towns and small communities of their countries of origin. The dispersion of the population of Yemenite and Kurdish Jews and the Bene Israel (from southern India) in Israel took place when the bourgeois immigrants and members of the liberal professions had already adapted themselves to the change, and the simple Jews, those who remained in their traditional frameworks, found it difficult to strike roots in the new society. Kahanoff was not afraid to make the assertion, which gave rise to controversy among scholars, that "the well-to-do mainly went to various countries in the West and the great majority of the poor, less adapted to the modern world, went mainly to the State of Israel."[256] In her opinion, the immigrants lacked their traditional leadership—it was "an immigration without a head"—because the guiding elites were missing. Only the Jewish communities from Yemen and Iraq immigrated to Israel with their leadership. The adaptation of the affluent sections of society that immigrated to the west took place through the acquisition of the English or French language and a distancing from Judaism. The immigration (Kahanoff used the term *uprooting*) to Israel of the less affluent sections of society took place at the height of the crisis of the fragmentation of the communities. It was a sudden uprooting and immigration to a new country.

If the exiles from Spain, said Kahanoff, had the impressive leadership of people like Abravanel and Don Joseph Nasi and enjoyed cultural and religious unity, the members of her generation were, in her words, "hybridized people, gnawed by doubts, seeking a path in life and given to self-questioning."[257] Unlike the Jews of Eastern Europe, the Mizrahi immigrants had not experienced any collective movement such as Zionism. They had to adapt themselves quickly to twentieth-century Israel where a process of rapid modernization was in progress, whereas in their countries of origin the process of westernization took place gradually. The uprooting and the westernization destroyed the structures of the conservative world of many families and communities. Kahanoff acknowledged that it was perhaps in Mandatory Palestine and Israel that the Mizrahi Jews were first seen as a distinctive group. At the same time, the Mizrahi communities coming to Israel lacked the social and cultural fusion of the Jews of Egypt. These communities, which were exposed in Israel to the heritage of the Eastern European Jews, felt the lack of a common cultural infrastructure, an infrastructure that existed in the Jewish Diasporas of North and South America, in Europe, and even in Egypt. Kahanoff's optimistic temperament and her sociological analysis brought her to the conclusion that "the revival of Israel makes possible, for the first time in a long period, the creation of a [Jewish] civilization—one with the surprising image of a mixed Jewish-Jewish [sic] symbiosis."[258]

In a series of visits to the periphery of Israel, to the poorer city neighborhoods, to the moshavim and the development towns in which the immigrants from the eastern countries were concentrated, one sees Kahanoff's journalistic, psychological, and anthropological talents: her capacity to discern the difficulties of absorption, her capacity to understand the complaints of the new immigrants, her reproach of the absorption authorities for their insensitivity, and, together with that, an uncompromising demand for the people she interviewed to exercise self-criticism and to attempt to surmount their difficult conditions. She noticed what she regarded as the main problem of the Mizrahi immigrants, and that was their isolation in Israeli society. Each community lived in isolated cultural, social, and cultural clusters, without any connection with other communities, and certainly without any affinity or connection with people from Europe. For example, she noted with regard to a cultured family from Iraq that had a splendid lineage in their old country, some of their children had what she called a "Mizrahi complex," a sense of systematic and deliberate deprivation that resembled the "Jewish complex." Kahanoff maintained that there was no comparison between their hardships and the persecution of the Jews in Central and Eastern Europe, but she also sorrowfully noted that European Jews often failed to extend a fraternal embrace to Mizrahi Jews. "People who experienced such great suffering because of prejudice in Europe should not have prejudice themselves."[259] The Mizrahi immigrants, Kahanoff observed, were understandably traumatized by the failure of many Israelis to warmly welcome them, and by the difference between Zionism as they had imagined it would be and the disappointing actuality of Israel. The immigrants from Europe felt at home with the old-timers of the Yishuv, the Yiddish they spoke (Kahanoff ignored the fact that most of the old-timers did not know Yiddish or preferred not to speak it), the food with which they were familiar, and the basic concepts of modernity, nationalism, and secularism they were used to. The Mizrahi immigrants, on the other hand, were expected to adapt to an alien culture and customs strange to them. Moreover, in contrast to the European Zionists, the Mizrahi immigrants still saw the Jews as constituting a religion rather than a nation, for the idea of nationhood that developed in the Muslim countries under western influence still had a religious affinity with Islam.

The feeling of exile that the Mizrahi immigrants had as a result of their uprooting and replanting in an alien culture gave rise to a cult of longing for the place they left behind as they went to their old-new motherland. The sufferings they had experienced in the gentile environment were forgotten, and there was a nostalgia for

A TALE OF FOUR CITIES

an imaginary wholeness of life that was said to have existed in the countries in which they had lived for millennia.

Nonetheless, the Mizrahi Jews did not want to be silent witnesses or victims of the Zionist revolution.[260] They wished "to make history instead of being carried by it." Their ambition was to be equal partners in a new interpretation of their Jewishness—a vision that Kahanoff endorsed by offering a psychological observation. The Mizrahi Jews, in her opinion, needed self-liberation. Just as psychoanalysis can help a patient to gain a healthy self-understanding, the Mizrahi Jews must meet the challenge of gaining a secure and self-respecting foothold in Israeli-Zionist society. Accordingly, Kahanoff reasoned, they have to break the wall of isolation and near-pathological contempt of the Ashkenazi-Zionist elite. Kahanoff went a step too far in placing a whole community on the psychologist's couch. The Mizrahi Jews, who in her opinion suffered from a collective neurosis, needed a receptive ear and a sympathetic approach. The Mizrahi Jew, like a patient in psychoanalysis, could come to terms with himself if there would be "a two-way bridge of give and take, a bridge over a river both of whose banks would be in the same country and not in two different countries."[261]

Regina, a new immigrant from Tunisia, served as an example for Kahanoff of the assimilation of the Mizrahi immigrants in the 1950s. Kahanoff was both charmed by and critical of the special quality of Regina, a bourgeois Tunisian Jewess who came from a cultured family, spoke French, and in her own estimation belonged to the social elite. Regina, who had personal charm, social abilities, and feminist drive, came to Israel in 1952 and settled with her five children in a development town in the Negev. Although she recognized the importance of education, she had a wasteful lifestyle and a penchant for Oriental hospitality that was exaggerated and exorbitant, to say the least, and that obliged her children to neglect their studies to work to support the family. Despite her talents and her industriousness, Regina found no way to channel her energies and talents. Kahanoff tried to persuade her to become a kindergarten teacher or a teacher of the culinary art, but without success.

Regina did not allow her children to speak Hebrew at home, making the French she spoke a matter of pride and also a "revenge" against the Israelis, who were unable to accommodate a woman like her. She compared the local clinics and schools to the French ones in Tunis, and the comparison was not complimentary. Her children were allowed to be absent from school, although she knew that her daughter, who had abandoned her studies and refused to serve in the army, "had gone back to the Mizrahi habits that she herself had been weaned of . . . and now it was too late to repair the damage."[262] Kahanoff came to the conclusion that the "Reginas," as she called them, would find their way in Israel only if they were treated with respect and appreciation from the start.

Regina was an excellent cook and knew how to prepare inexpensive and tasty food, but she refused to entertain the idea of teaching cookery: "Who understands cooking here? Who knows if food is good or tasteless? Give them *lebeniye* and salt fish and they call it a feast!"[263] In her article titled "Claude Lévi-Strauss, Culture and Cooking," Kahanoff observed that in many Mizrahi communities there is a rich, varied, and refined culinary tradition. The reason there was no Israeli cuisine—one should remember that this was written in the 1960s—was connected, in her opinion, with the pioneering tradition. The early settlers did not create a refined culinary culture, for "they eat only because they had to, and that was more important than what they ate." The plain, egalitarian kibbutz meals were part of their communal, ascetic lifestyle. She thought that indifference rather than simplicity was the reason for the Israeli neglect of cuisine, for good soups and salads are not difficult to prepare. The Israeli substitutes for the original eastern food were forced and unsuccessful. For instance, instead of the Mizrahi cakes being made with peanuts or honey as they had been originally, they were made with a sugar syrup. What was needed, in her opinion, were personal initiatives in setting up restaurants and a continuation of the culinary traditions that youths could learn from their mothers and their grandmothers. This type of cooking went together with a family atmosphere, as it originated in an environment in which fish, olive oil, wine, and vegetables such as artichokes, tomatoes, and eggplant were the order of the day.

Another stop on her anthropological tour of the Mizrahi immigrants in Israel was a new moshav in the Galilee where Kahanoff was received by a young immigrant couple from Marrakesh, Morocco, and their four children. They were told that they were sent to the moshav because of their poverty: "They never told us that what we would find in Israel would be stones and isolation."[264] In Morocco, only underprivileged people worked in agriculture, and thus as graduates of the French primary schools they felt degraded by this kind of work. Kahanoff said that those responsible for absorption had not told them about the importance of agricultural settlement and were certainly unable to instill in them pioneering values. One cannot demand pioneering from people not brought up on Zionist ideals. The matter was further complicated when the couple was suddenly infected with the "racist virus" and refused to mix with Yemenites for fear that "people would think we are dark-skinned like them."[265] Kahanoff thought that if the Europeans had seen the immigrants as equals, it would have prevented a sense of "white" superiority from the beginning.

A stratum of misunderstanding overlaid a stratum of lack of knowledge. The secretary of the moshav answered the mistaken ideas of the couple with some mistaken ideas of his own: "The Yemenites work, but these people are beggars from birth."[266] His lack of knowledge of the immigrants from Yemen and North Africa, said Kahanoff, led him to respect one of these communities over the other, without understanding the difference between that community and the other. The Yemenites, she explained, have a conservative cultural tradition and code of behavior that has never been questioned, and thus their adaptation to Israel is not a threat to their identity; but the partial assimilation to European ways that the Moroccan immigrants have experienced weighs on them and makes it difficult for them to adapt to the Zionist new collective identity. There is no precedent for how they should behave, and their self-image is what others think of them. They want to be westerners, but others see them as Moroccans. They have a mixed identity, part secular European and part traditional Jewish, an incongruity that was not resolved by their immigration to Israel and that makes it difficult for them to relate to a third element: their Israeli identity.

In two Galilee settlements in the south, Kahanoff found an example of the opposite of this friction. The southern settlements of Moshav Gila and the town of Dimona had homogeneous populations; in Gila the residents all came from Tunisia, and in Dimona they mainly came from Morocco. The secretary at Gila said that a group of Jews from Tunisia who had fought in Israel's War of Independence founded the moshav, which became a success. Although it seemed strange to him to live in Israel in the company of his former Tunisian countrymen, the objectives they set for themselves—the adaptation to a new way of life, the acquisition of the Hebrew language, and participation in a major war—filled him with pride, and he hoped that the next generation would take on new challenges. In Dimona, the educated North African leaders also demonstrated local patriotism: "This settlement has grown from one day to the next, before our very eyes. We are doing in the Negev what the first settlers from Europe did in the north. We are true pioneers."[267] Kahanoff warned against sneering at the declarations of these young leaders, who were proud of their settlements. She believed in the authenticity of the speakers and their words.

In Beersheba she visited a school in which most of the pupils, who were poor, were the sons and daughters of new immigrants.

On her way to the director's office she observed some unpleasant incidents that involved children of the school, and she doubted "if it was at all possible to educate children like those I met."[268] But the director, Ephraim, an educationalist through and through, dispelled her fears. When she accompanied him on a tour of the classrooms, he gave personal and warm attention to each pupil. She thought that "these things essential to education, being a means to a better life, must have a permanent effect on people who never knew them before. Moreover, I felt that the children were not 'Mizrahi Jews' but individuals with their own qualities and problems, and because of their past and the demands now made on them by society, they needed special care and understanding in order to overcome the difficulties of adolescence."[269] Skepticism and indifference on the part of the parents were liable to make the school lose its children, and it was therefore important to gain the confidence of the parents and make them active partners in their children's education. As she visited the places where new immigrants from North Africa were settled, Kahanoff's motivation surfaced when one of the pupils asked her why she had come to their class: "I told them that I am a new immigrant, and I thought that there was no better way to improve my spoken Hebrew and increase my knowledge of Eretz-Israel than to get to know the pupils of her school as much as possible."[270]

After she had spoken about the settlements of the new immigrants of the 1950s, Kahanoff sought out the old-timers, and for that purpose visited the neighborhoods of Tel Aviv, which had a concentration of Mizrahi immigrants totaling sixty thousand, about 10 percent of the city's population. By and large, they had a low self-image. Many of the inhabitants of the Hatikvah neighborhood were of Yemenite origin, former members of the right-wing underground military "Lehi" and "Etzel" organizations that had fought against the British, but individuals from Iraq gradually became the majority in the neighborhood. The inhabitants constituted an organic community, most of whom were gainfully employed, some of them (the more well-to-do) in stalls in the city's open-air food market. Nonetheless they were angry and frustrated, claiming that their neighborhood was being deliberately neglected.

In contrast to these neighborhoods in South Tel Aviv, Kahanoff portrayed North Tel Aviv as European, educated, and prosperous, with fine buildings and well-maintained public facilities. On the other hand, the south of the city, which was mainly populated by poor, uneducated Mizrahi Jews, was lacking in public facilities— its streets were unpaved and unlit and the Ezra neighborhood had no sewage system. However, contrary to the stereotyped perception of the Hatikvah neighborhood of the 1960s and 1970s as a place of organized crime, drug addiction, and delinquent youth, she presents a complex, warm, and empathetic picture of its inhabitants, but without ignoring their problems.[271]

Kahanoff was struck by the friendly and intimate atmosphere of the crowded Hatikvah neighborhood, characterized by a vibrant Israeli Mizrahi way of life. The neighborhood, where few academics lived, was also characterized by an education gap (only one in eight children in secondary school was of Mizrahi origin). In the whole area, there was no secondary school or public library. She opposed the view of the urban authorities that it was better for the young to leave the neighborhood and mix with others. A local secondary school could, in her opinion, have contributed to the creation of a local leadership. Because the Hatikvah was the largest and most active neighborhood, naturally it was the one with the most potentiality. Kahanoff saw it as a "ghetto community" characterized by "warmth, mutual loyalty, intimacy, a special sub-culture, segregation, and suspicion of the outside world." The residents of Hatikvah felt as a community, and it was therefore easier for them to do things together. Although the organizational ability of the neighborhood was still in its infancy, it already had an amateur theater and a local newspaper.

The neighborhood's problems were due to its history. It was sparsely populated at first, but during the War of Independence it was filled with Jews fleeing from Jaffa. Many of them were of Yemenite origin, and they built their homes piecemeal, a warren of little low houses to which they added many rooms, without sewage, without gardens, and with bad sanitary arrangements. The root of the trouble was the absence of planning in the neighborhood, and the lack of an overall plan. New buildings next to old ones were inhabited by many people on welfare, and there was no possibility of demolishing these slums. In contrast, although Neve Shalem, another community that Kahanoff visited, was a planned neighborhood, it was planned "without imagination and without love, and it did not represent the clearance of a slum but its adaptation to modern conditions." In other words, suddenly a new slum had come into existence: there was now a large population on a smaller area. On her visit to Neve Shalem neighborhood, in the home of a poor family of eight people, Kahanoff encountered the personal and social problems of the new quarter. In the older neighborhood, Hatikvah, she talked to the parents' committee of a school that for three years had been an educational experiment. Many of the parents had lost faith in the municipality and the authorities, who ignored the inhabitants' desire to be equal partners in the social development of their place of residence.

Complaints arose from the Hatikvah neighborhood that the Barbour Youth Center built between Kfar Shalem and Yad Eliyahu was too far away from the neighborhood. The youth center was, in their opinion, intended not for Hatikvah but for the immigrants from the affluent countries and the Soviet Union who lived in the new buildings in Yad Eliyahu. Unlike the Barbour Center, which looked foreign to its surroundings, the Hatikvah neighborhood theater, which was suited to the place, had a direct connection to the inhabitants and had a first-hand knowledge of their problems. Because of this two-fold relationship with the public, it succeeded in conveying a message to the audience. But the success of the center and the theater did not prevent Kahanoff from discerning a lingering and serious problem: Many parents who saw the local school as a cure-all, and who adopted the competitive norms of the middle class in Israel, were liable to push their children toward competition of the capitalist norms, "but that does not mean that one has to accept these norms uncritically."[272]

To be sure, there was a new spirit in the neighborhood. There was a social sensitivity to special human problems and an understanding of the needs of those with low incomes and of the price that society pays for poverty. Newly recruited social workers were professionally trained young people who encouraged community self-awareness and collaboration between the citizens and the city authorities. The inhabitants' awareness that they could make a difference caused the authorities to be more responsive to their requests for change. A new concept of independent action that gives self-respect and self-confidence took root in the Hatikvah neighborhood as well.

One cannot overlook Kahanoff's sense of social concern, which was primed by her optimistic spirit. She believed in the Zionist project, which aimed at creating a new society in a new land, but she was not blind in her belief. She was not unaware of the social price that weak people had to pay for the implementation of a modern ideology.

Ramat Hadassah-Szold

Six years after she immigrated to Israel, in 1960, the hundredth anniversary of the birth of Henrietta Szold, Kahanoff's book *Ramat-Hadassah-Szold: Youth Aliyah Screening and Classification Centre* was published. In the book's introduction, she pointed out that the influx of two streams of immigration had diminished in the course of the 1950s. One stream was the immigration of Jews from Europe, composed mainly of concentration camp survivors, and the other was Jewish immigration from the Muslim countries. To Kahanoff, the absorption of these groups in Israel was a drama with both difficulties and achievements. She wrote, "I have not been trained as an educationalist, sociologist or psychologist. I do not have the means to evaluate the experience of children of non-European origin when they enter a new society, or how they adapt when going from one environment to another, or how they feel in their new environment. As someone born in the east and educated in the west, I know the difficulty of fusing a number of different worlds into a single world."[273]

This honest declaration of Kahanoff's motives in writing the book on the educational center reflected her Levantine viewpoint and was in keeping with her journalistic work, which focused on the absorption difficulties of new immigrants. The book *Ramat Hadassah-Szold* was not intended to be a critical analysis or a scholarly work but was a methodical and informative description, a sort of long and detailed report on the history of the institution founded by the American Zionist educator Henrietta Szold (1860–1945)—its aims, activities, structure, methods of operation, and decision-making process. Kahanoff observed the activities of the center for about a month and wrote a comprehensive professional account of its work. Her writing did not contain any criticism or offer advice or point out defects, but rather provided the genealogy of the institution and described its activities. It was a work on the educational institution and the movement behind it from a public relations point of view. No less and no more.

The book, accordingly, limited its focus on the institution's program of preparing immigrant youth for life in Israel. It was thought that the young people would need a number of weeks to accustom themselves to their new surroundings, but the educators and instructors clearly lacked the tools to evaluate the situation, in part because there was no precedent for an absorption of this kind. Kahanoff dryly noted the missionary zeal of the ideological movements, which demanded maximum coverage for themselves. Most of the kibbutzim absorbed the children from Youth Aliyah, a nonparty organization, despite the knowledge that the period of training to be given was too short to prepare the children and young people for an independent life.

This was especially true where children from Arab counties were concerned.[274] Kahanoff pointed out that many of them—those of a low socioeconomic level and from outlying areas—were far from the Zionist ideology, the kibbutz movement, and Youth Aliyah. The children and youths felt they had been uprooted from the environment they knew and replanted in a society that was completely alien to them. They came from conditions that had been shattered and from traditional societies that had broken up under the influence of western culture, modernity, secularism, and assimilation—processes that affected many Jewish communities in Islamic countries. The children discarded their families' values and did not succeed in exchanging them for new ones. Many of them, Kahanoff argued, were illiterate and felt lost in the new environment. A transitional framework was therefore set up to help them to acclimatize themselves more rapidly. Although it helped them, it was not adequate.

The Jewish-Arab Conflict

In a seminar in memory of Martin Buber (1878–1965) at the educational center Giva't Haviva, Kahanoff called for a dialogue between the Jews and Arabs in Israel. The starting point of her discussion of the Jewish-Arab conflict was pessimistic: "Today it seems that there is hardly any possibility of a dialogue between Israel and the neighboring Arab countries because their leaders do not recognize Israel's existence apart from wanting to destroy it."[275] But with the Arab citizens of Israel, she surmised, a dialogue was possible and, indeed, necessary. Kahanoff thought that the aim of the dialogue would not be to reach an agreement between the positions of the two sides but to develop each side's

A TALE OF FOUR CITIES

awareness of the other—an awareness that would render the relationship between them more amiable. A new generation of Jews and Arabs had arisen in Israel for whom the tragedies of the past had lost much of their intensity, and they wanted to find a way to live together in Israel regardless of the conflict with the neighboring Arab countries. The Israeli Arabs' strong attachment to their towns, villages, and fields was the reasons they remained in Israel. Statistics showed an increase in the Arab birth rate as compared with that of the Jewish population. Young Arabs increasingly participated in industry, and they were beginning to resemble the Jews in their speech and outlook. Kahanoff warned of the danger of apartheid, which she called a "divided society," and she agreed with the view expressed by those present at the seminar that if the division between the Jews and Arabs in Israel continued, Israel would become a series of "mutually exclusive ghettos." Among the proposals made at the seminar, those favoring a fusion of the populations included the creation of mixed schools with common programs and the provision of equal educational and economic opportunities.

Her dialogic approach was inspired by Martin Buber, "whose philosophy and outlook" she wrote, "derived from his concept of a dialogue between man and God and man and man."[276] Already before the First World War, Buber had called for a dialogue between Jews and Arabs. Kahanoff believed that in his article "The Spirit of the East and Judaism" (1912), Buber foresaw the reawakening of the peoples of the Orient and called on Jewry to affirm its Oriental origins.[277] Buber, she added, together with his friend Akiva Ernst Simon and other members of the Ihud (Unity), a small but vocal binationalist Zionist political party founded in 1942, worked for Jewish-Arab understanding grounded in a mutual acknowledgment that they were both descendants of Abraham and thus were destined to share the Holy Land in a fraternal bond. She did think, however, that Buber may have gone too far in asking Israel, a country fighting for its survival, to demonstrate "unselfish idealism." Years later, she noted with a measure of contrition that Buber's vision was not dated. Kahanoff recalled that when she delivered her earlier address at Giva't Haviva, she fancied that Buber "was looking down at us from a highly enlarged photograph. His bright, happy eyes gleamed at this evidence of his wise and friendly presence."[278]

Another peace activist who commanded Kahanoff's affectionate regard was the Iranian-born Abie Nathan (1927–2008). In February 1966, he flew from Israel to Egypt in his personal single-engine airplane with the hope of bringing the message of peace to Abdel Nasser. His dramatic flight to Egypt in a small, flimsy aircraft fired the imagination of young Jews and Arabs in Israel and made him a national hero. At a time when the majority of young Jews were indifferent to the Zionist project, idealism like that of Abie Nathan had an effect on people's thinking; it snowballed and found new forms of expression. Especially promising examples thereof were seen in the Knesset debate on Nathan's exploits. In their speeches, the heads of the Israeli Arab communities of Baka and Nazareth enthusiastically declared that they were open to receive visitors, and they invited those present to be guests in their towns.

Kahanoff wondered if a fusion of the Jewish and Arab populations would make Israel lose its Jewish character, and so anticipated by many years the debate about post-Zionism in the 1990s: "Underlying all difficult questions there is the debate about whether Israel sees itself as a modern state which grants equal rights to all its citizens or as an exclusively Jewish state in which non-Jews are a tolerated minority."[279] At the end of the Six-Day War, she was eager, like many Israelis, to see the captured Palestinian territories, in particular the Gaza Strip.

At the beginning of her article "Nothing Sweet Comes Out of Gaza," she asked, "How is Gaza to be described?" She did not mince her words: "How can one describe such ugliness, such filth, so devastated a population?"[280] Nothing existed in Gaza except hatred, disorder, poverty, and a refugee atmosphere, although something could have been done about it since 1948. It would have been possible to have set up "scientific institutions, agricultural stations, irrigation centers, canning factories and the production of fruit-juices and things for export." Although western intellectuals (she called them "leftists") made a distinction between "Arab socialist regimes" and "feudal regimes," to her great surprise the Hashemite regime in Jordan turned out to be more progressive than the Nasserist regime in Egypt. In the West Bank, which she called "the areas of western Jordan," the Palestinians worked in agriculture and various trades, but in Gaza most of the people for the last twenty years had been unemployed and had degenerated for lack of work. She asked: "Can't building works be undertaken, and can't anything be done to promote hygiene and cleanliness?" While the refugees lived in dire poverty, the rich lived contentedly in their villas. Gaza was a subcolony of Egypt, which itself had passed through a process of decolonization, and the Nasserite regime had not improved the lives of the masses there. The socialist slogans were a modern cosmetic for a society in deep crisis. In view of the wretchedness of the life there, what use was Nasserite socialism?

A true revolution, she concluded, would take place only with a liberation from the past, with abandoning ways of thinking that are unsuitable to the modern world. There is no point of speaking of socialism until the government and society are guided by common sense. The sight of books whose covers display a brave Palestinian fighter with a machine gun, or of kindergartens whose walls show paintings of Jews being slaughtered brought her to the conclusion that "the real problem is not the existence of Israel or the fate of the refugees but a stubborn refusal to accept the modern world."[281] Israel is only an alibi. An excessive use of Marxist discourse combined with Nazi-type slogans had no bearing on the reality of Gaza, where "an obsession with a Muslim society goes together with a rejection of the modern world."

If turning one's back on modernity was in her opinion the reason why Gaza was in such a terrible state, then, in conformity to her view that modernity was the solution to the miserable condition of the Palestinians, the Golan Heights presented the opposite picture. Progress and modernity were both reflected there by the conditions of life of the Druze, the inhabitants of the former Syrian area. Many of the Druze worked in building construction. They received the same wages as the Jews, insurance coverage, severance pay, and other allowances. In the villages of the Golan Heights, there were mother and child health clinics. Their school curricula resembled those of the Druze and Arabs in Israel. Their years of compulsory education were lengthened from six, as was the case in Syria, to nine as in Israel. The number of private cars jumped from eleven in the time of Syrian rule to two hundred. The Golan Heights was administratively linked to Israel, and roads were built there that connected to the Israeli network. Water sources were found, a new pipeline was laid, and electrical generators were installed. Kahanoff was provided with all these facts by the military administrator, who was proud of the Israeli achievements. She did not ask him any critical questions. On the contrary, she said that "the administrator . . . , who resembled a Roman jurist, spoke with great satisfaction about these developments, and rightly so. Israel constitutes a new factor, active and revolutionary, in the Middle East."[282] She saw the official as an example of the kind of Israeli officers who are not only excellent administrators but "give much thought to the relations between the Jews in Israel and the other peoples of the Middle East." Her bottom line was this: "Israel has brought prosperity to the Golan."

Israeli rule in the Golan also brought prosperity to the "extraordinary and inspiring young [Israelis]" who in establishing Jewish settlements in the Golan Heights, dealt with "steel, stone, barbed-wire fences and the placement of weapons." They were a "select group" of settlers who planted apple orchards and grew flowers and vegetables, proud that their place was known as "a little Ukraine" or "a little Texas." Kahanoff saw settlement as a pioneering act that testified to a renewal of Zionist initiative: "New roads have been laid, trucks and tractors are on the move, bulldozers roar, hammers strike, buildings rise, and, above all, the Israelis have produced a new crop of babies who were born here." Although Arab "terrorists" still planted mines and settlers were killed, this did not affect the spirit of development "of the well-mannered young men with untidy hair."[283]

In the romanticism of her description of the young soldiers, she followed in the footsteps of the poet Nathan Alterman, who in his glorification of the prestate Jewish fighters of the Palmach eulogizes the young men as "a poem in themselves," and the poet Dahlia Ravikovitch, who effusively describes "the soldiers in an embattled bunker" on the northern front as bearing "the [angelic] face of a youth." Kahanoff, likewise, visiting a unit stationed on the Golan Heights, gave effusive descriptions of the soldiers: "One tried to conceal the picture of a beautiful, scantily-dressed girl, others told jokes and read detective novels," and there were some who painted on the walls slices of watermelon, sunsets, flights of birds, and fields in flower. "These are the things they miss most, although in civilian life they are hardly aware of them." Ravikovitch also described "an old motor-car that became a club-house with soft lights—yellow, green and red. And those who have nothing to do at night hammer nails and stick in pictures."[284] It is not surprising that there was a warm friendship between the two women, as Ravikovitch saw Kahanoff as someone "who was able to write about painful matters of importance without the anger and bitterness with which it is usually done."[285]

TWO

—⚬—

LEVANTINISM
A Cultural Theory

FROM THE LEVANT TO LEVANTINISM

Kahanoff constructed a mythic narrative in support of an idyllic image of Levantism to inspire Israel to affirm a Mediterranean Levant identity. Toward the end of her life, when she gathered her articles together to publish them in English with a comprehensive critical perspective on her past writings, she expressed her belief that Levantinism was a "mythical dimension." For her, Levantinism was not only a territorial "mythical space" but also a "mythical time," or, more precisely, a "psycho-historical time."[1] The mythical reconstruction of a culture requires a radical break with conceptions of continuous time and space. Every great cultural myth requires a starting point—a *fons et origio*—to endow the present time with a spiritual force. "Mythical time" is complete, harmonious time, while present time alone is partial, defective time.

What Kahanoff proposed with her modern perspective was the simultaneous adoption of the various points of time and space of the Levant, made up of different viewpoints, relationships, and cultural dimensions. Thus, the Levant is revealed as a rich mosaic, a mirror in which many different spiritual perspectives are reflected, a fertile and creative cultural kaleidoscope that is not restricted to a one-dimensional ideology of east or west. She continually stressed the eastern part of the Mediterranean as the Levant; it may be said that she saw this geographic region as a distinctive cultural space that made possible a productive dialogue between East and West.

At the end of her introduction to her projected collection of essays in English,[2] Kahanoff confessed that her articles reflected a certain ambivalence about a past that was not entirely free from the outlook of the period between the two world wars or the dilemmas of an immigrant to Israel from an Oriental country who was none too enthusiastic about her experience of integration. Hence, her gaze, she wrote, was perforce focused on the past rather than the future. The 1967 war, however, had brought Israel back to the Levant as a force that could change the old order. She hoped it would be a positive force, a modern and progressive one.

Kahanoff expressed the hope that Israel had changed its approach to the Levant, that it was integrating into its surroundings and would not be too preoccupied with the Jewish aspect, as it had been in the past. She did not delude herself that the adoption of a Levantine sensibility and consciousness would ipso facto defuse Israel's conflict with its Arab neighbors, but at the same time her vision was directed toward the *longue durée*, a view advanced by Fernand Braudel, the historian of the Mediterranean: "In the long run, it might help Israel integrate in the Levant."[3]

The Levantine option is not only a cultural possibility but also a concrete political proposal. In place of pan-Arabism, on the one hand, and Zionism in its European-Ashkenazi articulation, on the other, Kahanoff proposed a political culture of the Levant, the essence of which was "live and let live." The reconstruction of the Levant, the product of the ancient encounter between Byzantium, Islam, and Judaism, could help to redefine the relationship of the Israelis to the political and cultural space in which they reside.

Cultural mutations, Kahanoff argued, are of course not exclusively an Israeli or modern phenomenon. For example, in the Middle Ages scholars argued against the "corruption" of language, but this corruption and the mixing of languages with other idioms finally produced the majority of European tongues. Are there still people who argue in favor of preserving the purity of Latin? After generations, or at least in a gradual manner, a people in a declining culture can adopt a living culture as its own and in that way can amalgamate that culture with the living elements in its own culture. Cultural mutations are thus one of the major tools for the preservation of cultures in the course of history.

Israel, for Kahanoff, was a meeting place of the west, represented by American technology, and the east, which was in competition with the west. She criticized the tendency of the Yishuv to aim at "purity," which she regarded as unrealistic in view of the State of Israel's dependence at that time on the immigration of Jews from all over the world, and especially from the Oriental countries. One should therefore be on one's guard, she felt, against the prejudice against Levantinism. An example of the historical consciousness of the Levant is found in the Romans, who had respect for the civilizations of the Levant, and an attraction toward them, that still exists in modern Italy.

—∿—

Kahanoff saw the climate as an important element in her cultural theory (in a vein similar to Montesquieu's ethnological theories). A certain climate creates the character of a culture in a particular geographical region. In hot countries, people tend to spend a great deal of time outdoors, where they mingle freely with others, and thus they tend to be noisier than the inhabitants of Northern countries, where weather conditions necessitate living indoors in private dwellings. The Jews, she added, Mediterranean in origin and in temperament, were looked down on by the Europeans because of their "rowdiness, their emotionalism and their gesticulation."

However, although Israel was never a "little Switzerland," climate and temperament do not justify the impoliteness of the Israelis. As an observer from outside, Kahanoff criticized the tendency of the Israelis to shout at one another in the street and, generally speaking, to be inconsiderate to others. In her opinion, calling this "Levantinism" is to ignore the question of why the Israelis behave in this way and why they evade educational responsibility.

She also examined the "double standard" of the Israelis toward immigrants from Arab countries. After all, it was the American immigrants who brought the use of drugs to Israeli culture. Similarly, the attempts of the Israeli artistic elite to imitate American fashions was seen by Kahanoff as "a superficial Levantine adoption of Western cultural practices." She also noticed that in time of war, or immediately after, the "Levantine problem" disappeared from the public sphere. This disappearance obscures the fact that Israel had not yet succeeded in fully absorbing the Jews from the eastern countries as equal citizens, as was evidenced by phenomena like the Black Panthers protest movement of Mizrahi youth in the seventies and the riots of indigent Mizrahi Jews in the Wadi Salib neighborhood of Haifa in 1959.

In Kahanoff's cultural theory, the scientific and technological revolution was deemed to be more radical than the revolution of literacy that preceded it. While in the revolution of literacy, religion could be the factor that served as a bridge between the outlook of the educated and the outlook of those who were not, the scientific and technological revolution also embodied a change of outlook. But there was a huge gap between those who adapted themselves to the latter revolution and those who did not. To characterize the fraught problems of the Mizrahi acclimatization to life in Israel as "Levantinism" is simply insufficient for the purpose of finding a local solution to the global sociological problems attendant on the scientific and technological revolution.

Kahanoff believed that the gap between the creativity of the culture of the European Jews and the creativity of the Jews of the Mizrahi countries could be explained by the fact that the Jews of Europe were to a large extent part of European culture at a time when it developed from a scientific, technological, and intellectual point of view. The Jewish communities of the eastern countries, on the other hand, were, generally speaking, part of a population oppressed by the forces of European conquest.[4] But as the Jews were a minority with extensive connections to the world of culture as a whole, they were more open than others to changes in their outlook. The reaction of the Jews of the eastern countries to the European influence was different from the reaction of most of the Muslim population. For the Muslims, the European forces were mainly occupiers, and thus their influence had to be resisted, but the Jews, said Kahanoff, like other minorities, saw colonialist rule as an opportunity to regain their freedom and develop culturally. The problem, according to Kahanoff, was largely the poverty and disease of the Muslim population, and the colonial rulers were unable to find a solution for it. Into this vacuum entered militant Muslim and nationalist forces such as the Muslim Brotherhood, which by means of xenophobia united the masses under various imported forms of local socialism and thus rose to power.

The minorities in the Muslim world, Kahanoff maintained, did not adopt the European ideals in a superficial way but became truly westernized and so were an element that aroused suspicion among the local population. In her opinion, a similar process occurred in Europe when the Europeans disdained the intellectual and communist Jews, preferring the fascists. The Jews and Copts in North Africa, she claimed, were annihilated just like their counterparts in Hungary and Germany. In the east, the rise of pan-Arabism and Muslimism destroyed any vestige of true Levantine culture, a culture combining east and west that was found among the Jews, the Copts, and the Christians. In that way, the opportunity was missed for these minorities to serve as a bridge to bring the general population closer to an open and free society that would benefit one and all.

In Kahanoff's opinion, the Jews from the Mizrahi countries who came from places rife with hunger and poverty clung to the traditional outlook that accompanied these things. The human condition of the lives of the Jews from Arab countries at the beginning of the 1950s reflected the fate they shared with the Arab environment from which they came. Kahanoff thought that Israel and the Arab countries needed to undergo the same processes of rapid adaptation to westernization, technology, and a new economic system. Perhaps these processes would be the bridge that would unite them in the future. She envisaged the possibility that the combination of east and west to be found in Israel, if developed in the right way, might serve as a bridge between east and west in general, and in this way, Israel would realize a vision almost as powerful as that of the prophets. At the same time, it does not seem that Kahanoff was in any haste to see such things, and what she said in her article "Israel's Levantinization" remained only speculation.

Only nine years after the State of Israel was founded, Kahanoff beheld the development of Israel with amazement. It seems that all the children were clothed, most of them were not immediately hungry for bread, and most of them received an education and learned a profession. This salutary process gained added impetus, Kahanoff held, with the Sinai Campaign of 1956, uniting the European and Mizrahi Israelis and the westerners into a single people. Nonetheless, Kahanoff decried, most of the economic and educational problems had not yet been solved and remained a festering wound in the body politic of Israel.

Kahanoff wrote that the process of socioeconomic integration seemed—but only seemed—to succeed because of an agreement between the Mizrahi Jews and the Zionist leadership not to discuss the educational, housing, and economic needs of the immigrants from Arab countries. At the same time, when these objectives were more or less attained, neither side understood that what had been achieved was nothing less than a revolution that had brought Israel onto the threshold of the modern world. The Zionist establishment, she contended, was afraid that the Jews from the eastern countries would drag Israel down to the level of the Arab countries. This fear caused the leaders of the country to make many mistakes, such as the rapid integration of the eastern Jews without consideration for their cultural sensibilities.

This rapid mechanical integration without consideration resulted in feelings of shame and resentment among the younger generation of Mizrahi Jews, who experienced their "re-education" as a humiliating act of noblesse oblige.

Kahanoff pointed out that, ironically, the common experience of deprivation gave the Jews from the eastern countries a sense of solidarity that had not existed before. The Jews from Egypt were obviously not the same as the Jews from Morocco or the Jews from Tunisia. At the same time, their common experience gave them a common identity-in-struggle. Kahanoff quoted the declaration of a conference of young politicians of Iraqi origin: "As long as you old settlers do not let us share power with you, you bear the responsibility for the mistakes committed in the policy of integration which you conceived and applied without consulting us."[5]

Kahanoff believed that the great challenge in the following years was to create a leadership of people from the Arab countries from among their communities. After the more superficial problems had been solved (a common language, education, etc.), there remained deeper problems that the integration of the immigrants had not addressed: spiritual and social identification with Israel, and what values the people from the Arab countries should retain and even contribute to Israeli society.

Kahanoff considered the Zionist leadership's response to criticism as reflecting a certain ignorance. The criticism was seen as a form of ingratitude; they were hurt by this criticism, for they failed to appreciate that it was part of a necessary process whereby a society with different values tried to protect itself and to bring into the open the values that it thought were important. Kahanoff saw the Israeli society of the time as the result of many years of work and hard experiences. The Zionist establishment considered this as being to its credit and did not take into account that the Israel of that time was also the basis of the Israel of the future, and that as such Israel had to change to adapt itself both to the new population and to future conditions. The Jews from the eastern countries, for their part, did not understand the complex feelings of the members of the Zionist (Askhenazi) establishment; they interpreted the establishment's reaction as simply rejection, and they were even less able to understand the European Holocaust survivors and their suffering.

Generally speaking, Kahanoff perceived a new positive direction that was evolving before her eyes: an increasing awareness of the Americanization of Israeli culture, a cultural sensitivity on the part of the establishment, a new respect for exilic traditions, and so on. She saw all this as a positive demonstration of the forces of Israel's Levantine identity. Kahanoff put forward the vision of a pluralistic, free, and egalitarian Levant.

Kahanoff began her postscript to *From East the Sun* by pointing out the unity of this collection of articles. The unity, she said, was due to their Levantine perspective. She affiliated herself with the Levant by noting that although her education was entirely western, her deepest feelings were eastern, and thus her identity, like that of many others of her background, derived from this basic tension—a tension that could yield in Israel a fruitful synthesis of Jewish traditions with technological western modernity. Israel could then serve as a model for the surrounding Arab countries. At the same time, Israel has to move past Zionism, which has fulfilled its function. Israel has to recognize that it is situated in the Levant, and it must attempt to adapt itself to its position. Levantinism, thought Kahanoff, could help it to do so.[6]

Kahanoff also promoted an archetypal view of the perception of mythological time in the Middle East. One should remember not only that the Jewish, Muslim, and Christian calendars show that we are at a different date in relation to some founding event but also that this view of the date reflects something essential with regard to the culture that created this conception of time. Kahanoff suggested an examination of prehistorical history as a way to determine the possible root from which the religious archetypes emerged. In this way, the local mythologies might be seen as part of the same cultural family, each of whose branches grew in a different direction. She believed that in order for the Levant to share in the creation of a shared future, it would first have to discover its shared past.

THE LEVANTINE OPTION

Levantinism as a geocultural construct emerged in the eastern Mediterranean during the twentieth century, when the colonial presence of the French and the English brought about a dialectical interaction of cultures, representing diverse languages and literary traditions. The roots of Levantine culture date from the late Middle Ages, but already at the beginning of the modern era, the Levant began to be a defined geographical area where the European west was involved commercially, militarily, and culturally with certain Mediterranean countries such as Egypt and Lebanon. The colonial encounter was preceded by the Orientalist ideas of the western elites about an imaginary East. In the late 1950s, Kahanoff presented the Israeli cultural elite with a radical theory of cultural identity that was appealing to all Israeli communities equally: Levantinism. She formulated her theory in a series of articles titled "The Levantine Generation," published in the journal *Keshet* in 1959. There Kahanoff described the historical connotations of the concept "Levantinism," its cultural ramifications, and the as-yet-unrealized options it provided.

In a collection of articles written in English, which she prepared for publication in 1968, Kahanoff adumbrated her editorial guidelines:

> Because of its diversity, the Levant has been compared to a mosaic—bits of stone of different colours assembled into a flat picture. To me it is more like a prism whose various facets are joined by the sharp edge of differences, but each of which, according to its position in a time-space reflects or refracts light. Indeed, the concept of a continuum is contained in the word Levant as in the word Oriental, and perhaps the time has come for the Levant to re-evaluate itself by its own lights, rather than see itself through Europe's sights, as something quaintly exotic, tired, sick and almost lifeless.[7]

Kahanoff viewed modernity not as a purely western phenomenon, which Marx, Weber, Emile Durkheim, and other western thinkers assumed it was, but as the manifestation of varied cultural expressions. In this respect, she anticipated the concept of the renowned sociologist of modernity Shmuel Eisenstadt's "multiple modernities." In the year 2000 he wrote this: "In different periods of their development, [they gave] rise to multiple institutional and ideological patterns. Significantly, these patterns did not constitute simple continuations in the modern era of the traditions of their respective societies. Such patterns were distinctively modern, though greatly influenced by specific cultural premises, traditions and historical experiences.... The idea of multiple modernities presumes that the best way to understand the contemporary world . . . is to see it as a story of continual constitution and reconstitution of a multiplicity of cultural programs."[8]

Kahanoff's own view of multiple modernities was drawn from an autobiographical perspective. In her childhood and youth in Cairo in the 1920s, she saw pluralism and universality not as contradictory but as two sides of the same coin: "When I was a small child, it seemed natural that people understood each other although they spoke different languages, and were called names—Greek, Moslem, Syrian, Jewish, Christian, Arab, Italian, Tunisian and Armenian."[9]

And what in fact *is* the Levant? There are as many interpretations of the concept as there are interpreters, but here we may consider a scholar who refers to Kahanoff in developing her conception of the Levant. Tiziana Carlino says that the Levant, as a geographical area, is identified with part of the Mediterranean; the Levant is a form of adoption of modernity, a way of fusing several modernities, a combination of different metanarratives. In modern times, Levantines have been Europeanizing people engaged in commerce with the northern Mediterranean, cosmopolitans of the colonial world who spoke many languages.[10] Kahanoff, in Carlino's opinion, saw the Levant as a geographical space with actual cultural characteristics and not merely symbolic ones.

As a result of her experience of immigration to France and the United States, and influenced by western intellectuals like Albert Camus and Claude Lévi-Strauss, Kahanoff formulated the idea of a Levantine culture as a hybrid identity that could serve as an alternative to the contradiction-ridden reality of Israel. Levantinism was proposed as a possible form of rapprochement between controversial issues like religiosity, rationality, progress, and Middle Eastern culture. The modernistic Levant proposed by Kahanoff, in opposition to the western cultural hegemony, which also prevailed in Israel until the 1970s, comprised definite elements of modernity: an aspiration to universality, a commitment to progress, a vision of social and economic equality. In her Egyptian colonialist education, she was introduced to and adopted a mélange of modernistic principles from Marxist ideology, feminist teachings, the revolutionary tradition, and the history of national movements.

The Levantine figure parallel to Kahanoff, said Carlino, is the Italian woman writer Fausta Cialente (1898–1994), who lived in colonialist Egypt and published the novel *Ballata Levantina* (The Levantines).[11] The protagonist of the novel, Daniela, is an orphan raised by her grandmother Francesca, an Italian mistress who had a child—Daniela's mother—sired by a wealthy Jew from Alexandria. Daniela, a typical Levantine, is very reminiscent of Kahanoff: she commands several languages, leads a cosmopolitan existence, has had a European education in an Islamic country, and has independent characteristics and a feminist consciousness. Her doubts of whether Egypt is truly her country show a sense of alienation from the land in which she lives. The ending of the novel is mysterious: Daniela disappears close to the Nile. Her disappearance signifies the end of the colonialist era. She may have drowned, and thus her memory was obliterated like that of other Levantine authors. An obsessive concern with identity—cultural, national, feminist—is common to Kahanoff and Cialente, and both of them chose a literary medium through which to express their hybrid self-awareness.

A postcolonialist reading suggests a combination of Levantinism and modernity, at a time when Levantines were regarded as agents of colonialism and victims of modern nationalism. The urban anthropologist Daniel Monterescu developed an anthropological categorization of the Jewish Levant as exemplified by the life and letters of Kahanoff. He first diagnosed a characteristic, seen in Kahanoff, of a cosmopolitan liminality that blurred the imperial and cultural boundaries of the Jew and the Arab. Modern nationalism regarded this as a danger and made the liminality into a stereotype of rootlessness. The second characteristic Monterescu diagnosed is a rejection of historical identity in the form of Arab peoplehood or Jewish peoplehood, and an affinity with the Levantine qualities of cultural mixture and mutation and compounds. The third characteristic he discerned is the Levantine concept of the "foreigner"—defined by Georg Simmel and Albert Memmi as a "stranger" who came to stay yet remained a stranger: the first communities expelled from Egypt and North Africa were "foreign" communities, although they had been there for centuries. The fourth characteristic is exemplified in Kahanoff's promotion of hybridity, an idea that challenged a confined, organic conception of nationhood.

How did Monterescu see the Levantine? The Levantine, characterized "by categorical transgression and restless mobility, is a 'fishy' type inhabiting the shores of the Mediterranean since the early modern period."[12] The Levantine in popular culture represents a stereotype of "the other," moving between east and west, changing allegiances, not a real human being but a cultural object labeled as a member of an ethnic minority dwelling in the midst of the host nation, a stranger who does not belong and is a client of a colonial power. The Levantine is viewed by the national and anticolonialist imagination as threatening and dangerous. The Levantines, products of transnational migration, were not an immanent part of the nation-states, and the Mediterranean space gradually became their home. The cosmopolitan Levantines crossed national lines, engaging in boundary-crossing activities such as commercial and cultural mediation.

In this respect, Kahanoff personifies the rise and fall of the cosmopolitan Levantine generation. She extended the limits of the Israeli discourse on ethnicity, multiculturalism, and hybridity in the area. In Monterescu's opinion, the aggressive nativism of the "Sabra," the product of Zionist nationalism, was an imitation of the normative option of the Jewish immigrants, the Levantine "foreigners." The "foreigner" was not the immigrant who is here today and gone tomorrow but the one who is here today and will stay tomorrow. The foreigner is a "marginal man," a cultural hybrid, who is sacrificed on the altar of national purity—"blind nationalism," as Kahanoff called it.

In her article "The Mediterranean Option: On the Politics of Regional Affiliation in the Current Israeli Cultural Imagination,"[13] Gil Z. Hochberg, a professor of comparative and Hebrew literature, portrays Kahanoff as a hybrid of east and west.

She describes Levantinism as representing not only a call for an acceptance of cultural pluralism but principally an appeal for "a rethinking of culture as such by regenerating a discourse suspicious of claims of cultural purity and authenticity." The decision of the advocates of the "Mediterranean option" to adopt Mediterraneanism—a concept that Kahanoff, in Hochberg's opinion, never used—was a byproduct of the rejection of the Levantine option, a deliberate erasure of the recent postcolonial past of the region. Levantinism is now depicted as having a history of violence and as lacking a tradition of colonial minority groups such as the Jews, the Copts, and the Greeks, while Mediterraneanism is identified with the glorious past of the Hellenic civilization, leisure tourism, poetic inspiration, and a flourishing economy. From that point of view, Kahanoff does indeed go beyond cultural pluralism to a rethinking of culture itself.

In another article, "Permanent Immigration: Jacqueline Kahanoff, Ronit Matalon and the Impetus of Levantinism,"[14] Hochberg declared that Kahanoff's aim was to replace the colonial connotations of the term *Levant* with a radical new cultural and sociopolitical meaning. For Kahanoff, Levantinism was not only, in Hochberg's words, "the experience of hidden self and loss of language but also the way out of this state of loss." Kahanoff, in this interpretation, found colonialist oppression in Israeli-Jewish society: the "internal colonialism" of the Ashkenazi toward the Mizrahi, "'a complex illness' based on racism and phobia." Kahanoff wished to cure this colonialist sickness by reclaiming "Levantinism," transforming this concept, which had previously signified a lack of authenticity and cultural stability, into a positive cultural force with therapeutic power.

Hochberg claimed that because Kahanoff found the geographical definition of *the Levant* constricting, she broadened it to include the temporal dimension. She challenged the geographical formulation and applied it to history as well. By bridging the glorious civilizations of the past and recent European colonialism, the Levant laid a basis for a cultural encounter between east and west. There are differences of opinion concerning the geographical borders of the modern Levant. It is identified with the countries of the eastern Mediterranean, but it can also include Iran, Iraq, Yemen, and Libya, and in different contexts Turkey, Greece, Cyprus, and the Mashrak (the eastern regions of the Arab world). As a temporal bridge between cultures of different eras, the Levant gave rise to cultural fusions that reflected "the necessity of living, not a nostalgia."[15] Hochberg sees Kahanoff's Levantinism as an area of literary production, cultural dialogue, and creative cooperation transcending national, linguistic, and geographical frontiers. Her Levant is a time-related cultural concept, a vibrant political and cultural force, and is not conceived in nativistic-spacial terms. As further evidence, Hochberg cites Shlomo Elbaz and Mikaél Elial, the editors of the journal *Levant*, who saw a similarity between the Levantine option and the Andalusian school of thought: that is to say, it is a model of interpretation, a way of writing, reading, and thinking, an area of literary creativity giving rise to "surprizing meetings" like that of Amos Oz and the Moroccan-French writer Tahar Ben-Jelloun, or Palestinian Israelis writing in Hebrew like Naim Araidi, Atalha Mansour, Muhammad Watad, Salman Massalha, and Anton Shammas (today one could add the Israeli Palestinian Sayed Kashua).[16] Israeli Palestinian writers writing in Hebrew like Anton Shamas and Sayed Kashua are good examples of liminal literature.[17]

Such manifestations not only represent a reality that crosses ethnic, religious, linguistic, and national lines but also break down the barriers between east and west, the Middle East and Africa, Arabs and Jews. Thus, a cultural conception of the Levant is offered as an alternative to the existing national, geographical, and ethnic options. Another intellectual who supports the idea of the Levant as a cultural space rather than a geographical one, Edward Said, envisions the Levant as marking the possibility of a productive interplay of "nationalism" and "exile," as "home is always more than a territorial location." "Home" and "place" are broader concepts than as perceived by the nationalist outlook.[18] In Jewish thought, the contrasting concept of "home as territory" is that of "the text as home."

In his book *After Jews and Arabs: Remaking Levantine Culture,* Ammiel Alcalay opposes "the modern myth of the Jew as pariah and wanderer [that] has ironically translated into the postmodern myth of the Jew as 'other,' an other that collapses into the equation: writing = Jew = Book. . . . the Jew was native, not a stranger but an absolute inhabitant of time and space."[19] Alcalay distinguishes between the European intellectuals and writers—Kafka with his preoccupation with law is but one example—who deal with the abstract, and the Levantine writers with their "concrete and sensual attachment to the fact and memory of a native space." Alcalay sees the Levantine Jew as the native Jew "at home," who lives in his natural eastern environment and is able to share that space with the Muslims. Hochberg links Alcalay's spatial conception with those of Hannan Hever and myself. Hever asserts that "the spatial reality of the Mizrahi Jew, unlike that of the Ashkenazim . . . is local,"[20] and I am cited as saying that in his writing the Mediterranean Jew "is a natural son to his surroundings . . . and cultural origins." Hochberg sees the spatial approach of Alcalay, Hever, and myself as liable to degenerate into an ideology of national aggression.

Deborah Anne Starr critiques their approach by saying that the late success of Kahanoff's Levantinism is due to "a particularly relevant paradigm in its attempt to undermine persisting hegemonic, unitary national discourses."[21] These critiques seek to appropriate Kahanoff for their political purposes by turning her into the mother of the Mizrahi Israelis.

A more balanced and sympathetic profile of Kahanoff is proposed by Alexandra Nocke in her book *The Place of the Mediterranean in Modern Israeli Identity*: "In her unique vision of Israel as an integral part of the Mediterranean or Levantine world, she promotes an open, pluralistic society in the Levant."[22] The aura surrounding Kahanoff, explains Nocke, transfers a nostalgia for a world of cultural coexistence to the harsh realities of the Israeli present. Kahanoff revaluated "Levantinism" by describing it as a model of a rich multiculturalism and a long cultural heritage. Nocke concludes with this: "The Levant is being rehabilitated and presented as an alternative, even conciliatory way to approach the different existing maps of the region."

The Levant was characterized by exchanges of intellectual goods and mutual influences and affinities resulting from conquests, alliances, expulsions, discoveries, and wanderings on the eastern shore of the Mediterranean Basin. According to Kahanoff, the culture of ancient Greece penetrated Egypt, Asia Minor, and Palestine. There was a meeting of Jews and Greeks in the Hellenistic culture of Alexandria, and that dialectical encounter formed the intellectual basis of Christianity and western civilization. Greek, the language of ancient civilization, was dominant in the Levant long after Greece became a province of the Roman Empire, and the Greek Byzantine Empire became the center of the civilized world after Rome fell to the barbarians of the north. The Byzantine Empire adopted Christianity, and Greek became the liturgical language of the eastern churches. Kahanoff continued to trace the Levantine "mythical time" that existed in the Levantine "mythical space" up to the Alexandria of the time of her youth.

Kahanoff saw herself as belonging to that generation of the colonialist Levantines whose task, but also privilege, it was to spread European culture to the rest of the world. For her, and for other Levantine women, the truth lay beyond religion or western civilization. In the article "Europe from Afar," Kahanoff wrote that the philosophy course in the French lycée was bon ton among the members of the minorities in colonialist Cairo. It was fashionable to know the names of famous philosophers, but, Kahanoff confessed, "We never read any of the works cited in our textbooks,

LEVANTINISM

and knew no one . . . who ever had or would. . . . Who then read the books which had made people so famous? This was one of the mysteries of Levantine culture."[23] The writer who aroused the most resentment in her, and who perhaps most represented western rationalist thought, was Darwin. The following provocative passage was omitted by Aharon Amir when he translated Kahanoff's essay: "If Darwin were right, then the Nazis were right. There was a master race, and when it had destroyed all mankind it could only destroy itself. The last man would die, triumphantly asserting his domination over the devastated earth."[24] Amir continued his translation only from the passage beginning with the questions "How could our professors, good Socialists most of them, waste our time on Darwin? What was there I didn't understand?" To Darwin, Kahanoff added Nietzsche: she saw both of them as leading to the swastika. She predicted that not only the Jews would be crucified on this symbol but also Christian Europe itself. She thought the Levantines should be selective in their use of the European heritage: they should take out the poison and emphasize "Thou shalt not kill."[25]

Secularism was an important principle of modern Levantinism for Kahanoff. The following sentence is taken from the original manuscript of "Europe from Afar": "We had a religious approach to the problems of our day, transposed to the secular world, for we despised the stale old beliefs."[26] Amir took liberties and condensed this complex sentence as follows: "At the same time, I despised religion."[27] Kahanoff's secularism did not mean atheism, and in all her writings she was respectful of the Jewish religion as well as all other religions, and one also finds in her writings a basic belief in an omnipotent God. Kahanoff treated the hope of national independence in Egypt and the attempt to liberate the country from British colonialism with great skepticism. She was critical of the Egyptian elite for its superficiality in wanting to obtain the modern luxuries without doing the hard work of building a new society: "We compared this to the situation in Palestine, a place where they were building a new society from the foundation, at the same time as in Egypt they were beginning at the top floor in the hope that the foundations could be built on it."

In the modern Levant that Kahanoff envisaged, feminism was a cornerstone. With a critical retrospective glance, she followed the stages of her awakening up to the crystallization of her egalitarian gender consciousness. She wrote candidly of the patriarchal structure that her mother attempted to bequeath to her. When she asked to be allowed to work independently, her mother answered, "You can't. People would think your father was ruined."

In a later article, "Greetings to the Little Woman," Kahanoff suggested that the message of the movement for women's liberation was perhaps the idea that in the future women would no longer have to bear children and bring them up. Perhaps fertility itself would be unnecessary in the humanity of the future. Uncharacteristically for her, Kahanoff followed her conclusions ad absurdum in the hope of arriving at a radical analysis and of opening up possibilities that religion at that time did not provide. This may have been an ironic essay critical of the women's liberation movement: "Almost without knowing it, the women's liberation movement prepares women spiritually and intellectually for the day in which their traditional role will not only be ineffective but will even be a stumbling-block to evolution and progress."

The title of Kahanoff's essay "Ambivalent Levantine," a meaningful expression of her complex perspective, was unfortunately rendered by her Hebrew translator Aharon Amir as "Black on White." Here, in a short paragraph she conveys the essence of the Mediterranean worldview, whose starting point is in the dialogue between, and the mutual enhancement of the east and the west: "I am a typical Levantine in that I appreciate what I inherited from my Mizrahi origins and what is now mine of western culture, I find in this cross-fertilization, called disparagingly in Israel 'Levantinization,' an enrichment and not an impoverishment. It is from this vantage point that I wish to try to define the complex inter-related malady of both Israel's Sephardic [Jews of Mizrahi / Middle Eastern origin] and Ashkenazi [East European] communities."[28]

Kahanoff produces a sociohistoric genealogy of the Jewish Diaspora, which went its separate ways in the East and the West. Part went into the Christian-western world, part to the Levantine-Muslim. Only in Israel did these two streams join one river. Each of the Jewish Diasporas was influenced by the cultural and national character of their respective geographical surroundings. Thus, the eastern Jews came to Israel without technological proficiency or professional expertise, and lacking western culture's capitalist impetus. At the same time, they were influenced by their traditional surroundings in many other spheres: social organization, the individual's relationship with the general public, their practices of worship, and their philosophy of meekly accepting God's judgment.

The first expression of this attitude—an expression that was virtually racist—appeared in a series of articles by the journalist Aryeh Gelblum in the newspaper *Haaretz* in 1949 on the subject of the great wave of immigration that took place at that time. In these articles, Gelblum displayed a patronizing attitude that viewed the Mizrahi immigrants as "Levantines" who represented the wretched, primitive culture of undeveloped countries, and also as dangerous elements that could lower the cultural level of Israeli society to that of its enemies. If the Israelis were fated to live in the Levant, they should at least protect themselves from its inhabitants and the negative culture they represented.

MEDITERRANEAN ISRAEL

The Mediterranean option has virtually disappeared from the Israeli discourse. The Hebrew literary historiographies, which are known to be exercises in canonization, fixed the boundaries of the "republic of letters," which contribute decisively to the shaping of Israeli society. The writers, poets, and essayists within this territory are given their due of attention, and those who were excluded from it are regarded as "others." The voice of many of the "others," such as Arabs and Mizrahis, was not heard directly but merely heard via the citizens of the republic. The Mediterraneans, however, are not even recognized as "others" but are thrust beyond the boundaries of the discourse. A dominant or hegemonic culture necessarily creates some "other," in contrast to which or in opposition to which it defines itself. It also results in a disappearance or an absence. A classic example of this historiographical absence was Jacqueline Kahanoff and the Mediterranean option.[29]

Kahanoff's biographical distress has not remained unresolved but finds a solution in the Mediterranean option she proposed to the Israeli society in process of formation. She played an active role in the debate on Israel's Mediterranean identity. As a precursor of this cultural identity, Kahanoff may become a paradigm facilitating an understanding of the different forms of identity in Israel's culture in the making, of questions of east and west and the intermediate areas, and of the place of Israel in the Mediterranean geocultural space. Kahanoff's identification with Israel's Mediterranean image is so self-evident that she has been called "the bearer of the Mediterranean spirit," "the First Lady of the Mediterranean," and "the representative of the Mediterranean idea."[30]

Those who view Jacqueline Kahanoff as the representative of Mediterranean culture are immediately confronted with one of the major obstacles of advancing the Mediterranean idea in Israel. The advocates of the Mediterranean option claim that those who oppose it are attempting to evade the issue of Israel's proximity to the Arab states and the Palestinians, and to escape into an amiable, pleasant relationship with the Europeans. But this escape, say the critics, has no basis in reality. It is an evasion of the basic problems of Israel and its Arab neighbor. Those who reject this criticism, for their part, claim that the Mediterranean option is a real cultural and political possibility, which can therefore serve as a viable basis for a dialogue with the country's neighbors. This option offers a new and fresh perspective that is not dependent on the basic assumption of two contending, adversarial sides. The validity of this option is contingent on the idea that there is a rich fabric of geocultural affinities between the peoples living in the Mediterranean Basin—affinities with a vital political significance that can facilitate the creation of a broad dialogue and regional channels of communication, and thus to some degree can moderate the Israeli-Arab dispute. This dispute is often said to be insoluble, and it is possible that this negative verdict may be due, among other things, to a disregard of the general Mediterranean context, of the things that are common to the heritage of all the peoples of the region and of the widely different geopolitical interests these peoples have. Unlike the constricting old-new Middle Eastern option, this new option does not regard the Mediterranean as a "contested" space, the arena of a conflict between Jews and Arabs. But this option is by no means confined to the external relationships between the peoples.

It is interesting to consider the degree to which Kahanoff's early views on Mediterranean culture—one that she saw as a "cross-influence" and "cross-mutation" of east and west, forming a "dynamic unity"—resemble those of the historian of the Crusades, Joshua Prawer. In his article "Jews, Christians and Muslims in the Mediterranean Basin," Prawer described Mediterranean culture as a symbiosis of the cultures formed on the shores of the Mediterranean: "Mediterranean culture is a synthesis or confection of religions and cultures that were formed on the shores of the sea or close to them, and that influenced each other until there was a kind of symbiosis, a cohabitation, a sometimes uncomfortable but always productive symbiosis of these cultures."[31]

Kahanoff described Israel's Mediterranean option in similar symbiotic terms: "Israel's situation is unique, because this process of cross-influence and cross-mutation takes place in the same country, which is Levantine with regard to its geographical position between East and West, and because of the mixture of its population. For that reason, it can fuse the two main elements in its composition into a dynamic and productive unity, like the outstanding Levantine cultures of the past—Byzantium and Islam—which were also a fusion of inhabitants and cultures, as Western Europe also was in its formative period."[32]

The public discussion of the Mediterranean identity of Israeli society began in 1995, with the founding of the Forum for Mediterranean Cultures at the Van Leer Institute in Jerusalem. In the heat of this discussion, parallels were drawn between Jacqueline Kahanoff and Albert Camus. In his lecture "False Mediterranean Harbor," the essayist Meron Benvenisti compared Kahanoff— to whom the opening evening of the forum was devoted—with Camus, and quoted from Kahanoff's works and from "the nice but worthless writings of the young *pied noir* on Mediterraneanness."[33] Benvenisti saw the Mediterranean option as an escape from the Middle East.

Benvenisti said that Camus and Kahanoff made us see the essential point. The promotion of a "Mediterranean culture" is an escape from the true and only viable option, which the mature Camus advocated and fought for and whose failure broke his heart. This was the possibility that the various communities in Algeria could coexist and establish cultural links between them; the hope that cross-fertilization, intimate coexistence, and a sense of belonging to the common homeland would prove stronger than militant tribalism and seclusion in national ghettos. The conclusion Benvenisti drew from this analogy was clear: despair of the possibility of coexistence, escape to a purely cultural form of cross-fertilization, and on a deep level, a pessimistic acknowledgment of the correctness of the deterministic philosophy of the school of the pessimistic thinker Carl Schmitt, which postulated an eternal opposition of "friend" and "foe."[34] Benvenisti claimed that under the pretext of "reverting to the original, regional basis," an attempt had been made by intellectuals, writers, and artists to fabricate a cultural approach that was detached, unrealistic, and cut off from the local life and culture—an attempt, in short, to see value in Levantinism. In his opinion, the choice of Kahanoff by the academic director of the Forum for Mediterranean Cultures was no accident: "A forgotten Egyptian-Jewish writer, Jacqueline Kahanoff, is being touted as a model personage 'who was ahead of her time.' The atmosphere of Lawrence Durrell's *Alexandria Quartet*, which celebrated the life of a 'cosmopolitan community' that moved in its own circles among a sea of children with which it had no social or cultural connection, and whose whole identity was borrowed, has become a source of inspiration for the new Israeli cultural identity."[35]

The literary critic Nissim Calderon also saw points of similarity between Kahanoff's Mediterranean approach and that of Camus. Both, he observed, see a real possibility of a multiplicity of cultures, and for that reason the Israelis would do well to return to Kahanoff and Camus as they give an exact account of cultural pluralism.[36] Camus belonged to a minority group in Algeria just as Kahanoff belonged to a minority group in Egypt. The Jews in Egypt lived under conditions different from those of the million French in Algeria, but at the same time a critical distance was common to both Kahanoff and Camus. Kahanoff called this distance "Levantine" and Camus called it "Mediterranean." In his lecture "A Trip in the Mediterranean," Calderon explained that in the places where Kahanoff and Camus lived, movement was a necessity. Immigrants traveled from place to place in the Mediterranean, intellectuals excelled in "trading" facts. Thus, Kahanoff's and Camus's procedure was distinguished by a cultural pluralism, not a relativism in which all is permitted. Neither of them made an idealization of the place they came from: they in person experienced the contradictions that the Mediterranean region contains. Who like them is able to personify the idea of cultural pluralism?

In the mid-1950s, Aharon Amir helped to found the "Tsohar Publishing House," which was to serve to change the literary order of priorities in the country, to diminish the influence of the Anglo-Saxon world on Israeli culture, and to bring the reader closer to the Mediterranean Basin. Amir saw the Mediterranean as the arena of conflicts, hostility, and armadas, but also as a sea of pleasantness. He seized on Camus as someone who perceived the fanaticism that existed in the Mediterranean countries but who also sought the "sense of proportion" of ancient Greece and tried to find a balance between religious differences, ethnic tensions, and national confrontations.[37]

According to the Israeli author Sami Michael, Camus was the product of the Mediterranean as a sea of escape: of the despairing, of poor Frenchmen who immigrated to Algeria in the nineteenth century to find redemption. "The Mediterranean region produced Moses, Mohammed and Jesus, who failed to make peace in their area. It is a sea of wars and conquests more than a sea of peace and trade." The Israeli author Dan Tsalka is less unambiguous than Sami Michael. He sees the Mediterranean as a sort of snare. On the one hand, it is the classical sea, *Mare Nostrum* (Our Sea) of the Romans, the sea of wandering and return home, and on the other hand, fascism and other such evils sprang up on its shores. Camus, thinks Tsalka, had an intellectual tendency to create heroes, philosophical figures who could express his longings and desires—that is to say, a kind of humanism that had a certain poetic force associated with the Mediterranean.[38]

A cultural critic who made great efforts to bring the Mediterranean aspects of Kahanoff and Camus to the notice of the Hebrew reader was the essayist, translator, and journalist Yoram

Bronowski. Bronowski always presented the "Mediterranean option" as a suitable one for the Israelis. *Me-Mizrah Shemesh* (*From East the Sun*, the collection of Kahanoff's essays) represented for him "an idea of culture," which Kahanoff called "Levantinism."[39] This provocative epithet was meant to contradict the usual associations of this term in the western Israeli culture, which were the opposite of culture, a lack of authenticity, and even something caricatural. Levantinism was a mishmash of cultures that came into being in the eastern Mediterranean over hundreds of years as elements of European culture came together with scraps of Arab, Turkish, Jewish, Greek, and Egyptian culture.

Kahanoff represented the Levantine culture as having the right to a full, authentic independent existence, although one that was not without problems. Levantinism, said Bronowski, echoing Kahanoff, is a culture in the making, a cultural configuration that will come into being after a prolonged encounter between Europe and the east. This cultural encounter takes place over a long period, but only in the postcolonial era does it begin to constitute a truly new culture. A true culture is always heterogenous in its beginnings, made up of contradictory and even opposing elements, and it is not surprising if the members of the initial generations have difficult problems of identity.

Years after Bronowski wrote this piece on Kahanoff, he read Camus's *Le premier homme* (The First Man) and wrote that the book "was apparently intended to be a lament for the death of a culture, and perhaps also for the death of a certain option—the Mediterranean option." Bronowski believed that the readers of Camus in Israel would see an analogy between the Algerian problem and the question of the territories in Israel: "In the public debate in Israel, the memory of the Algerian War of Independence has been brought up again and again in recent years, and the episode of France severing ties with its old colony. Many suggested to then Prime Minister Yitzhak Rabin that he should take

France's President, Charles De Gaulle as an example. When one compares an exodus from the occupied territories with France's departure from Algeria and becomes better acquainted with the attitude of the French to the events of thirty years ago, it is difficult not to be drawn into vexing thoughts."[40]

The Israeli author A. B. Yehoshua connected Kahanoff's Levantinism with Israel's evolving Mediterranean identity: "Kahanoff gave depth and force to the scorned concept 'Levantine' and was also sober and critical in her attitude towards it. We felt closed in and besieged, and she transmitted openness, aroused hope that after the peace there will be someone to talk to."[41]

The Israeli author Haim Be'er was of a similar opinion: "[Kahanoff] set a surprising succulent new dish on the small Israeli table. She did not preach, but she gave you to understand that Ashkenazi pride was based on an error, and that the Levantine option is much better than what we have to offer. She presented a world whose beauty lay in its complexity—French, English, Mediterranean, Judaism, Mizrahi aristocracy. In her personality and in her writings, she proposed connections we were not aware of, a possible model for life in the region. Not one of self-effacement and servility and not one of pride. Only afterwards did we read Cavafy, Durrell, etc."[42]

In 2011, a collection of articles, *Mongrels or Marvels: The Levantine Writings of Jacqueline Kahanoff*, edited by Deborah A. Starr and Sasson Somekh, appeared for the first time in English. The editors highlighted Kahanoff's early vision of a revival of "the Levant as a geographic entity comprising many genuinely native peoples and cultures," against the Zionist vision of the creation of a new Jew with a new Israeli identity. The editors cited the words of Yaira Ginossar: Kahanoff "caused a revolution in the term from a shameful word to a possible description of honor for people who exist in two cultures."[43] After the Six-Day War in 1967, Kahanoff broadened her vision of the Levant to that of a cosmopolitan society that embraced the whole region. The editors concluded that "although Kahanoff devoted a great deal of effort to unmasking legacies of European imperialism and internal forms of colonialism within Israeli society, she never recognized her own colonizing tendencies towards Arab-Islamic culture. Her social model is derived from a notion of a Levantine subculture composed primarily of minorities that served as a bridge between East and West but had little direct contact with the majority culture outside their milieu."[44]

As a promoter of the Mediterranean idea, Kahanoff branched out or deviated from the prevalent adversarial or oppositional reality toward a broad, rich, and polyphonic mesh of geopolitical cultural elements. Her grasping of Israel, together with her biographical and creative journey on the threshold, made Kahanoff the herald and initiator of a different cultural possibility, far more extensive than was offered in her time, and also, perhaps, than is being offered now.

Joseph Shohet, Jacqueline's father. By permission of Ms. Laura d'Amade. All rights reserved.

Yvonne Shohet, Jacqueline's mother. By permission of Ms. Laura d'Amade. All rights reserved.

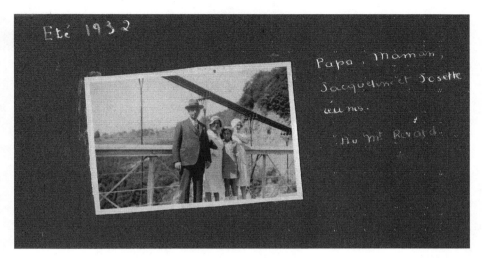

Shohet family, 1932, from family photo album #1. By permission of Ms. Laura d'Amade. All rights reserved.

Shohet family. By permission of Ms. Laura d'Amade. All rights reserved.

Jacqueline in white dress. By permission of Ms. Laura d'Amade. All rights reserved.

Jacqueline in Cairo. By permission of Ms. Laura d'Amade. All rights reserved.

Jacqueline and her sister Josette. By permission of Ms. Laura d'Amade. All rights reserved.

Jacqueline on the beach. By permission of Ms. Laura d'Amade. All rights reserved.

Jacqueline on the beach.
By permission of
Ms. Laura d'Amade.
All rights reserved.

Jacqueline's wedding
photo, Cairo. By
permission of
Ms. Laura d'Amade.
All rights reserved.

Jacqueline, probably in Boulder, Colorado, 1944. By permission of Ms. Laura d'Amade. All rights reserved.

Portrait of Jacqueline, between 1946 and 1948. By permission of Ms. Laura d'Amade. ©Photo by Eugène Rubin.

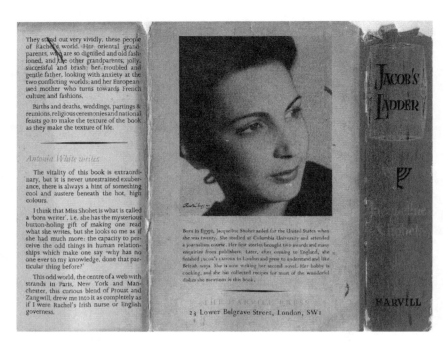

Portrait of Jacqueline, reproduced on the original book cover of *Jacob's Ladder*. By permission of Ms. Laura d'Amade. All rights reserved.

Jacqueline on board the RMS *Queen Mary*. By permission of Ms. Laura d'Amade. All rights reserved.

Jacqueline in Paris, 1950s. By permission of Ms. Laura d'Amade. All rights reserved.

Jacqueline Kahanoff. By permission of Ms. Laura d'Amade. ©Photo by Devora Hirshfeld.

Jacqueline in her study, 1970s. By permission of Ms. Laura d'Amade. ©Photo by Yael Rosen.

Jacqueline and friend Diane Jorland in Jerusalem. By permission of Ms. Laura d'Amade. All rights reserved.

THREE

KAHANOFF'S POETIC JOURNEY

KAHANOFF AND DAHLIA RAVIKOVITCH

Both Kahanoff, who immigrated to Israel, and the poet Dahlia Ravikovitch (1936–2005), born in Israel and widely accepted as the most "Israeli" of the female poets of that time, are considered Levantine writers. Yet whereas Ravikovitch's poetry was rife with analogies between Zionism and the Crusades, which bespoke of an existential dread regarding Israel's future, Kahanoff, as a recent immigrant, did not share these anxieties; indeed, she was sure of herself and of the future of the nation, albeit also critical.

Kahanoff was, however, an intellectual challenge and source of inspiration for Dahlia Ravikovitch. In May 1963, Ravikovitch wrote a letter to Kahanoff:

> Dear Mrs. Kahanoff,
>
> Three years ago, when I first read your article, "The Levantine Generation," I intended to write to you, but because I was three years younger than I am now, I was also more shy. This time—simply—after I read your "France Chronicles" published in *Keshet,* I had a clearer idea of what I wanted to write to you. In all your articles, from "The Levantine Generation" to your latest articles, there is a basic quality which gives rise to admiration and envy: you

are able to write about painful and essential matters without the tempestuousness and bitterness with which people generally write about them. This subdued approach is the correct historical perspective, and because you already have it, you do not know how difficult it is to attain. Moreover, and perhaps for that very reason, you have a good balance between abstract ideas and concrete details. I have specified the qualities you possess not because you need my appraisal, but because I have a particular interest in them.

You write, among other things, that this country is twenty years behind Europe, and you describe this backwardness not only as a cultural backwardness but as a backwardness also connected with the way of life, the outlook and ideas, and tensions in [Israeli] society. Because I was born in this country and have not been out of it, with the exception of one year, this fact has a painful significance for me. This fact is something irreparable because I have no doubt that the main deficiencies of cultural life in this country also necessarily apply to me. Like all provincials, I too lack a proper sense of proportion in assessing things, and I even find it hard to relate to ills like ethnic or national deprivation as I should. I either exaggerate the evil or I ignore it for a long period.

The matter you described in your last article—the matter of the new way of life in France with a modern but almost anti-revolutionary approach—made a very deep impression on me. I would like to hear more about it, and I would like to hear from you many things about matters with which I am not familiar.

You should realize that every Tuesday I go to Jerusalem to complete my B.A. Owing to the material of my studies and the lively discussions in the classes and the slight excitement of the journey I sometimes refresh my way of thinking, but on the other days of the week I read newspapers and talk about the things that everyone else talks about.

If my Hebrew is too difficult [for you] I am ready to translate my letter into English, in which case it will be shorter and there will also be a few mistakes. I would be grateful if you would answer me in any way whatsoever. My telephone number is 35587 and I live in Ramat Hen, so the geographical distance between us is not great.

Thanking you in anticipation,
Dahlia Ravikovitch[1]

Where did Kahanoff and Ravikovitch stand at the time in which the letter was written? The twenty-seven-year-old Ravikovitch was in a period of intense spiritual awakening. Four years earlier, in 1959, her first book of poetry, *Ahavat tapuah ha-zahav* (The Love of an Orange), had been warmly received in the literary world. One critic wrote that in the author of the book "we are witnessing a great and a true talent."[2]

In the year in which Ravikovitch's letter was written, Kahanoff was already known to the readers of *Keshet*, particularly for the series of articles "The Generation of Levantine," published in the same year as *The Love of an Orange*. In October 1962, Kahanoff was introduced to the readers of the journal *Amot* for the first time through her travel essay "Wake of the Waves," in which she opened a window on the Mediterranean:

> This is my first trip abroad after living in Israel for seven years. The Mediterranean Sea, which is much bluer than I remember, whips up foam—a dense white foam that thins out, disperses, and disappears. I have often been on voyages like this, watching the ship's greenish wake as it dissolves, amazed again and again by the way these expeditions of ours leave nothing behind them, even the memory of them erased, unless something happens, a tremor that sends bubbles rising to the surface of our minds. How strange it is that we wander over this vast expanse until one day we reach some shore, some place, which carries back to me, like the spray of sand or water, scenes of our life to together, and now we know that everything we have assembled will scatter like a wave, and soon our fragments will be cast up at random. I try to find some shape in those scatterings, like the fortune-teller on the beach in Alexandria many years ago, who with her henna-stained hands would toss shells onto the sand to read our future and would say, as we children listened in rapt attention: "Long journey ... sorrow ... good luck ... love ..." And indeed, who among us did not know all of these?[3]

These descriptions of Mediterranean Israel may seem, in retrospect, a tad colonialist. Inner tensions and contradictions in her developing identity affected her literary image and her life as an adult.

At the time, Ravikovitch, twenty years younger than Kahanoff, was still crystallizing her critical understanding of the Israeli identity. In her poem "Karnei Hattin,"[4] she describes the voyage of the crusaders, identifying it with the voyage of Jason and the Argonauts to steal the golden fleece—the image of the kingdom of Jerusalem. The crusader pirates are depicted as bringing with them an Apollonian wisdom, but Christian compassion, which they came to preach, changed into lawlessness, and they were carried away by their madness and simple cruelty. The Christians were soon defeated by the Muslims under the leadership of Saladin, who "passed judgement on them at the battle of Hattin." Finally, justice was done, as is seen in the sound of the poem. In Hebrew, the meaning of Saladin (*Salah Ed-Din*) is "the success of faith" (*din* is "religion" or "faith"). Ravikovitch switches roles in this poem. Contrary to Jewish tradition, which warns that kindness to the cruel is likely to end in cruelty to the kind, the poetess pitied the crusaders, who were far from their homes, exposed to dangers, disillusioned, and deprived of their good name.

Ravikovitch's letter to Kahanoff provides us with a significant glimpse of the attitude of the generation of secular Sabras who came of age with the founding of the State of Israel. Many of the leading writers and poets of that generation would turn to Kahanoff, as it were, to find a bandage to dress the existential wounds they suffered in forging an Israel. A. B. Yehoshua (b. 1936) described the fascination Kahanoff exerted on his generation: "Within the crystalizing Israeli identity, she opened a window for us on worlds with which we were not familiar; not Mizrahi folklore but the intellectual Levant."[5]

Ravikovitch could be rescued from the cultural and intellectual confines of Israel only through imaginary journeys to the Bible and the world of mysticism, to Hannibal and Saladin. But Kahanoff, who came to Israel from the world at large, brought to her new country the scents of the region and the wonders of the west: the streets of Cairo and the pavements of Alexandria, the cafés of Paris, the jazz clubs of Chicago, and the intellectual atmosphere of Manhattan's New School and Columbia University.

In 1954, the year she immigrated to Israel, Kahanoff was free of the spiritual oppression that weighed on Dahlia Ravikovitch and her friends, the writers and poets of her generation. She did not feel a "crusader anxiety" about the possible destruction of the state, nor did she have feelings of "crusader guilt" about appropriating the property of others. She had finally reached the land of her heart's desire. The calm assurance of her Jewish identity enabled Kahanoff to publish her essays with a Canaanite editor at *Keshet* without fear of harming her self-image. She rejected Canaanism on the one hand, but she also rejected the encomium to exile of her friend from Egypt, the poet Edmond Jabès: "In order to be whole we of course need books, but also houses, fields, streets, schools, work, in order not to be simply a race, but a people."[6]

The patriotism shown by Kahanoff in making her home in Israel in its twenty-seventh year of independence was less evident in the writers of the Sabra generation. Those writers, who came of age with the birth of the state, asked critical questions about the state's crusader-like isolation, its relationship to the Arabs, and the ethical and existential quandary of securing national identity. They sought ways of escaping the burden of Jewish history; Kahanoff was comfortable in her Judaism. They were used to living in a masculine world; she embodied a feminist spirit. The kibbutz and the army were quasi-sacred institutions for many Sabras; she scrutinized these foundations of Israeli culture with a critical eye. They closed their eyes to the Mizrahi immigrants of the state; she was alert to and wrote about the distress of the new immigrants. They closed themselves in a Hebrew shtetl and often felt stifled by it; Kahanoff opened for them a window on the Mediterranean. As a Levantine woman, she wrote about herself

166 JACQUELINE KAHANOFF

and about many of her generation after their wanderings in the world and in the Mediterranean: "How strange were our wanderings in that vast space, those who went as far as Paris and New York, and those who closed the circle and returned to the port of departure, have left us as we go on our way."

RELIGIOUS EXISTENTIALISM

In an unpublished French poem, apparently written in her later years, Kahanoff sounds an existential resignation to a life unfulfilled: "What can one say? What can I say? I love life / I didn't love life enough / So much the worse, so much the worse." Although she seems to have written very few poems, none of which she published, the style she wrote in indicates that she was drawn to French poets of a religious existential temperament. In particular she enthralled by the poetry of Charles Péguy, which read as a form of prayer.[7] She compared Péguy's "poetic cathedral" to Noah's ark. The ark carried the best of all that the spirit of humanity had produced and that was worth saving. But Péguy's life and poetry, she mused, did not always dwell on the lofty heights of the spirit. His contempt for the modern world, which he felt was lacking in any divine beauty, was in telling contradiction to his poetry, which bordered on mysticism. Péguy's hope to rescue the modern world from total degradation, Kahanoff held, was inspired by Joan of Arc, the martyred French saint who symbolized spiritual fortitude and integrity.[8]

Like Joan of Arc, Kahanoff held, Péguy "believed in a world in which the elements of emergency and drama of a battlefield were at work, a perpetual campaign of God, whose soldiers were always in a state of preparedness to attack the enemy, to fight a righteous war and a war for the greatness of France."

The poet's patriotism did not contradict a special kind of socialism that in Kahanoff's words was closer to Saint Francis than to Marx. The full greatness of humanity, Péguy said, would come about when the soil of life in this world would be duly prepared for the realization of the kingdom of heaven.

The religious poem "Eve,"[9] which Péguy wrote a year before his death, was celebrated by Kahanoff as "a flood of eight thousand lines" that brought his religious vision to a nigh-eschatological crescendo: "Happy are those who fall for cities of flesh and blood / for they are the body of the city of God."

—⁂—

Kahanoff discerned in Péguy's religious existentialism a continuous meditation on the mystery of God. In his essay *L'argent* (Money)[10] (1913), he acknowledged his attraction to religion already from an early age: "There is no greater mystery than that of the obscure years of preparation when every man stands on the threshold of his life." Palpitating behind his religious affirmation, Kahanoff noted, were intimations of existential despair. He felt as a child, as he lay on his back on a hill and gazed up to the heavens, God speaking through France, and he described the scene as follows: "A little man putting his sorrows before God / with all the seriousness in the world / and consoling himself as though it were the consolation of God." Paradoxically, perhaps, Kahanoff observed, Péguy's poetry served to inspire a "militant Catholicism in France," whose advocates found in his poems "a spirit both religious and revolutionary."

According to Péguy, militant Catholicism refuses to distinguish between the world of the spirit and the world of matter or to recognize the distinction between body and soul. This, in Kahanoff's opinion, was the reason for the poet's identification with Joan of Arc, who fought for both this world (*politique*) and the next world (*mystique*).

From this perspective, Péguy's biography exemplifies the historical continuity of France. He was not "an anarchist who mixed holy water with petrol" but, as Kahanoff said, a traditionalist who knew that tradition is only effective when it is active. He was born in Orléans, the town from which Joan of Arc is traditionally said to have sallied forth to rescue the French kingdom. The French national mythology went as far as Greek mythology, concluded Kahanoff, and saw Joan of Arc as a kind of Antigone. Péguy himself thought that the tragedies of Oedipus and Antigone had nothing to do with Christianity but represented an existential situation: "The tribulations of Péguy's Joan of Arc, the pariah of pariahs, are expressed in her cry, 'How will the redeemed be saved?'" Kahanoff believed that these thoughts of the poet and his literary encounters enabled him to anticipate modern literary criticism by some fifty years.

Kahanoff saw Péguy as an original thinker, an individualist, a wandering pilgrim of France who was before his time. As a prophet, he warned against a disastrous fusion of mysticism and politics, a combination that foreshadowed the phenomenon of political theology in the twentieth century. As a pioneer, he paved the way for a return to simple values, to a mystical approach to life. As a returning Catholic, his intellectual faculties were unharmed and he criticized the politics of both the Church and the socialist party. Kahanoff astutely described him as "the controversialist who wrestled in the arena of concrete reality while the poet expressed his vision in another world, but the two were always linked."[11] She explained his support of Dreyfus, for example, by the fact that he thought that the latter was excluded from the national society because he was Jewish and by his belief that the honor of France took precedence over the honor of its army.

Kahanoff's view of Péguy voiced a regard for the Jewish people as exemplifying the prophetic dialectic of quotidian political concern with affirmations of the divine mystery. He sadly noted, however, that contemporary Jewry failed to honor this dialectic: "Israel has given the world innumerable prophets, saints and warriors, but in normal times the children of Israel do not raise their eyes, are not enthusiastic as in periods of great and wonderful deeds."[12]

KAHANOFF'S POETIC JOURNEY   169

In his book of essays, *Notre Jeunesse* (1910), he softens this critique by sympathetically noting that the Jews' "exile of many years" is compounded by "the exile of modernity."

For Kahanoff, Péguy was "a prophet who remembered the future,"[13] and who, like the "anti-intellectual intellectuals" of his generation, preferred myth to reason. His critique of progress derived from his belief that "the most marvelous inventions and discoveries could be made by man into instruments of destruction and ruin."[14] According to Kahanoff, his mystical poetry was directed against technical progress, party politics, the corrupt bureaucracy, the intellectuals, the "dukes of the Sorbonne," a church only for the rich.

If with Péguy Kahanoff had a taste for mystical poetics, she shared with the poet Edmond Jabès sensibilities nurtured by common provenance in colonial Egypt and the legacy of its Jewish community.[15] Aside from her life-long friend Jabès, Kahanoff wondered why the Jews of Egypt, who lived in the cosmopolitan Egyptian cities, produced hardly any literature. With surprising honesty, she said, "It seems to me that we looked upon ourselves as too inferior—or as they say in Israel, too 'Levantine'—to express ourselves in writing. Gide and Malraux were our idols, but it never occurred to us that our task was to tell our story in our own words, not to imitate them."[16]

Someone who did tell his story in his own words was Edmond Jabès, whom Kahanoff regarded as the best of the Jewish writers from Egypt. Though his family lived in Egypt, they held Italian nationality and were wedded to French culture. Jabès worked in the Cairo stock exchange, was active in the Jewish community, and played a prominent part in antiracist and antifascist political activities. He was finally expelled from Egypt after the Suez crisis. Kahanoff remembered Jabès ("Eddie") as "a handsome young man, a dreamer and charming, whose blue eyes strayed far into the distance." He entitled his first book of poetry *Je bâtis ma demeure* (I'm Building My Home). At the time, he thought it was possible to build a home. But all that remained was "a broken people."[17] The abiding theme of Jabès's poetry is what remained of "Judaism after God." In *Le livre des questions* (Book of Questions), Surrealism and Kabbalah are in dialogue with imaginary rabbis pondering the misfortunes of the Jewish people.[18] Although Kahanoff considered the book "an exceptional achievement," it lamentably depicted a barren world, a world of total isolation in which there was no trace of the vitality that had enabled the Jews to survive. Everything led to nothingness, and the human cry of despair that was so well expressed by Nietzsche's "Where shall I feel at home?" reverberated in emptiness and received no reply.

The need to identify the Jew with the east from which Jabès came, Kahanoff ruefully noted, is seen in the Mediterranean names of the rabbis in his work. It was not fortuitous that the path of Yankel and Sarah crossed the Mediterranean world in Corfu, Cairo, and Marseilles. According to Kahanoff, a reading of Jabès reveals the code connecting the Mediterranean world and the Jewish world of her youth: "I again see with the eyes of my spirit these names, these landscapes, these streets, these buildings, these faces, issuing from the *Book of Questions* and reflected there. I know the place of the tear where the pages of his life were torn out, and I know that there are many wounds that will never be healed."[19] This tear and this wound caused her to consider the meaning of Jewish existence: "Can we do otherwise than to ask ourselves to explain the insoluble equation of Jewish existence, due to which we are here but also there, everywhere and nowhere?" Kahanoff rejected the "nihilistic conclusions" of the hymn sung by Jabès to exile, and she hoped that the wandering pilgrim would at last find his dwelling place: "His very foundation is the fulfillment of the Jewish soul in the harsh and gentle concrete reality of the land of Israel."

In the second half of the twentieth century, Jabès exemplified the image par excellence of the alien in French literature. This basis of foreignness, refugee status, or exile, which Nietzsche and Camus called "homelessness," was very characteristic of the culture of the Mediterranean Basin in the period of colonialism.[20] The changes that took place in the Maghreb and Mashrak forced thinkers, writers, and political activists to be exiled from their country. The paradox is that many of them felt good in exile and were comfortable in their alienation, perhaps a central principle of the cultural and political history of the Mediterranean Basin. Jabès expressed it well: "My mother tongue was a foreign language. Thanks to that, I have both feet in alienation." This formulation is also valid for the political exiles who had to continue their anticolonialist activities outside their country.

The work of the French poet Claude Vigée, an Alsatian Jew who fled to the United States in the Second World War, then settled in Israel, and died in France in 2020 at the age of ninety-nine, is also characterized by religious existentialism. Kahanoff wrote essays on his works, befriended him, and interviewed him in 1963, the year when Dahlia Ravikovitch wrote to her. Kahanoff regarded Vigée as "the most outstanding of the Jewish poets in France" who struck roots in Israel.[21] Through him, she examined the nihilistic and narcissistic roots of the modern sensibility as reflected in the poets, writers, and philosophers of her time.

The title of his book *Les artistes de la faim* (The Artists of Hunger) was inspired by Kafka's story "The Hunger Artist," in which a character deprives himself of food as a way of refusing the duties of life.[22] Through examining man's experience in modern life and his relationship to the world and to God, Vigée came to the conclusion that Christianity is a life-denying tradition, whereas Jewish tradition honors life and sees it as a blessing. In the book of Genesis, God blesses his creations, but Christian tradition stresses rejection, the duality between spirit and matter. Augustine's "City of God" is not located in this world, and in his *Confessions* he hopes for salvation in the next world. For modern man, even this hope is not in the realm of possibility.

Kahanoff examined the way in which Vigée presents the modern heroes or antiheroes who cling to their arrogant personalities, hating them and worshipping them at the same time.[23] The Don Juans, for example, feel they exist only when they humiliate other people. An ego of this kind can be victorious only through contempt of the "other." Vigée's knowledge of European literature and thought leads Kahanoff to follow him into the depths of the hell of suicidal Werthers, of Fausts whose lusts cannot be satisfied, and of "accursed" poets (*poètes maudits*), for all of whom the heavens are cold and gray, as if they needed a roof over the dungeon in which they are condemned to live. This is the voice of modern poetry.

Kahanoff regarded Vigée's poetry as a prism for a critical appraisal of the nihilistic sentiments of modern French poets: Romantics like Alfred de Vigny, who only admired God's eternal silence; Stoics like Baudelaire, who described life as "an oasis of horror in a desert of boredom" and who finally locked himself up in a darkened room to escape from the hellish fire of the outside world; poets like Mallarmé, who claimed that women are no more worthy of respect than the dead; Valéry, who declared that his love was narcissistic, the love of a man who was curious only about himself; and Rimbaud, who ceased to write poetry and became a slave trader. The conclusion of all this was that the negation of life ends in the degradation of the human personality and of poetry itself.

In marked contrast to this onslaught on the part of Vigée, Kahanoff underscored his hymn to life in his book *Révolte et louanges* (Revolt and Praise),[24] in which he celebrated real people who lived in the real world. The supreme example was the Spanish poet Jorge Guillén (1893–1984), whose poetry heralded the morning after the malignant disease that had overtaken Europe. It is as though this poet discovered in his first steps in nature the sunrise, fragrant scents, birdsong, and the human voice. This Spanish poet took each of the *poètes maudits* ("accursed poets") and turned them on their head.

Vigée was on the verge of adulthood, like another poet of the same age, René Char (1907–1988), when the Second World War

KAHANOFF'S POETIC JOURNEY

173

broke out. A new generation of poets looked with horror at the former cultural tradition motivated by an abhorrence of life and hatred of the human race. This, wrote Kahanoff in her reading of Vigée, was an abyss in which some poets were still ensconced. Samuel Beckett's human puppets waited for Godot in vain. He was a god who would never come.

These nihilistic poets of emptiness enjoyed degradation and rolling about in the muck, but Vigée was one of those who prefer songs of praise. This vital Jewish ethos does not reject the world or distinguish between the real and the spiritual. Kahanoff understood Vigée's attempt to reconcile man with the world in which he lives. "The recentpoetry, said Kahanoff, has removed the roof in its language to show that while the skies are gray, one can also find an abundance of light. That is the greatness of the Jewish tradition, which has never betrayed the world, not even the one known to Job."[25]

Kahanoff's own unpublished poems resonate with those of the French poets who addressed her existential religious longings. In the Gnazim archive in Tel Aviv, I discovered the few poems she wrote. This was a startling discovery, since Kahanoff was known first and foremost for being a writer, an essayist, an author of a novel, a journalist in the Israeli media, and an interviewer of important figures. These existential poems do not seem to require a sophisticated elucidation—they are simple, personal, and moving.

KAHANOFF'S POEMS

Until now, Kahanoff has been chiefly known for her essays and her novel. Her poems, appearing here for the first time, shed light on another dimension of her lust for life.[26]

Life Was
A fabric fabulous
Bolts and bolts
Velvets sumptuous

Cool linens
Warm woolens—
I could choose

I didn't know, I swear.
I'd have nothing to wear
But odds and ends
Hand-stitched end to end
So little to choose!

Take life as it comes?
When it goes?
Nothing is left
But remains
For the graveyard:
There's nothing to choose.

To Kiss the Light
A child who pranced
And danced
To catch the sun
And bite the light
With such delight!

Remember? The two
of you
The spot of light
That pierced
Through the shuttered room
On that hot afternoon?

You danced and pranced
Twisted in trance
To catch the spot of light
That slipped upon his lips.
You kissed the light
Right on his lips.

He kissed the light
That moved on my lips

Spot of light that slipped
And fell when . . .
The door opened a crack
creaked
A voice hissed
We no longer kissed
But fled in flight
And dropped the light

I had wanted his son
The son of the sun
I kissed on his lips
Before it slipped
And was gone.

Ciaò
What can one say? What can one say?
It hurts to die
No longer the courage to write
But the wish to feel
Feel life
That, yes! Life
I desire

What can one say? What can one say?
One has to suffer
Before one dies
It's the rule of the game
To die on a low flame
A little every day,
A very little.

What can one say? What can one say?
I love life,
I didn't enjoy it enough
So much the worse! So much the worse!
The world passes and passes me by
Me, it passes by, like
Life itself!

What can one say, what can one say
To the flowers that die?
Flowers that go from red to black
White, blue, pink, then black!
Are the flowers afraid?
Do they know they're dying
A little, day by day?

Nothing to Wear
When young, I thought I'd die
Of love.
I tried three times,
But how can one die
Sought out by love?

When life was a sumptuous fabric
Velvet, satin, silk,
Rolled out, unrolled,
Delicate hangings,
Rough wool,
Fresh linen,
Confectionery of all kinds,
Tangible,
Which I loved
To feel
With my hands,

I never imagined
That all that was left
Of all this
Would be odds and ends.
Nothing to wear
But these odds and ends
Sewn and re-sewn.

How
Can one take life aright
When all that remains
Of all these lengths

Are these odds and ends,
A mere nothing
That one has to wear?

I submit myself
To the Lord on high
And in the end
Beyond these scraps
I give back
What remains.

Stitches
They cut me up
They sewed me up
With their little stitches.
Ho! Ho!

I wouldn't give up
They stood me up.
I'm now in stitches!
Ha! Ha!

Ritornello
The surgeons do *petit point*
With their little stitches,
little stitches.

They sew up life with threads
But life slips away, step by step,
with little steps
To the dustbin, my beauty.
Life slips away.

Forbidden Fruit
The good Lord has hung
The pomegranate
With its ruby pips
Crammed with juice
On the tree of life.

Man, you defile
The pomegranate!
You load with lead
The wings of Life
Which explodes
with scarlet drops
Like the rubies
of the pomegranate
On the tree of life.

Ah, if the good Lord knew
That man would load
His pomegranate
With lead,
He would have said, "No, no,
My man. That's not allowed!"

But man would have disobeyed.

The Sound of the Horn
I hear the sound of the horn
The horn in the depths of the woods
the sound

Voice of the body of the body
on wood
Of the billiard . . .

The sound of the horn of the body
from the depths
Of the hearse

FROM THE LEVANT TO AFRICA

The poetic journey that we have undertaken with Kahanoff,
which begun with Dahlia Ravikovitch's letter to her, and continued with her few poems influenced by the religious existentialism of French poetry, has now reached its final port of call:
her dealings with African poetry and literature. In the works of

writers and poets from Africa, which she analyzed in the 1960s, two contradictory yet complementary principles of the cultural theory Kahanoff was developing were discovered: on the one hand, something she called a "literature of social mutation" and, on the other hand, something she called "black literature."

Kahanoff is known as an essayist, a writer, and a critic, and she also wrote poems, but another aspect of her work is also worth considering: her role as a theoretician of culture. The "literature of mutation," she declared, reflects a cultural process and social change that has not been sufficiently noticed. A search for identity and a refusal to be confined by a narrow definition characterizes the literature of writers whom we call crossbreeds. In their personalities and writings, these writers mix the various elements that molded them, without any desire to renounce any of them. We are speaking here not only of Levantinism, but there is no doubt that Kahanoff's Levantine starting point with its mixture of cultures served as an inspiration for her to develop a universal model of culture. In her opinion, a large part of literature was produced by writers who found themselves at an intersection of different countries and cultures, and who therefore cannot be described as "national" authors. These writers and poets are the product of a long period of colonialism, and their works reflect a transitional mentality, a mutation from the traditional culture of their predecessors to a new culture that would not exist if not for a long drawn-out, if ambiguous, connection with the western world.

V. S. Naipaul (1932–2018), for example, an Anglo-Indian writer who lived for many years in Jamaica, is not an English writer or an Indian writer, nor is he a Jamaican writer.[27] As a displaced person, he reflects a "mutation," a transitional situation: he has one foot in his community and the other in England. The connection between them is his writing. India has likewise produced a number of writers who do not feel at home in their motherland: Santha Rama Rau, an Indian emigrant writing in the United States and the author of *Gifts of Passage*; the writer Dom Moraes, an Indian Christian; and Ved Mehta, brother of the conductor Zubin Mehta—both Oxford graduates. The Tunisian-French-Jewish writer Albert Memmi was also given by Kahanoff as an example of what she called the "literature of social mutation."[28]

In 1963, the year in which Ravikovitch wrote to her, Kahanoff edited the book *African Stories*, and it was published by Am Ha-Sefer. It was an anthology of stories, poetry, and essays, and its aim was to introduce the then-new culture of the peoples of Africa to the Israelis. It did not represent the whole of Africa. For editorial reasons South Africa, where apartheid prevailed, was not included, nor were the countries of the Maghreb and Mashrak, but it presented the writings of the new African countries south of the Sahara. Examples were also given of the work of Caribbean writers, who, together with those from the former French colonies in Africa, played an important part in the creation of a new literature that is African in inspiration and French in expression. According to Kahanoff, both past suffering and hopes for the future are to be found in this literature.

Kahanoff said she found that the preparation of this anthology was a kind of "voyage of discovery towards what is perhaps one of the most exciting human adventures."[29] In her comprehensive introduction, she declared that she witnessed the birth of "something especially hopeful in an old and weary world." In her words, the book revealed the African "essence" that neither slavery nor colonialism could suppress, an essence that was expressed first and foremost in new languages. Historically, there were hundreds of spoken dialects in Africa, but there was no regional written language except for Arabic. In modern times, French, English, and Portuguese were the main languages. The colonial cultures had some influence on the literature, but the style and content were typically African, expressed via the European languages. For instance, a syncopated African rhythm runs through the poem

"Rama Kam," by the Senegalese poet David Diop (1927–1960): "I love your look, a wild look / and your mouth which tastes like mango / Rama Kam / And your body, black pepper / which makes desire sing out / Rama Kam."[30]

When the writer Camara Laye (1928–1980), from French Guinea, told the story *L'Enfant noir* (The Dark Child), about a boy's longings for the lost world of his past, Kahanoff felt she was present at an invocation of the mysterious life forces and magical atmosphere of his adolescence. The evocative phrases, repetitive, chantlike, sounded to Kahanoff like a hymn. The child had gazed spellbound at his father who fashioned gold into a jewel, but was unable to do what his father did. He dared not fondle the black serpent, the embodiment of the spirit of the ancestors of the tribe, from which his father gained his strength. The child, who went to a French school, felt he could never be at home in his father's world. The ceremonies for his coming-of-age, which he recalled as a student in France, were associated in the story with his long absence from Africa.

Aimé Césaire (1913–2008), a French poet born in Martinique who studied at the École Normale Supérieure and opposed French colonialism, was one of the founders of the Francophone "black literature." Kahanoff relates that when Césaire was asked to write a sonnet, he replied, "Believe me, it would be better for us to beat on tom-toms as we have always done."[31] Together with Léopold Senghor, he wrote the essay "L'étudiant noir" (The Black Student), in which he coined the term *Négritude*, denoting "Black identity." As a surrealist poet whom Kahanoff saw as representative of the Africans who emerged from a preliterary culture, Césaire broke through directly into the modern world. In his poems he sought to speak of the kernel, the root, the beginning, claiming that the Africans were truly the "firstborn of the world" because they had not cut themselves off from their roots: "Possessed, they are inebriated with the essence of all things / They are truly the firstborn of the world."[32]

Senghor, Césaire's partner in the Négritude movement, was the first president of Senegal, the first African appointed to the Académie Française, and a permanent candidate for the Nobel Prize in Literature. Kahanoff was impressed by the comparison he made between the intuitive and sensory ways of Africa and the antirationalist tendencies of science and philosophy in our time. Senghor stressed emotion as a way of knowing the world, in which subject and object are not separated but connected. Césaire and Senghor represent what Kahanoff called "integral humanism." The changes that took place in tribal Africa occurred against the background of the trials and tribulations of slavery, colonial exploitation, and racial oppression. The phenomenon of the new culture embraced the whole continent, the entire race: "Africa possesses an abundant and joyful self-confidence which is as refreshing as the dew after the excessively pessimistic intellectualism of contemporary European literature." There was new life, she felt, in the African literature, and the Africans confronted their future with an almost mystical sense of awe, as though Africa was able to build itself up as a result of its martyrology.

Césaire from Martinique and Senghor from Senegal represented Négritude as a new form of universalism and integral humanism, a literature that according to Kahanoff was permeated with ambiguity: on the one hand, elements of the technological, individualistic, and rationalistic white civilization and, on the other hand, elements of the tribal and poetic Black civilization. Nevertheless, there was a synthesis between them. The best example she gave was the journal and publishing house *Présence africaine*, in which there were French-speaking writers and poets from Africa, the West Indies, and Madagascar. They were jealous of their artist friends, came together like them in Paris immediately after the Second World War, and then created a journal. Among the contributors were Senghor, Césaire, André Gide, Sartre, and Camus. The journal, which fostered nativistic self-awareness (somewhat like Aharon Amir's *Keshet*), provided a platform for many writers who promoted an understanding of the dark continent, its values and problems.

Kahanoff discerned in the journal something of the existentialist idea of *engagement* in the African poets writing in French. The attitude of the African poets writing in English was perhaps healthier and more rational, but the "French," in her opinion, attained a higher degree of intensity, power, and compassion in works like those of Césaire and Senghor. The colonial cultural differences were reflected in the African works of literature. The French wished to pass on their culture to their disciples, and the ideals of the French Revolution played a crucial role in molding the educated African elite. But because this happened in a colonialist regime, it was not fully accepted, and the consequent frustration produced the reaction of the radicalism of Négritude. The British, who to a certain extent were idealistic, sought to be honest though distant rulers, and thus left their African protégés less divided and hesitant about identity, race, and legacy than their French-speaking counterparts did.

The Kenyan anticolonialist leader Jomo Kenyatta (1897–1978), who became the first president of Kenya, had a practical approach—unlike the abstract and intellectual approach of Senghor, the disciple of French culture—and most of the French-educated writers were the same. Kahanoff, whose sympathies in the matter are obvious, thought that she detected something false in the facile optimism of English-educated writers such as Michael F. Dei Anang. Anang wrote, "I will die for the world, / a wonderful world. / There is no other country / in the East or West / that will give me continuation here. / Only Africa can do that."[33]

In contrast to him, the inhabitants of "color" in apartheid South Africa, where there was an intense racial conflict, produced literature that in Kahanoff's opinion was the most polished in form and the most western in its ideas and concepts. She viewed top-ranking South African writers, such as Peter Abrahams and

Can Themba, as having a certain obsession with the subject of racism. Abrahams wrote about a Zulu child who retained the memory of the glory of the Black kings who reigned before the coming of the white man. This child, a proletarian, cut off from his tribal society and dwelling in slums on the outskirts of a city or in mines, refused evacuation to a native reservation. Themba, for his part, gave an excellent description of African aspirations in his introduction to *African Voices*, a literary anthology published by the African journal *Drum*: "Here we are, Africans addressing Africa and the world, / Dreaming of the great things we will do in the future: / a new civilization, / a new African culture."

Kahanoff opened a window on the literature of the dark continent, a world born in a violent, ambivalent dialogue between Black and white, between the neolithic and the technological. The continual tension between the two could lead to a symbiosis, to what Kahanoff called a "literature of mutation," or it could lead to the adaptation or isolation of "black identity."

It would seem that Kahanoff saw the various ramifications of multiculturalism very early on, several decades before it was discussed in the postmodernist discourse.

The tales of the African people, which were passed told from generation to generation, were regarded both as instruction and as entertainment. Kahanoff saw them as a special blend of morality, humor, and common sense. The Nigerian writer Amos Tutuola (1920–1997) succeeded in rendering this literature in English. In his story *The Palm-wine Drinkard*, a man is observed wrestling with death. It is an example of an African narrative full of imagination, which, like surrealistic poetry, blurs the western boundary line between external reality and subjective feelings. In the story *Over the Wild River*, by the Ghanian writer Amankwa Andrew Opoku (b. 1943), the hero of the story, who leaves his village to create a cocoa plantation, justifies his action before the members of his tribe with popular sayings.[34] These modern African writers did not break away from their popular roots, but

Kahanoff noticed that the traditional foundations of their stories and poems underwent a change in the transposition to European languages.

The African thread was entwined with another, far from Africa, in the Caribbean and on the eastern American seaboard, among the descendants of African slaves.[35] The collective African American memory has been preserved despite the attempt to efface it. The former Africans made an impact on America that is seen in jazz, in Negro spirituals, and in the combination of African art and Christianity found in the Haitian cult of voodoo. After the American Civil War, when a need was felt to rehabilitate the liberated slaves, there was a debate about their education and whether it should be based on professional instruction or given a broader humanistic character. If in the history of the Negroes in the United States after the Civil War there was much hope for assimilation, already at the beginning of the twentieth century one could perceive a desire to strengthen the African roots of the Negroes. Kahanoff called this "African Zionism." Already in 1903, in his book *The Souls of Black Folk*, W. E. B. Du Bois declared, "The problem of the twentieth century is the problem of the color-line, the relations of the darker to the lighter races. . . . The American Negro . . . would not Africanize America. He would not bleach his Negro soul in a flood of white Americanism. . . . He simply wishes to make it possible for a man to be both a Negro and an American."[36] Kahanoff said that these sentences express a "black humanism," an outlook developed by African and African American writers a generation later.

Writers from the Caribbean islands under French rule—Haiti, Martinique, Guadeloupe—and writers from Guiana played an important part in the flowering of the new literature, producing an impressive list of authors and poets. In an interesting insight, Kahanoff pointed out that the colonial status and the consciousness of color were often less pronounced in Catholic countries than in Protestant ones. The French, she said, had less racial consciousness than other European peoples. This cultural tolerance permitted young writers to give expression to their "Négritude" and to their revolt against the artificial order that the white man had imposed in Africa. Many of them played central roles in the continent—in the colonial administration, in the revolt against colonialism, and in the postcolonial society that they created.

In the 1930s, writers from the Caribbean founded a journal in Paris called *Légitime défense* (Legitimate Defense). Kahanoff followed up with a few of the many African contributors who participated in the cultural revolution in France, a revolution encouraged by French men of culture, including André Breton, the French "pope of surrealism." Senghor declared that this "would not be just a journal, but a cultural movement." He wrote a poem, "Femme noire" (Black Woman), about a mother who he feared was lost. Longings for the good old order of life are aroused by the Black mother, who also represents the earth, the principle of the renewal of life—Africa itself. The mother, who embodies simple, unsophisticated life, is contrasted with the cold, corrupt world of the west. As a soldier, Senghor had been crushed by columns of tanks in Europe and had rotted in prisons where "the sheets were white and cold." He prayed for recovery and for a consciousness of his value as a human being to be restored to him. In the 1960s, Senghor sought to heal this breach; in the article "The African Path to Socialism," in an almost mystical way, he reconciled traditional African values with the thinking of his time.

The reconciliation reappears in the work of the Nigerian poet Gabriel Okara (1921–2019), who represents this dual legacy, of which he does not renounce any part. In the poem "Piano and Drums," he listens to the drums of the jungle together with a piano concerto. The African, according to Kahanoff, is not only a man "who has lost everything" but also one who has acquired new tools. His literature touches people's hearts and influences them through its spontaneous joy and poetic enthusiasm. He longs to rediscover a lost magic, seeks pure waters to quench the thirst of modern man who feels alienated from his world because contact with the cosmos has been taken from him. Here, Kahanoff's existentialist discourse reaches a climax, but it is a discourse that says yes to life. Like the ancient Hebrews, the African believes that life is good and holy, in the spirit of "God saw all that he had done, and, behold, it was very good." He does not turn his back on the world, does not differentiate between God and the creation, and refuses to see man as an irremediable sinner. African man is in Kahanoff's opinion a pilgrim constantly engaged in a tireless search.

But there is another option in Kahanoff-type existentialism. Jean-Joseph Rabearivelo (1901–1937) is considered one of the most important African poets and Madagascar's leading writer. His poems appear in the anthology *From the Poems of the Great Island Madagascar* (1964), in which all the introductions were written by Kahanoff.[37] Rabearivelo published a few poetic anthologies in French and Malagasy, as well as literary criticism, an opera, and two novels. As a young man and as a poet under the French colonial regime, he was deeply humiliated when his request to participate as an artist in exhibitions in Paris in the early 1930s was turned down. He was a sensuous poet who was infatuated with symbolist poetry; adored the "accursed poets," especially Rimbaud and Baudelaire; and translated works by Edgar Alan Poe and Paul Valéry into Malagasy. Kahanoff understood his affinity with the post-Christian and nihilistic culture of his time, in which the isolation and *sacro egoismo* (sacred selfishness) of the genius lead him into nothingness and suicide.

In his works, Rabearivelo interwove Malagasy culture and western culture. As he was trapped in colonialism—western culture that gave him cultural benefits without gaining him social acceptance—for lack of choice he returned to his sources, from which he took his pick. The humiliations endured by the wounded soul of this writer and intellectual were documented in the eighteen hundred pages of his *Calepins bleus* (Blue Notebooks). In a letter to a friend before committing suicide, he referred to a fable of La Fontaine in which the death of a grasshopper that had sung all night aroused the pity of the ants. Responding to this, Kahanoff saw a link between Baudelaire and modern African poetry: "What poet of that period did not cultivate, groaning, the flowers of evil of his despair?"

FOUR

"WHERE CAN I FEEL AT HOME?"

JUDAISM, FEMINISM, CULTURE

Kahanoff's writings in many ways revolved around Nietzsche's poignant question, which was also Albert Camus's point of departure: "Where can I feel at home?" Modern man is cast out of the world: conscious of his frailty, he is homeless in his universe. This modern feeling is quite different from the outlook of the ancient Greeks or of Christian theology where man was anchored in the cosmos or the *civitas dei*. The reversal of this situation causes mankind, the "lord of creation" in the Greco-Christian world, to find himself in the position of being "not at home"—or "being outside," as Heidegger expressed it. Martin Buber spoke of the alienated individual as one living "in the world as in an open field under the vault of heaven, and sometimes unable to find even four pegs to set up his tent."[1]

In the Mediterranean option that Kahanoff presented to Israeli society, Judaism had a special place. In her review of *Quatre lectures talmudiques* by Emmanuel Lévinas, many years before he became well known in Israel, Kahanoff observed that "many Jews live, culturally speaking, in a sort of cultural no-man's land in Israel and abroad." Israelis, the French Jewish philosopher

189

averred, were part of western culture, and at the same time, they were adrift, shorn of a firm grounding in Judaism and its religious teachings. "Neither the Orthodox culture, nor the narrow Zionist culture disseminated by our institutions, nor that of the native Sabras, which is too introverted—none of these provide a real answer to the modern Jew's sense of loss, to his feeling of alarm at being cut off."[2]

Lévinas addressed himself to this question, thought Kahanoff, first of all because he himself experienced this sense of loss. In his opinion, a knowledge of the continuity of the Jewish religious tradition can in itself open up a channel of communication between traditional Judaism and modern Israel, between Jewish culture and the culture of the west. Kahanoff's review was structured as a dialogue with an Israeli Air Force pilot, a Sabra to whom Jewish culture was alien.[3] In their discussion of Lévinas's opening essay, "The Promised Land or the Permitted Land," whose subject was the Talmudic tractate *Sotah*, Kahanoff and the pilot discovered that though the essay was written in 1966, its subject—the debate over Greater Israel (embracing the Palestinian territories captured in the Six-Day War)—was still actual.[4]

Kahanoff's conclusion on reading Lévinas's essay was an acknowledgment of the importance of human "engagement" and an understanding that absolute moral purity in any political action involves a certain violence. She commented on Lévinas's view that the Bible and the Talmud are not merely a collection of myths but that they have at their core universal significance. In Kahanoff's opinion, Lévinas's greatness is manifest in his capacity to make the Talmud relevant in the present day, by sharing Talmudic wisdom in a modern idiom, and to indicate how the teachings of the rabbis may help address contemporary problems. Furthermore, Kahanoff endorsed Lévinas's view that a Jewish religious culture closed to the non-Jewish world condemned Jewry to spiritual death, just as assimilation condemned them to a spiritual desert. Only an independent Jewish political and cultural existence, Lévinas affirmed, would permit the birth of what he called a "post-Christian Judaism."

Zionism, according to Lévinas in Kahanoff's interpretation, makes possible the simultaneous existence of "the Jew of faith" (beholden to divine revelation) and "the Greek" (bound by rational precepts). The drama of our existence as Jews as envisioned by Lévinas, concluded Kahanoff in her review of his writings, alas, is not taking place now in the context of the western Christian world ("post-Christian Judaism") but in the context of the eastern Muslim world—"post-Islamic Judaism," as she called it. In her opinion, many Jews, including Lévinas, failed to reckon with the fact that the rebirth of Israel had shaken the Islamic world to its foundations. She therefore thought that new means had to be created to challenge the Islamic world, and to create a connection with it through an open debate on its tradition. The dispute between the Israeli Jews and their neighbors had generally been conducted in terms of western national and ideological concepts that were not amenable to the mentality of the Muslims. Kahanoff suggested that a solution to the Arab-Israeli conflict might be found if the Israelis were to conduct an intercultural dialogue with the Arab world.

In the essay "On Jacob," Kahanoff dealt with the Israeli-Arab dispute as it unfolded in the wake of the end of the Six-Day War by referring to the Hebrew Bible and the interrelationship of myth and history: "Again, like many, many Jews in Israel, I often turned to the Bible during these days of June and afterwards. . . . This prayer or belief was almost the same as absolute faith in the I.D.F. [Israel Defense Forces]."[5] The Bible invaded history, the past was fused with the present, prayer and military might overlap. "We found a way to go from the bygone historical time to the temporality of myth. After this victory, which was quite extraordinary, myth again superseded history." Kahanoff turned to the Bible to find an allegorical answer to the worrying questions concerning the Palestinian territories that had been conquered, and to the attendant question of Israel's identity and its Jewish origins. She turned to the biblical figure of Jacob to look for new answers, or perhaps to ask new questions in a period in which myth once again overflowed into historical, finite, limited time: "It was impossible not to think of Jacob, who struggled with his brother Esau as we struggle with our brethren/enemies over the same rights to the same land."[6]

Jacob personifies the dilemma of the choice between force and morality, a dilemma that, according to Kahanoff, lies at the heart of the collective identity of the Jewish people returning to their land. She examined the approaches of the Christian religion and the Islamic religion to the story of Jacob. While in the Christian tradition there is some theological legitimization of Jacob's deception, the Muslims borrowed the Christian depiction of Jacob the deceiver and applied it to modern Israel. To the dual claim of the Arabs and Israelis that the Israelis are alien to the region, Kahanoff replied, "If we see ourselves as wholly European here, others will also thus see us, and do indeed see us, as wholly alien, and in that case the common heritage we struggle over is in fact denied."[7]

The mythical rivalry of Jacob and Esau has in our days become a metonymy for the political-historical dispute.[8] In the mythical story, the brothers are twins born to the same mother, and the choice is between the brotherhood of these two rival brothers and the possibility that one of them will do to his brother what Cain did to Abel. As was her custom, Kahanoff added an original feminist perspective: although Rebecca loved both her sons, she knew that their characters were different: "And so perhaps the time came when, after the men had had their say, the mothers rose to speak, so that the sons would know that they were brothers to each other, contending, rival brothers, but within the limits set by nature and culture."[9]

Kahanoff examined the interrelationship of biblical myth and the political history of the State of Israel from the Six-Day War in 1967 to Anwar Sadat's visit to Israel in 1978. In her essay "My Brother Ishmael," she regards the historic decision of the Egyptian leader as an act transcending mere political significance, and one that touched on mythological themes: the struggle of Isaac and Ishmael over the claim to the title of "son of Abraham."[10] An ancient Semitic myth common to Jews and Arabs, about a father ready to sacrifice his own flesh and blood to his God, now divides the Arabs and Israelis. Kahanoff interpreted Sadat's message on his arrival in Jerusalem as a revolutionary proposal for a mutual recognition between the sons of Isaac and Ishmael. The sons would live side by side, and each would recognize his brother's legitimacy and birthright. Here she once again indicated that the sources of the political dispute in the region are to be found in the Semitic identity and have as much to do with theology as with politics. The Mediterranean geopolitical space is ensnared in the patriarchal tradition of the single, exclusive heritage of Abraham's legal son.

According to Kahanoff, the appearance of Zionism confronted the Muslims with the question of the right of Abraham's son to claim and reconquer his inheritance. This sentiment was complicated by the fact that the Islamic countries gave refuge to the Jews from the time of the Inquisition and up to the Second World War. The rebirth of Abraham's estranged son and his return as a refugee from the Nazi concentration camps were seen as a challenge to the Islamic belief that Ishmael was the sole heir of Abraham's patrimony. Although the Muslim national opposition is modern, its roots are ancient and steeped in mythology and in the theology of rivalry. Both national movements, the Jewish and the Arab, came into being at roughly the same time. One was supported by Europe, and the other rose up against European colonialist rule. The ancient myth of Ishmael and Isaac emerged once again in the age of nationalism.

Ishmael was seen by the Palestinian Arabs as representing the exclusive heir to the country—Ishmael dispossessed of his rights.

It is fascinating to see to what a degree symbolism taken from the patriarchs contributed, according to Kahanoff, to the present-day rejection of the "Other," the other son. For Kahanoff, Sadat was the first Muslim Arab leader to recognize the right of "Isaac" to exist in Israel, after years of denial. This position differed radically from that of Arab nationalism, and also from that of Islam. The Israelis were now no longer seen as foreign invaders, but as one of the legitimate sons. It was not by chance that Sadat chose to come to Israel on the festival of Eid al-Adha, commemorating Abraham's readiness to sacrifice Isaac, but with the difference that this time the father proposed *himself* as the sacrifice, to save the lives of his sons. In this, Sadat specifically went counter to the patriarchal tradition that only one son can be heir. The Egyptian leader thus made a radical break with this patriarchal tradition in asserting that all the sons were rightful heirs, and by way of compensation Kahanoff added that "the daughters and mothers also had a legitimate claim." One should remember that Sadat came from the patriarchal Muslim societies, and his revolutionary breakthrough in the political arena stands out even more in light of the prevailing conservatism.

Kahanoff's "post-Islamic Judaism" is also reflected in her feminist approach and her openness to eastern cultures. These three elements bear witness to a self-confidence that permits openness, curiosity, and dialogue—the Levantine model, which does not efface itself before the hegemonic power of the "Other." The source of her understanding of the cultural context of the Jewish position, the feminist position, and the Mizrahi position is her refusal to accept the radical stance of "Let justice be done though the heavens fall!"

In her youth, Kahanoff experienced the life of the Egyptian Jewish "aristocracy" as assigning an inferior, physical, functional role to women in a society managed by men. The life of women was circumscribed to "marriage, child bearing, adultery and possibly divorce."[11] Despite her criticism of the "inner colonialism" responsible for the European attitude that was dominant in Israeli society in its dealings with the immigrants from the Islamic countries, in Israel Kahanoff identified "the one country in which there has taken place, in less than twenty years, an enormous permutation in the status of Mizrahi women, when they are Jewish." Already in monarchical Egypt in the 1920s and 1930s Kahanoff had adopted a feminist position, which found intellectual expression in her late essays.

In her article "The Tragedy of the Eastern Woman," the religious and political leadership of Egypt was revealed as fostering a regime of slavery and oppression of women. Operations on little girls to prevent sexual enjoyment, the public consummation of marriage, the encouragement of polygamy, the widespread use of hashish among men, and so on—all this bore witness to the patriarchal nature of Egyptian society, deeply entrenched in Islam.[12] Kahanoff drew attention to the status of women as objects of pleasure and "machines" for bearing children, and she criticized the conditioning that condemned women to a life of constant fear.

Kahanoff herself admitted that she had "very often used the writing of a book review as a pretext for writing about the position of women in that society." Examples of this can be found on two separate occasions when Kahanoff enthusiastically praised two Frenchwomen who were famous for their feminist activities. In her review of Françoise Sagan's *Aimez-vous Brahms?* she describes the heroine Paula as "a vibrant figure, a modern woman, free, not dependent."[13] The inner pattern of the book is seen as a wavering between two factors: one, protection of norms created by selfish men, and two, "the whisper and echo of the liberation of woman." Her article "The Great Couple in French Literature" was unique by virtue of her treatment of the writings of Jean-Paul Sartre and Simone de Beauvoir on a basis of equality. The two of them "entered into the contemporary battlefield with courage and generosity of spirit, and at the same time preserved their image as human beings."[14] They raised their voices on behalf of those in need of freedom, justice, and compassion, values from which the modern world keeps at a distance—outmoded ideas in comparison with ideology, technology, and efficiency. De Beauvoir's "road to liberty" was for Kahanoff the path of a woman fighting for her freedom in a patriarchal world.

Did Kahanoff herself practice what she "preached" to other women? One of her friends thinks that "all her life she entered into one relational framework in order to escape from another. Her tragedy was that she lived in the pre-feminist generation, a generation in which economic dependence on men solved what can be solved today by a cheque book."[15] The Israeli novelist Ronit Matalon viewed Kahanoff as a new type of individual, an inhabitant of the world at large who does not live in continual disapproval of the human landscape and environment. In these respects, "Kahanoff was first and foremost a writer, and only afterwards a feminist publicist."[16]

Dolly Benhabib, a founder of the Mizrahi Democratic Rainbow Coalition, was more grudging in her account of Kahanoff's feminism, which she felt to be selective, and was critical of the following observation by Kahanoff, written after a visit to the occupied territories: "I once observed that it was a hopeful sign that women's skirts had got shorter in [Arab] East Jerusalem, so that it is now difficult to distinguish one girl from another by her style of dress."[17] Benhabib saw the shortened skirts as a sign of a cultural change among oppressed Arab women similar to the cultural change that once took place among Israeli Mizrahi women during the process of "internal colonialism."[18] The Mizrahi women had exploited the chance of modernity that Israeli society offered them. According to Benhabib, Kahanoff's blindness to the situation of the Arab women laboring under the dual burden of military occupation and internal colonialism reveals the limits of the vision of the Israeli national collective, although Kahanoff did show sensitivity toward women immigrants and the new immigrants from the Islamic countries who were "headless," or in other words no longer enjoyed the Jewish Levantine leadership.

Kahanoff was a great believer in modernity. In her opinion, modernity would liberate both the Mizrahi women in Israel and the Palestinian women in the Occupied Territories, "the objects of colonization," as Benhabib called them.[19]

Although Kahanoff's education and formal culture were European, the environment in which she was born was not, and the first sounds she remembered were those of the muezzin.[20] The classical music in the concert halls did not move her like the sound of the muezzin at sunset did. Her ears were always attuned to Mizrahi music, and a long time had to pass before she could get a feeling for western music and appreciate it. It was hard for her to grasp the complex western musical structures, but the endless variations of Mizrahi music, "which drive most western people crazy," gave her a sense of elevation. In her article "Mizrahi Music in Israel," Kahanoff threw some light on her cultural and musical roots in the Levant, and related that in her first years in Israel she used to travel to the Mimouna festival to listen to the old people playing the oud.[21] She knew that thousands of people living in Israel felt the same way she did and were more receptive to the east than to the west.

Mizrahi music in Israel—prophesied Kahanoff in 1977—"is likely to prevent the blocking and obstruction of the channels of communication which bind together elements in the population common to us and our neighbours and even our enemies. The language of music at least does not divide as do words, politics, and ideology." Almost thirty years before the process took on flesh and blood in Israeli society, she understood that Mizrahi music in Israel, which "developed in a sort of ghetto, is being renewed on various paths far from the high road of the official culture." True to her Levantine outlook, Kahanoff approved of a meeting of cultures, for "it is a fact that these cultures intermingle, and it is almost impossible to preserve a tradition in its purity, especially when people of different cultural regions meet and mix."[22]

Kahanoff was quick to discern that while Israeli Jews of European descent play the role of the white brother in the Levant, they deny the cultural contiguities summoned by the Zionist project and experience a sense of inferiority toward the west.[23] Similar inversions of Levantinism were presenting themselves from circles unknown to Kahanoff at the time, particularly in art music of the 1950s. In 1953, for example, the composer Alexander Uria Boskowitz deemed *Levantinism* a derogative term for musical formulations lacking stylistic unity, as in the accompanying of an eastern melody with Eurocentric devices, rendering such pairing as inadequate matchmaking.[24] And what was signaled in Kahanoff's and Boskovich's texts resonated in the compositional praxis of composers who, according to the musicologist Assaf Shelleg, refused to subjugate music from the east to ethnographic quarantines and peripheral masks. Kahanoff's Levantinism was realized in the works of Mordecai Seter, who sought to liberate ethnographic imports from their materiality so that they would condition the music from *within* and cease to function as an exotic frill. A similar idea has shaped the works of Betty Olivero since the 1990s; her music became a solvent of Levantine musical traditions that not only muted Zionist territorialism but also wounded the very criteria of westernness (with which Zionism had aligned itself), all while comprising non-Jewish musical traditions from the Levantine space and recalibrating national Identitarian qualities.[25]

THE LITERATURE OF SOCIAL MUTATION

The importance of the liminal writers and the literature of mutation, Kahanoff foretold, would increase, not diminish. These hybridizations of peoples and cultures (in now the era of globalization) reflect a new relationship between the former native and yesterday's conqueror, to use Kahanoff's expression.

In her essay "The Literature of Social Mutation," Kahanoff gave a name to a particular trend in mid-twentieth-century literature:

> In recent decades, a great deal of literature has been produced by writers who found themselves at the crossroads of many cultures,

"WHERE CAN I FEEL AT HOME?"

of various civilizations and countries, and who cannot be placed in any "national" category. These writers are the product of a long period of colonialism, and the books they write represent a transition from or mutation of the traditional culture of their predecessors to a new culture whose crystallization is aided by their works. This literature represents a shift towards a new culture in the process of formation, a culture which would not have existed without the prolonged though ambivalent connection with the western world, for these writers do not write in their mother-tongues but in one of the western languages—generally English or French—which they used during their period of studies. Some of them have been politically involved in revolutions or national struggles, but not all of them. Decolonization did not necessarily bring them to a complete identification with the national ideologies of their countries which had just been liberated.

These writers often have bifurcated souls, torn between the various forces which moulded them, and writing often serves them as a means of fusing these elements into a more significant whole, and of creating order both in the subjective inner reality and in the objective outer reality. They often give expression to a new internationalism which suddenly reveals new connections between existing cultures, just as chemical compounds have their own qualities that are completely different from the qualities of the elements composing them.[26]

The literature of social mutation, said Kahanoff, represents a cultural and social trend to which, she argued, insufficient attention has been paid and which is not limited to the Levant but is a worldwide tendency. The writing of these hybrid cultures is characterized by a "search for identity" and a refusal to accept an alien, arbitrary definition of themselves. In their personalities and writings, its creators blend the different elements that formed them, while allowing no element to be relinquished. Kahanoff welcomed these "cultural hybrids" and "the challenges of the new combinations"; without their vitality and surprising mutations, culture, she thought, might freeze up. The writers of the "literature of social mutation" did not submit to what Kahanoff called the "hegemony" of the western model, despite its great influence, but produced multicultural and multinational compounds instead.

The Jewish Franco-Tunisian writer Albert Memmi (1920–2020) is an edifying example of the "literature of social mutation." Kahanoff considered the questions Memmi raised in his book *Portrait d'un juif* (Portrait of a Jew) concerning Jewish existence both in North Africa, his place of birth, and in France, his new place of residence. Memmi, said Kahanoff, saw many "shadowy figures" among the Jews, and he claimed that in comparison with other subjugated peoples, their dispersion had made them the most persecuted people in history.

Kahanoff, like Camus, detected in Memmi a ruptured identity that colonialism had created in him, many years before the diagnoses of Homi K. Bhabha. She also reflected on Memmi's investigation of Jewish identity in his book *La libération du juif* (The Liberation of the Jew). Lost in bewilderment, sunk in disappointment and despair, Memmi considered his attitude to the Church, to the Left, to the Muslim countries that had recently been liberated, to mixed marriages, and to Jewish hesitancy with regard to assimilation. The only way out of the maze, said Memmi, is an independent national entity where one's consciousness would not be dependent on others. Kahanoff quotes Memmi in a conversation with Jewish students who asked his advice on what to do: "I am glad that I belong to the generation that has understood where our liberation can come from. Our task is to complete that liberation. Israel—that's your business! That is the only real way out for us, our only trump card, our last chance in history. Anything else is a diversion."[27]

The significance of this appeal, thought Kahanoff, lay in the fact that it was addressed to people like herself, born in North Africa and drawn toward French culture—people who thought they could assimilate among the citizens of France without losing their Jewish identity. Despite the optimism to be found in *La liberation du juif*, Kahanoff saw the book as personally tragic. Despite the career he had made in France, Memmi's children, who came from a "mixed marriage," asked him, "Daddy, what are you? An Arab? A Frenchman? A Jew?" Kahanoff said that, set against this background, he had "the courage of a cornered animal."

He showed courage in his refusal to renounce France, on account of what it had given Jews like him who had come from the Tunisian ghetto; courage in his persistence in shattering Jewish illusions about improving the attitudes of the Church; and courage in destroying the illusions of Jews who wished to make their situation more tolerable.

After discussing the question of Memmi's identity and that of people like him, Kahanoff moved on to a broader subject: the possibility that Jewish writers, who typify the "literature of social mutation," might write works of Jewish-universal significance. There can be no doubt, she said, that the Bible is a great work, but a long time had passed since the Jews had produced a significant work in the Jewish cultural context, for the works of Kafka, Freud, Marx, and Einstein are not specifically Jewish works. And here Kahanoff came to a surprisingly Zionist conclusion: "A whole and vital culture can only spring up from the connection between the people and its soil." Equally surprising was her declaration that if French literature has been released from its obligation to "Frenchness," "the same will happen in due course to our culture in Israel." Can this Israeli-French analogy be said to be Canaanite? The Canaanites were a minor ideological movement in the early 1940s of Palestine that conceived of Hebraic identity as being defined by nativism rather than ethnicity or religion. They looked to France as the model of a local national identity that was a fusion of country and language and nothing more.[28] Kahanoff also drew an analogy with Greece: the Hebrew sacred literature is to the land of Israel what Greek mythology and the Christian sacred writings are to western culture—a source of symbolism and poetic inspiration.

Kahanoff rejected Memmi's claim that the inner tensions arising from his problems with his Jewishness prevented him from doing what he wanted to do most of all—to write novels. In her words of criticism, one may clearly discern an idea she had already expressed in her article "The Literature of Social Mutation." Even though her starting point was Memmi, her conclusions were universal:

> But the time is coming when we as adults will have to come to terms with the full scale of our personal tragedy instead of trying to run away from it. From this sublimation many works of art have come into being, whose virtue is that they are honest towards all the people involved in the drama.... This book [which will be written] can be truer than Memmi's last book, *La libération du juif*, because it will contain less mutual recrimination and more generosity of heart. It can be part of the great current of good Jewish literature being written today, parallel with the Hebrew literature being written in Israel. An acceptance of the impossible situation man is condemned to and which he has chosen has not only given birth to good literature. but it also effects a sublimation of the raw material of feelings to the point where it is given a form.[29]

Many see Memmi's first novel, *La statue de sel* (The Pillar of Salt), as his best book, and, as Kahanoff wrote, "his most exciting and convincing."[30] In the years of Nazi occupation, when the Tunisian Jews were rescued at the last moment from being sent to the death camps, Memmi, together with other Jews, was taken to a work camp. The chapter "The Camp" in *La statue de sel* describes the time of imprisonment in the camp and the escape from it. This book, in Kahanoff's opinion, movingly describes the conflict experienced by a Jewish child in the ghetto of Tunis who learns French at school and is torn between the three dimensions of his inner world: the Jewish, the Arab, and the French. As a Jew he identifies with Israel, although he does not emigrate there; as an Arab he sympathizes with the North African liberation movement, although he is critical of the Arab hatred of foreigners; and finally, the fascination of French culture tips the scales.

Three more authors who may be considered representative of the Mediterranean enlightenment tradition are Albert Cohen (1895–1981), Jorge Semprún (1923–2011), and Najib Mahfouz (1911–2006). Although Cohen lived for most of his life in Geneva, his origins, his experiences, the conflicts in his works and in his biography, the characters in his books, and his outlook belonged to the Mediterranean world. He was born in the island of Corfu (called Kerkyra by the local inhabitants) in northeastern Greece. In 1900 his family moved to Marseille after anti-Jewish riots in Corfu. After antisemitic disturbances in the island in 1881, five thousand Jews from the island fled to Trieste, to Alexandria, and to other places. Albert's grandfather was head of the Jewish community in Corfu, but his grandson was educated in a Catholic school in Marseille and studied law in Geneva, where he acquired Swiss citizenship and became editor of the journal *Revue juive*. He was also Chaim Weizmann's representative in Paris. In the Second World War, he escaped to England where he served as a legal adviser on refugees and, as a representative of the Jewish Agency, he met General de Gaulle.

In Cohen's novel *Solal* (1930), the members of the rabbi's family were strange *Luftmenschen* who bought and sold almost everything, conversed in French, and told each other about "the great world far away, its dangers and its legendary riches." The crumbling beauty of the island, the apathy of the Greeks, the lazy Albanians, the dirty priests, and the poverty, pride, and romanticism of the Jewish inhabitants are skillfully portrayed. Solal, the rabbi's son and protagonist of the story, fell in love at the age of thirteen with the wife of the French consul, ten years his senior. Kahanoff wrote that for all his life Solal was torn between allegiance to the Jewish people and a platonic attraction to the "other world," personified by a blonde Christian woman with an aristocratic and antisemitic background. With the help of this woman, Ariane, "remembered as a beautiful golden idol," Solal reached France, received an education, and became secretary to a diplomat who became prime minister. He fell in love with the diplomat's daughter, Aude, but before he could marry her, the members of his family arrived in Paris and came between them.

Solal, who wanted to break away from Judaism, greeted his aged father with the sign of the cross. He acquired a run-down chateau in the country and built an altar to his Jewish past in the cellar (in his book *Ô vous, frères humains* [O Humans, My Brothers], he also built a shrine in a cupboard, but this time to the glory of France).[31] His wife became Jewish in his honor, and, according to Kahanoff, he felt that "the conquest of this Christian woman was like conquering the world,"[32] but she was nevertheless foreign to the Mediterranean world of Solal's family, and he wanted to bring her back to Paris. He told her, "I'm just like them, a humorous people, a poetic people, hungry, scattered, desperate . . . , a people of thorns." Aude left Solal and he committed suicide. Kahanoff said that she was moved by the novel: "Here, finally, is a tragic Jewish novel with a capital T. The very name "Solal" evokes a Jewish rebirth which is at once delicate and harsh like the sun-drenched lands where Sephardic Judaism sprang up before and after every persecution. It is as though it were about me."

Jorge Semprún, in a manner similar to Cohen, exhibits a Mediterranean hybrid identity in his writings.[33] He fought in the French Resistance and was a survivor of Buchenwald, the German concentration camp. From the time of his release onward, he documented the horrors that had taken place in Europe but also preached for its unification. He opposed the fascism that had seized control of his homeland Spain and he defended dissidents, freedom fighters, and citizens everywhere. He also protested in his writings against the political trials in Prague and the Colonels' regime in Greece, and he warned against the intellectual justification of terror wherever it appeared, from the Russian Nechaev to the Leninists in France. In the cemetery at Portbou, overlooking the Mediterranean Sea, one hundred years after the birth of Walter Benjamin and fifty years after the end of the world war that had cut short Benjamin's life, Semprún, as Spanish Minister of Culture, laid the cornerstone for Dani Karavan's sculpture in honor of the Jewish philosopher who had been trapped in the Pyrenees.

Like Semprún, Najib Mahfouz is not the kind of writer to take refuge in a tub. Mahfouz took his place as Egypt's leading writer with his work *The Cairo Trilogy* (1956–1957).[34] At first, in an attempt to embrace the totality of history, he wrote of Pharaonic Egypt, but in the 1940s and 1950s he turned his attention to the new, poor Cairo, the city where he was born. An allegory about the Mediterranean prophets Moses, Jesus, and Muhammad was situated in modern Cairo. The historical novel opened the way for social realism. The trilogy described the development of the new Egypt and its lively metropolis between the two world wars, focusing on the history of a single family, that of the petty merchant Ahmed, over several generations and the growth and development of modern Egypt from the first king, Fuad, to the revolution of Saad Zaghloul. What is special about Mahfouz's work is his description of the banality of daily existence, which raised the question of why Egyptians chose to submit to their fate, and his attempt to answer this question through a candid depiction of the moral, religious, and ethnic factors and socioeconomic conditions peculiar to Egypt.

THE TEXT AS MY COUNTRY

As noted, Kahanoff was perplexed as to why the Jews who lived in cosmopolitan Egyptian communities produced so little literature. She surmised that the reason was paradoxically due to the multilingual culture abounding in these cosmopolitan centers. English was the language of the occupying power, French was the language of culture, Greek was in common use, and Italian was used by the members of the important Italian Jewish community, who sent their children to Italian schools, and many of whom belonged to liberal professions and had been encouraged to contribute to the modernization of Egypt. In the Jewish families, mixed marriages with non-Jews abounded. Kahanoff well observed that "this complexity gave the minority culture its piquancy, diversity, and subtlety. However, no common ethnic or linguistic base was strong enough to bring the many minority groups to some form of unification."[35] In a confession of surprising candor, Kahanoff explained why the Egyptian Jewish immigrants did not produce much literature: "Why did we have an attitude at once so touchy and denigrating towards ourselves? I think we considered ourselves too inferior—or, as we say in Israel, too 'Levantine'—to dare express ourselves in writing. Gide and Malraux were our standard, but it didn't occur to us that the point was not to emulate them, but to tell our own story in our own words."[36]

For Edmond Jabès, writing—an act that, in his opinion, reflected the divine creation in human creativity—was a desperate investigation of the world and of man, who lives there lost and alienated.

Kahanoff thought that through Jabès's fluent French he had crossed all the intersections he had come upon as a Jew. "Did he not find this world again when he went into exile?" she asked, referring to Egypt. "Was not this world dormant within him without his knowing?" In the outskirts of Paris he described desert landscapes, sand dunes, the shade of palm trees. The need to identify the Jew with the east, from where he had been uprooted, was shown, said Kahanoff, in the Mediterranean names of the rabbis in Jabès's book *Le livre des questions* (The Book of Questions). It was no accident that the travels of Yankel and Sarah were across the Mediterranean world: Corfu, Cairo, Marseilles, and so on. Kahanoff said that reading Jabès revealed to her the code that linked the Mediterranean world with the Jewish: "I see again with my spiritual sight these names, these landscapes, these streets, these faces peering and appearing out of *Le livre des questions*. I know the place of the rupture, where the pages of our lives were torn out, and I know that there are many wounds that will never be healed. This Jewish world was written and inscribed within us but not known, like a page that is turned without being read."[37]

The rupture and wounds she described caused Kahanoff to reflect on her Jewish existence: "Ought we not to question ourselves about the meaning or lack of meaning of our Jewish existence: we who resided in Egypt but did very little and did not speak the language properly? Did we not see it as strange or even scandalous to celebrate the exodus from Egypt when we had come back to it after being swept up into huge wanderings far away from the Promised Land? Ought we not to ask ourselves the meaning of the insoluble equation of Jewish existence, because of which we are here but also there, in every other place and nowhere at all?"

Kahanoff objected to the romanticization of the exile that was found in Jabès: "I had a strong desire to shut the door on the closed world of this sterile and arid book, to escape from this cruel exile closed in upon itself." In Paris, Jabès told her, when she asked him, how he came to think of the imaginary rabbis: "I feel that they were always with me, but they only spoke when I learnt what exile is." She rejected the "nihilistic conclusions" represented by Jabès's song of praise for the exile, and she pitied Sarah for the following lines taken from her diary: "I set against life the / hollow truth, / waterless shores." In reaction to these shores of death, Kahanoff rhapsodized: "I know of other shores, alive with the freshness of our waters, which are not stagnant beneath the well of memory, but waters of our ambitions, seas, rivers, which sparkle with thousands upon thousands of new and turbulent questions."[38]

In *Le livre des questions* Kahanoff discerned a hidden path that in a short while would bring its author to Israel, where he would sit by the well with his brothers. She hoped that the erring pilgrim would ultimately find his home there: "Our basic principle is to fulfil the Jewish soul by fusing it with the sensuous, strong and tender reality of Eretz-Israel." These thoughts occurred to her when she was interviewing Jabès's wife Arlette for the Institute of Contemporary Jewry. Kahanoff, Jabès, and his wife visited Jaffa, "which sometimes slightly resembles Alexandria. The same sort of churches were built at the same time by Italian architects. We heard Greek music." Jabès said, "Here in Israel there is a place called Yabetz, which we came from, according to the tradition. The name Jabès is a corruption of Yabetz." Perhaps, thought Kahanoff, one of Jabès's ancestors had studied Kabala in that place, and it was his voice that spoke through the imaginary rabbis in *Le livre des questions*.

THE DIALOGIC GENRE

In her essay "My Brother the Rebel," Kahanoff related how two North African anticolonialist revolutionaries had visited her family in Cairo. They were Habib Bourguiba (1903–2000) and Ahmed Ben-Bella (1916–2012). Habib Bourguiba, who later became the first president of Tunisia, was a guest of her cousin Julian. Ahmed Ben-Bella, eventually one of the leaders of the Algerian underground and the first president of independent Algeria, lived for a few years in her room in her parents' home.[39] Kahanoff revealed with unconcealed envy and a certain pride the special relationship between these historic figures and her family. Only after her mother had immigrated to Israel did she dare to tell her daughter about their close friends, the North African patriots, students from friendly countries "who fill the space a little created by the silence of the children we left behind." Kahanoff was intrigued by the thought of a stranger who lived in "my room . . . as if it were his."

The way Bourguiba and Ben-Bella are described reveals Kahanoff as an essayist of dialogue, not a rhetorician of "Otherness."

This article shows a culture of openness, dialogue, and positive symbiosis. A negative symbiosis takes place when the dominant party needs an "Other," not to be enriched but to be confirmed. The process resembles the Hegelian dialectic of master and slave, in which each person defines himself in terms of the other. This model is not productive but schematic: the "Other" is an objectification of your fears, your insecurity, your lack of an existentially secure identity. When this is the case, how can you hold a discussion with someone else, enter into intellectual negotiations with him, trade cultural merchandise with him? Because the attitude of the "Other" has been predetermined, there can be no dealing with him: he is fixed, unchanging. As a stereotype he even defines *you* in a one-dimensional way, like a kind of caricature.

Kahanoff provided a different option, a model of *positive* symbiosis and dialogue. She had sufficient self-confidence to open herself up to that "Other." She did not assume a hegemonic identity that defines itself through an adversarial "Other," an entity that, even when attractive, remains dark and demonic. Kahanoff proposed a different structure: radical, not in the exegetically erroneous sense of extreme, but representing a wish to get to the root (Latin *radix*) of things, or, as the Hebrew poet N. H. Bialik put it, "The place where opposites join their roots." Kahanoff's Mediterranean option is radical because its structure necessitates the renunciation of something very basic in the dominant identity.[40] The model proposed by Kahanoff is Jewish, feminist, Mediterranean; a model based on mutual sympathy, mutual inspiration, and egalitarian attitudes. In such an outlook there is no need to set up barricades against the outside world and foreign cultural influences consciously and in an exaggerated manner. There is no need to imagine an "Other," and one can efface boundaries and be liminally in several different worlds at once.

Perhaps Kahanoff was thinking of herself when she concluded her article "The Literature of Social Mutation" as follows: "The writers I have mentioned here look beyond one kind of world to another and reflect much more than isolated individual cases. They express new and complex cultural forms that are at one and the same time marginal with regard to the national literatures and important as international statements because they fuse wide geographical and cultural areas in new and unexpected combinations. They represent an aspect of contemporary literature and culture which is worth following closely, and whose existence we are only just beginning to be aware of now."[41]

In any case, she was referring to a literature that moved between borders, that embodied immanent tensions both in the lives of the writers themselves and in the subjects they wrote about. Kahanoff, as we have said, was of Tunisian and Iraqi Jewish extraction, grew up in a Jewish community in a cosmopolitan British society in Egypt, went to a French high school, conversed with governesses in English and with servants in Arabic. In the formative years of her life, she lived both in the national society of France and the pluralistic immigrant culture of the United States and in Israel in its early days when there was a cultural-political hegemony. These cultural changes could have destroyed the identity and creativity of many writers, but in Kahanoff's case they served as an abundant source of vitality and interiorization of many national, class, and cultural perspectives. Her ideas move between the frontiers of the universal (the cosmopolitan) and the Levantine, the Levantine and the Israeli, the Israeli and the Jewish, the Jewish and the Muslim.

This liminality characterizing Kahanoff was expressed not only in the wanderings of her life and her spiritual divagations but also in her deep affinity with cultures that lay outside Israel's hegemonic discourse in those years. Kahanoff was, perhaps more than anything else, in almost all respects "both outside and inside," a Jewish intellectual who was an "outsider as insider," to use the expression of the historians who wrote about the Jewish intellectuals in Germany.[42]

At the same time, Kahanoff always sought a place that would be a home, a place where her polyphonic identity would find rest, where east and west would have a fruitful meeting. The biographical and spiritual stages on the path to her identity did not cause a tear in her personality, but gave rise to a Mediterranean outlook combining various places in a kind of multilocational culture.

FIVE

BEING A MODERN WOMAN

A WOMAN'S LIFE IN EGYPT

There were some feminist inclinations in the young Jacqueline Shohet in the conservative Jewish society of monarchical Egypt, but only years later, after a marriage and divorce, did Kahanoff (Shohet's name by a later marriage) declare that Muslim society maintained a regime of oppression and subjugation of women. Jewish conservatism, on the one hand, and Muslim oppression, on the other hand, caused her to state, in the high-flown Marxist phraseology of those days, that no distinction could be made between the freedom of the Egyptian citizens and the freedom of women in Egypt: "In a society that held women in a state of servitude, no one was really free."[1] She came to understand that the Islamic leadership accepted customs she considered barbaric, such as female circumcision, that the Egyptian government shut its eyes to those primitive norms, and that the United Nations was indifferent to these norms and customs. The patriarchal character of Egypt with its deep roots in Islam found expression in circumcision of girls to prevent sexual enjoyment, the existence of public marriage nights, the encouragement of polygamy, the widespread use of hashish, and so on.

Youssef el Masry's 1962 book *Le drame sexual de la femme dans l'Orient arabe* (The Sexual Drama of Women in the Arab Orient) gave Kahanoff a deeper understanding of Islam.[2] Islam, in the author's opinion, "surpassed" the other monotheistic religions, which by nature were not favorable to women, in degrading women's humanity. It created a "system of terror of male imperialism." Woman became a sexual object and a childbearing machine who could be married without her consent. The possibility that a man could marry a number of women caused many women to live in continual fear of being divorced if they failed to give birth to a son.

Kahanoff said that in her opinion there was a paradox in Egyptian society. Old women could dominate the paternal home by providing the family with order and stability. Many men preferred the stability provided by the mother to the despotism imposed by the father. The old mother exerted control by suppressing any signs of rebellion and by making the major decisions. There was thus a matriarchal logic at work within the patriarchal Egyptian society. But in Kahanoff's opinion other tendencies were also operative in Islamic society, one example of which was the revolutionary steps taken by Habib Bourguiba, the president of Tunisia at that time, to restrict the authority of the ulama (the sages of the Muslim religion) and to enact laws to prevent polygamy and divorce without a trial. Similarly, in the time of Abdel Nasser, who was more conservative than Bourguiba, the women and female students in Egypt gained in self-awareness and demanded recognition of their rights. With regard to the matriarchal element, said Kahanoff, education was the feature that distinguished the Jewish minority and the other Levantine minorities from the Islamic society as a whole.

Her feminist awareness began to develop when she observed social events in which women would "cast away virtue together with their veils . . . defiantly asserting the most precious of all freedoms, the easiest to conquer—conjugal infidelity. . . . We learned then that a girl who sat at a bar was putting her reputation at stake, and that she should never accept a dance with a Muslim. . . . We [were] . . . ardent feminists, aggressive, [and] proud to sit in the classroom with our male contemporaries, taking notes on Descartes, Kant and Spinoza."[3] They bandied about the names of these philosophers without actually reading their works, which according to Kahanoff was a typical Levantine characteristic. Françoise, a French Christian girl, aroused jealousy among her friends by her inner tranquility. She went to mass and occupied herself with poetry, embroidery, and recipes, "as if women were not fighting to be liberated from domestic enslavement." Their self-assertive conduct gave Jacqueline Kahanoff and her friends the feeling that they were affirming something that had eluded them. The years of adolescence were characterized by confusion and contradictions among the girls and boys, despite the fact that their relationships were much freer than those of their parents had been. Education was the ideal of the leisured class, although Jacqueline and her friends knew that education for girls served no practical purpose. Nevertheless, they hoped for some miracle, some great love or courageous action that would fire them with the strength to rebel.

But the miracle did not happen. After the matriculation exams, the girls went on holiday to Alexandria, where they were without the boys they knew at school, who went to study in universities overseas and came back knowing more than the girls did and treating them like older sisters. "We'd go to parties, flirt and drink, outrageously bored, disappointed, waiting for husbands, tempted, but without daring to cut the silken cords which tied us to our well-to-do families. We'd read, play cards, be pessimistic, and continue in that vein through marriage, childbearing, adultery, and possibly divorce."[4]

Jacqueline knew what she was talking about. Her mother tried to console her by saying there was much for a girl to do—parties, nice clothes, sports, concerts, learning to sew and cook. As a married woman who knew how to run her home, she could attend courses in literature. Seeing these narrow horizons in store for her and those like her, she was deeply frustrated. She suggested to her mother that she should marry an Ashkenazi—"Ashkenazis are intelligent"—and as an example of the path she wished to follow, she put forth her friend Sylvie, who was permitted to study at the Sorbonne. Her mother answered, "Geniuses don't make good wives," and refused to allow her daughter to work: "People would think your father was ruined." She sometimes envied girls who had to work.

Legal studies and a knowledge of European law also seemed to young Jacqueline superfluous in view of the imminent end of European colonialism. She was well aware of the significance of the choice between colonialist Europe and Islamic nationalist Egypt. In her description of a traumatic incident she experienced, she exemplified what was likely to happen with the exodus of the Europeans from Egypt: During a demonstration of Muslim students against British rule, she found herself closed in with them in a locked chamber. When she rushed to the door, she was finally let out by one of them. She told him, "It is not right to lock girls up with so many men. You wouldn't like it to happen to your own sisters."[5]

This incident did not prevent Jacqueline from volunteering to do community work in a clinic in a Cairo neighborhood. She soon left this occupation, however, because of rumors of Zionist activities spread by Islamist circles and because of the fears of the parents of the girl volunteers that they would gain the reputation of being "well-meaning but dangerous revolutionaries."[6] Without the clinic, their lives seemed futile, and parties and flirtation were less exciting. They despised themselves and "the smug young men who at least had the satisfaction of making money." Some of them joined antifascist groups and made contact with "unmarriageable, fascinatingly disquieting young men," but they still had the feeling that they lacked self-realization. A girlfriend expressed the opinion of many of them when she said, "Our grandmothers knew how to make rose water, and we, not even that."

The more Jacqueline's feminist consciousness developed, the more frustrated she became. Gossip about a friend who rejected the advances of King Farouk made another friend remark, "I wish I had the guts to be a naked cabaret dancer. We all behave like whores anyway once we're married—except for the poor queen."[7] A complaint against another girl, Diana, was an additional cause of feminist fermentation among the young Jewish girls. A young assistant professor of philosophy asked for Diana's hand before he divorced his wife, and she became a heroine in Jacqueline's circle because she did not give in to her parents, who refused him. Her insistence became "the rallying cry of a generation of young women who wished to be masters of their own bodies as they saw fit." The young women, who rejected the patriarchal norms, told their male critics that "the system is all to your advantage, but we won't stand for it any longer." Even the Muslim women saw an analogy between this affair and the case of the Duchess of Windsor. This "evil spirit," as Kahanoff called it, the self-awareness developing among Muslim women, created a great disturbance among the Egyptian men.

The Second World War revealed how much Egypt was changing. The girls who throughout the whole period of Tobruk and El Alamein had enjoyed the company of Allied soldiers hoped that the war would never end. When Kahanoff came back to Egypt for a short time as a young divorcée (a "thoroughly enviable position"), she found that many of the young women she had known had married Allied soldiers and left.[8] This visit to Egypt closed a circle. Leaving her conservative home and going to the New World were possible due to what she called a "marriage of convenience." When this marriage no longer met her expectations, however, she decided to divorce. Her return to Egypt as a woman who decided her own fate was another stop on her long journey on the circuitous path of a young feminist.

"WOMEN, WITH A PEN OF THEIR OWN"

The autobiographical novel *Lovers and Tyrants* (1976), by Francine du Plessix Gray (1930–2019), a left-wing Franco-American journalist and intellectual, describes the struggle between a woman's love for a man and her desire to be independent.[9] Kahanoff said that in contrast to the situation in the militant protest literature of the past, which was very necessary, and in which "the women writers were feminists who had to break the bonds of their situation of inferiority," the western women of her time enjoyed a great deal of freedom.[10] Unlike these writers, Gray, who was sent to prison for her protests against the Vietnam War, went beyond "the dogmatism of the Women's Liberation movement." In her travels between her native country, France, and her country of choice, the United States, Gray had a number of experiences involving love and eroticism, marriage and politics.

Stephanie, the heroine of the novel, follows Søren Kierkegaard's precept, "If so, then choose despair, for despair is a choice, and when a man despairs, he chooses . . . the absolute."[11] Existential decisions exist within despair, not in avoiding it. She continues to quote the Danish philosopher: "Woman chooses herself." While liberation makes woman into a "bad child," the same society makes the liberated man into a hero. Parallel with the description of Stephanie's various erotic adventures, "old women, with their conservative outlooks, their naive religious faith and their parochial respectability," are depicted "with a whimsical mixture of affection, understanding, humor and respect."[12]

Gregory, a friend from her days at university and a Jesuit priest, rebukes Stephanie: "Don't hide beneath your inferiority as a woman. Don't seek refuge in your repressed status. That is the worst form of cowardice. Get off the wagon of women's liberation." She respects him because she did not succeed in bringing him over to her side. Stephanie, the liberated woman, abandons her husband and wanders all over America in the company of a handsome homosexual drug addict. Kahanoff commented on the absurd aspect of women's liberation: mature women keep young men who could be their sons just as elderly men keep girls who could be their daughters. She favors Stephanie's personal choice as a reflection of her life. Many husbands leave their loving and faithful wives, so why should wives not leave their loving and faithful husbands? This was a modern choice reflecting the right of a woman to reject a comfortable existence, as the painter Gauguin did in his time. Stephanie chose to be herself and at the same time a strong individual who, regardless of any pride or snobbishness, aimed at a kind of universalism in keeping with the modern world in all its perversity.

Another woman writer Kahanoff considered was Françoise Sagan (1935–2004). In her criticism of Sagan's 1959 book *Aimez-vous Brahms?* (Do You Like Brahms?), she saw the heroine of the novel, Paule, who was mature and unattached, as "a vibrant figure, a modern woman, free and independent."[13] Paule's choice between two lovers was regarded sympathetically. On the one hand, there was Roger, her old lover who exploited the idea of mutual liberty for his own advantage, and on the other hand, there was Simon, a young man who worshipped her. She chose her old lover, not because she loved him but because "she recognized him as her partner." Kahanoff understood Paule, who preferred a permanent, orderly relationship to the fervor of youth, which in the final analysis is not the main thing. What motivated Sagan as a writer was the attempt to understand the ethics behind the man's dominating role.[14] This modern story with its musical title conjures up the myth of Orpheus, the musician in Greek mythology whose love was taken from him. The world of art and music represented by the young lover Simon is set against the daily life represented by Roger. These are confronted by Paule's freedom of choice. Kahanoff examines the internal game described in the book, which fluctuates between two principles: defense of the norms established by self-centered men, and "the promptings and echoes of women's lib."

Kahanoff had the feeling when reading books by certain women writers that they very often try "to resemble men as much as possible." In her essay "Women, with a pen of their own," she wrote about Sagan again and observed that her special quality lay in her emotional diagnosis of human feelings and not in sociological analysis, in her writing as a woman artist and not in intellectual reflection.[15] Her style is connected to her femininity, and her writing is no less sophisticated than that of men, to which it owes nothing. Her primary concern is her art in writing and not the depiction of beautiful things, as is the case with certain woman writers. Because she sees Sagan as a seemingly "simple" woman of the people, she prefers her to an intellectual like Simone de Beauvoir.

In her opening sentence of *The Second Sex*, "A woman is not born a woman; she becomes a woman," Simone de Beauvoir (1908–1986) distinguishes between sex and gender.[16] The belief that womanhood is something acquired is the foundation of modern feminism. The "otherness" of woman is expressed in de Beauvoir's statement that "woman is the 'other' in a whole in which two components are necessary to each other." Many people have seen Jean-Paul Sartre and de Beauvoir as two parts of a single whole, and Kahanoff also thought that the grand couple of French literature could not be separated. She saw both of them in the light of equality; they both "went forth into the battlefield of their time with courage and a generous spirit, and they always retained a human image."[17] They spoke up on behalf of those who needed freedom, justice, and compassion. Kahanoff regarded de Beauvoir's "path to liberty" to be that of a woman fighting for her freedom in a patriarchal world. Despite her severe image, she was generous and sensitive to others, and she had the capacity to combine love and friendship with the pleasures of life.

De Beauvoir and her partner were seen by Kahanoff as contemporary prophets like the members of the Russian intelligentsia in the past, intellectuals who aroused the displeasure of their fellow countrymen, a voice crying in the wilderness. At the same time, in her *Memoirs of a Dutiful Daughter* (1958), de Beauvoir, in Kahanoff's opinion, submitted to Sartre's ideas, and failed as an artist because she preferred abstract ideas to emotions.[18] She expressed her thoughts but not her feelings. A female philosopher among men, she looked down on women who chose "feminine" occupations such as art. Her book "lacked backbone, was pretentious, lacking in humor." She was analytical and decadent rather than intuitive and poetic. When a woman deliberately tries to resemble a male intellectual, she reaches an impasse. Paradoxically, it was only "when she found a man who dominated her with his personality—namely, Sartre—that she finally felt herself to be a woman."[19]

Unlike de Beauvoir with her "flimsy verbiage," Mary McCarthy (1912–1989) in Kahanoff's opinion was an intellectual distinguished by a combination of spiritual alertness and poetic imagination. This American critic, writer, and political commentator was known for her sharp criticism of twentieth-century totalitarian ideologies and her condemnation of the involvement of the United States in Vietnam. She published articles and essays in the best American journals and was a close friend of Hannah Arendt (she was appointed her literary executor). Kahanoff said that McCarthy's articles were cutting and virulent and that she did not defer to any male intellectual. This also applied to her autobiography, *Memories of a Catholic Girlhood* (1957).[20] It would seem that Kahanoff had Simone de Beauvoir in mind when making the following statement: "Mary McCarthy, who is a beautiful woman and not only talented, is not ashamed to write with charm and magic, with pleasure and a sly feminine power of persuasion because she knows that when one uses these tools correctly, it is more effective than a punch on the nose."[21]

Another woman writer and countermodel to Simone de Beauvoir was the American anthropologist Ruth Benedict (1887–1948), who was teaching in Columbia University in New York at the time Kahanoff studied there for her master's degree. In her classic anthropological study of culture, *Patterns of Culture* (1934), Benedict treated cultures as expanded personalities.[22] Each culture has its own particular character traits. The Pueblo cultures of the American Southwest, for example, are characterized by restraint, whereas abandon is the character trait of the Native American cultures of the Great Plains. In this school of "culture and personality," regarded today as outmoded, there was a cultural relativity. Benedict was a successful anthropologist, said Kahanoff, "because she used her feminine qualities in her creativity and did not force herself to wear the garments of a totally unnecessary masculinity."[23] Her ability to perceive different cultural expressions led her to the conclusion that national liberty cannot be distinguished from the various forms of expression. Kahanoff's conservative feminism is again seen in her statement that "women need freedom and creativity as much as men, but they work more harmoniously when the two sexes complement one another rather than compete with each other."[24]

SEXUAL FREEDOM

Kahanoff thought that sexual freedom was an expression of equality between the sexes. Moreover, permissiveness creates a more open relationship between a couple. In several articles, she addressed the question of how sexual freedom between a man and a woman, which is not confined to their mutual relationship, can bind a couple together. Sexual relations were in her opinion no longer something to be hidden or concealed, and in her time they had become a widespread social phenomenon. For the young, "eternal love" was just a flowery expression. "Already people do not worship a young woman, and she is already not 'protected' as she was in the past, but she is also not exploited as in former times. Today she is more experienced and able to run her life on her own."[25]

In the 1950s, the apocalyptic fear of the nuclear bomb after the Second World War led Kahanoff to feel that one had to enjoy whatever life had to offer. Counter to this was a growing tendency to rein in what was seen as the danger of anarchy and unlimited freedom and to prefer a conservative way of life. "After it goes on an extended joy-ride, mankind is liable to tire of erotic and political extremism."[26] A generation later, in the 1970s (Kahanoff passed over the permissive 1960s), there was a great change. There began a wave of eroticism and pornography expressed in literature, in art, in advertising, and in films like *The Decameron* and *A Clockwork Orange*.

In the film *A Clockwork Orange*, directed by Stanley Kubrick (1928–1999), Kahanoff saw an aestheticization of violence, and especially of violence against women.[27] The women in the film are objects of perverted lust, suffering, and vindictiveness, and this reaches its sadistic climax in the rape, torture, and murder of a young woman, the wife of a writer, by the young man Alex and his friends. Kahanoff saw this scene as a "negative" (in the photographic sense) of the Christian myth of the immaculate conception, the model of the Virgin Mary, but here it was not a son who was crucified, but a woman was crucified by a man. This motif, which recurs, in her opinion, in the films of Federico Fellini (1920–1993) and Luchiano Visconti (1906–1976) and in the books of Alberto Moravia (1907–1990), castrates the Christian ethos and western culture as a whole. This motif of deliberate destruction and violence was anticipated by the Nazi myth.

The women in *A Clockwork Orange* are the object of a murderous madness because in Kahanoff's opinion "the men unconsciously hope that nature would protect them."[28] While the young men hoist the flag of sexual freedom, the woman is not a free and equal partner but an object of sexual exploitation and masculine aggression. In Kahanoff's opinion, the artificial décor and the absence of nature from the film symbolize the loss of the value of woman—the severance of man's connection with nature, which gives life. All that is left is the flaying of the flesh and soul of the woman. But Kahanoff's main contention was that it is all represented too aesthetically, in a way that tends to give the viewer an empathetic view of violence. Soon, she said, with the noble intention of revealing the rottenness of society, people will enjoy the sight of babies dying of hunger. Was Kubrick's fantasy just a violent cinematic spectacle that could not be judged by moralistic criteria, or, in the words of his widow Christiane, was it "a supreme example of evil"? It would seem, however, that Kahanoff's judgment was too moralistic and to a great extent simplistic.[29]

Kahanoff, as was her custom, sought the golden mean: neither violent eroticism nor moral rigidity. In her opinion, eroticism and pornography reflect normal needs of human nature. When a society attains a high degree of affluence, people tend to seek a variety of sexual experiences and be excited by the human body, phenomena that do not necessarily contradict feelings of love or monogamous relationships. The democratization of eroticism is of course also seen among women, who are more exposed to sex in the newspapers and the cinema, and who are almost as experienced in sexual relations as are men. Kahanoff offered a sociological explanation: the birth rate has increased, there is no longer a need for women to give birth at an early age; there is birth control, and having children can therefore be postponed.

Kahanoff's feminist conservatism or conservative feminism gave her the idea that a time comes when couples want to consolidate the relationship between them by creating a home and raising a family. Although the younger generation of the 1970s had fewer complexes than its predecessor, it was just as subject to mixed feelings. It too was attracted to a stable environment and a disciplined way of life. Kahanoff sought a middle path to happiness: neither a conformist ideal of sexual relations nor total sexual freedom. There was a dual fear: that a reaction to sex would cause puritanical repression and deny a basic human need, and that a licentious life would be lived at the expense of human feelings. Both obsessive eroticism and excessive puritanical coercion represented only one aspect of human nature.

In a somewhat poetic passage, Kahanoff gave a description of her fears and those of other women:

> Perhaps the passing of the years has something to do with it. The older I become, the more it seems to me that roses are no longer what they were. The roses of the older generation knew how they should be: large, scented garden roses were like masses of blonde women trembling at the climax of their passion. The wind, which scattered their petals, seemed to give relief to their desires. Red roses on their long stems were like proud queens, and when they withered, they held their heads aloft, and their perfume made them even more like tragic heroines.[30]

Unlike these withered roses, young women have a bright, assertive femininity and look down on anyone over twenty years old. Kahanoff's conservatism can also be seen in her attitude to the dress fashions of the young, and also to the politics of the rebellious younger generation: "Students' demonstrations by their very extremism can faithfully reflect the confusion of a well-off and frightened generation which sometimes behaves like a small child who smashes his toys in his anger." She ironically added that young men and women choose their partners as though matching colors. She thought that sexual confusion reached the point of absurdity in negative descriptions of great figures: A woman like the indomitable Israeli politician Golda Meir (1898–1978) "may be a far more representative figure than we think of a society in which women had not yet renounced their right to be something of value rather than just pretty young things."[31]

ON BEING A COMPLETE HUMAN BEING

Kahanoff did not speak only of the theoretical aspects of feminism or the intellectual consequences of distinguishing between sexual freedom and the female gender. Women of flesh and blood interested her as much as the heroines of novels. She was annoyed, for instance, at the statements of some participants in the Israeli radio program *A Moment of Truth*, in which the subject of "women without men" was discussed, because three or four young women complained of loneliness. Their social life before their separation from their spouses, they said, was that of a partner in a relationship, but after the separation their connection with the social environment of their former partner was gradually cut off. Kahanoff's astonishment at their lack of self-esteem—their lack of their sense of their own value—was soon replaced by the impression made on her by an older woman who also appeared on the program and took up an independent position. She ordered a man who was traveling with her to leave a motorcar. For the women younger than herself, who were not feminists like her, a woman without a partner was not a complete human being. Kahanoff quickly concluded that social status and spiritual status are closely interconnected.[32]

In Kahanoff's opinion, the fact that a woman's dependence on marriage is a normal value in Israel required women to develop a critical attitude to customs and norms that had taken root in society. In the past, people were able to deal with loneliness. In Israel's War of Independence, women reacted differently from the way they did in other wars, despite the many casualties. They felt necessary to society, which was more united in those days. In the Yishuv in Mandatory Palestine women also enjoyed solidarity, and in the Jewish shtetls the women also stood firm when the men sailed to the New World. The society of affluence and welfare that succeeded the society of want enabled women to perform tasks that previously only men had performed: "They will have to develop a different psychology, to learn to depend on themselves and on other women and reject the idea of being someone's wife first of all in order to become someone themselves."[33]

Kahanoff went on to say that in Israel the men were absent in wartime, as also happened elsewhere, and she spoke of the situation of women at such times: the women have to take the place of the men, which they do successfully, but when the war ends, they revert to their previous roles. It is not surprising that a generation later, when their children leave home, the women are at a loss. This gave rise to the radical women's liberation movement in the United States. Kahanoff said that the women of her time wanted to be full partners in society, to function as complete human beings, and to regain their self-esteem. What prevented them from doing so was the lack of an infrastructure for training in practical subjects; at vocational schools girls were taught only "feminine" professions, and at universities women mainly studied the humanities while the men went in for engineering and science. Israel needed women mechanical engineers no less than housewives.[34]

A population surplus, a shrinkage of resources, and inflation had in Kahanoff's opinion made women's fecundity a disadvantage, as a high birth rate requires many resources to satisfy needs, from food to education. Women were forced to seek interests and employment outside the home, and they needed to feel that they were useful not only as mothers. Large families became a problem, because they were generally made up of women with few resources and many children. Families with means were more able to increase in size, and families with few resources had to reduce their birth rate. Effective birth control would prevent a proliferation of children, would take many people out of poverty, and would allow women to find employment. In Israel in the 1950s and 1960s, women of the eastern communities did not have the possibility of rebelling and did not have access to the media—unlike in the United States, for example, where women were less repressed because they were more able to express their opinions.

Even before she wrote on these matters in the 1970s, Kahanoff volunteered to assist the Organization of Sephardic Women, a society whose aim was to encourage talented children of families of the eastern communities and enable them to study in a high school. An example of such children was a fourteen-year-old girl called Dora who had seven brothers and sisters and whose father was a cleaning worker in a small town. Dora, who wanted to study, understood that a grant would not be enough as the family needed two extra working hands. The purpose of the "Organization of Sephardic Women" was to help such families.[35] Elsewhere, Kahanoff summarized the change that had taken place in the status of women in Israel:

> Israel is the one country in which, in less than twenty years, there has been a radical change in the status of eastern women, when they are Jewish, and it may be assumed that things are better for the majority of young people, seeing that they can earn their living and have a freedom to choose and decide which their mothers did not have. . . . This is Israel's revolution which took place as though by chance, but whose consequences are far-reaching. One can blame the dominant "Europeanism," which has also been accused of a kind of internal colonialism, but altogether, young people, and especially girls, have been quick to seize the opportunity they were offered.[36]

SCHEHERAZADE AT THE DAMASCUS GATE

At the end of her article "With the Return to the East," discussing the situation of Palestinian women in East Jerusalem, Kahanoff declared, "After all, women's protest is already present in *One Thousand and One Nights*."[37] But this statement is surprising in two respects. First, in this article the "women's protest" was not that of Palestinian women. On the contrary, Kahanoff deplored the lack of any Palestinian feminine self-awareness. Second, what had Palestinian women after 1967 to do with the tales of *One Thousand and One Nights*, a collection of legends, some of which are from the period of the Abbasid caliphate and some of which are from the period of Harun al-Rashid the Tenth?

As we know, Scheherazade was a highly educated girl and the daughter of a vizier, who for a thousand nights provided the caliph Shahryr with a thousand wives. To spare the women of the kingdom their fears of the fate awaiting them—one night's marriage, after which they would be killed—Scheherazade decided to marry the caliph and every night tell him a story that would be continued the following night. Thus, the caliph, after a thousand and one nights, found himself married to Scheherazade, with three children. These stories, said Kahanoff, were like a psychiatric treatment: a healing process in which the fears and neuroses of a sick patient are cured—a process that takes place in *One Thousand and One Nights*.

In these stories, Scheherazade investigated the characters of women, both strong women and traded women (bought and sold), who were like objects. In this way, for example, she made a criticism of a society that traded in female slaves. Thus, a corrupt social order was revealed in which the sexual life and self-respect of women were trampled underfoot. As against this, there was a manipulation whereby a female slave, considered an object, could rise to the level of a queen, an independent personality. Cunning, lies, and infidelity became weapons in the hands of the women avenging the denial of their instincts, their freedom of choice, and their self-respect. These stories, said Kahanoff, contain lessons on the improvement of women's status: the obligation to keep faith with a man only if the man does likewise, or the promotion of the ideal of monogamous love to the displeasure of the man of means who exploits his power to practice polygamy. *One Thousand and One Nights* is a series of lessons on women's attempts to find solutions to their plight.

Thus, Islamic society sees woman as a sexual object—an attitude that exists in other societies as well. The moral lesson we learn from Scheherazade, as from psychoanalysis, is that one cannot impose absolute moral values but must teach the understanding and ability to accept contradictions and habituate oneself

BEING A MODERN WOMAN

to compromises. In *One Thousand and One Nights* one finds a living society with its defects and compromises, and, according to Kahanoff, it contains an ironic implied comment on motherhood. Mothers are women but not objects. Although rebellious women were usually Christian, the lesson was not lost on Muslim women. The folktale provided the feminine morality "in which the mother, and especially the grandmother, was the real wealth of the family." There, stories reflect the great ages of Islam in which educated women of quality—a type that never completely disappeared in the east—lived and worked.

Kahanoff said that despite the polygamy and slavery, the perception of women in Islam was in some measure commendable because it accepted an important feature of popular feminine morality. Islam does not ignore the sexuality of women, does not regard sex as a sin, and does not see it as merely a means of procreation. Carnal desire is viewed as a hymn to the creator, who gave men and women splendid bodies to be enjoyed. Sexual pleasure is a gift of God, providing it is not indulged in to excess. In contrast to the Christian view that the flesh is shameful, in *One Thousand and One Nights*, Christian girls are attracted to Islam because it regards their womanhood as a sign of God's love and not as a source of sin.[38]

The lessons of *One Thousand and One Nights* are alluded to once more in Kahanoff's article "With the Return to the East." "Like the mothers of sultans and the grandmothers of *One Thousand and One Nights*, she [the traditional Muslim woman] is allowed to use her brain when her beauty and charm are gone."[39] Kahanoff met that traditional Muslim woman when she entered the Damascus Gate immediately after the Six-Day War. She was once again exposed to the scents, sights, and sounds of the Cairo of her childhood and adolescence. Kahanoff indulged in colorful descriptions of "the cymbals of the tamarind-drink seller with his checkered multicolored apron, the bazaar atmosphere, the veiled women emerging from the winding streets,"[40] but shortly afterward she lost her enthusiasm: "I was not, and did not want to be, part of that world, but a modern person belonging to her own century." She now no longer saw the place as picturesque and romantic but merely as poor and backward, a place where children dressed in rags became objects of exoticism.

Arab East Jerusalem was in her opinion a wretched copy of the past. "In that world, petrified by tradition, a revolution must take place, the only valid one—the revolution of modernity—and that will necessarily include women and influence them."[41] Kahanoff had grown up in an Islamic environment. She knew that the situation of women had not changed much, despite all the men's talk about freedom and revolution. Here is a poetic description by Kahanoff of the Arab women in the eastern part of Jerusalem: "Shadowy figures; silent, secretive, as if they had disappeared from the world, and it is possible, indeed, that their strength is all the greater because they are not visible and their intentions are seen and not seen. There are some who look with disfavor at the new vision we offer them."

In the streets of East Jerusalem, Kahanoff discerned the power of the Muslim woman, a power that should not be underestimated. Within her home, she governs the life of the family and her children rely on her. It may be that her power is diminished when she "loses her beauty and charm," as that is the tradition. Generations of subjection to religion—an ideological cover for male imperialism—have made the Muslim woman into a female prisoner. It is a paradox (and here Kahanoff returns to a motif she already mentioned in connection with the Cairo of her youth) that a woman can retain her power in Islamic society on condition that she observes tradition and opposes change. It is an even greater paradox that in Arab-Muslim society there are an increasing number of women who work and study, and also women with political awareness like those who protest against the Israeli occupation. Why are they silent when one speaks of the repression of women in the patriarchal Muslim society? She muses, "What do they think, the women in the villages, resplendent and beautiful in their embroidered dresses? What are their hopes? They are the image of an ancient world which preserves itself with determination, and it may be that, where they are concerned, Israel represents the revolutionary power of modernity."[42]

For the Palestinian women, Israel represents the spirit of change, which does not seem to them such a bad thing. In the early days after the conquest of the Old City, with the masses of Israelis buying in the Arab markets, there was a slight hope among women on both sides that the future would provide some solution. "The women showed a more developed feeling for politics than the men and independently chose a policy of peaceful coexistence,"[43] but the conservative Islamic structure based on men was not made for change. However, it is possible, hoped Kahanoff, that women will be the source of change despite the fact that they are not allowed to express themselves.

On an autumn excursion to the Arab village of Latrun, Kahanoff encountered a group of Palestinian women who were surprised that she spoke Arabic (although a "broken" Arabic) and was born in Egypt, but their "Easternness" as a common denominator between them did not count for anything. It is possible that they and the young Israeli women who emigrated from the Arab countries want to escape from the world of tradition, but the Israeli girls have a horizon of change whereas the Palestinian girls are imprisoned in their patriarchal heritage. Already before 1967, Kahanoff thought that Arab girls wanted to abandon their traditional society for a modern one. A little Arab girl she met in the countryside told her she hated working in the fields and her dream was to become a secretary in Haifa and wear modern clothes. Her family did not allow her to do so, however, and girls like her had no chance of choosing their path in life.

In the excursion to Latrun mentioned above, a "wonderfully beautiful" little Arab girl went around with the Israeli women and, "looking at our skirts, hinted that she had shortened her dress a little and would soon shorten it a bit more."[44] The motif of shortening a dress as a symbol of modernity was repeated by Kahanoff in a passage that has frequently been turned against her: "I once observed that it was a hopeful sign that women's skirts had got shorter in East Jerusalem, so that it is now difficult to distinguish one girl from another by her style of dress. . . . The shortened skirt is perhaps a symbol of cultural change, exactly as happened in Israel with girls of the Mizrahi communities."[45]

In her criticism of Kahanoff's article "With the Return to the East," Dolly Benhabib wrote sarcastically, in a tone that is a sort of parody of Kahanoff, or at any rate sounds like it: "As long as skirts get shorter, all hope is not lost. We can continue to play at shooting and weeping, at girls who shoot and shorten their skirts, at the girl-occupier with the explosive short skirt, an accessory which becomes a symbol of the hoped-for dialog between the occupying Israeli girl and the occupied girl from East Jerusalem."[46] Benhabib thought that in this Kahanoff resembled Ataturk, who in his modernization of Turkey at the beginning of the twentieth century wanted to throw out the red, fez-like men's hat called the *tarbush*. "Can an article of dress really serve as a symbol of cultural change?" she added. One can answer this by saying that Kahanoff at an early stage foresaw the continuation of the existence of radical Islam, with all its consequences for the situation of women, in the nonadoption of modern practices. The rejection of the tarbush and the lifting of the "accessory" of the woman's hijab, or veil, symbolize Islamic democracy in the manner of Erdogan, heir to Ataturk's modern secular republic.

Details like styles of dress can indeed symbolize a society, a culture, or a civilization. The rise of Islamic fundamentalism in Gaza, in towns in the Palestinian Authority, and in other places in the Arab world is reflected in the veil that effaces the humanity of the Muslim woman. Kahanoff came to a definite conclusion: the tradition of protest that is clearly seen in *One Thousand and One Nights* no longer exists for the supporters of Palestinian

BEING A MODERN WOMAN

self-determination. As far as they are concerned, the women can continue to wear long skirts and preferably a hijab. The intellectuals of the Left, said Kahanoff, who defend every national demand, end by defending the most abject and repressed societies: "It is doubtful if it enters their heads that the women in Muslim societies may want their liberation, and if it does not, they are reactionaries who want to impose a backward male imperialism on the feminine half of mankind."[47]

WOMEN NOT FROM HERE

Kahanoff examined the condition of the modern woman and possible solutions to the lack of gender equality. Her conservative feminism excelled at eliminating class and racial divisions. It was a universal feminism that was not at all confrontational, far from provincialism or political or national considerations, and was balanced, like most of the ideas representing that feminism in her articles.

Véronique, a French friend, was an independent woman who was notable for making bold feminist statements ahead of their time. An example: "If we accept the idea that a number of women can live together happily with the same man, the women most conversant with the matter say that it is a slavery imposed by a male imperialism of which colonialism is only a sub-species."[48] What was withheld from her—the capacity to be a writer because she raised five children—was a legacy to her daughter. Véronique's reaction to an article she read about a congress of emancipated African women who called for a ban to be placed on polygamous husbands was to say that African women influenced by western culture now spent their time and money on educating and caring for their children, whereas previously they spent them on potions concocted by a witch doctor. Spreading the task of bringing up children among many women made their self-realization possible.

The process of emancipation of women in Africa was paralleled by the process for Asian women, who were motivated by the dual ideal of women's liberation and national liberation. Kahanoff looked at this struggle described in a book that contained a collection of letters and was published under the auspices of UNESCO.[49] Princess Adjeng Kartini (1879–1904), the daughter of a local Javanese nobleman, wrote these letters at the beginning of the twentieth century (*Letters of a Javanese Princess*); the collection was published in Holland in 1911 thanks to Princess Kartini's friend J. H. Abendanon, the director of children's education in Java. Abendanon promoted a liberal colonialist policy, and thus Kartini, who advocated women's education, became a symbol of children's liberation in Java and the Netherlands. *Letters of a Javanese Princess*, which was translated into many Asiatic languages, led to the founding of the Kartini Foundation and the establishment of a girls' school in Java, and it also had an influence on the Indonesian struggle for independence. Today Kartini's ideas are regarded as conservative because they directed women toward the designated vocational fields of domestic science, bookkeeping, and handicrafts, but these first steps paved the way to women's leadership in Asia.

Kahanoff felt much sympathy for Kartini's attempt, which resembled her own, to bridge two worlds: on the one hand, a revolt against tradition and an attraction to western culture and its values and, on the other hand, an identification with the religious faith and landscape of her homeland. Kartini, although critical of Java's feudal society, was bound by Buddhist mysticism. The letters alternate between a desire for freedom and a sense of failure, between the old and the new, between her Dutch friends and the members of her family. Kahanoff saw her as "fleeing to the shelter of conformity. A small, tragic figure whose story is highly significant because it touches in a decisive way the psychology of people who grow up under the influence of two or more cultures."[50] In a slightly similar situation, Kahanoff's fate was different, but she

BEING A MODERN WOMAN

understood the feelings of Kartini, who stood at a tragic cross-roads. Conservative forces, or, in Kahanoff's words, "frozen and automatic ways of behaving," overcame the young Javanese lady. The transition from an ancient and refined Asiatic culture to modernity was not easy, and it was a long time before it happened. Kahanoff's conclusion was this: "The women fighting in the women's liberation movements are much freer than Kartini ever dreamed of being, but they are nevertheless not contented, for otherwise, why are they protesting?" Kartini lived and died in the prison of her home, yet, despite that, her voice is heard, a feminine voice that passes on an old story from Java.

For a time, Kartini attended a western school run by a western woman, but she was soon taken out and confined to her home. The gate to modern life was locked behind her, and according to Kahanoff, she felt "sentenced to death in a sort of Javanese palace." She went, like others, from her parents' home to that of her appointed husband. Nevertheless, her father allowed her to learn embroidery from the wife of the deputy Dutch governor, a socialist and feminist who had a great influence on Kartini, and through this woman she made the acquaintance of liberal Dutch intellectuals. Although she won a scholarship to study, the pressures from home and her father's bad health proved to be decisive. She returned to her country, very soon adopted a traditional way of life, and married according to her father's wishes. What is interesting about Kahanoff's description is that in writing about Kartini she did not adopt the tone of an all-knowing feminist, and she was able to appreciate Kartini's relative progress, a slow route sometimes involving retreats that many women often have to make.

A more successful Asiatic woman, who also became an author, was Santha Rama Rau (1923–2009), who dramatized E. M. Forster's book *A Passage to India* (1924) for the London theater and Broadway. The stage play also became a film directed by David Lean. Rau was better known among English readers than among her own people, most of whom were poor and uneducated. Like many writers from India, she was connected to her country of birth (her father was the first Indian ambassador to Japan) but preferred to live in the United States. In her book *Remember the House* (1956), the Indian heroine, unlike the author, chose to adhere to her original culture. In her youth, before India's declaration of independence, Rau lived in the highest circles in Bombay, which despite their British appearance had a traditional way of life characterized by self-effacement and acceptance of fate. Although she was uncertain in her youth whether to consent to the bridegroom chosen for her in accordance with the Indian social order, she finally submitted to the old order and made a loveless marriage to a young man of means. Kahanoff saw Santha Rama Rau as an example of a woman who combined eastern traditions with new western elements, attempting to find a common language and attain a cultural equilibrium. She drew an analogy between the Indian writers and the Levantine idea: "And what is Levantinization, really, if not the search for a balance between the ways of life and mentalities of the west and east?"[51]

SIX

BEYOND THE LEVANT

JAPAN

Kahanoff made a long bibliographic journey from the Near East, the location of her Levantine world, to the reading and study of the literature of the Far East, where she encountered worlds unfamiliar to her but close to her heart. In making this journey, she broadened the perspective of her writings and anticipated the era of the backpackers and globe-trotters. She was fascinated by Japanese literature. In a series of articles, she traced its development from the earliest period, where it was chiefly popular in character, consisting of myths, legends, and poetry, to the period after the Second World War, with the suicide of the poet and playwright Yukio Mishima (1925–1970), whom she called "the last samurai."

Kahanoff was also intrigued by the great poetic compendium *Man'yōshū* (Collection of Ten Thousand Leaves), which contains poems reaching back to the eighth century, when Indian Buddhism and Chinese culture began to leave their mark on Japanese thought. Drawing inspiration from nature and the Japanese landscape, these pantheistic poems bespeak human moods and their analogous manifestations in nature.[1]

Between the thirteenth and fifteenth centuries, the Japanese succeeded in fusing the different elements of their culture, and under the influence of the Zen priests and the masters of the tea ceremony, who prized a rustic simplicity, they again drew from their sources in the past. The period was inaugurated by *The Tale of Genji*, by Murasaki Shikibu, the ceremonial name of an unknown authoress who wrote the great work between the years 1000 and 1008. It was the first Japanese novel, in which one of the empress's ladies-in-waiting reported on events in the Imperial Palace in the Heian period. The novel relates the amorous adventures of a Japanese Don Juan—Genji, a youth of seventeen, the heir apparent to the throne. In one story in the novel, Genji hid his identity from a shy girl he fell in love with who lived near his home. The lovers concealed their love, but the girl died of a mysterious illness, and her tragic fate haunted Genji until the day he died. Though the story is a simple one, Kahanoff regarded it as the pivotal moment in the novel, determining the emotional life of its principal protagonists: "There is something ambivalent about them which is never completely resolved or understood. Their motives are not clearly analyzed, but, as in a Zen painting, a number of lines indicate the basic truths about a character. It is a spontaneous and controlled way of seizing the reality of a person."[2]

Women in the Heian period had a special character. In the days when the Imperial Court, with its rites and ceremonies, was established in Kyoto, women flocked to the palace and competed for honors and status. Kahanoff saw a similarity there with the court of Louis XV in eighteenth-century France, and also mentioned, in this connection, the 1678 novel *La princesse de Cleves* (The Princess of Cleves), by Madame de Lafayette, the first French historical novel and "perhaps the best novel written by a woman."[3] Kahanoff commended the novel as characterized by restraint and psychological delicacy; in this respect, it reminded her of Murasaki, who lived in the shogunate period (1192–1867) and was a friend of the Empress.

The Story of the Lady Ochikubo (The Lady in the Basement), written in the tenth century by an unknown author, was employed by Kahanoff as a peg on which to hang her sociological curiosity concerning the imperial regime, the nobility, and the common people in Japan.[4] Ochikubo's stepmother, who mistreated her, forced her to live with a female servant in a basement, where she wrote poems and fell in love with a nobleman who suddenly appeared. Here we have a stereotypical heroine, beautiful, abandoned, who was rescued from her distress by a nobleman who took her away. As in the story of Cinderella, she now lived in wealth and happiness, but the strong realism of the story, mingled with a certain humor, gives this simple story a special flavor. The woman-servant Akogi describes the chief characters in the story as violent and arrogant but also vulnerable. This contrast between their appearance and their real nature makes the tale into a sort of social comedy. For instance, Ochikubo's dying father begged his illustrious son-in-law to obtain for him an elevated rank in the imperial hierarchy so that upon his death he would receive the highest honors. The description of the ceremonial splendor of the funeral, which took place after Ochikubo's father had received his title, is intentionally astounding. According to Kahanoff, this ironic tone turns the legendary tale of the Japanese Cinderella into a social satire in which the middle class observes the aristocracy.

Kahanoff saw a similarity between the medieval theater in Japan—in which drama, wit, and religiosity were combined—and the passion plays of medieval Europe, but the difference, in her opinion, was that in the Japanese plays there were sometimes comic interludes, initially provided by the court jesters, and their pranks gave an element of humor to the ceremonies of the Imperial Court and the Shinto temples. The foolery was accompanied by songs, jugglery, and lively music called "monkey music," and these little acts resembled those of Harlequin and Figaro in Europe. Typical figures in the Japanese theater were the foppish feudal lord, the rural gentleman, the wise servant, and the cowardly samurai. There was a kind of "wild speech" (*kyogen*) in the popular tradition, and writers declared that speech of that kind "should make one laugh without giving rise to vulgarity."

Similarly, Sei Shōnagon (966–1025), whose diary described court life in a lively and intimate way, reminded Kahanoff of one of the famous letter-writers of seventeenth-century France, the Marquise de Sévigné. The Japanese court described by Sei, characterized by wild festivities, intrigues, and a dubious morality, reminded her of the court of the "sun king" (*Roi Soleil*), Louis XIV. She made an analogy between this epithet and the emperor of Japan, who according to tradition was a descendant of the sun goddess—goddess of the "land of the rising sun." She described Shōnagon's writing as being like a "flowing brush-stroke." One should remember that in Japan, as in China, the script is pictorial, and calligraphy was the art considered closest to painting. The form of Sei's book was unconventional: in her system, she recorded series of things connected to her thoughts or feelings, like a number of anecdotes involving religious festivals connected with the Japanese calendar, or anecdotes involving court ceremonies or excursions in nature. Shōnagon was perspicacious and outspoken, and she gave an amusing description of people of the court who performed an imperial ballet so that they could be seen. She remained loyal to the Empress Sadako after the palace coup in which she was deposed. Sei displayed humor, wisdom, and even depth. Kahanoff thought that "much of the vitality and scintillating beauty of her admirable style is no doubt lost in translation, but enough remains for us to show appreciation, to raise a smile and to consider what this extraordinary woman has to tell us about all kinds of subjects."[5]

The Pillow Book of Sei Shōnagon, a diary from the beginning of the tenth century that can be read with pleasure even today, is made up of perceptive glances at situations in the Imperial Court, expressed in a style of poetic charm. *The Pillow Book* contains descriptions of many contemporary people, objects, and letters, and is a diarylike "blog," recording in no particular order, for instance, contemptuous views of the lower classes. Shōnagon touches on everything, from galloping horsemen, to exchanges of letters, to pouring rain.

The beginning of Japan's Heian period (the first part of the classical period, 794–1185) closely resembled the Meiji period (the time of "Enlightened Rule," 1868–1912), when the encounter under Emperor Mutsuhito with western civilization inaugurated a major outpouring of creativity in all spheres. Kahanoff boldly asserted that the encounter of east and west in the Meiji period had the same qualities of fertility and plenitude as the meeting of the cultures of the east and the west in the Levant.

In Kahanoff's time, hardly any Japanese literature had appeared in Hebrew apart from an anthology of modern Japanese stories issued by the publishing house "Am Sofer" and a couple of novels published by "Am Oved." She claimed that Japanese literature was worthy of the attention of the Israeli reading public, for it was "fascinating, with a continuous development for hundreds of years, and it had a wide variety of genres. Without being by any means an expert in the subject, I have long been fascinated by Japanese literature because of its inner beauty and special feelings, different from those of European literature, and also because of some remarkable similarities with products of European literature of roughly the same periods."[6]

Japanese literature, like its European counterpart, had a continuous development from its original popular and religious sources, producing folktales and plays, poetry and novels. Kahanoff found an interesting parallel between Buddhist and Christian influences. Just as Christianity spread in Europe and took various peoples under its wing, so Buddhism spread throughout Asia. Both religions experienced divisions into various sects. Japan developed the school of Zen Buddhism, and monastic orders were founded in Europe. Rituals, festivities, and men of religion brought civilization and joy to the feudal societies of both cultures. There were comic characters in Japan just as the Grand Guignol and the commedia dell'arte existed in France and Italy. Japan absorbed not only Indian Buddhism but also Chinese culture and writing, as is shown by the fact that Japanese poets in the Heian period wrote poetry in Chinese. Kahanoff also found a similarity between the Chinese model that fashioned Japanese culture and the role played by the Latin language in Europe.

In the modern period, Japanese literature often had an existentialist character. Kahanoff saw a similarity between the relationship of certain Japanese authors—Yukio Mushima, for instance—to the Buddhist or Shintoist tradition, and the relationship of Sartre and Camus to Christianity. These postwar writers, in Japan as in Europe, expressed the absurdity and anxiety of the modern world. Their view of the world was based not on faith but on a despair resulting from a collapse of values—values that had once been dear to them. One cannot fully understand Sartre's thinking without a knowledge of the Christian context he rebelled against, and similarly one cannot appreciate Mishima without taking into account the Zen tradition that pervaded his work and outlook. The reactionary Mishima and the revolutionary Sartre are two facets of the same post–Second World War skepticism.[7]

In many ways, the history of modern Japan bears more resemblance to that of the western countries than to that of any other Asiatic people, and because they were an island people, the Japanese achieved national unity at an early period. Until the Second World War, no European power succeeded in conquering Japan, which even defeated czarist Russia. Japan was the first Asian country to embark on a large-scale industrialization, and it embraced an abominable form of imperialism and an extreme nationalism that made it an ally of Nazi Germany. After its defeat, it concentrated, like Germany, on the rehabilitation of its economy and the democratization of its national institutions. It is significant, Kahanoff claimed, that Japan took its place in the modern world not as a satellite of the European powers, but as a competitor. A hundred years before most of the Asian peoples developed industry or liberated themselves from European colonialism, the Japanese were sufficiently flexible and enterprising to be able to adapt to the world after Hiroshima.

Mishima, an outstanding writer and an extraordinary personality, chose to end his life at the age of forty-five by hara-kiri or seppuku, an ancient custom of the samurai, the warrior class of feudal Japan. This awesome form of death included Mishima disemboweling himself, followed immediately by his beheading by a friend. Nowadays, his extreme right-wing views are dismissed as having no political significance, but his suicide had a sensational symbolic impact, which Mishima intended. He wished to remind his people that Japan was more than a country that manufactured cars, cameras, and tape recorders, and its culture could not be evaluated solely in terms of material wealth. He warned that if the Japanese embraced the new affluence, they were liable to lose their particular culture, their souls. While Kahanoff saw him as belonging to the reactionary right in Japan, she pointed out that Dostoevsky, Gogol, and Tolstoy were not liberals either. Each in his own way rejected the westernization of his country, just as Mishima opposed the Americanization of Japan. The cultural influence of Russian authors like Pasternak and Solzhenitsyn was tremendous despite the communist ideology that prevailed in their time. From this Kahanoff concluded that the power of a writer is different in kind from the power of a party leader: "It would be strange to confuse political positions with cultural influence."[8]

A samurai's suicide is said to be an act of great significance for the Japanese. Hara-kiri is one of the traditional subjects of Japanese painting: old prints show the lofty status of the man committing suicide by his ceremonial costume and the ritual pose he adopts, and by his distorted, spellbound face; they express an inner truth that realism cannot convey. That is how Kahanoff understood the effects of Mishima's suicide. In support of her argument, she quoted the statement by Herbert Marcuse, in his book *One-Dimensional Man*, that one of the means by which the technological society dominates people is by reducing an action perfect in attractiveness, beauty, and truth to a series of ascertainable facts, a reduction that negates its symbolic significance. Thus, Mishima was depicted as crazy, although he was not. He was really an aristocrat impregnated with the culture of Japan, permeated with the philosophy and sensitivities of Zen Buddhism. As a creative individual obsessed with noble actions and thoughts of self-immolation, and as a writer with modern perceptions, he wanted to put his ideas into practice. As Kahanoff added ironically, "And without any help from Sartre or Heidegger, he was a Japanese-style existentialist and nihilist."[9]

Mishima wrote so provocatively on Japan and on the Japanese condition, said Kahanoff, that he gave the impression he was the person in the Japanese prints. These prints were produced by an artist so eager to know the essence of beauty that that very beauty became destructive. Mishima's novel *The Temple of the Golden Pavilion* (1956) was about an object of tremendous beauty, a beauty destroyed because someone understood its magical power to be an affirmation of destruction, an affirmation so integral to beauty that it was disconnected from life. The story was based on a real incident that took place in 1950 when a young Buddhist acolyte called Mizoguchi set fire to the Kinkahu-ji, a beautiful pavilion near Kyoto.

This story made Mishima reflect on the person of the young Mizoguchi, the son of a poor village priest, an ugly, stammering youth whose stammer kept him away from other people. Closed in on himself, he dreamed of the destruction of those who laughed at him, and of the time he would be a great artist who created eternal beauty like that of the golden pavilion his father had told him about. His father took him to see this pavilion, and Kahanoff gave a fine description of "the ancient green and gray beams smeared with gold, the delicate symmetry of the tiled roofs, the palm-tree rising up into the heavens, and all this reflected in the shining waters of the small pool beneath." The youth was disappointed because he did not feel the special quality of the beauty, but eventually he became obsessed with the pavilion, and this obsession cut him off from life.

Mishima was by no means advocating a return to ancient Japan and Zen Buddhist monasticism. Far from it: the unfortunate Mizoguchi embodied the decay of Zen Buddhism and its lack of relevance. On the day Japan surrendered to Allied forces in the Second World War, the head of a monastery told his students the story of a cat that he had killed because the monks quarreled over it. Mishima's pessimism reflected the state of depression felt in Japan following the country's defeat, a defeat accompanied by much disillusionment and the doubting of many assumptions of Japanese culture. His descriptions are "Japanese" in that they are delicate and poetic. The Golden Pavilion is described with its dark chambers reflected in the pool, illuminated by the light of the sun and moon. This description is a preliminary stage for the development of Mizoguchi's act of destruction. Mishima was capable of describing, in accordance with the laws of Japanese aesthetics, a bee entering the heart of a yellow chrysanthemum, a dark and stormy day, or water lilies in a pond. When *The Temple of the Golden Pavilion* appeared after the war, it was purchased by more than four million readers, proof of the closeness the Japanese felt to this sensitive author.

Japan overcame its defeat, and Mishima, according to Kahanoff, "succeeded in expressing the mystery of a life based on nothing."[10] In other words, creation and destruction were seen as changing forms of an unchanging universal order or disorder. "Thus, Mizogushi destroyed the Golden Pavilion in the hope that this would give him life, and Mishima killed himself in order that the Golden Pavilion and what it represented could continue to exist in all their splendor. Mishima may have yielded to the forces of destruction that possessed him, but he chose to destroy himself rather than destroy the beauty he loved." In Japan, which respects the values of the past, the Golden Pavilion was rebuilt. Kahanoff concluded that Mishima similarly wished to embody his image of beauty. He knew how easily the tragic can degenerate into the ridiculous, and perhaps it was precisely for that reason, she suggested with a touch of romantic regret, that he abandoned a hopeless enterprise and died heroically and honorably like the last of the samurai.

Kahanoff touched briefly on mid-twentieth-century Japanese literature, seeing it as "a stormy, living, vibrating image of contemporary Japan, Japan after the war, its people and literature."[11] She also discussed its affinities, its nature, and its position between east and west in their historical context. From the beginning of the seventeenth century, Japan adopted an isolationist policy under the rule of the shoguns, the rulers who united the feudal aristocracy of the various provinces. In 1853, when the United States sent its fleet to compel the shogunate government to open the ports of the country to trade with the west, the Japanese were confronted for the first time with the power of a western country. Japan became a modern country, and its people willingly accepted this far-reaching change in their lives. The Japanese did not call industrialization a revolution but a "renewal." This development naturally affected culture and literature, and the gates of the country were opened wide to western influences. Japan is the only non-European country in which industrialization and the influence of western culture have been active for more than 150 years. "The fusion of east and west has been unusually successful there," wrote Kahanoff.

In Kahanoff's opinion, an anthology of stories she reviewed represented the spirit of modern Japan despite the western influences. For instance, in the story "Nightingale" by Einosuki Ito, there is an entertaining and tragic description of people going to a police station to relate their troubles; the story "Machine," by Riichi Yokomitsu, describes the relationships of workers in a workshop; in "A Letter Found in a Cement Barrel" by Hayama Yoshiki, a letter by a female worker relates how her boyfriend fell into the stone cement-crusher in a cement factory. The girl wrote, "I did not have time to realize how much he loved me . . . , and now I am sewing him a shroud—no, I'm really sewing up a sack of cement."[12] According to Kahanoff, the stories of the war period were exemplified in "The Idiot," by Ango Sakaguchi, "which reflects the atmosphere of gloom and nausea of the war years, the absurdity and lack of purpose, in a style resembling that of Camus and Sartre." She said that other stories interpreted the Japanese aristocratic tradition in modern psychological terms. With a mixture of violence and delicacy, impulse and fatalism, the foreign reader is presented with human types of a special Japanese kind.

INDIA

Yukio Mishima and Mahatma Gandhi (1869–1948) are national heroes of two Asiatic countries. The first, the major Japanese writer of the twentieth century, maintained a small private militia and promoted an aestheticization of violence. The second, the leader of modern India, stood by the principle of nonviolence in leading his people's struggle to gain independence from Britain. Despite Kahanoff's literary appreciation of Mishima, she saw how, in his case, a heroic ethos could be subject to a poetic manipulation. With regard to the leader of the Indian independence movement, who began his political life in South Africa, this is how she felt about him when she was still a teenage girl in Egypt:

> Gandhi was the hero of my adolescent years. I snapped up the English-language newspaper *The Egyptian Gazette* in order to read about him every time he began a hunger strike or was

248   JACQUELINE KAHANOFF

imprisoned. I prayed for him with great fervor, and I was convinced that the prayer would reach him and give him whatever he
needed for his struggle against the British. I made little sacrifices
for him like not eating sweets and not eating dessert after meals.
In Egypt in the nineteen-thirties, there was something wonderfully appealing about the photograph of this little brown-skinned
man with the protruding ears mounting the steps of the British
governor of New Delhi on his way to negotiate with him. Gandhi
was the great symbol of the victory of the poor, ignorant, oppressed colored peoples over the proud white man who ruled
over them. . . . It was all we could do not to make him into a
tortured saint, the local British said with a certain bitterness, as if
that was not what mattered, but that was precisely what mattered!
Passive resistance, non-violence forced the British to withdraw in
the face of a mass of unarmed children.[13]

When writing reviews of two articles on Gandhi and India by
two authors of Indian origin whom she admired—Ved Mehta
and V. S. Naipaul—she used her reviews as an occasion to sketch
a portrait of Gandhi as she saw him. In slightly exaggerated terms,
she wrote that "this ugly, feeble little man, brown as a nut, clad
in a *dhoti*, represents the power of those who succeeded in rising
against that empire, forcing it to withdraw." That "holy man,"
she believed, had something to say to every man and woman
in the east and west, to the various Indian castes, to the British
and the Muslims, the Christians and the Jews, to idealists and
to decent people who believed in the brotherhood of man. But,
in Kahanoff's opinion, the Mahatma had failed. The prophet of
nonviolence was killed by a Hindu fanatic, and then India and
Pakistan engaged in mutual bloodshed. His vision dissipated in
a fog of war, terror, and violence, and the collective memory of
him became an idolatry. Despite his failings, which were human,
all too human, Gandhi remains "one of the few political leaders
and social reformers who, at least for a certain time, did not shed
blood in order to achieve their ends." When there was violence in
India, Gandhi would fast and pray. What other leader in the east

or west would in such a situation think of prayer and repentance? Despite his many mistakes, Gandhi had an aura of sanctity. "Is that a thing of no consequence?"[14]

In her reviews of the essays by Mehta and Naipaul she discussed, regarding Mehta's essay, the significance of Gandhi in the sad context of India in the days of Indira Gandhi (1917–1984) and, regarding Naipaul's essay, the significance of Gandhi in relation to the impaired Indian civilization caught between the need to solve its perhaps insoluble problems and the desire to honor its past. Both Mehta and Naipaul went to prestigious British and American universities, knew the world, and wrote their books in English. They sometimes returned to India and looked at their former homeland with a critical and sympathetic eye. They both belonged and did not belong, and their point of view was therefore complex: they saw India from the inside as Indians and from the outside as westerners. This dual vision prevented them from adopting the apologetic and sentimental approach of a local patriot, but it also prevented them from making India the object of harsh criticism and self-hatred.

The historian and essayist Ved Mehta (1934–2021) wrote a great deal about contemporary thought and about western historians and theologians. His essay on Gandhi, the product of a visit to India and careful research, is an outstanding historiographical portrait. It describes Gandhi's slow development and insecurity as a law student in England, the courage and political astuteness he displayed in South Africa in his fight for the rights of the Indian settlers, his return to India and his laying of a path to Indian independence, his hunger strikes and imprisonments, his murder by one of his people, and his beatific death. It is far from an idealizing portrait, but it is one that does not hold him up to ridicule. What impressed Kahanoff was the depiction of the character traits and actions of a leader who was not one-dimensional, a depiction that did not hide contradictions such as the discrepancy between his ideals and his practice of political realism, and between his true nature and his self-image as a saint. His belief that one could attain sanctity through self-mortification did not prevent him from surrounding himself in his old age with young female disciples.

Kahanoff critically assessed Gandhi's legacy: his obsession with cleanliness, for instance, which was to influence the modern approach to hygiene in Indian villages; his constant preoccupation with diet and with bowel movements, with vegetarianism, with taking baths, and with massaging with oil; his "craziness" in playing with children; his "insensitive, possessive" treatment of his wife; his intolerant attitude to his eldest son. One also finds in Gandhi an incompatibility between his abstinent image and his journeys throughout India, which cost a huge sum that was underwritten by wealthy Indians. While he advocated dressing in a few simple clothes, he was supported by a textile tycoon who lived in affluence on a magnificent estate. When Ved Mehta interviewed this millionaire in his old age, the man described a visit to the factories he managed in which the workers inhaled a thick layer of dust and in the evening returned to their broken-down huts.

Kahanoff did not have a self-righteous attitude toward Gandhi, and she understood that "Indian life is permeated with the Hindu version of Buddhism which links the caste-system to belief in reincarnation. The believers have the idea that the members of the lower castes have been reborn in a subhuman state because of their sins in a previous incarnation. It is a kind of purgatory, a furnace of purification of the soul before one goes to paradise where one's sins are judged. In this world, one has to work for the redemption of one's soul and ensure its status in the next world." Kahanoff thought that Gandhi never believed that these depths of degradation and situations of dire poverty were preordained. He mobilized resources to finance his movement, and Kahanoff believed he had to compromise his principles for that purpose. The dilemma Gandhi faced was whether he should remain unknown or should create a financial foundation that would enable him to act. Despite Gandhi's personal failings, Kahanoff thought that the movement he founded was impressive and certainly less corrupt than the political movements founded by the Congress Party of India or other modern Indian organizations.[15]

Her forgiving attitude to the personal conduct of this great leader is seen in her explanation of his sexual behavior in old age: "It is possible that this old man, seeing the failure of his vision when India was submerged in a bloodbath after its declaration of independence, needed any consolation he could get, just as King David needed the caring attention of Abishag in circumstances less tragic than those of Gandhi." She felt that Gandhi's weaknesses enhanced his image, and revealed his humanity in all its greatness and flawed sainthood. She declared that the Mahatma was "human, all too human," as Nietzsche would surely have put it: an extraordinary man who became the living symbol of India.

Kahanoff's discussion of Japanese tradition, of the skin color of the Indians, of the slanting eyes of the Chinese, and of European culture led her to reflect on the diversity of mankind, and to ask this: "If man is the crowning glory of creation, why are human beings different in color, and why do these colors appear to symbolize the different values that humans ascribe to their neighbors?"[16] She wanted to find the reason for the inconsistency between the deep religious impulse that gives a common divine origin to all men and the human need to justify prejudice and explain inequality. People in different countries told themselves many stories connected with the color of their skin. She related some of them and, as was her custom, made philosophical observations on the nature of the human race.

Santha Rama Rau (1923–2009) was an Indian writer and journalist. Among her writings were travel books that contained autobiographical elements revealing a clash between the western tradition and the Indian tradition. She is also known for her successful 1960 film adaptation of E. M. Forster's novel *A Passage to India.* In her book *This Is India* (1954), she described how the Naga, an Indian mountain tribe, explain the origin of human skin color. According to the Naga, God created man out of dough, put the dough in an oven to bake, and took it out too early. That is how the first white man was made. On another occasion, God left the dough in the oven too long and it came out burnt, and that is how the black man came into being. Having learned from experience, God put the dough in the oven a third time, and on taking it out saw that it was the correct brown color. That is how the Indian, the perfect man, was made.

Nirad Chaudhuri (1897–1999) was a writer and author from Bangladesh. His book *The Autobiography of an Unknown Indian* recounts a number of episodes from his childhood in which attempts were made to explain why the British were light-skinned.[17] To the astonishment of the other children, one child said that originally all children were born dark, but the British fathers cooked the babies in wine to make them white. They used pitchforks to put them in the vat, and if the baby did not turn white, the father stuck the pitchfork in his throat and killed him. In this episode, Chaudhuri linked the question of color to the anger of the subject populations at the prejudices of the white colonialists. He saw this anger as the emotional reaction of the Hindu deeply connected to Indian history. When the light-skinned Aryans invaded India, they subjugated the dark-skinned inhabitants. The Aryans made color into a criterion for the organization of Indian society and created a caste system to prevent an admixture with the color of the darker race. Chaudhuri observed that to people as proud of their race and color as the members of the Indian upper castes, the domination of the white Europeans was seen as insulting. Kahanoff mused that when one considers the fact that discrimination has very often accompanied colonialism, one can only wonder at the persistence of racial prejudice among peoples like the Hindus and the Europeans, who created great civilizations.

AFRICA

In a short article titled "Where Does One Get the Color of One's Skin?" Kahanoff declared that the Africans also believe that initially all humans were black.[18] In Gabon there is a story about a hunter who chased an animal until it was caught in a place far from his village. He was thirsty and drank water from a spring and washed his body with it. Every place where the water touched his body turned white. He liked the color, washed his whole body with the water, and became the first white man. He told the people he met about it, and they too washed themselves in the spring and turned white. The masses of people who came to the spring finally found little water, and only with great difficulty succeeded in removing a little of the black color. That is why there are people with different shades of brown, from the lightest to the darkest. The last to arrive found only a little muddy water, with which they washed the tips of their fingers and toes. That is why the Africans have remained black apart from the tips of their fingers and toes.

In her article, Kahanoff referred to Sartre's essay on African poetry, in which he speaks of the emotional ambiguity produced by the juxtaposition of western and African concepts of color.[19] In the French schools, African children were read stories about people whose souls are white as snow or black as coal—similes natural to the Europeans. Kahanoff said that until they came into contact with Europeans, it had not been usual for Africans to associate the idea that light color is good and dark color is bad with skin color. As a result, the Africans and American Blacks have many stories about the incongruity of black souls in white bodies and white souls in black bodies.

In the collection *African Stories*, Kahanoff saw an opportunity "to penetrate a little into the soul of the awakening continent."[20] The stories in this publication represent a few examples of the rich literature of sub-Saharan Africa and reveal the roots of its culture. She thought that to be acquainted with this new African literature was to discover a continent and a world. In the past, the explorers of those lands followed the paths of the great rivers and "tore that continent to shreds," but by the 1960s it was possible to discover the actual people living in Africa. Like the sound of tom-toms going from huts to the towns and the bustling new ports, these voices assail the western world from every side. The removal of the veil of ignorance that previously existed between the west and the many peoples of Africa permits us "to hear the voices weeping over the afflictions of the past, raging with anger, singing songs of hope, and then, in joyful rebellion, demanding their share in human culture."

In the United States and the islands of the Caribbean, African voices have again been heard after silence descended on the continent when the great bass drums stopped, as the Liberian poet H. Carey Thomas put it. Black Americans lived in very close contact with western culture, but many of them felt that it was no longer their objective "to prove their intellectual abilities in the court of white society." They began to draw on African sources while using the languages and literary forms of the surrounding societies. They expressed their special feelings in terms of their Black heritage.

The writer and civil rights activist W. E. B. Du Bois (1868–1963) wished that everyone could have an ambiguous identity so that one could be Black and American at the same time. Kahanoff proposed substituting the word *white* or *western* for the word *American* in Du Bois's statement and, in that way, describing the nature of contemporary African literature. The new African writers do not want to reject the positive values and universality of western culture, but they are also unwilling to abandon the legacy of their ancestors and their emotional world.

Kahanoff warmly observed that many Africans were immigrating to Europe: the colonization of yesterday has become an immigration to the mother country, as if to say, "Once you came to us, now we come to you." France, said Kahanoff, is the most racially open country in the world, but it must integrate the hundreds and thousands of immigrants and refugees properly so that the American tragedy with regard to the Blacks will not be repeated there. In France in the 1950s, the time during which Kahanoff observed it, there were hundreds of thousands of Muslims, Algerians, and Africans living on the edges of the dominant culture of the host country. In her opinion, they suffered from a lack of technological skills due to the failure to integrate them into the modern world. In a journey by bus from Marseilles to Aix-en-Provence, she heard a young boy whisper to a friend, "Do you see that apartment block? Not a single Frenchman lives there!" A group of Black youths in the bus were mistreating a child, an incident that prompted a Frenchwoman to say to her husband, "Just imagine what kind of citizens they will be in twenty years' time!"

In Aix, Kahanoff saw huge apartment blocks, and next to the railway station she spied a row of cafés in which most of the waiters were African. In the streets of the old town, groups of young people wandered about aimlessly, and one square was filled with Muslim youths. These manifestations reached a climax in Marseilles, where a large concentration of non-European immigrants could be found next to the port and by the Saint-Charles railway station. At the port, there were stevedores, dockworkers, street cleaners, and garbage collectors, all of them new immigrants of foreign origin who were needed for work requiring physical strength.

Kahanoff thought that the tragedy of the colonialist situation, and especially of the postcolonialist situation, is that "the native receives only part of the culture of the settler, and that diminishes his already limited capacity for action." The colonized do not think of having an identity of their own with social and political institutions that reflect their collective will. Racism creates a "colored" subproletariat both in undeveloped countries and in developed, industrialized ones. While Kahanoff firmly believed that the cultural and technological backwardness could be overcome, she hoped that the price for it would not be the further weakening of the collective and personal identity of the immigrants. She feared that the colonialist situation had not disappeared but had merely been transferred to the heart of the empire.

In reviewing Charles V. Hamilton's *Black Power: The Politics of Liberation in America* (1967),[21] Kahanoff quoted Stokeley Carmichael and Charles Hamilton, leaders of the Black Power movement, who claimed that white groups tended to form a single block in their fear of Black racism. First of all, Kahanoff thought that one should distinguish between racism and collective identity. Second, human groups have "complex, constantly changing identities which include language, history, memories of the past, various cultural influences, religion, race, moving from one area to another." People are divided into individuals, ethnic groups, and cultural units. Her conclusion was that one can go from a hegemony to a symphony in which performers on many different instruments create a symphonic whole.

Kahanoff added that the Industrial Revolution and colonialism were based in the nineteenth century, fired by a belief in infinite progress. Europe, which created a surplus from the conquest of new countries and the domination of old ones, did not take into account the rights of native populations. Technically advanced peoples gave other peoples an inferior status, seized the riches of the world, and not only denied others their basic rights but depleted the world's resources. Paradoxically, the possibilities of the Industrial Revolution were used to destroy the supply of food that people had in their natural environment and to upset the balance between man and nature that protected the subsistence of both man and beast. Competing ideologies dominated the masses and destroyed their adversaries or attempted to reduce them to a subhuman condition.

Against the background of what Kahanoff called the "regimented humanity" that exists in a world ever more depleted of space and resources, many writers in the second half of the twentieth century emphasized human freedom. They declared that man will be free only if he recognizes his dependence on nature, and if he recognizes the rights of others, including animals, to enjoy their place in the universe. Han Suyin (1917–2012) set forth this problematic in her somber story "The Sparrow Shall Fall," in which she described how in Peking a war was waged on sparrows, the birds that ate the grains that were an essential food for the population. She also described the millions of cows in India that have no pasture while millions of people die of starvation, and she ended with this question: Is it necessary for one species or another to remain alive, for sparrows to fall in order that man may live, or that in Asia one always has to decide between one species and another?

In his novel *Les racines du ciel* (The Roots of Heaven), Romain Gary (1914–1980) depicts the elephant as a symbol of freedom. Elephants are described as proud, moving in the depths of a forest, while safari hunters in armored cars hunt and slaughter them for the purpose of making ashtrays from their ivory. A French underground fighter declares war on the elephant-killers because they deny the right of every creature to life. As against this, the son of a former tribal chieftain, a member of the French parliament, who regards the elephant as a symbol of African nationalism, is ready to kill elephants and even many members of his own people to attain his national objectives. This question of the mutual relationship of man and nature was also discussed by Kahanoff in her review of the book *Apologies to the Iroquois* by the American author Edmund Wilson (1895–1972), who condemned the "rapacious civilization" of the white man for its treatment of the American Indians who still remained.[22] He took as an example the white Americans' appropriation of the Indian reservations in the state of New York, an area whose population shrank in two centuries from eighteen million to seventy-eight thousand people. Wilson supported his criticism with texts and descriptions of the leaders, legends, and beliefs of the Indians, reflecting their identification with nature in contrast to the destructive approach of the authorities.

Kahanoff's anthropological interest led her to study the internal grammar of Muslim theology and to discern how the principles of Islam were similar to and different from those of Judaism and Christianity. In the Muslim community, there is an aspiration to unity expressed in an uncompromising faith, a common language, a sacred literature, and a network of ordinances covering all areas of life. The *haj*, the pilgrimage to Mecca, strengthens this unity through companionship and the arrangements for lodging and sanitation. The Muslim leaders meeting in Mecca prepare political campaigns for the glorification of Islam and, Kahanoff adds, "for the greater vexation of the western imperialists and the State of Israel." For Muslim believers, religious faith, law, politics, and national sentiment are not separate categories but different aspects of the will of the One God. The political preaching in the mosques generally mixes these areas together. This lack of separation makes innovation and reform difficult, and new interpretations are rarely accepted. An example of this nonacceptance is that of the innovation of Habib Bourguiba, the first president of Tunisia, himself a great expert in this sphere, who asserted that one need not fast on Ramadan because, with the founding of the republic, Tunisia waged a jihad against the greatest apostasy of all: backwardness.

Many articles that have been written on the subject of decolonization have quoted the assertion of the Algerian writer Malek Bennabi (1905–1973) that to carry out the colonization of a place, the place has to be suitable.[23] A fatalistic and uncritical acceptance of tradition created a stagnation that was a suitable condition for colonization, which was furthered by the many divisions in the tribal Muslim society. These divisions among the Arabs and Muslims often made them look for a scapegoat. A disregard of moral prohibitions is very destructive for any religion, including Islam. Kahanoff quoted an article by an Armenian priest who accused the "Young Turks" of the murder of a million Armenians and compared this massacre to Hitler's murder of the Jews. She thought that the megalomania of the Young Turks served as a model for a generation of "Pan-Islamist" fanatics, and, she added, "Father Masirian was not wrong when he saw this national madness as a crime against humanity, whether its perpetrators were Christian Nazis or Muslim pashas." In her opinion, the time had come to pass judgment on both the colonialists and "the liberators from colonialism who often show a tendency to become imperialist colonialists themselves." Kahanoff was not afraid to leave the anthropological ivory tower and adopt a normative position toward the subject under discussion.

Kahanoff adopted a normative position, this time positive, toward the Jewish communities that lived for two thousand years among the Berber tribes in southern Morocco. She based herself on the 1959 book by Pierre Flamand, *Diaspora en terre d'Islam: Les communautés Israëlites du Sud Marocain* (The Diaspora in the Lands of Islam: The Jewish Communities in Southern Morocco).[24] Flamand was an inspector in the French Ministry of Education, and he provided testimonies, photographs, stories, and proverbs concerning the life of these southern Jews. The photographs show craftsmen at work in the markets, patriarchal rabbis and holy sites, amulets for the protection of babies, and scenes of lessons in the sacred tongue for pupils in the *heder* (religious primary school). There are also legends from the days when the little Jewish-Berber kingdoms succeeded in warding off the Berber tribes that had converted to Islam. Within the limited possibilities they had available in their geographical, cultural, and economic environment, the Jews always adapted themselves to the ways of their hosts. One of the negative characteristics of the Jewish communities was an extreme conformism, which was a means of survival in conditions of great adversity. Kahanoff's description is full of compassion for her people: "The communities were too poor and remote to provide their children with more than scraps of Jewish education, and their cultural life was restricted to the repetition of the same *piyyutim* (liturgical poems), the same customs, the same thoughts, until they became used to always doing the same thing."[25] The changes introduced by French colonialism that made the special professions followed by the Jews redundant, and the awakening of nationalism, among both Muslim Arabs and Zionist Jews, hastened the disintegration of these Jewish communities.

EUROPE: ITALY AND PORTUGAL

Kahanoff did not break her ties with Europe, the continent she loved. She returned to the places of her youth, cities on the shores of the Mediterranean that she first visited as a girl. She and her friends "sailed from Alexandria and disembarked in Naples, Genoa or Marseilles, and sat in a café until it was time for the train to leave. In childhood, I always liked to explore and get to know new places, but father and mother couldn't bear the thought that we would miss the train (as if there would be no others, I thought to myself). We had reserved seats, and in the days when the Italian trains were known for their frequent delays, father thought that our particular train would come on time."[26] Above all, she loved Europe in the autumn, because at that time friends and relatives returned from their summer vacations. In the end, she nearly always reached the places where the people she loved, and who loved her sufficiently to receive her, were to be found: "I had reached the stage in my life when the people I longed to see were more important to me than landscapes and monuments."[27] In autumn, she wrote, one feels the pulse of the earth, "and I would say that in Italy the pulse is rapid and irregular."

On her way to Naples, she stopped in Rome and wandered around in the streets near the Roma Terminal Station. The sight depressed her, the street was badly lit: the Roman municipality saved money on electricity. She also found the people in the

BEYOND THE LEVANT

streets and espresso bars depressing. Youths in trendy clothes and some well-dressed elderly people were milling around. There were a few prostitutes, chiefly male ones. She grabbed her handbag and waited impatiently for the train. Most Italians had a negative opinion of Rome, and the inhabitants of the city thought it parasitic, a city-not-a-city that had grown up because it was the seat of the government and the Vatican. As a result of Rome's dual governmental profile, there were two kinds of diplomatic representation and two forms of social life, which gave it a cosmopolitan character of a world-in-itself. Rome was also the center of the film industry, but the Italians liked to say that Visconti was a Milanese and Fellini came from Ravenna.[28]

At the time she was in Rome, the film director Piero Pasolini (1922–1975) was murdered, a violent death that stunned Italy. There were rumors of neofascist aggression against the Marxist director, and about his habit of "ambushing" youths from the suburbs or from the Roma Terminal Station area. "As the story came out of his cruel murder by a youth who had been captured, it was hard to see [Pasolini] as someone solely motivated by social justice, the victim of a fascist conspiracy." At the same period, youths from the well-to-do areas of Rome seduced working-class girls and tortured them to death. She thought that this aggressiveness of Pasolini and the youths transcended their political orientations and reflected the mood in Italy at the time she was there. An economic crisis gave rise to a social crisis that led thousands of young people to break with the traditional frameworks of family, school, and church.

Despite all the violence, the young Kahanoff had the impression that the Italians were much more likable, honest, and considerate than their counterparts elsewhere. She chatted in Italian with the travelers in second-class carriages of the trains, and it never happened that the people next to her did not offer her food or drink from their provisions. "They said: 'Would you be so kind as to accept this?' when it was really *they* who were treating *me*."

She considered the Italians a generous people who behaved politely to one another and almost never spoke aggressively to each other. "They have sufficient culture to know that, while life is full of troubles, little acts of generosity, little shared pleasures are what make it tolerable and sometimes even agreeable for yourself and your neighbor."[29]

She always loved Naples. Despite its pollution, disorder, poverty, and congestion, it had a nobility, beauty, color, and kind of extravagance all its own. Naples, she wrote, was the capital of the Kingdom of Naples and the Two Sicilies under the Spanish Bourbons. There are many royal palaces in the city, and, judging by the number of visitors, it seemed to Kahanoff that the people of Naples were proud of the lavishness of their rulers. Dozens of brides were photographed with their partners and families in the rooms and gardens of the palaces. Her cousin Miriam told her that the people of Naples had lived for long periods under the occupation of one country or another and were always defeated and exploited—so that they came to believe that they could never be victorious. Although the folk hero got a bad name because of the favors he received from the Spanish authorities he rebelled against, the Neapolitans knew that they would act in the same way as he did if they had the opportunity. Miriam said that "the people of Naples seem light-headed and superficial only because they have been in deep despair and do not believe that their condition can ever improve. But they have a style, they have imagination."[30]

"How beautiful the Italian cities are!" wrote Kahanoff. Her visit to Florence did not prompt her to write a conventional description of the city. Rather, she saw Florence from a special, personal perspective, with the marble stripes of the cathedral and the Duomo glistening under a thin veil of mingled sun and rain. Her description included the variegated texture of the tiled roofs, the wooden Ponte Vecchio over the River Arno, and the choicest paintings in the galleries. She appreciated the fine craftsmanship of the objects in the shop windows. The dominant color was gray: there were elegant women's costumes in pearl gray, dove gray, steel gray, shoes and gumboots in gray suede, gray leather wallets, gray skirts, coats, hats, umbrellas. "This delicate gray seemed to reflect the sober mood of Italy, but it was a sobriety of a most subtle and exclusive kind." In her opinion, there was a class dimension to this subtle and elegant symphony of gray, and this class association was typical of Florence. Gray is not obtrusive and has a kind of hidden distinction. She thought that the economic crisis in Italy had no effect whatsoever on the standard of living of a small number of fortunate people, but it brought classical good taste back into fashion after the previous neglect of it. Kahanoff enjoyed her stay with her friend Margery in Florence, and she soon devoted herself to her hobby of painting: "Tubes of paint, brushes and paper I had ordered lay on the table in my room. I was sorry I had to leave."[31]

She thought that the beauty of Italy lies in its variety. The country is still a patchwork of provinces known for their different styles of art and influenced by the main city of the province at a certain period. For instance, the north and south have different kinds of food, wine, and cheese. The same language is taught in schools but the dialect changes from one area to another. As soon as one crosses the River Magra, Tuscany and Liguria begin, as though they were part of an international frontier. The anthropologist in Kahanoff turned her attention to the relationship between the northerners and southerners, a relationship resembling that of the old-timers in Israel, who came from Europe, to the immigrants from the eastern countries. On the one hand, there was an interest in improving the lot of people who came from backward places, and not only because of the knowledge that too great a gap gives rise to social agitation. And on the other hand, there was a fear that their backward social structure, their high birth rate, and their unsuitability for jobs in industry and technology could endanger the existing order. The people in Milan and

264 JACQUELINE KAHANOFF

Turin claimed that industries were more successful in the north than in the south because of the fatalism and irresponsibility of the latter. This sounded familiar to Kahanoff: the tension that exists between an advanced technological society and a backward society takes no account of frontiers.[32] The transition from a way of life based mainly on religion to one based on a materialist, rationalist ideology and the development of science and technology has a difficult birth.

Despite the different character of each province, the Italians were united in their love of beauty and their admiration for the great Italian artists and men of culture. Almost everywhere between Florence and Ravenna, Kahanoff found touching reminders of the life of Dante, whose statue is found in many churches. The town of Ravenna, she noted, is understandably proud of the fact that Dante lived there after he was banished from Florence. At Positano, her guide showed her Dante's room in a palace on a high hill. In the great hall of the palace, next to Dante's worktable, a sheet is rolled out containing the story of his life. Although the palace was badly hit in the world war, the poet's room is wonderfully preserved, which according to Kahanoff is evidence of the Italians' reverence for Dante's genius. Italy's unstable political scene and the fact that the land is steeped in culture led Kahanoff to the conclusion that the country prizes artists and cultural figures more than military heroes. This was perhaps an oblique criticism of the cult of political commemoration in her homeland, Israel.

Venice, which was once a major power in the Mediterranean, she describes as follows:

> Like a polished diamond ringed with lakes and islands, it is embedded in the glistening sea. Its domes and towers, its arched roofs and turrets are bathed in a pale, pearly light that reflects the Adriatic. Its streets, intersected by canals, are spanned by wide-arched bridges, and beneath them are black gondolas with their gondoliers who steer them standing upright with a single

oar. The gondolas glide past the wonderful facades of the palaces whose faint shadow is seen in the landscapes of Venice reflected in the water. . . . The waters of the canals reflect their windows with their arches and columns, the balconies with their white stone pillars, the endless variety of the Venetian roofs, sculptures and churches, the marvelous architectural ensemble of the city in which the Byzantine style is softened under the influence of the Italian style, creating a delicate combination of straight and curved lines, bathed in the special light of Venice, pink, blue and gold, as though blended by an artist of genius. The city is a dream, a vision liable to disappear into the sea from which it emerged like a mirage.[33]

To Kahanoff, Venice seemed like a phantom ship filled with treasures from the past, slowly sinking into the depths of the sea. This former great power was "wealthy, full of the desire for gain, shrewd, treacherous," but it also loved beauty to the point that it devoted its considerable wealth to the creation of a monumental and cosmopolitan city. One saw there Mizrahi figures, Moors, Turks, Jews. Venice, she mused, is "a magical city in which many styles blended into a wonderful whole, a gay city, lightheaded, nostalgic, sad, decaying, magnificent." She attributed the cosmopolitan character of the city to the many visiting tourists, and also its Mediterranean character reflected in St. Mark's Basilica, the patron saint of Venice, whose remains were traditionally said to have been brought there from Alexandria.

On leaving the gallery in the Doge's Palace, she saw a youth vigorously cleaning the long blonde hair of his girlfriend after "a dove had mistakenly thought her a saint and dropped something on her head."[34] On another occasion, she saw a little girl whose doll had fallen into a canal. At that moment, a Venetian came out of his house dressed in a white suit, with a straw hat on his head and a cane in his hand. On hearing the little girl cry, he went back into his house, brought out a stick with a net attached to it, rescued the doll from the canal, and returned it to its owner.

There was once a large Jewish community in Venice. Kahanoff visited the ancient ghetto, which she thought "the most depressing, poor and ugly area of Venice." One could find Jewish sacred utensils there, but they were imitations of Venetian handicrafts. There were also miserable dolls representing praying rabbis. In view of the splendor of the city, it was hard for Kahanoff to see the wretchedness of the Jewish Quarter, and she envisaged the difficulty the Jews had in the past preserving their identity in the Christian world: "If one sees the poverty of the ghetto, one is surprised how many of the Jewish merchants were actually wealthy, and one is thankful for the existence of Israel and one respects the generations which had to withstand the temptations of the world-at-large, and in Venice, one of these temptations, and not the least of them, was its stunning beauty."

Capri was also outstandingly beautiful, and it reminded Kahanoff of the setting of an Italian opera. The beautiful island is a village tucked between huge rocks, with villas standing out in the landscape, surrounded by vineyards. But she disregarded all this and went up by bus to "Anacapri," the home of the Swedish doctor, humanist, and author Axel Munthe (1857–1949), writer of *The Story of San Michele* (1929).[35] Munthe's house made a great impression on her, especially the sculptures in the garden, "stone figures one could fall in love with."[36] His moving story of the house concerned the actions of a solitary man and what a man with imagination and a deep sense of the past could achieve. Kahanoff concluded that there are not many people who, even if they are rich, create beauty for others and do not keep it only for themselves.

She heard of the town of Livorno ("Leghorn") from her maternal grandmother. Although her grandmother was born in Turkey, she spoke fluent Italian, proudly declared that her family came from Livorno, and looked down on her uneducated "Tunisian" relatives, who prattled in a North African dialect mixed with a little broken French. Thus Kahanoff, influenced by her memories, got off the train at Livorno; she was disappointed to find that it was just a small port and nothing special. She went into a shop, where she saw dates of the kind she used to receive from her relatives in Tunisia for the festivals, and she quickly bought some to bake a date-and-walnut cake in the home of her hostess, a non-Jewish friend. The cake, though not up to her grandmother's standard, was nevertheless a success, and the cat, who smelled it, was driven away with the shout, "Marrano! You're a Marrano!" On seeing Kahanoff's bewilderment, the maid explained that "in the Florentine dialect, the term 'Marrano' means someone who can't be trusted." Although Kahanoff pointed out that it was a term used for Jews who had been forced to convert to Christianity in Spain and Portugal, the maid's interpretation is supported by an Israeli philologist who said it was a term used by merchants and sailors in the Mediterranean to describe people with whom it is best not to have any commercial dealings. Kahanoff, realizing that the maid was "a Levantine from Tuscany," said that "if a descendant of the Jews of Berdichev dared to speak to me about these matters, I would call him a 'Marrano' in the Florentine sense, of course, and let him guess what I meant."[37]

Lisbon reminded Kahanoff of Rome, although the pace of life there was slower than in the Italian capital and the atmosphere was less intense. The middle-class Portuguese women bore an extraordinary resemblance to their sisters in Rome. In her long and detailed article, "Summer in Portugal," Kahanoff elaborated on this theme to indicate both the similarities and the differences between Portugal and other places in the world.[38] For instance, the policemen directing the traffic in Lisbon reminded her of the police in Tel Aviv and Jerusalem in the time of the British Mandate. They were dressed in white from head to foot and stood on a pedestal, they had a colonial-style helmet on their heads, and their hands in white gloves directed the traffic with an elegant authority as if conducting an orchestra. The Salazar Bridge over the Tagus River reminded her of the Golden Gate Bridge in San Francisco Bay.

Portugal, in her opinion, was a European country that had absorbed many elements of other cultures, and she knew Jews who were proud of their Portuguese origins and had Portuguese names, but their physiognomy resembled that of American Indians, and one should remember, she said, that Brazil, the largest country in Latin America, speaks Portuguese. African ancestry is perceptible in many faces, in a variety of shades from café au lait to chocolate brown, and there are Portuguese who call themselves "the Africans of Europe." One of the people she spoke to told her, "Mozambique and Angola are extensions of ourselves overseas, dear lady. They have been part of Portugal for five hundred years."[39] She replied that in Israel too there was a fierce debate about the definition of the "occupied," "liberated," or "held" territories. Isolated at the tip of Europe, Portugal is separated from the rest of Europe by Spain and the Pyrenees, and to circumvent that, the Portuguese became a nation of seafarers. Like the Italians, the Portuguese are great artists, but unlike the Italians they do not use ancient art for modern purposes. The kitchens in the palaces are dark like those of Versailles; the blue and white tiles decorating churches, castles, and houses depict, as in Italy, the lives of saints and historical events. Her general impression was that Portugal, unlike other European countries, had not been disfigured by progress and modernity.

Kahanoff's real and imagined journeys beyond the Levant enriched her world and her creativity. In her article "On Being a Tourist," she wrote, "What a great loss for the senses is city life which, with all the excitement, cuts us off from the phenomena of nature!"[40] This journey, the easiest and most comfortable she made, was less interesting than it would have been in the days when one went by foot or by carriage, stopped at inns by the wayside, and met the local people. Tourists, she contended, want to see too much in too short a time and do not have the leisure to gain a deep knowledge of other ways of life. Most of the shopping centers resemble one another, the kind of entertainment is one-dimensional, and many places have lost their special character. Thus, many young people rebel against the banality of this type of tourism and prefer to go by motorcycle and stop where they please. "The day is not far off," predicted Kahanoff, "when they will go on foot, as that is the best way to know a country or get the feeling of a city." Like these young people, she preferred to experience things in her own way, to touch them and feel them, to enjoy a bicycle ride or a journey by local bus to a village on a mountainside, to wander in a forest, to lose her way and find it again, to see the world.

SEVEN

LIFE AT THE EDGE OF THE LINE

OLD AGE AS A METAPHOR

In her book *Illness as Metaphor* (1978), the American essayist and writer Susan Sontag (1933–2004) called for a demystification of cancer and for cancer not to be portrayed as an uncontrollable affliction, a harbinger of death, comparable to such phenomena as Stalinism and Watergate.[1] A portrayal of cancer as a sickness like any other and not as an incurable disease, she wrote, could help in overcoming the despair and helplessness felt by those who are affected by it. A normal terminology rather than an overwrought emotional vocabulary could persuade those afflicted by cancer, who regard it as debilitating, lethal, and incurable, to relate to it in a rational way and discuss it in a rational and balanced manner.

In a similar vein, Kahanoff saw the prolongation of the life expectancy of the old as a metaphor for the technological possibilities of the modern age and, at the same time, as a symptom. In keeping with her discussion in her youth of the illusions of progress and the disadvantages of technology, in her maturity she came to the conclusion, following her father's confinement to an old-age home and his condition in his final years, that advanced technology does not necessarily bring happiness and comfort, but often brings unnecessary pain and suffering to the old, their families, and those around them. The literary document she produced as a result, the article "To Die a Modern Death," published in two parts in two issues of *Keshet*, describes that tragic, vulnerable, and degenerate stage of her father's life, which could have been avoided, as a metaphor for modern death, a lingering death, not for the purposes of life, which is really over and is a mere shadow of one's former life, ending with the loss of one's human image.[2]

One of the most mistaken ideas of contemporary civilization, in her opinion, is that scientific and technological development, regardless of its influence on people's lives and human values, is a form of "progress." Proper medical treatment has given way to a bureaucratization of medicine that is inconsiderate of the humanity of the ill. In the manner of the "Frankfurt School," she declared that life in the modern capitalist era has become a kind of commodity. The greater the demand for it, the more of it there should be, whether it involves pains or pleasures. She wondered if we have the right to prolong a man's life beyond a certain limit, and if we have a greater right to do that than to shorten it. And who decides what the limit is?

Kahanoff began her article as follows: "People often make the blessing, 'May you live to a hundred and twenty.' They believe, or claim to believe, that life is an absolute good. But today, when I hear this well-meaning proposal, I say to myself, 'God forbid!,' for I have learned from the death-throes of my father that the life of people in old age is not always and not in all circumstances an absolute good, and that how you live is more important than if you live."[3]

The days have over when the death of old people was brought on by tuberculosis. From the time antibiotics were invented, they have delayed the process of physical, social, and spiritual degeneration. Life can be extended because of the medical sciences, because of surgery, and because of chemical interventions in the processes of life and death. Comparing the peaceful and dignified death of her grandfather with the prolonged, painful death of his son, her father, she came to the conclusion that "a time has come when even dignity in death has been taken from a man and it has become a mockery and a derision."

Her grandfather, who one Passover had reached the age of a hundred, told his family that evening that his days were fulfilled: "I have grown old, my time has come. This is my last Passover." After he had blessed them all, he died that very night. That, in her opinion, was a dignified old-fashioned death, a death that everyone can understand and accept. But the death of his son, her father, who died at the age of eighty-three after months of agony, in a room not his own, a bed not his own, in clothes that did not belong to him—that kind of death was something she could neither accept nor forgive, although she did not really know whom or what she could not forgive. Her father, an old-fashioned man who died a modern death, died in what is called "a hospital for chronic diseases," a type of place she compared to a concentration camp, where people dumped their old folk, out of the way, out of sight, when they became infirm and senile and when family could no longer look after them at home, or simply were unwilling to. Here the victims were not an ethnic or religious minority, but a most defenseless group—the aged.

This is how she described them:

> Bent down, trembling, dribbling, the patients were wheeled, dragged, pushed, pulled, like mules to water, to sit blank-eyed at the table. Their unsteady coarse hands spilled food on their worn clothes, which had been picked up at random. Some spat on the floor, others had a tube hanging down the opening of their trousers. A wizened old couple kept squabbling, whining and groaning, not listening to each other. Here and there, middle-aged children helped their parents with their food. One caring son carefully picked up the slop from his mother's hairy chin. With an unsteady hand, he conveyed a twisted tin spoon loaded with gefilte fish from the plate to that forlorn port, his old mother's mouth. There were no forks or knives.[4]

LIFE AT THE EDGE OF THE LINE

Here we see Kahanoff as a sharp-eyed naturalistic essayist who seized on small items in the life of the elderly, reporting them without sentimentality but with a stark realism and a capacity for close observation of details without any attempt to soften their effect. This harsh realism is not employed for its own sake, but to make us realize that old age accompanied by degeneracy is not becoming for those who experience it. It is unnecessary, and there is no need to prolong it even if we are able to do so.

At first, she and her mother hesitated to send her father to a facility for the old. Kahanoff explained that she was not able to have him in her home because her husband had rights over the house: "There's a limit to what a woman can ask of her husband."[5] Finally, after her father caught pneumonia and after they had examined some alternatives, it was decided to send him to Beit Miriam, an old-age home in one of the rural settlements near Tel Aviv. They soon became aware that "he was deceived, and so were we."[6] They had failed to see the difference between saving a life and prolonging a death-agony.

On her frequent visits to Beit Miriam, she was shocked to find her father dazed from medication, with bits of food on his mouth, his personality effaced. She did not mind giving details, like other patients' use of his clothes and underwear, the wretched, torn garments he wore, his incontinence. He was surrounded by "non-humans" whose eyes exuded a vague animosity. There were days she regretted she was not an orphan because she discovered that there are limits to a daughter's love. She was subject to a whirlwind of contrary feelings: on the one hand, love, and, on the other hand, "anger, physical revulsion at her father, emotions which occasionally boarded on hatred, mingled with self-pity and a perpetual longing to be freed from the heavy burden of this worry."[7] Kahanoff looked at herself in the mirror, and she did not spare the reader the ugly reflection she saw.

There was no hope for Kahanoff's father. However devoted the staff may have been, there is no denying the fact that death and dying are intrinsic to life, a fact that renders the medical staff understandably inured to the torment of the dying and the distress of their family. How could they have attended to our feelings sympathetically "when they are looking after eighty living corpses"? But, nevertheless:

> The description of this experience may help people to understand the nature of modern death, and what those who reach a bad, decrepit old age can expect. If, as a result, it is possible to prevent an iota of the suffering of our old people and relatives, the suffering experienced by my father will not have been totally in vain. I do not know what can be done about this sadistic prolongation of the death-agony which we impose on people in the belief that life is sacred, but it is just as well that people should know what modern death is like and can decide if it is suitable for their parents or themselves.[8]

On the Saturday before he died, Kahanoff rocked her father in her arms as if he were her child. She stroked the tortured skeleton with the broken hips and dry skin. His whole body was covered in sores and the stench was dreadful. "But when his wandering eyes focused on me, they were my father's eyes, brimming over with tenderness."[9] Her description from this point onward was the finest and most moving in all her writings. It seems that only in his last moments was she able to have these feelings and to write them down: "Weak as he was, it was his smile, despite the gaping pit that was his mouth, and that blueish and transparent hand which found the strength to bring my cheek closer to his—it was my father's hand. We held each other tight, but I could not stop the tears."[10]

Her father asked her to go home, and about an hour later they rang up to say that it was all over. "All I felt was tremendous relief. It was all over at long last." After the family had paid their last respects, she felt that her father was now free, "and so was I free, free to live and to remember him not only at Beit Miriam but also in the 'happiest days,' of which this was one."[11]

During her father's stay in the home and after his death, she thought a great deal about the meaning of his death and especially about his life at death's door. Death nowadays, she thought, is a variable and difficult compromise between the natural order and the demands of culture. Technology, which prolongs old age indefinitely, is undoubtedly part of the contemporary cultural landscape. In her opinion, a balance must be found between the enjoyment of life, as far as possible, and an acceptance of the inevitability of death. One may ask whether the saying "Where there's life, there's hope" applies in all cases. Kahanoff gave findings from the 1951 book *Les 40 000 heures* (The 40,000 Hours) by Jean Fourastié on life expectancy at the time of the French Revolution. People lived from twenty to twenty-five years on average, less than a third of the children lived to the age of eleven, most children were orphaned by the age of fourteen, and only one person out of four reached the age of forty-five. At the time when she recorded her reflections on death (in 1967), when human life expectancy had greatly lengthened, she wondered how much old-age insurance would be needed to cover the added twenty to thirty years of inactivity.

Life is regarded as sacred, but Kahanoff asked if this is the case everywhere. The Eskimos of the polar regions at the beginning of winter send out some of their old people to freeze to death. To us this may seem cruel, but while an old Eskimo's agony of dying is brief, a modern death in an old-age home can last many months or even years. Another example she gave was that of pious Jews living on the verge of starvation who think birth control is sinful and that birth must be regulated by faith. There are also, she added, groups who shorten the lives of their members when the food supply is in danger of running out.

The increase in the birth rate and the lengthening of the life span have taken place through the development of medicine along with developments in agriculture, livestock breeding, and technology. Traditionally, our beliefs about death had been molded by an economy of relative scarcity, an economy that preceded the Industrial Revolution and the technological revolution. That is why we regard the refusal to lengthen a human life as killing, a reprehensible shortening of life. But these additional years of life very often inflict sadistic tortures on old people. We are also unwilling to make the arrangements and sacrifices needed to deal with such torture. The sick, she said, are generally not entrusted to medical science but to a system, a complex bureaucratic process, and they often complain about the lack of human contact, about being treated as objects or numbers:

> The red lights go off in the eyes of the Cyclops of electronic surveillance. We are mere bundles of flesh, limbs with something added or just limbs, not human beings, but these mysterious, frightening machines have saved many of us. Our human reactions—fear, anguish, pain, anger, depression—are alien to this technology. Perhaps one cannot ask the system for something it was never meant to provide. Its treatment is technical, efficient, but not personal. Perhaps the patients, the families, the public as a whole, should be more knowledgeable about modern medical treatments and embrace them wholeheartedly.[12]

From this perspective, Kahanoff also anticipated the later discourse on vegetarianism, the treatment of animals, and the approach to nature in general. She thought that it was precisely because our direct dependence on nature for the supply of food had lessened that the opposition between nature and culture had increased. The rearing of poultry and cattle in huge quantities is meant to provide us with protein, and we feel no need to apologize for killing these animals to supply our needs. We have the technological means to produce much larger quantities than we could in a state of nature. The human solidarity with nature has diminished. "What driver of a car will slow down in order to avoid running over the entrails of stray dogs and cats lying on the road?" In many ways, man has become indifferent to the way animals die.

LIFE AT THE EDGE OF THE LINE

The same applies with regard to the old. They are "run-over dogs," the scapegoats of modern society.[13] Just as the new affluence has diminished the solidarity between man and nature, so the solidarity between the generations has disappeared. The treatment given to the old is technical, inhuman, and we atone for it at a low emotional and financial cost. We pride ourselves on being cultured: "Look," we say, "at how we treat these human wrecks!" But our dominance of nature and the way we force it to supply our needs is not in contradiction with our revolt against the reality of death. The approach of death reminds us night and day that nature is still in control, that humans are far from being sons of God on earth, that "we are simply creatures that are born, reproduce and die like any others." We artificially extend the length of old age, and at the same time we despise it and glorify youth. Young people, who are more familiar with the world of space and with the media than their grandparents were, fear that if they accept their grandparents' concepts of right and wrong, they will be seen by their friends as primitive. How can a grandchild be respectful to a grandfather and other old people whose lives seem to go on endlessly? "In cultural terms, the question of whether we have the right to prolong the agonies of the dying and humiliate them at a time when medical technology is creating such a change in the conditions of existence, is a moral and metaphysical one. Is there any room for patience or hope when man gives or compels acceptance of something provided by God or nature?"[14]

Kahanoff also expressed herself on different aspects of old age. In her opinion, we should take another look at our ethical presuppositions and their influence on modern life where old age and death are concerned. Every person has a name, but in old-age homes the old people are stripped of their identities and are called "grandpa" or "grandma" by everyone. And that is the opposite of the situation in Tunis in her grandmother's time, where the dead belonged to the community. They would visit them in the cemetery every month, and they ate, sang, and laughed next to the grave. The dead were part of a living community and their death was not anonymous.

Kahanoff was critical of the Israeli rabbinate's prohibition of the inscription of secular dates on Jewish tombstones and its opposition to autopsies, and also of its failure to give an opinion on the conditions under which doctors could prolong life. She was ahead of her time in her proposal for nurses and caretakers to treat old people in their own homes. The aim was "to ensure that the old would not prolong their lives in a state of total or relative neglect, and as long as they lived, and even if they did not live so long, they would feel themselves to be part of the human community."[15]

In April 1976, three years before she died, Kahanoff began to keep a diary in which she described her sufferings from cancer. As in her description of the suffering and loneliness of her father in his old-age home, a meticulous portrayal of the last stage of his life, here too she pulled no punches in describing her experiences in a hospital during her surgery and afterward. She recorded a nightmare in which a huge man wearing a black raincoat and carrying a black case sat down on her bed. She screamed, pleading for him to leave, but "he put the case on the ground and it grew hair all over his body and like some terrifying seaweed."[16] When he was chased out of the room, she woke up covered in sweat. "Then I knew I was very ill." It was two o'clock in the morning on January 1, 1976. "I said to myself: 'What a beginning to the year!'"

It all began with a flu accompanied with a great deal of coughing. The examinations she underwent revealed lumps on her stomach. "You must see a gynecologist at once," a female doctor told her. "That's how it all started." The pain worsened from day to day. The endless proceedings of her divorce from Kahanoff also weakened her, and she postponed medical treatment again and again because she feared that she would not have enough physical strength when the time came to go to court. In the background was the chaotic post–Yom Kippur War atmosphere, which did not allow her to recover from her father's long stay in his old-age home, and at the same time she had undertaken to look after her mother, who kept falling.

As a child, she had loved her mother very much, but, as she said, "There were many changes in my feelings towards her in the course of my life."[17] In her youth, she rebelled against her mother's attempts to make her into an educated, submissive young lady preparing herself for a good match. She was very angry that her mother had not allowed her to carry out her dream of becoming a doctor or anything else she wanted to be. She also remembered the way her mother had treated her in the difficult period when she returned to Egypt from the United States, divorced from Izzy and brokenhearted by the dissolution of her romantic interlude with Claude Lévi-Strauss. Her position as a divorcée in Cairo at that time certainly did not enhance her reputation. She enveloped herself in silence for many months and from that time forward found it difficult to forgive her mother.

"I envy my mother having two daughters," she would say to Sarah Rippin, editor of the magazine *At*, in which she published articles from time to time.[18] Alone in the hospital or in care homes, she was sorry she had not raised a family. She forbade her mother to visit her in hospital and even cut off relations with her. Her mother nonetheless continued to try to visit her, standing by her door in the corridor and waiting, but in vain because Kahanoff did not allow her to come in. They did not see each other again until the day of Kahanoff's death.

When she recovered from the surgery, she traveled to Europe for a month. "I was haunted by the idea that I would never again see the ones I loved."[19] In Europe she recuperated somewhat, but when she returned to Israel the pains came back. "What was I to do? I was so eager to enjoy life a bit after years of struggle, disappointment, uncertainty." When she went about in the streets, weeping between one medical examination and another, she worried that writing another long article would not be of any benefit to her. And then she had another dream. She was lying in a grave. People came to the funeral, and among them was a "friend" who had abandoned her when she was in trouble. When he was delivering a funeral oration and speaking about their friendship, she leaped out of the grave and shouted, "Hypocrite! Liar!"

More than she feared that the surgeon would dismember her on the operating table, she was frightened that she would leave the surgical theater incapacitated, connected to tubes of liquid. She felt lonely, despite the fact that friends telephoned and encouraged her all the time. Eva Weintraub, a close friend who worked at the American embassy in Tel Aviv, and Sarah Rippin were her only companions during that period. She had great faith in her doctor, and she refused to seek advice from any others, or to go to Paris, as her sister wished.

The surgery took place on February 8, 1976. The operation was successful, but other treatments were required at the Hadassah Hospital in Tel Aviv. When Eva collected her for treatments, Kahanoff insisted on sitting beforehand at a café and enjoying a coffee and a piece of cake.[20] In the oncology department, she did not want to be like the other patients, so she disregarded various instructions such as those on the sheet of paper given to patients on leaving the hospital, telling them what to do and what not to do. Most of the time she was tired, and she consequently did not receive many friends in her home. Even reading was more than she could manage, and she sometimes wondered why she did not use the time to do what she had always wanted to do—write another book. She avoided intellectual effort, and preferred to care for plants, listen to music, draw, and paint. It was enough for her at such times "to live a passive life, to enjoy the sheer fact of being alive." A few days before her birthday, a nurse told her that the treatments had ended. "I was so happy that I kissed her," she said, and in her diary she noted, "This was the opportunity to do what I should have done and did not do all these years—write a book.

But I don't have the strength or the desire. I am living passively. What I have done I have done, and what I haven't done, I haven't done. It makes no difference. The world can continue without books by Jacqueline Kahanoff. It won't lose or gain anything by that. Even if I will never write another line, I have lived, and I am still alive."[21]

Aleksandr Solzhenitsyn said in *The Cancer Ward* that a private doctor is better than public medicine, but in Kahanoff's opinion only the well-to-do can afford private treatment, and one therefore cannot return "to the system of medical treatment that existed before the birth of sophisticated medical technology. Medical treatment prolongs our lives, and that too is a gift."[22] These words seem to contradict what she said in connection with the prolongation of her father's life. If this appears to be a slip of the pen, Kahanoff adopted this position once more, and this time more forcefully: "It is precisely impersonal medical technology that has enabled me not only to live a few more years (hopefully), but to experience something that is a kind of revelation, an almost mystical celebration of life."[23] How can one resolve the contradiction between this praise for the technology that had prolonged her life and her condemnation of this technology in the case of her father?

Perhaps there is no contradiction. People want to live, and they seek by all means to extend their life expectancy. Jacqueline Kahanoff was no exception, especially as she was only sixty-two years old when she died. In her last days, when cancer consumed every part of her withered body, she was hospitalized in a care home, where she was laid on a wooden bed with a fencelike partition, like a baby's cot. She was moving toward her slow, lingering death, her "boring death" as she called it, but she did not give up. When they gave her a hard-boiled egg, she took only the yolk, saying that it was a concentration of healthy substances. She clung to life on the verge of death and looked in the end like a diminutive Egyptian mummy.

EPILOGUE
Kahanoff and the Humanist Mediterranean Heritage

THE "MEDITERRANEAN HUMANISM" WRITERS EXPRESSED what Albert Camus called "a sense of measure." "Mediterranean humanism" was not a branch or species of European Enlightenment, and its characteristics as a whole differentiate it from its older northern counterpart. The Mediterranean idea of humanism was led by a diverse group of writers who immigrated to Paris: Albert Camus from Algeria, Albert Memmi from Tunisia, Tahar Ben-Jelloun from Morocco, Edmond Jabès from Egypt, and Jorge Semprún from Spain. Another important Mediterranean center in Egypt included Taha Hussein, Louis Awad, Constantine P. Cavafy, and Najib Mahfouz; the writer Orhan Pamuk, who connected between Turkey and Europe; the writer Albert Cohen from Corfu in Greece; and Kateb Yacine from Algeria. Jacqueline Kahanoff is an essential part of this Mediterranean humanist school.

These Mediterranean humanists valued the warm, unmediated contact of dialogue between peoples and cultures. Rather than dreaming of a "new man," they considered the problems of existing human beings in Mediterranean societies. The biographies of most of them represent a kind of migration that endowed them with a creative approach, a critical perspective, and moral

EPILOGUE

values with which to oppose the illusions of many Europeans concerning the emergence of a "new man" in a context of radical ideology that justified violence.[1]

The Promethean passion of the European Enlightenment sought to create a new humanity, a western man who would be his own master and use his reason to rule over nature and mold the world as he pleased. This passion inspired the political ideologies of the nineteenth century and prepared the way for the regimes that arose in their wake in the twentieth, from the "new man" of the Enlightenment (Jean-Jacques Rousseau) to the Nietzschean Übermensch and the idea of a "man-machine." The Mediterranean humanists rebelled against this tradition.[2]

Albert Camus's description of the diminished position of modern man anticipated the analysis of Michel Foucault. According to Camus, the Enlightenment, a liberating concept, ensnared modern man in a prison of his own making as both victim and executioner.[3] From the Renaissance and the humanism of the early modern period to the nationalisms and political ideologies of the nineteenth century and the dictatorial regimes of the twentieth, the unfettered will affirmed the creation of political churches, complete with priests, dogmas, rites of passage, and the hope of redemption. All these different churches—among them the nation-state, the dictatorship of the proletariat, and modern technology—reflected the same phenomenon: man overpowering himself. Recognition of this self-enslavement appeared only with post-Kantian thought: modern man with his liberated consciousness discovered that he was enslaved to a reality that he himself had created.

Camus believed that the human experience of the twentieth century was to be found in the fluctuations of modernism from the desire for freedom to the will to power, from Promethean humanism to Prometheus unbound. Modernism, with self-deification at its center, was self-destructive. From the time of humanism onward, modern man places himself at the center of creation as creator. When he murdered his God and that God's representative on earth, the king, man shook off his metaphorical chains. Like Nietzsche, Camus saw the characteristic condition of modernity as homelessness and alienation: men who have rejected God are, dangerously and paradoxically, liable to seek the certainty that only God can provide. By crowning himself Caesar, Prometheus changed from friend to enemy of mankind.[4]

Toward the end of the nineteenth century, in certain intellectual circles in Italy, France, and Spain, there was an ever-intensifying feeling that the Latin peoples were unable to withstand the power of the Anglo-Saxon countries. This feeling was augured by France's ignominious defeat by Prussia in 1870, and Spain's loss of its colonies. The challenge to Latin identity and honor sowed the seeds of fascism, yielding the likes of Benito Mussolini and Francisco Franco. After the Second World War, the Russian-born French philosopher Alexandre Kojève (1902–1968) broached the idea of a Latin empire, and sought to convince General de Gaulle that France, Italy, and Spain and the Mediterranean countries should unite, under French imperial tutelage, to resist the hegemonic ascendency of America and England.[5] It transpired, however, that the postwar end of colonialism and the concomitant desire of the former colonies of the Maghreb to create independent national identities would run counter to the envisioned unification of the northern and southern sides of the Mediterranean.

In the aftermath of the Gulf War of 1990–1991, the crisis in the Muslim countries requickened the Mediterranean cultural discourse. There was a marked flowering of cultural initiatives and artistic collaboration, and the founding of intellectual institutions promoting a cultural dialogue among the peoples of the Levant. The vibrant dialogue is attested by *Quaderns de la Mediterrània*, issued by the Institut Europeu de la Mediterràneo (Barcelona) and the publication of the anthology *Representations of the Mediterranean Spirit* and the *Enciclopedia del Mediterraneo*.

The attack on the Twin Towers in 2001 marked the end of a decade characterized by dialogue and a search for cultural bridges between the Mediterranean countries. The first two decades of the twenty-first century represent a reaction to the Mediterranean idea, and the Mediterranean Sea once again became a border between the north and south. This tragic border is typified by ships overflowing with desperate denizens of North Africa crossing the sea to southern Europe. In scenes remote from the vision of the intercultural fraternity of the Levant, the European countries turn their backs on their southern European neighbors. Some Mediterranean intellectuals offered an explanation for the alienation of the southern European countries, and repeatedly suggested an intercultural dialogue among the peoples of the Mediterranean as the most efficient remedy.

The Lebanese writer Amin Maalouf (b. 1949) claims that the identity of each of us is formed by numerous affinities, but instead of being in contact with all these affinities and gaining an understanding of them, we choose only one of them—religion, nationality, ethnicity, and the like—which becomes a totality. The chosen affinity becomes the only one, and occasionally we kill in its name.[6] The Indian American anthropologist Arjun Appadurai (b. 1949) contends that today it is easier to kill than to conduct a dialogue, concluding that "nobody can enter a dialogue without taking serious risks."[7]

It was Erasmus of Rotterdam (c. 1466?–1536) who first defined *Christian humanism* based on the principle of universal human dignity, individual freedom, and the importance of happiness as essential and principal component of the teachings of Jesus. In certain respects, the Lebanese Christian writer and poet Charles Corm (1894–1963) continued the line of Erasmus in his attempt to locate the place of the Christian faith in Mediterranean civilization. In his opinion, the humanism of the Renaissance, Christian humanism, and Mediterranean humanism are links in a single chain.

Corm promoted the humanist and Mediterranean aspects of Lebanese nationality, embracing the country's diverse religious communities, through the Circle of Friends of Lebanon and *La Revue Phénicienne* (The Phoenician Review). Two of his articles are deemed seminal in the articulation of his vision: "L'Humanisme et la Méditerranée" (Humanism and the Mediterranean) and "The Humanism of Lebanon."[8] The first text was read in Monaco in 1935 at a congress organized by the Mediterranean Academy. He opened his lecture by declaring that "The presence of Lebanon in the Mediterranean scene is always of concern to her."[9] He continued to argue that one has to "define the strategic principles of that presence in history and especially its task in the service of humanism." For him, the meaning of Mediterranean humanism was "to understand, to permit, to forgive and not to condemn everything in human nature. Humanism is man's destiny, superior to all riches. It fosters all virtuous qualities, promotes reflection and truth, justice and human solidarity which concerns us all." One discerns in these words a resonance of Erasmus's Christian humanism.

Returning to Beirut, Corm elaborated his conception of a Mediterranean humanism, in which he argued that Arabism was above all an ideology that preceded the Muslim religion. True to its Arab patrimony so conceived, Lebanon had to aspire to be the spiritual center of Mediterranean civilization: "What is the use of all the cultures [of Lebanon and the Mediterranean] if they do not instill respect for man and improve the quality of human society?"[10] The Mediterranean identity, he said, is single and multiple at the same time, and is characterized by a humanist spirit of abiding cultural and spiritual values of *Mare Nostrum*. The two world wars, he held, should have taught us that wars and violence were to be avoided and should have strengthened the imperative of the cultural and national communities of the Levant to overcome mutual enmity by an irenic dialogue.

EPILOGUE   287

Eminent Lebanese writers actively contributed to Corm's journal *La Revue Phénicienne*. Among them was Michel Chiha (1891–1954), a banker, politician, writer, and journalist, one of the drafters of the Lebanese constitution, the ideas of which greatly influenced the formation of modern Lebanon and its Mediterranean outlook. In speaking of the significance of the Lebanese as a Mediterranean people, he claimed that boats and oars were Phoenician inventions, a tribute to Mediterranean seafaring, initiative, and trade. Chiha promoted the Phoenician, Mediterranean, and Lebanese myths to create an ideal image of modern Lebanon. In 1964 Michel Chiha described the Mediterranean as "the meeting-place into which peoples flocked and assimilated regardless of their origins; a crossroads where varied civilizations dropped in on one another, and where bevies of beliefs, languages, and cultural rituals salute each other in solemn veneration; . . . a Mediterranean construct above all, but like the Mediterranean itself, discerning and sensitive to the stirring of universal poetry."[11]

The writer and public activist Evelyne Bustros (1878–1971) wrote her booklet *Evocations* in memory of Michel Chiha. She lived in Beirut, Paris, and Cairo, and in her book *La main d'Allah* (The Hand of Allah) (1926), she called for Islamic-Christian rapprochement.[12] Bustros founded a number of literary, artistic, and feminist organizations in Lebanon; represented the country in international forums; and published the French-language literary journal *Ébauches* (Drafts), which dealt with Levantine subjects, among others. In 1942, she became president of the Lebanese Arab Women's Union (now called the Lebanese Women's Council), which grouped together the thirty organizations recognized by the government. A year later, she worked for recognition of Lebanese independence. Bustros also worked in the Association for Rural Development, together with the feminist activist and fighter for citizen's rights Anissa Rawda Najjar (1913–2016), older sister of the well-known Lebanese woman painter and sculptor

Saloua Raouda Choucair. These activists, who were close to Chiha and Corm, show the centrality of Lebanon in Mediterranean feminism.

However, Beirut, the capital of Lebanon, failed in its mission to be a multireligious and multinational Mediterranean city, whereas Haifa succeeded, becoming in this way a model in Israel of Jewish-Arab Mediterranean coexistence. From Hassan Bey Shukri, the Arab mayor of the city in the First World War, to the present liberal Jewish mayors, Haifa has been an outstanding example. There are many well-known Arab-Palestinian writers, poets, and musicians from Haifa whose names are connected with the Communist Party newspaper *Al-Ittahad* (The Union), such as Mahmoud Darwish, Samih al-Qasim, Tawfiq Ziad, Salman Natour, Salam Jubran, and Taha Muhammad Ali. There are also some of the outstanding Arab actors in Israel, such as Makram Khoury, Yussuf Abu-Warda, Salim Dau, George Iskandar, Norman Issa, and Yousef Sweid.[13] Three well-known Jewish writers lived in the city: A. B. Yehoshua, Natan Zach, and Sami Michael. Kahanoff's visits to Yehoshua in Haifa exposed her to this mixed city, which the theater, the university, the port, and the fashion industry have made into a secular, pluralistic, and open place. Unlike in Haifa, in Beirut the Mediterranean vision was extinguished with the Lebanese Civil War.

Rushdi Maalouf, a former member of the Lebanese French Academy, wrote that "Charles Corm was the first to show us how to love Lebanon."[14] His son, the writer and journalist Amin Maalouf, an editor of the journal *Jeune Afrique*, emigrated to France in the wake of the Lebanese Civil War of 1975 and soon became a member of the Académie Française. In his articles and books—notably, *Les Croisades vues par les Arabes* (The Crusades through Arab Eyes) in 1983 and *Les échelles du Levant* (The Ports of the Levant) in 1996—Amin Maalouf has fought fearlessly against racism and religious fundamentalism, proposing a multicultural Lebanese identity in conjunction with a Mediterranean dialogue.[15] Celebrating plural identities, he is also wary of the obliteration of local identities, ancient languages, customs, and traditions through globalization. In the introduction to the Hebrew edition of his 1998 book *Les identités* meurtrières (Deadly Identities), he warns against a "faith that becomes membership of a people or a religion, a religion that turns into nationalism, fanaticism, violence."[16]

Like Maalouf, the poet Adonis (pseudonym of Ali Ahmed Said Esber) left Beirut in 1975 during the civil war. Adonis was born in Syria in 1930s, went to live in Lebanon, and now lives in Paris. He is widely viewed as the world's leading contemporary Arabic poet. As a modernist poet, he has abandoned the Arabic traditions of rhyme and meter, and he has included in his poetry Phoenician motifs—this is also reflected in his nom de plume, which is the name of the Phoenician god Adonis, the god of renewal. Adonis says that he chose that name after he read the legend of Astoreth and Adonis, in which Adonis is killed by a wild boar. Apart from his identification with the victim, his choice reflects the Lebanese propensity for the adoption of different identities.[17] The eastern equivalent of Adonis is Tammuz. The late Israeli poet Natan Zach (1930–2020) declared that Adonis "founded the Canaanite school in Lebanon as [Yonatan] Ratosh did in Israel."[18]

The choice of a Canaanite identity, that is, a pre-Israelite Hebrew identity, by the poet Yonatan Ratosh (1908–1981) and his spiritual mentor Adia (A. G.) Horon (1907–1972) was in keeping with the Lebanese intellectual climate prevalent in the eastern Mediterranean in the1930s and 1940s. When he studied in Paris in the1930s, Horon, a scholar of the ancient east, developed a view of history according to which there was a Canaanite-Israelite unity in the ancient east.[19] He distinguished between the "Hebrews," defined by territory and culture, who dominated the entire Levant and extended even further, and the "Jews," an exilic community. The model for the Hebrews was classical Greece, which made its mark on the whole Mediterranean Basin. In his book *A*

History of the Hebrew People, he endeavored to demonstrate an affinity between the Mediterranean settlements of the Phoenicians (the "northern Hebrews") in North Africa and the children of Israel.[20] What attracted Ratosh, the founder of the Canaanite group in Palestine, to Horon was his non-Jewish Hebrew nativism with its Canaanite roots. Ratosh's encounter with Horon in Paris in 1938 was a turning point in his life in which, as he attested, from a Hebrew-speaking Jew he became a "Canaanite."[21]

In 1924, before the findings of Horon in Paris, Itamar Ben Avi (the first native speaker of the Modern Hebrew language, the son of Eliezer Ben-Yehuda) found correspondences between the Maronite Christians in Lebanon and the Hebrew "Canaanites," and wrote that "the creation of the Lebanese nation is a gift from heaven as far as we are concerned. Whether by design or by accident, the only possible way for them to move forward is to base themselves on a Hebrew Land of Israel, its foundations and principles."[22] About twelve years later, he praised the holy trinity of "Hebrew Judea, Christian Lebanon, and Muslim Arabia." In the 1950s, David Ben-Gurion supported an "alliance of minorities,"[23] and in the 1960s Eri Jabotinsky (1910–1969), the Zionist revisionist activist, the son of Ze'ev Jabotinsky, saw points of similarity between the Maronite people and the Jewish people. The Maronite community, he said, "closely resembles the Jewish people, first of all in its geographical situation. . . . Only a small part of it resides in its country. It also resembles us in its ethnic composition. They are descendants of the Hebrew speakers of Tyre, Sidon and Ugarit."[24] Likewise, Ratosh called for the establishment of a federation with the natives of the region, the Druze Mountains in Syria and Lebanon, which would serve as a basis for Brit HaKedem (Alliance of Antiquity) of the Levant.

The story of Kahanoff and Levantinism is set in a regional context that exceeds the Levant of her time. There were Levantines like her in the region as a whole, and in Egypt itself, like the Syrian-Lebanese community in Egypt before the rise of the

Egyptian president Abdel Nasser. There were also major Levantine communities that contributed to Egyptian culture, and which she encountered in Cairo, Mansoura, and Alexandria. The last two were ports of a cosmopolitan character where Kahanoff was exposed to Levantine communities like the Christian Levantine settlement, mainly composed of Maronites who had emigrated from Beirut and the Mountains of Lebanon in Ottoman times. In this group, there were members who were active in creating the Pharaonic-Egyptian identity that challenged the homogeneous Arab one. Three preeminent Israeli intellectuals in particular were friendly with Corm and were influenced by his conception of the Mediterranean Levant. Eliahu Eilat (1903–1990), Israel's first ambassador to the United States, studied in the American University in Beirut, where he first encountered Corm's writings.[25] Chana Orloff (1888–1968), a sculptress born in Russia, immigrated to the land of Israel in 1910, then lived in Paris, and was one of the major sculptors of the twentieth century. Her works gained primitivist inspiration from the Lebanese and Mediterranean region.[26] Nahum Slouschz (1872–1966), whom Corm persuaded to take an interest in his research on the Phoenicians, was a writer and scholar of Oriental languages and the author of *The Conquest of the Seas: An Aspect of the History of Civilization* (1948). In this book, published one year before Braudel's great work on the Mediterranean, Slouschz developed a philosophy of history that highlighted the activities of the Jewish communities in the Mediterranean Basin, and accordingly he spoke of "the Mediterranean Jew."[27]

The Mediterranean network was thus not confined to Corm and Lebanese intellectuals. The acclaimed Egyptian writer and literary critic Taha Hussein (1889–1973) passionately promoted the ideal of a Mediterranean Levant.[28] Despite the fact that he was blind, he was a founding official of the University of Alexandria, was head of the Academy of the Arabic Language in Cairo, and later became the Egyptian Minister of Education. From this prestigious and influential perch, Hussein was one of the leaders of the modernist renaissance in Egypt, which advocated the country's return to its pre-Islamic roots to develop a distinctive Egyptian cultural sensibility as a spur to enter the modern world. Among the sixteen volumes of his books and collected articles, in his autobiography *The Days* (1933) and his work *The Future of Culture in Egypt* (1938), he conjoined the Egyptian renaissance with the vision of Mediterranean Levant.[29]

The Moroccan author Mohammed Berrada (b. 1938) expressed surprise, and a measure of censure, that Hussein failed to note the Mediterranean affinity to Italian fascism. Berrada, a literary critic, essayist, and translator who was president of the Morocco Writers Union, is regarded today as one of his country's most important writers.[30] He is highly critical of the dominance of European colonialism in the Mediterranean countries.

Louis Awad (1915–1990), a well-known critical literary and academic figure in Egypt, and a former student of Hussein's, endorsed his teacher's vision of a modernist Egyptian renaissance. Like Hussein, he inherited two cultures, the European and the Egyptian, refracted through a cosmopolitan Mediterranean sensibility. He studied at Cambridge and Princeton and became Professor of English at Cairo University in 1947. Critical of Egypt's prevailing traditional and conservative literature, he wrote "free verse." Before the 1950s, Arabic poetry was still beholden to the neoclassical and romantic Arab poets. The "free verse" movement was the first to provide a new direction, and it was regarded as the only hope for Arabic poetry.[31] As a model of modernity Arabic verse, Awad translated T. S. Eliot into Arabic, and at the request by Taha Hussein, he published articles on modern writers in English.

Orhan Pamuk (b. 1952), the foremost contemporary Turkish author and a winner of the Nobel Prize in Literature, is also one of the critical Mediterranean writers. The Hebrew translator of Pamuk's novels, Israeli poet Rami Saari, noted that "dual

EPILOGUE   293

identities and a proliferation of voices" abound in Pamuk's novels, and that one finds in his writings "the style of traditional story-telling and retrospective elements, and the distance and blurring of modernist and postmodernist literature."[32] In his works, east and west, Islam and Christianity, religiosity and secularism, reality and imagination merge. In his novel *Istanbul—Memories and the City* (2005), Pamuk gives voice to the multiple layers of his identity: "I experienced the Istanbul of my childhood as a city in two shades, dark and grey, like a black and white photograph."[33] In the relationship of the author to the city, there are memories of the Byzantine Empire and the Ottoman Empire. At the present time, religion and secularism fight for the country's identity: restorative dreams of the glorious past, nationalist isolation, and fundamentalism versus entry into the gates of Europe.

Two European immigrant writers wandered in the Mediterranean region, which left its impression on their work: Albert Cohen and Jorge Semprún. Albert Cohen's book *Solal* depicts a Mediterranean world whose absurd and tortuous plot wavers between Christianity and Judaism, magic and realism, liberation from the ghetto and the search for education, wealth and status, and also touches on assimilation, heresy ("Thank God I'm an unbeliever!"), and suicide.[34] His subsequent books were a continuation to *Solal* and its Mediterranean settings. Solal was the only son of Gamaliel Solal, head of a disintegrating and scattered Jewish community in a group of islands in the Aegean Sea. For the Mediterranean settings of his novel, Cohen drew inspiration from his childhood in Corfu.

Likewise, the writer and intellectual Jorge Semprún emerged from Spain in a Mediterranean habitat. According to Jorge Semprún, ever since Plato's parable of the cave, in which nothing was visible but shadows, the quality of lucidity has been bound up with vision and perspective—or, in other words, with light. It is not surprising that Prometheus, who stole light from the gods and thus rejected a reality of transcendental values beyond man, has become a metaphor for an enlightened outlook. The Mediterranean sun was two-sided, representing the absurdity of the arbitrary and the enlightenment of lucidity. Semprún chose the latter option. Indeed, anyone, like the lark, can welcome the sun, and anyone, with Hegel, can compare the philosophy of history to the owl of Minerva that appears only with the onset of night—at the end of the historical process. However, Semprún is neither a lark nor an owl but an enlightened Mediterranean intellectual, one "who discerns the dawn in the darkness of night, who catches the light before it is truly visible."

The problematic nature of a modernist national identity, and ergo of the Mediterranean vision wedded to European cultural values, was poignantly articulated by the Algerian writer Kateb Yacine (1929–1989) in his critique of his countryman Albert Camus (1913–1960). The son of a Berber family who was educated in French educational institutions, as a student at a *collège* (secondary school) Yacine participated in a demonstration in which six thousand to eight thousand Algerians were killed by French colonial soldiers. In 1947 he published his first book of poems, and in that same year he joined the Algerian Communist Party. A decade later he published his first novel, *Nedjma* (1956), about the love of his childhood, an eternally unattainable woman, a metaphor for his motherland engaged in a bloody war for its freedom.[35] The book had tremendous influence on North African Francophone literature. Yacine was a writer, a poet, a playwright who traveled a great deal, met Bertold Brecht and Sartre, and wrote plays about Ho Chi Minh and Nelson Mandela. With his theatrical troupe, for five years he participated in tours throughout Algeria and appeared in front of workers, farmers, and students. Although he thought that French was a colonialist language, he said that the use of it did not make the speaker a foreign agent: "I write in French in order to tell the French that I am not French."

In 1957, when exiled in France, Yacine wrote a letter to Albert Camus, who that year received the Nobel Prize in Literature. He

EPILOGUE

approached the Algerian-French writer like a family member: "Dear son of my land," he said, "exiled from the same country, two rival brothers" who had the same heritage but did not wish to divide it. That heritage had now become a place of contention in which members of the same family killed one another. Yacine called on Camus to engage in dialogue.[36] In a recorded conversation, Yacine said that although Camus had criticized French colonialism, it was only on moral grounds. When it came to making a political decision, Camus preferred his mother (who was a French settler with Spanish roots) to justice (independence).[37] Yacine advised Camus's French readers to compare him to William Faulkner. Although in his opinion there was a racist tone in Faulkner's book *Light in August* (1932), the American writer provided details of the lives of Black people in the southern United States, tried to get to know them, and portrayed the image of a Black youth who was murdered.

In contrast, Yacine continued, Camus described the landscape and the sea at Tipaza but ignored its inhabitants. The native Algerians were not of interest to him, and the readers know nothing at all about the Arab killed by the "foreigner" except that he was called Said. Said was also the name of an Algerian worker in Sweden at the time when Camus received the Nobel Prize. Said broke into the journalists' party in honor of the prizewinner, saying that his disruption was prompted by Camus's famous statement that he saw no contradiction between his mother and his country.

—∿∿—

Kahanoff, like Camus and Sartre, spotted the inherent contradictions in Memmi's writings, and concluded, like them, that he was torn between the conflicting forces that shaped his personality and that he refused to relinquish any of his attachments. Where does he belong? To the Jewish people? To France? To North Africa? To the Mediterranean?

Albert Memmi alluded to the Mediterranean sun—hinting, of course, at the metaphor associated with Camus—but in an unexpected manner:[38] he warned against the shadow that it casts. The emigration, uprooting, colonialism, and wars so characteristic of that geopolitical area also sow seeds of racial trouble. Memmi believed that the struggle against racism went together with the struggle against oppression: for him, rejecting racism meant opting for a certain conception of humanity. Mankind could be united only on the basis of equality of all peoples and all persons. Universalism, according to Memmi, was "true mutuality," a rejection of particular values and the acceptance of a single principle: man as man. The Enlightenment sought to create a "new man" in its rationalistic image—something out of nothing. Its tool was ideology. Mediterranean humanism, in contrast, is concerned with real rather than abstract humanity, with experience rather than ideology, with the struggle against racism rather than hegemony.

Kahanoff considered the place of the Mediterranean writers in the literature of their countries of origin and in the literature of the countries that received them. In Albert Memmi, Edmond Jabès, and Claude Vigée, all of whom were her close friends, Kahanoff saw a group who cast light on a phenomenon that existed in France of the postcolonial era at a time when many immigrants from her former colonies settled there. Were they just a passing generation? For Kahanoff, these writers represented a cultural turning point with discernible consequences for the national cultures, whose defining characteristics they altered. Kahanoff's analyses were a prescient forecast of the situation in our time. At a time when groups of exiles and foreign workers have emigrated and settled in Europe (and, one may add, in Israel), one sees that they have not been completely assimilated into their new countries; instead, various "mixed" cultures have come into being that have consequently influenced the cultures of the host countries. Among the younger foreigners and economic migrants, the need soon arose to express their experiences and the crisis of identity that they were passing through.

Kahanoff and the Mediterranean writers serve as exemplars and intellectual seismographs of Mediterranean humanism's current and distinguished social critics—to use the term employed by Michael Walzer[39]—within the Mediterranean region. Although they do not constitute a formal school of thought, they share an opposition to violence, integral nationalism, dictatorship, and ideological radicalism; an antiracism stemming from their tolerance of the "Other" and their acceptance of the foreign and the different; a multicultural outlook that foreshadows postmodernist discourse; and an affirmation of dialogue as a form of human activity.

The Mediterranean humanist writers did their best writing in places where they felt great alienation.[40] They wrote about racism, multiculturalism, and dialogue. The Mediterranean for them evoked the Greek concept of *nostos*: the wanderer returning, the Odyssean hero ever longing for his Ithaca. Kahanoff had a tendency to create characters, philosophical personae, who could express their desires and longings. Her humanism was imbued with a poetic power identified with the Mediterranean. Readers of the Mediterranean humanist writers have found them sensitive barometers of their Levantine space who, while rebelling and protesting through their characters, their actions, their confessions, and the story of their emigration, at the same time embodied the region's Mediterranean humanism.

NOTES

PREFACE

1. Jacqueline Kahanoff, *Mongrels or Marvels: The Levantine Writings of Jacqueline Shochet Kahanoff*, ed. Deborah A. Starr and Sasson Somekh (Stanford, CA: Stanford University Press, 2011); Kahanoff, *From East the Sun* (Me-Mizrah Shemesh), trans. and ed. Aharon Amir (Tel Aviv: Yariv-Hadar, 1978) [Hebrew]; Kahanoff, *Between Two Worlds* (Bein Shnei Olamot), ed. David Ohana (Jerusalem: Keter, 2005) [Hebrew]; Kahanoff, *We Are All Children of the Levant* (Balevant Noladnu Kulanu), ed. David Ohana (Jerusalem: Carmel, 2022) [Hebrew]; Jacqueline Shochet, *Jacob's Ladder* (London: Harvill, 1951).

2. Kahanoff, "Childhood in Egypt—Memoire," *Jerusalem Quarterly* 36 (Summer 1985): 31–41. Also available in Kahanoff, "Childhood in Egypt," in *Mongrels or Marvels*, 1–13.

3. Judith Friedlander, *A Light in Dark Times: The New School for Social Research and Its University in Exile* (New York: Columbia University Press, 2019).

4. Emmanuelle Loyer, *Lévi-Strauss: A Biography*, trans. Ninon Vinsonneau and Jonathan Magidoff (Cambridge: Cambridge University Press, 2019); Maurice Godelier, *Claude Lévi-Strauss: A Critical Study of His Thought*, trans. Nora Scott (London: Verso, 2018).

5. Kahanoff, "Such Is Rachel," *Atlantic Monthly*, October 1946, 113–116. Also available in Kahanoff, "Such Is Rachel," in *Mongrels or Marvels*.

6. Kahanoff, "Cairo Wedding," *Tomorrow* 4, no. 11 (1945): 19–23. Also available in Kahanoff, "Cairo Wedding," in *Mongrels or Marvels*.

NOTES TO PAGES VIII–XVII

7. Kahanoff, "Wake of the Waves," in *From East the Sun* [Hebrew]; translated to English in Kahanoff, "Wake of the Waves," in *Mongrels or Marvels*.

8. Franck Salameh, *The Other Middle East: An Anthology of Modern Levantine Literature* (New Haven, CT: Yale University Press, 2018).

9. Philip Mansel, *Levant: Splendour and Catastrophe on the Mediterranean* (New Haven, CT: Yale University Press, 2012).

10. Fernand Braudel, *The Mediterranean and the Mediterranean World in the Age of Philip II*, trans. Siân Reynolds (New York: HarperCollins, 1972).

11. Kahanoff, "Introduction: From East the Sun," Gnazim Archive of Hebrew Writers, Israel (hereafter cited as G.A.), 1968.

12. David Ohana, "Jacqueline Kahanoff: Between Levantinism and Mediterraneanism," in *New Horizons: Mediterranean Research in the 21st Century*, ed. Mihran Dabag, Dieter Haller, and Nikolas Jaspert (Bochum: Brill Schöningh, 2001), 361–384.

13. Peregrine Horden and Nicholas Purcell, *The Corrupting Sea: A Study of Mediterranean History* (Oxford: Blackwell, 2000).

14. Shmuel N. Eisenstadt, "Multiple Modernities," *Daedalus* 129, no. 1 (Winter 2000): 1–29.

15. Kahanoff, "What about Levantinization?," *Journal of Levantine Studies* 1, no. 1 (Summer 2011): 13–22.

16. Aharon Amir, "Preface," in *From East the Sun* [Hebrew].

17. Kahanoff, "Between Two Worlds," *Yedioth Ahronoth*, December 9, 1977 [Hebrew]; Josette d'Amade, "Remembering Jacqueline," lecture given by Kahanoff's sister in Van Leer Institute's Forum of Mediterranean Cultures, Jerusalem, March 17, 1996.

18. Kahanoff, "Childhood in Egypt," in *Mongrels or Marvels*.

19. Gudrun Kramer, *The Jews in Modern Egypt, 1914–1952* (Seattle: University of Washington Press, 1989).

20. Kahanoff, "My America," in *From East the Sun*, 132 [Hebrew].

21. Kahanoff, prepublication version of "The Revolution in Education," Heksherim Archive, Ben-Gurion University of the Negev, Israel (hereafter cited as H.A.), undated [Hebrew].

22. Kahanoff, prepublication version of "A World View of Television," G.A., undated.

23. Kahanoff (under pseudonym Dina Monet), "Teacher's Teacher from Paris," *Jerusalem Post*, August 30, 1957 [Hebrew].

24. Kahanoff, "The Great Couple of French Literature: Jean-Paul Sartre and Simone de Beauvoir," *Maariv*, March 17, 1967 [Hebrew].

NOTES TO PAGES XVII–1   301

25. Kahanoff, "Welcome, Sadat," in *From East the Sun* [Hebrew]; translated to English in Kahanoff, "Welcome, Sadat," in *Mongrels or Marvels*, 239–242; Kahanoff, "My Brother Ishmael," in *Mongrels or Marvels*, 232–237.

26. Kahanoff, "Beersheba Story," *Reconstructionist*, G.A., undated.

27. Aharon Amir, "A Promise Rising on the Nile with Dawn," *Haaretz*, April 5, 1996 [Hebrew].

28. Kahanoff, *Ramat-Hadassah-Szold: Youth Aliyah Screening and Classification Centre* (Jerusalem: Goldbergs, 1960).

29. Kahanoff, "Israel's Levantinization," *Davar*, G.A., 1959 [Hebrew]; Ohana, "Levantinism as a Cultural Theory," in *Israel and Its Mediterranean Identity* (New York: Palgrave Macmillan, 2011), 77–97.

30. Ohana, "Mediterranean Humanism," *Mediterranean Historical Review* 18, no. 1 (2003): 59–75.

31. Kahanoff, "Charles Péguy," *Amot*, June-July 1963, 44–48, 50–65. See also "Charles Péguy," in *Between Two Worlds* [Hebrew].

32. Kahanoff, "Edmond Jabès, or 'The Book of Questions,'" *Davar*, June 4, 1973 [Hebrew].

33. Kahanoff, "Claude Vigée, a Portrait of a Poet," *Maariv*, January 4, 1963 [Hebrew].

34. Kahanoff, "A Literature of Social Mutation," *Haaretz*, December 8, 1972 [Hebrew].

35. Kahanoff, "From Egypt to Here," *Maariv*, October 4, 1967 [Hebrew].

36. Kahanoff, "The Tragedy of the Eastern Woman," *Maariv*, July 30, 1965 [Hebrew].

37. Kahanoff, ed., *African Stories*, trans. David Shahar (Tel Aviv: Am Hasefer, 1963) [Hebrew]; Kahanoff, introductions to *The Big Island—Songs of Madagascar*, trans. and ed. Shimshon Inbal (Tel Aviv, 1965) [Hebrew].

38. Kahanoff, "To Die a Modern Death," in *From East the Sun* [Hebrew].

39. Kahanoff, "Illness Chronicles," *At*, March-April, 1977 [Hebrew].

40. Ohana, Interview with Sarah Rippin, April 26, 2020.

INTRODUCTION

1. William W. Harris, *The Levant: A Fractured Mosaic* (Princeton, NJ: Marcus Weiner, 2005), xi.

2. Ibid.

3. Philip Mansel, *Levant: Splendour and Catastrophe on the Mediterranean* (New Haven, CT: Yale University Press, 2011), 1.

302 NOTES TO PAGES 2–12

4. "Levant," in *Encyclopedia Britannica*. https://www.britannica.com
/place/Levant.

5. H. Hagenmeyer, ed., *Fulcheri Cornotensis Historia Hierosolymitana* (*1095–1127*), lib. 3, c. 37 (Heidelberg: Carl Winters Universitatsbuchhandlung, 1913), 748–749.

6. Ibid.

7. Joshua Prawer, "Confrontation between East and West during the Crusaders Period," in *Lectures in Memory of Moshe Strossta R.I.P.*, ed. Joseph Geiger (Jerusalem: The Hebrew University, 1994), 28 [Hebrew].

8. Mansel, *Levant*, 6.

9. Ronnie Ellenblum, *Frankish Rural Settlement in the Latin Kingdom of Jerusalem* (Cambridge: Cambridge University Press, 1998).

10. Harris, *The Levant*, 118.

11. Mansel, *Levant*, 6.

12. Antoine Galland, *Voyage à Constantinople 1672–1673* (Paris: Maisonneuve et Larose, 2002), 1:261, 2:176.

13. Jon Calame and Esther Charlesworth, *Divided Cities: Belfast, Beirut, Jerusalem, Mostar and Nicosia* (Philadelphia: University of Pennsylvania Press, 2009).

1. A TALE OF FOUR CITIES

1. Jacqueline Kahanoff, "Testimony in Transition," in *From East the Sun*, trans. Aharon Amir (Tel Aviv: Yariv-Hadar, 1978), 61 [Hebrew].

2. Bat Ye'or, *The Jews in Egypt* (Ramat Gan, 1974) [Hebrew]; Ye'or, *Les Juifs en Egypt* (Geneva: World Jewish Congress, 1971).

3. Kahanoff, "Testimony in Transition," 62.

4. Kahanoff, "Between Two Worlds," *Yedioth Ahronoth*, September 12, 1977 [Hebrew]; also Kahanoff, "Between Two Worlds," in *Between Two Worlds*, ed. David Ohana (Jerusalem: Keter, 2005), 35 [Hebrew].

5. Kahanoff, "Childhood in Egypt," in *Mongrels and Marvels: The Levantine Writings of Jacqueline Shohet Kahanoff*, ed. Deborah Starr and Sasson Somekh (Stanford, CA: Stanford University Press), 8.

6. Kahanoff, "The Blue Veil of Progress," in *Between Two Worlds*, 60 [Hebrew].

7. Kahanoff, "Remembering Egypt," in *From East the Sun*, 64 [Hebrew].

8. Kahanoff, "Between Two Worlds," *Yedioth Ahronoth*; also Kahanoff, "Between Two Worlds," in *Between Two Worlds*, 35 [Hebrew].

NOTES TO PAGES 13–19

9. Kahanoff, "The Blue Veil of Progress," 50.

10. Kahanoff, "Childhood in Egypt," in *From East the Sun*, 11 [Hebrew].

11. Kahanoff, "Childhood in Egypt," in *Mongrels and Marvels*, 3.

12. Ibid.

13. Kahanoff, "Between Two Worlds," *Yedioth Ahronoth*; also Kahanoff, "Between Two Worlds," in *Between Two Worlds*, 35 [Hebrew].

14. Kahanoff, "Childhood in Egypt," in *Mongrels and Marvels*, 4.

15. Ibid.

16. Ibid.

17. Ibid., 11.

18. Ibid.

19. Kahanoff, "Europe from Afar," in *Mongrels and Marvels*, 103.

20. Kahanoff, "Childhood in Egypt," in *Mongrels and Marvels*, 12.

21. Ibid., 1.

22. Ibid., 8.

23. Ibid.

24. Kahanoff, "The Blue Veil of Progress," 49.

25. Ibid., 50.

26. Ibid.

27. Kahanoff, "Between Two Worlds," *Yedioth Ahronoth*; also Kahanoff, "Between Two Worlds," in *Between Two Worlds*, 34 [Hebrew].

28. Kahanoff, "Europe from Afar," 104–105.

29. Ibid., 110.

30. Kahanoff, "Between Two Worlds," *Yedioth Ahronoth*; also Kahanoff, "Between Two Worlds," in *Between Two Worlds*, 43 [Hebrew].

31. Kahanoff, "The Blue Veil of Progress," 60.

32. Ibid., 58.

33. Ibid., 57.

34. Ibid., 60.

35. Ibid., 53.

36. Kahanoff, "Childhood in Egypt," in *Mongrels and Marvels*, 5.

37. Ibid., 4.

38. Ibid.

39. Ibid., 5.

40. Kahanoff, "Passover in Egypt," in *Mongrels and Marvels*.

41. Kahanoff, "Between Two Worlds," *Yedioth Ahronoth*; also Kahanoff, "Between Two Worlds," in *Between Two Worlds*, 43 [Hebrew].

42. Kahanoff, "Europe from Afar," 107.

43. Ibid., 108.

304   NOTES TO PAGES 20–26

44. Ibid., 102–103.

45. Ibid., 103.

46. Kahanoff, "Childhood in Egypt," in *Mongrels and Marvels*, 11.

47. Kahanoff, "Europe from Afar," 107.

48. Ibid.

49. Ibid., 106.

50. Ibid., 103.

51. Ibid.

52. Kahanoff, "Between Two Worlds," *Yedioth Ahronoth*; also Kahanoff, "Between Two Worlds," in *Between Two Worlds*, 39 [Hebrew].

53. Kahanoff, "Passover in Egypt," 18.

54. Kahanoff, "Welcome, Sadat," in *From East the Sun*, 287 [Hebrew]; translated to English in Kahanoff, "Welcome, Sadat," in *Mongrels and Marvels*, 241.

55. On the subject of Messianism, Judaism, and Zionism, see David Ohana, *Political Theologies in the Holy Land: Israeli Messianism and Its Critics* (London: Routledge, 2009) [Hebrew].

56. Kahanoff, "Childhood in Egypt," in *Mongrels and Marvels*, 7.

57. Ibid. For further study of the Diaspora Jews' Messianic longing, see Arie Morgenstern, "Jews of the Diaspora and the Longing for Zion, 1240–1840," *Tchelet* 12 (2002): 51–100.

58. Ibid.

59. Kahanoff, "Europe from Afar," 103.

60. Ibid.

61. Kahanoff, "Passover in Egypt," 5.

62. Kahanoff, "Welcome, Sadat," in *From East the Sun*, 286 [Hebrew]; translated to English in Kahanoff, "Welcome, Sadat," in *Mongrels and Marvels*, 240.

63. "Welcome, Sadat," in *From East the Sun*, 286; see also Kahanoff, "My Brother Ishmael," in *Mongrels and Marvels*.

64. Kahanoff, "Welcome, Sadat," in *From East the Sun*, 286 [Hebrew]; translated to English in Kahanoff, "Welcome, Sadat," in *Mongrels and Marvels*, 241.

65. Kahanoff, "Europe from Afar," 109.

66. Kahanoff, "The Blue Veil of Progress," 47.

67. Kahanoff, "Between Two Worlds," *Yedioth Ahronoth*; also in Kahanoff, "Between Two Worlds," in *Between Two Worlds*, 35 [Hebrew].

68. Ibid., 39.

69. Ibid., 40.

70. Kahanoff, "Europe from Afar," 108.

71. Ibid., 110.

NOTES TO PAGES 27–36

72. Kahanoff, "Between Two Worlds," *Yedioth Ahronoth*; also in "Between Two Worlds," in *Between Two Worlds*, 48 [Hebrew].

73. Ibid., 47.

74. Ibid., 48.

75. Kahanoff, "Childhood in Egypt," in *Mongrels and Marvels*, 11.

76. Ibid., 13.

77. Ibid.

78. Kahanoff, "My America," in *From East the Sun*, 132 [Hebrew].

79. Kahanoff, "Between Two Worlds," *Yedioth Ahronoth*; also in Kahanoff, "Between Two Worlds," in *Between Two Worlds*, 45 [Hebrew].

80. Kahanoff, "My America," 132.

81. Ibid., 135.

82. Ibid., 138.

83. Kahanoff, "The Noble Prize, 1962—Why John Steinbeck?," *Maariv*, November 2, 1962 [Hebrew].

84. For a recent biography of Steinbeck, see William Souder, *Mad at the World: A Life of John Steinbeck* (New York: W. W. Norton, 2020).

85. Frederick Jackson Turner, "The Significance of the Frontier in American History," in *The Frontier in American History* (New York: Henry Holt, 1921).

86. Kahanoff, "The Noble Prize, 1962."

87. Kahanoff, "My America," 139.

88. Ibid., 140.

89. Ibid., 143.

90. Ibid., 144.

91. Ibid., 145.

92. For a recent study of the New School in New York, see Judith Friedlander, *A Light in Dark Times: The New School for Social Research and Its University in Exile* (New York: Columbia University Press, 2019).

93. For a recent biography of Lévi-Strauss, see Emmanuelle Loyer, *Lévi-Strauss: A Biography*, trans. Ninon Vinsonneau and Jonathan Magidoff (Cambridge: Cambridge University Press, 2019); also see Maurice Godelier, *Claude Lévi-Strauss: A Critical Study of His Thought*, trans. Nora Scott (London: Verso, 2018).

94. Kahanoff, "My America."

95. Ibid.

96. Kahanoff, prepublication version of "America—A Land of Plentitude and Absurdity," Heksherim Archive, Ben-Gurion University of the Negev, Israel (hereafter cited as H.A.), undated [Hebrew].

97. Paul Goodman, *Growing Up Absurd: Problems of Youth in the Organized Society* (New York: New York Review Books, 1960).

98. Herbert Marcuse, *Eros and Civilization* (London: Routledge, 2015).

99. Martin Jay, *The Dialectical Imagination: A History of the Frankfurt School and the Institute of Social Research,1923–1950* (Berkeley: University of California Press, 1996).

100. Jean Gottman, *Megalopolis: The Urbanized Northeastern Seaboard of the United States* (Cambridge, MA: MIT Press, 1961).

101. Kahanoff, prepublication version of "A City Named Megalopolis," H.A., undated [Hebrew]; see also Ohana, *The Intellectual Origins of Modernity* (New York: Routledge, 2019).

102. Ilan Troen, *Imagining Zion: Dreams, Designs, and Realities in a Century of Jewish Settlement* (New Haven, CT: Yale University Press, 2003), 176. I thank Ilan Troen for the remarks about the affinities between Kahanoff and Gottmann.

103. Kahanoff, "A City Named Megalopolis."

104. Ibid.

105. David M. Pollio, "Vergil and American Symbolism," *Classical Outlook* 87, no. 4 (2010), 145–146

106. William L. C. Wheaton, "Jean Gottman, Megalopolis: The Urbanized Northeastern Seaboard of the United States," *Annals of the American Academy of Political and Social Science* 341, no. 1 (1962): 166–167.

107. Stephen Graham and Simon Marvin, "Planning Cybercities? Integrating Telecommunications into Urban Planning," *Town Planning Review* 70, no. 1 (1999): 89–114.

108. Wheaton, "Jean Gottman, Megalopolis."

109. Kahanoff, prepublication version of "The Migration of the Peoples of the West," H.A., undated [Hebrew].

110. Ohana, "From Rousseau to Tocqueville: Janus Face of Modernity," in *Intellectual Origins of Modernity*, 29–79.

111. Kahanoff, prepublication version of "Planner of the Future, Buckminster Fuller," H.A., undated [Hebrew].

112. Stephen Mark Dobbs, "From Buck Rogers to Buckminster Fuller: On the Future of Art," *Art Education* 29, no. 3 (1976): 8–11.

113. Kahanoff, "Planner of the Future, Buckminster Fuller."

114. Ibid.

115. Norbert Wiener, *The Human Use of Human Beings: Cybernetics and Society* (London: Hachette Books, 1950).

116. Kahanoff, prepublication version of "The White Flag—Professor Norbert Wiener and the Science of Cybernetics," H.A., undated [Hebrew].

NOTES TO PAGES 43–54

117. Norbert Wiener, *God & Golem Inc.* (Cambridge, MA: MIT Press, 1964), chap. 8.

118. Ohana, *Intellectual Origins of Modernity*, 1–28.

119. Kahanoff, "The White Flag."

120. Ibid.

121. Michael Harrington, *The Other America: Poverty in the United States* (New York: Scribner, 1962); Harrington, *The Accidental Century* (New York: MacMillan, 1965).

122. Kahanoff, prepublication version of "Growing Up in America—M. Harrington's 'Accidental Century,'" H.A., undated [Hebrew].

123. Michael Harrington, "Fragments of the Century," *Kirkus Review*, January 1, 1973.

124. Kahanoff, "Growing Up in America."

125. Norbert A. Goman, "A Yankee Radical," in *Michael Harrington: Speaking American* (New York: Routledge, 1995), 1–24; Maurice Isserman, *The Other American: The Life of Michael Harrington* (New York: PublicAffairs, 2000).

126. Kahanoff, prepublication version of "The Revolution in Education," H.A., undated [Hebrew].

127. Ibid.

128. Kahanoff, prepublication version of "Television as a Springboard: To Swim or to Sink," H.A., undated [Hebrew].

129. Wilson P. Dizard, *Television: A World View* (New York: Syracuse University Press, 1966).

130. Herbert Schiller, "Television: A World View," *AV Communication Review* 15, no. 1 (1967): 122–124.

131. Dizard, *Television: A World View.*

132. Kahanoff, "Television as a Springboard."

133. Kahanoff, "Parisian Etchings," in *From East the Sun*, 83 [Hebrew].

134. Kahanoff, "My Paris in the Summer," in *Between Two Worlds*, 223 [Hebrew].

135. Ibid., 224.

136. Kahanoff, "Parisian Etchings," 81.

137. Ibid., 82.

138. Ibid., 83.

139. Ibid., 84.

140. François Villon, *Le Grand Testament* (Paris: CreateSpace Independent Publishing Platform, 2015 [1937]).

141. Kahanoff, "Parisian Etchings," 85.

NOTES TO PAGES 54–66

142. Ohana, *Nietzsche and Jewish Political Theology* (London: Routledge, 2019), 1–28.

143. Kahanoff, "Parisian Etchings," 85.

144. Ibid.

145. Ibid., 88.

146. Ibid., 89.

147. Ibid., 81.

148. Kahanoff, prepublication version of "Jules Romains, on his Seventy-fifth Birthday," H.A., undated [Hebrew].

149. Kahanoff, "What Happened to French Culture?," *Haaretz*, October 6, 1972 [Hebrew].

150. Kahanoff, "Jules Romains."

151. For a recent biography of Dos Passos, see James McGrath Morris, *The Ambulance Drivers: Hemingway, Dos Passos, and a Friendship Made and Lost in War* (Boston: Da Capo, 2017).

152. Donald Pizer, *Toward a Modernist Style: John Dos Passos* (New York: Bloomsbury Academic, 2013).

153. Kahanoff, "Parisian Etchings," 82.

154. Kahanoff, "Jules Romains."

155. Kahanoff, "Parisian Etchings," 95.

156. Ibid., 97.

157. Ibid., 98.

158. Ibid., 100.

159. Ibid., 101.

160. Ibid., 102.

161. Ibid., 103.

162. Ibid., 104.

163. Ibid.

164. Ibid., 105.

165. Ibid.

166. Kahanoff, "My Paris in the Summer," 227.

167. Ibid.

168. Kahanoff, "France Chronicles," in *From East the Sun*, 106 [Hebrew].

169. Ibid., 107.

170. Ibid., 118.

171. Ibid., 119.

172. Émile Ajar [pseud. for Romain Gary], *The Life before Us*, trans. Ralph Manheim (New York: New Directions, 1986).

173. Kahanoff, "France Chronicles," 121.

NOTES TO PAGES 66–80

174. Ibid.

175. Claude Lévi-Strauss, *The Savage Mind*, trans. George Weidenfeld and Nigel Nicolson (London: Weidenfeld & Nicolson, 1966).

176. Kahanoff, "France Chronicles," 122.

177. Ibid.

178. Ibid., 109.

179. Kahanoff, prepublication version of "The Algerian Exodus," H.A., undated [Hebrew].

180. Ibid.

181. Kahanoff, "The Algerian Exodus."

182. Ibid.

183. Ibid.

184. Robert S. W. Wistrich, *A Lethal Obsession: Anti-Semitism from Antiquity to the Global Jihad* (New York: Random House, 2010).

185. Kahanoff, "The Algerian Exodus."

186. Ibid.

187. Ibid.

188. Kahanoff, prepublication version of "I, General De Gaulle—A Fantastic Biography of the President of France," H.A., undated [Hebrew].

189. Kahanoff, "Charles Péguy," Gnazim Archive of Hebrew Writers, Israel (hereafter cited as G.A.).

190. Kahanoff, "I, General De Gaulle."

191. Lawrence D. Kritzman, "A Certain Idea of de Gaulle," *Myth and Modernity* 111 (2007): 158–168.

192. Kahanoff, "I, General De Gaulle."

193. Ibid.

194. Ibid.

195. Ibid.

196. See also Raymond Aron, *De Gaulle, Israel and the Jews*, trans. John Sturrock (London: Routledge, 2004).

197. Jane Hiddleston, "Kateb Yacine: Poetry and Revolution," in *Decolonising the Intellectual: Politics, Culture, and Humanism at the End of the French Empire*, ed. Jane Hiddleston, Edmund Smyth, and Charles Forsdick (Liverpool: Liverpool University Press, 2014), 205–249.

198. Kahanoff, "France Chronicles," 123.

199. Emmanuel Mounier, *Le personnalisme*, trans. Philip Mairet (Notre Dame: Notre Dame University, 1952).

200. Tony Judt, *Past Imperfect: French Intellectuals, 1944–1956* (New York: New York University Press, 2011).

201. Kahanoff, "France Chronicles," 126.

202. Ibid., 128.

203. Ibid., 129.

204. Ibid., 130.

205. Ibid.

206. Bernard A. Gendreau, "The Role of Jacques Maritain and Emmanuel Mounier in the Creation of French Personalism," *Personalist Forum* 8, no. 1 (1992): 97–108.

207. Kahanoff, "The Great Couple of French Literature: Jean-Paul Sartre and Simone de Beauvoir," *Maariv*, March 17, 1967 [Hebrew].

208. Ibid., 231.

209. Ibid., 233.

210. Ibid., 234.

211. Kahanoff, prepublication version of "Claude Lévi-Strauss: Culture and Cooking," H.A., undated [Hebrew].

212. Claude Lévi-Strauss, *Mythologiques: Le Cru et le Cuit* (Paris: Plon, 1964).

213. Ibid.

214. Kahanoff, "What Happened to French Culture?"

215. Ibid.

216. Kahanoff, "Jules Romains"; André Malraux, *La Condition Humaine* (Paris: Man's Fate, 1934).

217. Françoise Sagan, *Des bleus à l'âme* (Paris: Flammarion, 1972).

218. Romain Gary, *Europa* (Paris: Gallimard, 1999).

219. Kahanoff, "What Happened to French Culture?"

220. Laine' Pascal, *L'irrévolution* (Paris: Gallimard, 1971).

221. Kahanoff, "Waves," in *From East the Sun* [Hebrew]; translated to English in "Wake of the Waves," in *Mongrels and Marvels*.

222. Kahanoff, prepublication version of "Chicago: The Great Crowd Wept," *Maariv*, H.A., undated [Hebrew].

223. Kahanoff, "Welcome, Sadat," in *From East the Sun* [Hebrew]; translated to English in "Welcome, Sadat," in *Mongrels and Marvels*; Kahanoff, "My Brother Ishmael."

224. Kahanoff, "Waves," in *From East the Sun*, 148 [Hebrew]; translated to English in "Waves," in *Mongrels and Marvels*, 138.

225. Ibid., 149; translated in ibid., 139.

226. Ibid., 150; translated in ibid., 141.

227. Ibid., 149; translated in ibid., 139.

228. Ibid., 150; translated in ibid., 140.

NOTES TO PAGES 92–104

229. Ibid., 151; translated in ibid., 142.

230. Ibid., 152; translated in ibid., 143.

231. Kahanoff, "Chicago."

232. Kahanoff, "Waves," in *From East the Sun,* 155 [Hebrew]; translated to English in "Waves," in *Mongrels and Marvels,* 146.

233. Ibid., 15; translated in ibid., 148.

234. Ibid., 157; translated in ibid., 149.

235. Ibid., 158; translated in ibid., 150.

236. Kahanoff, prepublication version of "The Marakia Became a Sensation," in *Bamahane,* H.A., undated [Hebrew].

237. Ibid.

238. On the subject of the Beersheba School, see Kahanoff, "A Bridge towards the 'Olim' of the East," in *Between Two Worlds,* 167–174 [Hebrew].

239. Ibid.

240. Kahanoff, "The Marakia Became a Sensation."

241. Nissim Rejwan, *Outsider in the Promised Land: An Iraqi Jew in Israel* (Austin: University of Texas Press, 2006), 81.

242. Nurit Beretzky, "The First Lady of Mediterraneanism," *Maariv,* March 15, 1996 [Hebrew].

243. Dror Eydar, "Last Interview with Aharon Amir," *Haaretz,* February 27, 2009 [Hebrew].

244. A. B. Yehoshua, "The First Glass of Cognac," *Haaretz,* March 7, 2008 [Hebrew].

245. Aharon Amir, "Preface," in *From East the Sun,* 7–8 [Hebrew].

246. Aharon Amir, "A Promise Rising on the Nile with Dawn," *Haaretz,* April 5, 1996 [Hebrew].

247. Ibid.

248. Aharon Amir, "The Second Republic," *Haaretz,* October 19, 2006 [Hebrew].

249. Vered Kellner, "How Lovely the Nights," *Kol Ha'ir,* October 12, 2001 [Hebrew].

250. Tali Shiff, "Between Minor and Major Identity," *Theoria Vebikoret* 37 (2010): 143 [Hebrew].

251. Ian S. MacNiven and Carol Peirce, "Introduction: Lawrence Durrell: Man and Writer," *Twentieth Century Literature* 33, no. 3 (1987): 255–261.

252. Poem written by Amir on the subject of Kahanoff and her sister: "Two Sisters," *Yedioth Ahronoth,* published in April 1979, a week after Kahanoff's passing; see also Josette d'Amade, "Remembering Jacqueline," a

lecture given by Kahanoff's sister in Van Leer Institute's Forum of Mediterranean Cultures, Jerusalem, March 17, 1996.

253. Amir, "A Promise Rising on the Nile with Dawn."

254. Kahanoff, "A City Named Megalopolis"; see also Aharon Amir, "The Shock of Closeness," *Keshet—Chapters in the American Experience* 52 (1971): 6 [Hebrew]; Dan Laor, "I Hear America Singing: On One Aspect of the Canaan Worldview," *New Keshet* 11 (2005): 148–160 [Hebrew].

255. Amir, "A Promise Rising on the Nile with Dawn."

256. Kahanoff, "Testimony in Transition," 65.

257. Ibid., 66.

258. Ibid., 67.

259. Kahanoff, "A Bridge towards the 'Olim' of the East," 150.

260. Ibid.

261. Ibid., 154.

262. Ibid., 161.

263. Ibid., 158.

264. Ibid., 162.

265. Ibid., 163.

266. Ibid.

267. Ibid., 167.

268. Ibid., 168.

269. Ibid., 170.

270. Ibid., 172.

271. Kahanoff, prepublication version of "Hatikva," H.A., undated [Hebrew].

272. Ibid.

273. Kahanoff, "Preface," in *Ramat-Hadassah-Szold: Youth Aliya Screening and Classification Centre* (Jerusalem: Goldbergs, 1960), 13–14.

274. Ibid., 25.

275. Kahanoff, prepublication version of "Jewish-Arabic Dialogue in Israel," H.A., undated [Hebrew].

276. Ibid.

277. Ohana, *Nietzsche and Jewish Political Theology.*

278. Kahanoff, "Jewish-Arabic Dialogue in Israel."

279. Ibid.

280. Kahanoff, prepublication version of "Nothing Sweet Comes Out of Gaza," H.A., undated [Hebrew].

281. Ibid.

282. Kahanoff, prepublication version of "Four Aspects," H.A., undated [Hebrew].

NOTES TO PAGES 123–136

283. Ibid.

284. The song "In the Shaked Unit." Words: Dahlia Ravikovitch, meldy : Rafi Ben-Moshe, Performance: Southern Command Band.

285. Letter from Ravikovitch to Jacqueline Kahanoff, G.A., May 12, 1963 [Hebrew].

2. LEVANTINISM

1. David Ohana, "Jacqueline Kahanoff: A Mediterranean Portrait with a Lady," in *Between Two Worlds* (Bein Shnei Olamot), ed. David Ohana (Jerusalem: Keter, 2005), 14 [Hebrew]; also see Kahanoff's discussion of "psych-historical time" in Jacqueline Kahanoff, "Introduction: From East the Sun," Gnazim Archive of Hebrew Writers, Israel (hereafter cited as G.A.), 1968.

2. Ibid.

3. Fernand Braudel, *The Mediterranean and the Mediterranean World in the Age of Philip II*, trans. Siân Reynolds (New York: HarperCollins, 1972).

4. On Kahanoff's conception of Levantinism—as a European, as a modern woman, and as a Zionist—see David Tal, "Jacqueline Kahanoff and Demise of the Levantine," *Mediterranean Historical Review* 32, no. 2 (2017): 237–254.

5. Kahanoff, "Israel's Levantinization," Davar, G.A., 1959 [Hebrew].

6. Kahanoff, prepublication version of "A City Named Megalopolis," Heksherim Archive, Ben-Gurion University of the Negev, Israel, undated [Hebrew].

7. Kahanoff, prepublication version of "Introduction: From East the Sun."

8. Shmuel N. Eisenstadt, "Multiple Modernities," *Daedalus* 129, no. 1 (2000): 1–29.

9. Kahanoff, "Childhood in Egypt," in *Mongrels or Marvels: The Levantine Writings of Jacqueline Shohet Kahanoff*, ed. Deborah A. Starr and Sasson Somekh (Stanford, CA: Stanford University Press, 2011), 1.

10. Tiziana Carlino, "The Levant: A Trans-Mediterranean Literary Category," *TRANS-, a Journal of General and Comparative Literature* 6 (2006): 1–12.

11. Ibid.

12. Daniel Monterescu, "Beyond the Sea of Formlessness: Jacqueline Kahanoff and the Levantine Generation," *Journal of Levantine Studies* 1 (2011): 23–40.

314 NOTES TO PAGES 136–146

13. Gil Z. Hochberg, "The Mediterranean Option: On the Politics of Regional Affiliation in Current Israeli Cultural Imagination," *Journal of Levantine Studies* 1, no. 1 (Summer 2011): 41–65.

14. Gil Z. Hochberg, "'Permanent Immigration': Jacqueline Kahanoff, Ronit Matalon and the Impetus of Levantinism," *Boundary* 2, no. 31 (2004): 219–243.

15. H. K. Bhabha, *The Location of Culture* (London: Routledge, 1994).

16. Mikaél Elial and Shlomo Elbaz, "De Nouvelles Andalousies," *Levant: Cahiers de l'espace méditerranéen* 4, no. 1 (1991).

17. Ammiel Alcalay, *After Jews and Arabs: Remaking Levantine Culture* (Minneapolis: University of Minnesota Press, 1993).

18. Edward Said, *Orientalism* (New York: Vintage, 1978).

19. Alcalay, *After Jews and Arabs*, 1.

20. Hannan Hever, *Toward the Longed-For Shore: The Sea in Modern Hebrew Culture* (Tel Aviv: Van Leer Institute and Hakkibutz Hameuchad, 2007) [Hebrew].

21. Debora Ann Starr, "Ambivalent Levantines/Levantine Ambivalences: Egyptian Jewish in Contemporary Literature" (PhD diss., University of Michigan, 2000).

22. Alexandra Nocke, *The Place of the Mediterranean in Modern Israeli Identity* (Leiden: Brill, 2009).

23. Kahanoff, "Europe from Afar," in *Mongrels or Marvels*, 101.

24. Ibid., 102.

25. Ibid., 103.

26. Ibid., 103.

27. Kahanoff, "Europe from Afar," in *From East the Sun*, trans. Aharon Amir (Tel Aviv: Yariv-Hadar, 1978), 26 [Hebrew].

28. Kahanoff, "Black on White [Originally 'Ambivalent Levantines']," in *From East the Sun*, 48 [Hebrew].

29. Ohana, "Jacqueline Kahanoff: Pioneer of Mediterranean Culture in Israel," *Iunim Betkumat Israel* 13 (2003): 29–55.

30. Yair Sheleg, "The Princess of the Levant," *Kol Ha'ir*, March 15, 1996 [Hebrew]; Nurit Beretzky, "The First Lady of Mediterraneanism," *Maariv*, March 15, 1996 [Hebrew]; Yoram Bronowski, "The Levantines," *Haaretz*, April 5, 1996 [Hebrew].

31. Joshua Prawer, "Jews, Christians and Muslims in the Mediterranean Basin," *Pe'amim* 45 (1990): 5 [Hebrew].

32. Kahanoff, "Black on White," 53.

NOTES TO PAGES 146–165

33. Meron Benvenisti, "A False Mediterranean Harbor," *Haaretz,* March 21, 1996 [Hebrew].

34. Ohana, "Carl Schmitt's Legal Fascism," *Politics, Religion and Ideology* 20, no. 3 (2019): 273–300.

35. Benvenisti, "A False Mediterranean Harbor."

36. Nissim Calderon, "An Outing in the Mediterranean," *Haaretz,* May 17, 1996 [Hebrew].

37. Amir Aharon, "Preface," in *From East the Sun,* 7–8 [Hebrew].

38. Ohana, *Israel and Its Mediterranean Identity* (New York: Palgrave Macmillan, 2011).

39. Yoram Bronowski, "Lament over a Lost Option," *Haaretz,* May 27, 1994 [Hebrew].

40. Ibid.

41. Quoted in Beretzky, "The First Lady of Mediterraneanism."

42. Ibid.

43. Yaira Ginossar, "Otzmat Hakfilut," *Iton* 77 (1978): 14. Quoted in "Editors' Introduction," in *Mongrels or Marvels.*

44. "Editors' Introduction."

3. KAHANOFF'S POETIC JOURNEY

1. Letter from Dahlia Ravikovitch to Jacqueline Kahanoff, Gnazim Archive of Hebrew Writers, Israel (hereafter cited as G.A.), May 12, 1963 [Hebrew].

2. M. Golan, "In the Field of Poetry," *Al Hamishmar,* April 17, 1960 [Hebrew]. On the reception of Ravikovitch's first book of poems, see Giddon Ticotsky, *Dahlia Ravikovitch: Her Life and Literature* (Haifa: Haifa University Press, 2016), 68–86 [Hebrew].

3. Jacqueline Kahanoff, "Waves," in *From East the Sun,* trans. Aharon Amir (Tel Aviv: Yariv-Hadar, 1978) [Hebrew]; translated into English in "Waves," in *Mongrels or Marvels: The Levantine Writings of Jacqueline Shohet Kahanoff,* ed. Deborah A. Starr and Sasson Somekh (Stanford, CA: Stanford University Press, 2011).

4. Dahlia Ravikovitch, "Karnei Hattin," in *All Poems So Far* (Tel Aviv: Hakibbutz Hameuchad, 1994), 133–134.

5. Quoted in Nurit Beretzky, "The First Lady of Mediterraneanism," *Maariv,* March 15, 1996 [Hebrew].

6. Kahanoff, "Edmond Jabès or *The Book of Questions,*" *Davar* 30.4.1964" [Hebrew].

NOTES TO PAGES 166–183

7. Kahanoff, "Charles Péguy," G.A.

8. Charles Péguy, *Le mystère de la charité de Jeanne d'Arc* (Paris: Gallimard, 1921).

9. Charles Péguy, *Eve* (Paris: Gallimard, 2017).

10. Charles Péguy, *L'Argent* (Paris: Cahiers De La Quinzaine, 1913).

11. Ibid.

12. Ibid.

13. Kahanoff, "Charles Péguy."

14. Ibid.

15. Shimon Shamir, ed., *The Jews of Egypt: A Mediterranean Society in Modern Times* (London: Routledge, 2019).

16. Kahanoff, "A Culture Becoming," *Davar*, April 16, 1973 [Hebrew].

17. Ibid.

18. Edmond Jabès, *Le Livre du Dialogue* (Paris: Gallimard, 1984). For further reading see Steven Jaron, "French Modernism and the Emergence of Jewish Consciousness in the Writings of Edmond Jabès" (PhD diss., Columbia University, 1997).

19. Kahanoff, "Edmond Jabès."

20. David Ohana, *Albert Camus and the Critique of Violence* (Brighton: Sussex Academic Press, 2017).

21. Kahanoff, "Claude Vigée: Portrait of a Poet," *Maariv*, January 4, 1963.

22. Claude Vigée, *Les artistes de la faim* (Paris: Calmann-Lévy, 1960).

23. Kahanoff, "Vigée: The Frail Bridge between Man and World," *Davar*, Heksherim Archive, Ben-Gurion University of the Negev, Israel, undated [Hebrew].

24. Claude Vigée, *Révolte et louanges* (Paris: J. Corti, 1962).

25. Ohana, "Vige'e," *Haaretz*, October 14, 2020.

26. G.A., Kahanoff's Archive.

27. Ajay Kumar Chaubey, *An Anthology of 21st Century Criticism*, ed. V. S. Naipaul (New Delhi: Atlantic, 2015).

28. Kahanoff, "Albert Memmi, or a Twisting Road to Israel," *Maariv*, November 18, 1966 [Hebrew].

29. Kahanoff, ed., *African Stories*, trans. David Shahar (Tel Aviv: Am Ha-Sefer, 1963), 7 [Hebrew].

30. Ibid., 8.

31. Ibid., 9.

32. Ibid., 10.

33. Ibid., 11.

NOTES TO PAGES 184–196   317

34. Ibid.

35. Ibid., 12.

36. Ibid.

37. Kahanoff, introductions to *The Big Island—Songs of Madagascar*, trans. and ed. Shimshon Inbal (Tel Aviv: Eked, 1965) [Hebrew].

4. "WHERE CAN I FEEL AT HOME?"

1. Martin Buber, *I and Thou*, trans. Ronald Gregor Smith (New York: Simon and Schuster, 2000).

2. Jacqueline Kahanoff, "The Talmud as a Living Challenge," *Haaretz*, September 13, 1968 [Hebrew].

3. Emmanual Lévinas, *Quatre Lectures Talmudiques* (Paris: Minuit, 1968).

4. But see "Lest It, Too, Is Adopted by the 'Settler' Discourse," *Maariv*, April 12, 2002 [Hebrew].

5. Kahanoff, "On Jacob," in *From East the Sun*, trans. Aharon Amir (Tel Aviv: Yariv-Hadar, 1978), 194 [Hebrew].

6. Ibid. See also Yonit Efron, "In Search of Identity: A Historic Perspective of Hebrew-Writing Israeli Intellectuals from Iraq and Egypt" (PhD diss., Tel Aviv University, 2005) [Hebrew].

7. Kahanoff, "Of Jacob," 207.

8. See especially Debora Ann Starr, "Ambivalent Levantines/Levantine Ambivalences: Egyptian Jewish in Contemporary Literature" (PhD diss., University of Michigan, 2000); Efron, "In Search of Identity."

9. Kahanoff, "On Jacob," 209.

10. Kahanoff, "My Brother Ishmael," in *Mongrels or Marvels: The Levantine Writings of Jacqueline Shohet Kahanoff*, ed. Deborah A. Starr and Sasson Somekh (Stanford, CA: Stanford University Press, 2011).

11. Kahanoff, "Europe from Afar," in *Mongrels or Marvels*, 104.

12. Kahanoff, "The Tragedy of the Eastern Woman," *Maariv*, July 30, 1965 [Hebrew].

13. Kahanoff, "Do You Like Sagan?," *Maariv*, October 23, 1956 [Hebrew].

14. Kahanoff, "The Great Couple of French Literature: Jean-Paul Sartre and Simone de Beauvoir," *Maariv*, March 17, 1967 [Hebrew].

15. Ronit Matalon, "Uprooted from the East," *Haaretz*, August 1, 1986 [Hebrew].

16. Ronit Matalon, "The Sorrow of Possibilities' End," *Haaretz*, March 4, 1994 [Hebrew].

17. Kahanoff, "Upon Return to the East," in *From East the Sun*, 74 [Hebrew].

18. Dolly Benhabib, "Women's Skirts Had Shortened," *Theoria Ve-Bikoret* 5 (1994): 159–164 [Hebrew].

19. For further reading, see Homi K. Bhabha, *Nation and Narration* (London: Routledge, 1990).

20. Kahanoff, "Eastern Music in Israel," *Moznaaim* 3–4, no. 37 (1973): 217–221 [Hebrew].

21. Kahanoff, prepublication version of "The Maimona Festival," Heksherim Archive, Ben-Gurion University of the Negev, Israel (hereafter cited as H.A.), undated [Hebrew].

22. Kahanoff, "Eastern Music in Israel," 220.

23. Kahanoff, *From East the Sun*, 48.

24. Alexander Uria Boskowitz, "The Problems of Music in Israel," *Orlogin* 9 (1953): 290.

25. Assaf Shelleg, *Theological Stains: Art Music and the Zionist Project* (New York: Oxford University Press, 2020).

26. Kahanoff, "The Literature of Social Mutation," in *Between Two Worlds*, ed. David Ohana (Jerusalem: Keter, 2005), 109 [Hebrew].

27. Kahanoff, "A Twisting Road to Israel," *Maariv*, November 18, 1966 [Hebrew].

28. David Ohana, *The Origins of Israeli Mythology: Neither Canaanites nor Crusaders*, trans. David Maisel (Cambridge: Cambridge University Press, 2012).

29. Kahanoff, "A Twisting Road to Israel."

30. Albert Memmi, *The Pillar of Salt*, trans. Edward Rediti, preface by Albert Camus (Boston: Beacon, 2013).

31. Albert Cohen, *Ô vous, frères humains* (Paris: Gallimard, 1972).

32. Kahanoff, "Albert Cohen—Alone in the Storm," H.A., undated, 102–103 [Hebrew].

33. For example, Jorge Semprún, *Le Grand Voyage* (Paris: Gallimard, 1963); Semprún, *L'écriture ou la vie* (Paris: Gallimard, 1994).

34. Najib Mahfouz, *Palace Walk*, trans. William Maynard Hutchins and Olive E. Kenny (New York: Doubleday, 1990); Mahfouz, *Palace of Desire*, trans. William Maynard Hutchins, Lorne M. Kenny, and Olive E. Kenny (New York: Doubleday, 1991); Mahfouz, *Sugar Street*, trans. William Maynard Hutchins and Angele Botros Samaan (New York: American University in Cairo Press, 1992).

NOTES TO PAGES 206–218

35. Kahanoff, "Edmond Jabès or *The Book of Questions*," *Davar*, April 30, 1965. [Hebrew].

36. Ibid.

37. Ibid.

38. Ibid.

39. Kahanoff, "Rebel, My Brother," in *From East the Sun* [Hebrew]; translated to English in "Rebel, My Brother," in *Mongrels or Marvels*.

40. Ohana, "Mediterranean Humanism," *Mediterranean Historical Review* 18, no. 1 (2003): 59–75.

41. Kahanoff, "The Literature of Social Mutation," 113–114.

42. George L. Mosse, *Confronting History: A Memoir* (Madison: University of Wisconsin Press, 2000); Peter Gay, *Weimar Culture: The Outsider as Insider* (New York. W. W. Norton, 2001); Saul Friedlander, *When Memory Comes*, trans. Helen R. Lane (New York: Farrar, Strauss and Giroux, 1979).

5. BEING A MODERN WOMAN

1. Jacqueline Kahanoff, "The Tragedy of the Eastern Woman," *Maariv*, July 30, 1965 [Hebrew].

2. Youssef el Masry, *Le drame sexual de la femme dans l'Orient arabe* (Paris: Robert Laffonte, 1962).

3. Kahanoff, "Europe from Afar," in *Mongrels or Marvels: The Levantine Writings of Jacqueline Shohet Kahanoff*, ed. Deborah A. Starr and Sasson Somekh (Stanford, CA: Stanford University Press, 2011), 101.

4. Ibid., 104.

5. Ibid., 106.

6. Ibid., 109.

7. Ibid., 110.

8. Ibid., 112.

9. Francine du Plessix Gray, *Lovers and Tyrants* (New York: Simon & Schuster, 1976).

10. Kahanoff, prepublication version of "Lovers and Tyrants," Heksherim Archive, Ben-Gurion University of the Negev, Israel (hereafter cited as H.A.), undated [Hebrew].

11. On Kierkegaard's despair, see Søren Kierkegaard, *Fear and Trembling*, trans. Alastair Hannay (London: Penguin, 2005), 208–209.

12. Kahanoff, "Lovers and Tyrants."

13. Kahanoff, "Do You Like Sagan?," *Maariv*, October 23, 1956 [Hebrew].

NOTES TO PAGES 218–227

14. Kahanoff, "Castle in Sweden—Françoise Sagan's First Play," *Maariv*, July 1, 1960 [Hebrew].

15. Kahanoff, prepublication version of "Women, with a Pen of Their Own," H.A., undated [Hebrew].

16. Simone de Beauvoir, *The Second Sex*, trans. Constance Borde and Sheila Malovany-Chevallier (New York: Vintage, 2011).

17. Kahanoff, "The Great Couple of French Literature: Jean-Paul Sartre and Simone de Beauvoir," *Maariv*, March 17, 1967 [Hebrew].

18. Simone de Beauvoir, *Memoirs of a Dutiful Daughter*, trans. James Kirkup (London: Penguin, 2001).

19. Kahanoff, "Women, With a Pen of Their Own."

20. Mary MacCarthy, *Memories of a Catholic Girlhood* (New York: Harvest/HBJ, 1957).

21. Kahanoff, "Women, With a Pen of Their Own."

22. Ruth Benedict, *Patterns of Culture* (London: Routledge, 1934).

23. Kahanoff, "Women, With a Pen of Their Own."

24. Ibid.

25. Kahanoff, prepublication version of "Equality between Lovers," H.A., undated [Hebrew].

26. Kahanoff, "Onwards towards Chastity," in *From East the Sun*, trans. Aharon Amir (Tel Aviv: Yariv-Hadar, 1978), 212 [Hebrew].

27. Kahanoff, "Woman as a Mechanical Orange," in *From East the Sun*, 218–221 [Hebrew].

28. Ibid., 220.

29. Opposed to Stanley Kubrick, who solely described evil and immorality, Ferdinand Céline was wholly attracted to the aesthetics of evil, a fascination that brought him to a certain admiration of Hitler himself. See David Ohana, *The Fascist Temptation: Creating a Political Community of Experiences* (Abingdon: Routledge, 2020).

30. Kahanoff, "The Miniskirt and the Older Woman," in *Bamahane*, H.A., undated [Hebrew].

31. Ibid.

32. Kahanoff, "To Be or Not to Be . . . Independent," in *From East the Sun*, 213–217 [Hebrew].

33. Ibid., 215.

34. Ibid., 217.

35. Kahanoff (under pseudonym Dina Monet), "The Tinbox," H.A., undated [Hebrew].

36. Ronit Matalon, "The Sorrow of Possibilities' End," *Haaretz*, March 4, 1994 [Hebrew].

NOTES TO PAGES 227–244

37. Kahanoff, "Upon Return to the East," in *From East the Sun*, 74–75 [Hebrew].

38. Kahanoff, "A Thousand and One Realities," in *From East the Sun*, 188 [Hebrew].

39. Kahanoff, "Upon Return to the East," 69.

40. Ibid., 68.

41. Ibid., 69.

42. Ibid., 70.

43. Ibid., 71.

44. Ibid., 72.

45. Ibid., 74.

46. Dolly Benhabib, "Women's Skirts Had Shortened," *Theoria Ve-Bikoret* 5 (1994): 159–164. [Hebrew].

47. Kahanoff, "Upon Return to the East," 74.

48. Kahanoff, prepublication version of "Women Not from Here," H.A., undated [Hebrew].

49. Kahanoff, prepublication version of "Dreams of Freedom—Java 1900," H.A., undated [Hebrew].

50. Ibid.

51. Kahanoff, prepublication version of "A Two-Faced World," H.A., undated [Hebrew].

6. BEYOND THE LEVANT

1. Jacqueline Kahanoff, prepublication version of "Ancient Japanese Literature," Heksherim Archive, Ben-Gurion University of the Negev, Israel (hereafter cited as H.A.), undated [Hebrew].

2. Ibid.

3. Kahanoff, prepublication version of "The Golden Age of Japanese [Women] Writers," H.A., undated [Hebrew].

4. Kahanoff, prepublication version of "Folkloric Japanese Literature," H.A., undated [Hebrew].

5. Kahanoff, "Golden Age of Japanese [Women] Writers."

6. Kahanoff, prepublication version of "Of Japanese Literature," H.A., undated [Hebrew].

7. Ibid.

8. Kahanoff, prepublication version of "Mission: Last Samurai," H.A., undated [Hebrew].

9. Ibid.

NOTES TO PAGES 245–261

10. John Marmysz, "Yukio Mashima and Asian Nihilism," *Laughing at Nothing: Humor as a Response to Nihilism* (Albany: State University of New York Press, 2003). Regarding the analogy between Asian and European Nihilism, see David Ohana, *The Dawn of Political Nihilism* (East Sussex: Sussex Academic Press, 2009).

11. Kahanoff, prepublication version of "Japan—without Geishas: A Splendid Anthology of the Japanese Story," H.A., undated [Hebrew].

12. Ibid.

13. Kahanoff, prepublication version of "Ghandi," H.A., undated [Hebrew].

14. Ibid.

15. Guha Ramachandra, *Gandhi: The Years That Changed the World, 1914–1948* (New York: Vintage, 2019).

16. Kahanoff, "Ghandi."

17. Nirad C. Chaudhuri, *The Autobiography of an Unknown Indian* (New York: Macmillan, 1951).

18. Kahanoff, "Where Does One Get the Color of One's Skin?," *Maariv*, June 23, 1961 [Hebrew].

19. Jean-Paul Sartre, *Black Orpheus*, trans. S. Allen (New York: Présence African, 1948).

20. Kahanoff, ed., *African Stories*, trans. David Shahar (Tel Aviv: Am Hasefer, 1963) [Hebrew].

21. Kahanoff, "Review of 'Black Power: The Politics of Liberation in America' [by Stokeley Carmichael and Charles Hamilton]," Gnazim Archive of Hebrew Writers, Israel (hereafter cited as G.A.) [Hebrew].

22. Kahanoff, "Review of 'Apologies to the Iroquois' [by Edmund Wilson]," G.A. [Hebrew].

23. Badrane Benlahcene, *The Socio-Intellectual Foundations of Malek Bennabi's Approach to Civilization* (London: International Institute of Islamic Thought, 2013).

24. Kahanoff, "Jews amongst Barbarians—A Valuable Study of the Jewish Communities of South Morocco," *Maariv*, January 10, 1964 [Hebrew].

25. Ibid.

26. Kahanoff, prepublication version of "Visit to Capri," H.A., undated [Hebrew].

27. Kahanoff, "Europe, Autumn of '75," *At*, H.A., undated [Hebrew].

28. Kahanoff, prepublication version of "How Many Italians Are There in Italy?" H.A., undated [Hebrew].

NOTES TO PAGES 262–278

29. Ibid.

30. Kahanoff, "Europe, Autumn of '75."

31. Ibid.; see also Kahanoff, prepublication version of "The Word 'Marrano' in the Florencian Dialect," H.A., undated [Hebrew].

32. Kahanoff, "How Many Italians Are There in Italy?"

33. Kahanoff, prepublication version of "A Crumbling City of Enchantments," H.A., undated [Hebrew].

34. Ibid.

35. Axel Munthe, *The Story of San Michele* (New York: E. P. Dutton, 1930).

36. Kahanoff, "Visit to Capri."

37. Kahanoff, "The Word 'Marrano' in the Florencian Dialect."

38. Kahanoff, prepublication version of "Summer in Portugal," H.A., undated [Hebrew].

39. Ibid.

40. Kahanoff, prepublication version of "On Being a Tourist," H.A., undated [Hebrew].

7. LIFE AT THE EDGE OF THE LINE

1. Susan Sontag, *Illness as Metaphor* (New York: Farrar, Strauss and Giroux, 1978).

2. Jacqueline Kahanoff, "To Die a Modern Death," in *From East the Sun*, trans. Aharon Amir (Tel Aviv: Yariv-Hadar, 1978) [Hebrew].

3. Ibid., 225.

4. Ibid., 226.

5. Ibid., 233.

6. Ibid., 234.

7. Ibid., 237.

8. Ibid., 229.

9. Ibid., 250.

10. Ibid.

11. Ibid., 251.

12. Ibid., 213.

13. Ibid., 259.

14. Ibid., 261.

15. Ibid., 271.

16. Kahanoff, "Illness Chronicles," *At*, March-April 1977 [Hebrew].

324   NOTES TO PAGES 279–287

17. Kahanoff, "To My Mother, With Love," in *Between Two Worlds*, ed. David Ohana (Jerusalem: Keter, 2005), 195 [Hebrew].

18. David Ohana, Interview with Sarah Rippin, April 26, 2020.

19. Kahanoff, "Illness Chronicles."

20. Ohana, Interview with Eva Weintraub, April 20, 2020.

21. Kahanoff, "Illness Chronicles."

22. Ibid., 213.

23. Ibid., 217.

EPILOGUE

1. David Ohana, "The Anti-Intellectual Intellectuals as Political Mythmakers," in *The Intellectual Revolt against Democracy, 1870–1940*, ed. Zeev Sternhell (Jerusalem: Israel Academy of Sciences and Humanities Publishing House, 1996), 87–104.

2. Ohana, *The Intellectual Origins of Modernity* (London: Routledge, 2019).

3. J. C. Isaac, *Arendt, Camus, and Modern Rebellion* (New Haven, CT: Yale University Press, 1992).

4. Albert Camus, "Prométhée aux enfers," in *Essais* (Paris: Gallimard, 1965), 839–44.

5. Jef Love, *The Black Circle, a Life of Alexander Kojeve* (New York: Columbia University Press, 2018).

6. Amin Maalouf, "The Challenges of Interculturality in the Mediterranean," *Quaderns de la Mediterrània*, 1 (Barcelona: IEMed/Icaria, 2000); Maalouf, *In the Name of Identity: Violence and the Need to Belong*, trans. B. Bray (New York: Time-Warner, 2001).

7. A. Appadurai, "The Risks of Dialogue," *Quaderns de la Mediterrània*, 10 (Barcelona: IEMed/Icaria, 2008).

8. Charles Corm, *L'Humanisme et la Méditerranée* (Monaco: Cahiers de l'Académie, 1936).

9. Charbel Tayah, "L'Humanisme et la méditerranée dans la pensée de Charles Corm, écrivain libanais de l'entre-deux-guerres," Acts de colloque tenu à le 20–22 October 2001 (Lyon: Université Lumière-Lyon, Université de Chypre, 2003), 37:53–58.

10. Charles Corm, *6000 ans de génie pacifique au service de l'humanité* (Beyrouth: Les éditions de la Revue Phénicienne, 1950).

11. Michel Chiha, *Visage et Présence du Liban* (Beyrouth: Cénacle Libanais, 1964), 49.

NOTES TO PAGES 287–292

12. Evelyne Bustros, *La main d'Allah* (Paris: Bossard, 1926).

13. Tamir Goren, *Cooperation in the Shadow of Confrontation: Arabs and Jews in Local Government in Haifa during the British Mandate* (Ramat Gan: Bar-Ilhan University Press, 2008) [Hebrew].

14. Franck Salameh, *Charles Corm: An Intellectual Biography of a Twentieth-Century Lebanese "Young Phoenician"* (Lanham, MD: Lexington, 2015).

15. Amin Maalouf, *Les Échelles du Levant* (Paris: Grasset, 1996).

16. Amin Maalouf, *Les identités meurtrières* (Paris: Grasset, 1998).

17. Reuven Snir, *Adonis—Mafteach Peulot Haruach* (Tel Aviv: Keshev Leshira, 2012) [Hebrew].

18. Natan Sachs, "Of Adonis," *Haaretz*, August 30, 2011 [Hebrew].

19. Adia Huron, *Eretz Hakedem (The Ancient East)* (Tel Aviv: Hermon, 1970) [Hebrew].

20. Adia Huron, *Kedam VeArav: Canaan—The History of the Land of the Hebrews* (Tel Aviv: Dvir, 2000) [Hebrew].

21. Yonatan Ratoush, *Early Days: Hebrew Introductions* (Tel Aviv: Hadar, 1982) [Hebrew].

22. Itamar Ben Avi, *Canaan Our Land: 5000 Years of Israel in Its Land* (Jerusalem: Zion, 1932) [Hebrew].

23. Ohana, "David Ben-Gurion and the Messianic Idea," in *Political Theologies in the Holy Land: Israeli Messianism and Its Critics* (Abingdon: Routledge, 2009), 1–16.

24. Eri Jabotinsky, "Levant Club," Memorandum No. 2: April 1955, File Code: ISA-PMO-Arab Affairs Advisor-000fi3e, State Archive [Israel]; Jabotinsky, "Israel, Lebanon and the Maronites," *Maariv*, May 30, 1960.

25. Eliyahu Eilat, *Return of Zion and Arabia* (Tel Aviv: Dvir, 1974) [Hebrew].

26. Haim Gamzo, *Chana Orloff* (Tel Aviv: Masada, 1966) [Hebrew].

27. Nahum Slouschz, *The Book of the Sea: The Conquest of the Seas, an Aspect of the History of Civilization* (Tel Aviv: Hchevel Hayami Le Israel, 1948) [Hebrew].

28. Taha Hussein, *Taha Hussein and the Egyptian Revival: Selected Parts from His Writings*, trans. and ed. Immanuel Kopelevich (Jerusalem: Mosad Bialik, 2001) [Hebrew].

29. Taha Hussein, *The Future of Culture in Egypt*, trans. Sidney Glazer (New York: Hippocrene, 1954); Hussein, *The Days* (Cairo: The American University in Cairo Press, 2001).

NOTES TO PAGES 292–297

30. Mohammed Berrada, *Like a Summer Never to Be Repeated* (Cairo: The American University in Cairo Press, 2009).

31. *Levantine Arabic Verbs: Conjugation Tables and Grammar* (London: Lingualism, 2017).

32. Rami Saari, "Duplication and Fusion from Inside the Melting Pot," *Haaretz*, October 20, 2006 [Hebrew].

33. Orhan Pamuk, *Istanbul: Memories and the City* (New York: Faber and Faber, 2006).

34. Albert Cohen, *Solal* (Paris: Gallimard, 1989).

35. Kateb Yacine, *Nedjma* (Paris: Seuil, 1956).

36. Kateb Yacine, "Lettre à Albert Camus," in *Éclats de Mémoire*, Documents réunis par Olivier Corpet, Albert Dichy et Mireille Djaider (Paris: Editions de l'IMEC, 1994).

37. http:/www.youtube.com/watch?y=EpXExBh7URO.

38. Albert Memmi, "'La tête à l'ombre,' in Notre Méditerranée," *Le Point*, August 15, 1998, 86–87.

39. Michael Walzer, *Interpretation and Social Criticism* (Cambridge, MA: Harvard University Press, 1987).

40. Ammiel Alcalay, *After Jews and Arabs: Remaking Levantine Culture* (Minneapolis: University of Minnesota Press, 1993).

BIBLIOGRAPHY

INTERVIEWS WITH KAHANOFF'S ACQUAINTANCES

Josette d'Amade, Laura d'Amade, Aharon Amir, Betin Amir, Haim Be'er, Yoram Bronowski, Dian Gorland, Haim Guri, Yitzhak Livni, Albert Memmi, Amos Oz, Dahlia Ravikovitch, Micha Shagrir, Professor Amnon Shiloh, Prof. Sasson Somekh, Claude Vigée, Eva Weintraub, A. B. Yehoshua

KAHANOFF'S BOOKS

African Stories. Edited by Jacqueline Kahanoff. Translated by David Shahar. Tel Aviv: Am Hasefer, 1963. [Hebrew].

Between Two Worlds. Edited by David Ohana. Jerusalem: Keter, 2005. [Hebrew].

The Big Island—Songs of Madagascar. Edited and wrote forwards Jacqueline Kahanoff. Translated by Shimshon Inbal, Tel Aviv: Editions Equed, 1965. [Hebrew].

From East the Sun. Translated by Aharon Amir. Tel Aviv: Yariv-Hadar, 1978. [Hebrew].

Jacob's Ladder. London: Harvill, 1951.

Mongrels or Marvels: The Levantine Writings of Jacqueline Shohet Kahanoff. Edited by Deborah A. Starr and Sasson Somekh. Stanford, CA: Stanford University Press, 2011.

Ramat-Hadassah-Szold: Youth Aliyah Screening and Classification Centre. Jerusalem: Goldbergs, 1960. [Hebrew].

BIBLIOGRAPHY

We Are All Children of the Levant. Edited by David Ohana. Jerusalem: Carmel Publishing House, 2022. [Hebrew].

KAHANOFF'S STORIES, ESSAYS, AND ARTICLES

1945

"Cairo Wedding." *Tomorrow* 4, no. 11 (1945): 19–23.

1946

"Such Is Rachel." *Atlantic Monthly,* October 1946.

1951

"What's Going On: The Maharajah Turns Farmer." *Sunday Express,* October 14, 1951.

1955

"Strange Interlude." No source. 1955. Gnazym Archive of Hebrew Writers, Israel (hereafter cited as G.A.).

1956

[pseud. Dina Monet]. "Egypt Jewish Community." *Jerusalem Post,* December 21, 1956.
"Jewish Refugees from Difficult to Locate." *Jerusalem Post,* December 27, 1956.
"Nasser's Nazi Experts Efficient." *Jerusalem Post,* December 24, 1956.

1957

"Egyptian Refugees Reshaping Their Lives." *Jerusalem Post,* March 4, 1957.
[pseud. Dina Monet]. "Plan Needed for Egyptian DP's." *Jerusalem Post,* March 6, 1957.
[pseud. Dina Monet]. "Teacher's Teacher from Paris." *Jerusalem Post,* August 30, 1957.

BIBLIOGRAPHY

1958

"Reflections of a Levantine Jew." *Jewish Frontier*, April 1958.

1959

"Beersheba Story." *Reconstructionist*. G.A.
"Juvenile Delinquency in Israel." G.A.
"Ramat Hadassah Szold." *Hadassah Newsletter*. G.A.

1960

"SARINA." *Jewish Frontier*, 1960.

1961

"A Coat of Many Colors." *Hadassah Newsletter*. G.A.

1962

"Algeria—End of a Community." *Hadassah Magazine*,
    September 1962.
"Exodus from Algeria." G.A.
"A New Look to New Immigrants." G.A.
"Of People and Ceremonies." G.A.
"Recontres en Terrain Neutre." Papers from Journal. G.A.

1963

"Aspects of Contemporary French Judaism." *Jewish Frontier*. G.A.
A Response to Nissim Rejwan's Article "Bringing Art to the People." *Jerusalem Post*, August 20, 1963.

1965

"Dead Souls." G.A.
"Huckleberry Finn." G.A.

1966

"The Blue Veil of Progress." *Hadassah Magazine,* April 1966.
"The Oded Group." *Hadassah Magazine,* October 1966.

1970

"Communautés en Transition." G.A.
"Grandmother Was Militant Feminist." *Hadassah Magazine.* G.A.
"The Maimona Festival." *Israel Magazine.* G.A.
"Through Jewish Eyes." *Hadassah Magazine.* G.A.

1973

"Danger from Within." *Hadassah Magazine.* G.A.
"Hatikva—The Slums Whose Name Means Hope." *Hadassah Magazine.*
  G.A.
"Soldiers Try to Rebuild Their Lives." *Hadassah Magazine.* G.A.

1975

"La Paix." Translation from Arie Eliav Shalom's Book. G.A.
"Training Women for the New Technology." *Hadassah Magazine.* G.A.

1976

"Literary of Thomas Pynchon." *Dialogue,* Bnd. 9, Vol. 1, G.A.

1985

"Childhood in Egypt—Memoir." *Jerusalem Quarterly* 36 (Summer 1985):
  31–41.

2011

"What about Levantinization?" *Journal of Levantine Studies* 1, no. 1 (Summer 2011): 13–22.

BIBLIOGRAPHY 331

Undated

[pseud. Dina Monet]. "Absorption of Egypt's Aliya in Good Hands."
 Jerusalem Post. G.A.
"The Beduin Come to Town." No source.
"Beersheba Story." No source.
"Facing the Gaza Strip." [Other side of the page] "Facing the Gaza
 Strip(2)." No source.
"Finding Education in Patish." No source.
"Folklore in Israel." *Hadassah Newsletter*. G.A.
"How Integration Is Made Easier." *Alliance Review*.
"Integration in Israel." *American Israel Review*.
"Israel Can Be Fun." *Hadassah Magazine*. G.A.
"An Israeli Abroad." *Hadassah Magazine*. G.A.
"The Jewish Community of Egypt." No source.
[pseud. Dina Monet]. "Jews Emerged from Egypt's Ghetto."
 Jerusalem Post. G.A.
"The Jews of Egypt." No source.
"Letter from Israel." No source.
"Letters from Israel." *Reconstructionist*. G.A.
[pseud. Dina Monet]. "A Lot with the Hands." *Jerusalem
 Post*. G.A.
"Martin Buber Seminar on Arab-Jewish Understanding." *Hadassah
 Magazine*. G.A.
"New Setting for Padua's Ark." No source.
"North African Jews Hold Their Post-Passover." *Woodstock*.
 No source.
Papers from Personal Journal April 21, 1956. G.A.
"The Rabbi Loves Soccer." *Israel Magazine*. G.A.
"Round the New Settlements." No source.
"Settling Down." No source.
"The Stern Gun and the Book." *Jerusalem Post*.
"A Thing of Beauty." G.A.
"Trees Planted in Deserts in Israel." *Herald Tribune*.
"Two Little Gray School-Houses." No source.
"Visit to an Arab Village." *Jewish Frontier*. G.A.
"Vu Jerome Lindon Aux Edition de Minuit." With a Letter for
 Jerome Lindon, 28165/15, Catalog Id 195904. G.A.

BIBLIOGRAPHY

KAHANOFF'S ORIGINAL ESSAYS,
ARRANGED BY SUBJECT, G.A.

Art

"Buckminster Fuller: Exploring the Future"; "The Fine Art of Persuasion"; "The Mechanical Orange"; "The Rolling Stone"; "A Study of Modern Urban Growth"; "Suicide and the Artist"; "A Tale about Folklore"; "V for Venus"; "A World View of Television"

Literature

"Andre Malraux Remembers"; "Claude Vigée"; "Claude Vigée: Le Retour au Lieu Nu"; "Good Literature about Nothing"; "Introducing a Young Poet: Dom Morales"; "The Justinization of Laurence Durrell"; "A Magnificent Auto-Biography"; "A Many Splendored Book about Asia"; "A Novel about Nasser's Egypt"; "Poetry, Man's Frail Bridge to the World"; "A Psycho-Biography of Andre Gide"; "Required Reading for Conservatives: Norman Mailer's 'The Armies of the Night'"

Israel Society

"About 'Black Zionism' and 'the Fear of Assimilation'"; "L'Autre Cote, Vu d'Israel"; "The Beersheba Municipal Theatre"; "Dimona Revisited"; "The Hatikva Quarter"; "Immigrants from Egypt in Hatzor"; "Mizrahi Immigrants: Promise or Fulfillment?"; "Mizrahi Immigrants: Semitism Rediscovered"; "Mizrahi Jews as Key to Israel's Integration in the Middle East (with Particular Reference to Egyptian Jews)"; "Remembering Beersheba"; "The Ritual of Elections"

World Literature

"African Voices"; "Alfred Kazin"; "Ancient Japanese Literature"; "Andre Malraux, The Magician"; "Antisemitism in French Literature"; "Behold The Tropics"; "The Changing Culture of Africa"; "The Colour of Man"; "Cuba and the Magazines"; "The Eclipse of French Culture"; "French in the World Today"; "Impressions on Post-Franco Spain"; "Japanese Folk Literature"; "Japan's Golden Age and Women Writers"; "Jules Romains";

BIBLIOGRAPHY

"On Japanese Literature"; "On Love and Belief"; "The Quintessence of Japanese Artistry: Yasunari Kawabata"; "A Vivid Portrayal of Modern Japan"; "The Western Impact on Japanese Literature"; "What Is Happening to French Culture?"; "The World of Yukio Mishima"

Heroes and Myths

"After the Yom Kippur War: Soldiers and Civilians Adjust"; "Archetypes of National Heroes and Their Modern Projections"; "The Decline of Paris"; "The Story of the Two Eliahus"; "A Study of Post-War Rebellions"; "A Style Makes the General (De Gaulle)"

Thought

"An Alliance with Jupiter"; "A Contemporary View on Freedom"; "From the Tree of Knowledge"; "The Human Animal"; "The Life Ahead"

Judaism

"Aspects of Contemporary French Judaism"; "By the Western Wall: A New People Is Born"; "Contemporary French Judaism"; "A Jewish-Arab Dialogue in Israel"; "The Jewish-Berber Symbiosis"; "The Jewish Community of Egypt"; "Jewish Minorities in Moslem Countries in Relation to the New Nationalism"; "A Jewish Sociologist's Self-Portrait"; "Lanzman's Israel and Ours"; "A New Book of Job"; "On Jewish Self-Hatred"; "Sephardic Jewry Today: Permanence of the Sephardic Identity"
Alcalay, Ammiel, ed. *Keys to the Garden: New Israeli Writing* [includes excerpts from Kahanoff's prose, translated into English by Hannah Schalit]. San Francisco: City Lights, 1996.

SECONDARY SOURCES

Alcalay, Ammiel. *After Jews and Arabs: Remaking Levantine Culture.* Minneapolis: University of Minnesota Press, 1993.
Amir, Aharon. "A Promise Rising on the Nile with Dawn." *Haaretz*, April 5, 1996. [Hebrew].
Arad, Miriam. "Great Success of Literary Magazine." *Jerusalem Post*, October 1968.

BIBLIOGRAPHY

Arad, Miriam. "A Living Religion." *Jerusalem Post*, April 7, 1967.

Beinin, Joel. "On Kahanoff in the Dispersion of Egyptian Jews." In *The Dispersion of Egyptian Jewry: Culture, Politics, and the Formation of a Modern Diaspora*, chapters 1 and 2. Berkeley: University of California Press, 1998.

Benhabib, Dolly. "Women's Skirts Are Shorter Now: Levantine, Female Identity as Elitist Disguise in Jacqueline Kahanov's Writings." *Women's Studies International Forum* 20, no. 5–6 (September-December 1997): 689–696.

Benvenisti, Meron. "A False Mediterranean Harbor." *Haaretz*, March 21, 1996. [Hebrew].

Beretzky, Nurit. "The First Lady of Mediterraneanism." *Maariv*, March 15, 1996. [Hebrew].

Books of Today [review], December 1951.

Bronowski, Yoram. "Lament over a Lost Option." *Haaretz*, May 27, 1994. [Hebrew].

Bronowski, Yoram. "The Levantines." *Haaretz*, April 5, 1996. [Hebrew].

Calderon, Nissim. "An Outing in the Mediterranean." *Haaretz*, May 17, 1996. [Hebrew].

Carlino, Tiziana. "The Levant: A Trans-Mediterranean Literary Category." *TRANS-, a Journal of General and Comparative Literature* 6 (2006): 1–12.

"The Enigmatic Czar" [review]. *Glasgow Herald*, December 13, 1951.

Green, B. David. "A Conversation with Deborah A. Starr." *Haaretz: Books*, August 2011.

Guedj, David. "East, West and in Between." 2015. G.A.

Hacham, Shir. "Activists 'Rename' Tel Aviv Streets after Mizrahi Jews." G.A.

Halevi-Wise, Yael. "Mongrels or Marvels." *Sephardic Horizons* [online] 2, no. 1 (Winter 2012).

Hever, Hannan. *Toward the Longed-For Shore: The Sea in Modern Hebrew Culture*. Tel Aviv: Van Leer Institue and Hakibbutz Hameuchad, 2007. [Hebrew].

Hochberg, Gil Z. "The Mediterranean Option: On the Politics of Regional Affiliation in the Current Israeli Cultural Imagination." *Journal of Levantine Studies* 1, no. 1 (2011): 41–65.

Hochberg, Gil Z. "'Permanent Immigration': Jacqueline Kahanoff, Ronit Matalon, and the Impetus of Levantinism." *Boundary 2* 31, no. 2 (Summer 2004): 219–243.

Jewish Chronicle [review], November 2, 1951.

BIBLIOGRAPHY 335

John O'London's Weekly [review], November 23, 1951.

Matalon, Ronit. "Uprooted." *Haaretz Supplement*, August 1, 1986. [Hebrew].

Memmi, Albert. *The Pillar of Salt*. Translated by Edward Rediti. Preface by Albert Camus. Boston: Beacon, 1992.

Monterescu, Daniel. "Beyond the Sea of Formlessness: Jacqueline Kahanoff and the Levantine Generation." *Journal of Levantine Studies* 1 (2011): 23–40.

Ohana, David. *Albert Camus and the Critique of Violence*. Brighton: Sussex Academic Press, 2017.

Ohana, David. "Israel towards a Mediterranean Identity." *Munich Contributions to European Unification. Special Issue: Integration and Identity: Challenges to Europe and Israel* 4 (1999): 81–97.

Ohana, David. "Jacqueline Kahanoff: Between Levantinism and Mediterraneanism." In *New Horizons: Mediterranean Research in the 21st Century*, edited by Mihran Dabag, Dieter Haller, and Nikolas Jaspert, 361–384. Bochum: Brill Schöningh, 2001.

Ohana, David. "Jacqueline Kahanoff: Pioneer of Mediterranean Culture in Israel." *Iunim Betkumat Israel* 13 (2003): 29–55. [Hebrew].

Ohana, David. "Jacqueline Kahanoff: The First Lady of the Mediterranean." In *The Origins of Israeli Mythology: Neither Canaanites nor Crusaders*, 198–221. Cambridge: Cambridge University Press, 2012.

Ohana, David. "A Levantine Moledet." In *Birth-Throes of the Israeli Homeland*, 111–147. London: Routledge, 2020

Ohana, David. "Levantinism as a Cultural Theory." In *Israel and Its Mediterranean Identity*, 77–97. New York: Palgrave Macmillan, 2011.

Ohana, David. "The Mediterranean Option in Israel: An Introduction to the Thought of Jacqueline Kahanoff." *Mediterranean Historical Review* 21, no. 2 (2006): 239–263.

"On Matalon's Article." *Haaretz Supplement*, March 4, 1994. [Hebrew].

"On the Publication of 'Between Two Worlds.'" *Haaretz literary Supplement*, November 14, 2005. [Hebrew].

Pourgouris, Marinos. "Mongrels or Marvels." *Journal of Levantine Studies* 2, no. 2 (Winter 2012): 203–207.

Rejwan, Nissim. "The Denigrated" [review]. *Jerusalem Post*, September 15, 1978.

Rejwan, Nissim. *Outsider in the Promised Land: An Iraqi Jew in Israel*. Austin: University of Texas Press, 2006.

Segal, Mark. *Inside View of Israel*. 1960. G.A.

BIBLIOGRAPHY

Shapiro, Sraya. "A Woman Appreciating Her Many Worlds." *Jerusalem Post*, April 28, 1996.

Sheleg, Yair. "The Princess of the Levant." *Kol Ha'ir*, March 15, 1996.

Starr, Deborah Ann. "Ambivalent Levantines/Levantine Ambivalences: Egyptian Jewish in Contemporary Literature." PhD diss., University of Michigan, 2000.

Steinbach, Alexander Allen. "Two Worlds in Conflict within a Teenage Girl" [review]. G.A.

Tal, David. "Jacqueline Kahanoff and Demise of the Levantine." *Mediterranean Historical Review* 32, no. 2 (2017): 237–254.

Urouhart, Fred. "Time and Tide: Jacob's Ladder" [review]. December 1, 1950. G.A.

"Woman Fights Rabbinical Divorce in High Court." January 7, 1978. G.A.

GENERAL

Agnew, J. *Geopolitics: Re-visioning World Politics*. London: Routledge, 1998.

Ajar, Émile [pseud. Romain Gary]. *The Life before Us*. Translated by Ralph Manheim. New York: New Directions, 1986.

Amir, Aharon. "The Second Republic." *Haaretz*, October 19, 2006. [Hebrew].

Amir, Aharon. "The Shock of Closeness." *Keshet—Chapters in the American Experience* 52, no. 6 (1971): 6–8. [Hebrew].

Appadurai, A. "The Risks of Dialogue." *Quaderns de la Mediterrània*, 10. Barcelona: IEMed/Icaria, 2008.

Aron, Raymond. *De Gaulle, Israel and the Jews*. Translated by John Sturrock. London: Routledge, 2004.

Avineri, Shlomo. "The Presence of Eastern and Central Europe in the Culture and Politics of Contemporary Israel." *East European Politics and Societies* 2 (Spring 1996): 163–172.

Beauvoir, Simone de. *The Second Sex*. Translated by Constance Borde and Sheila Malovany-Chevallier. New York: Vintage, 2011.

Ben Avi, Itamar. *Canaan Our Land: 5000 Years of Israel in Its Land*. Jerusalem: Zion, 1932. [Hebrew].

Benedict, Ruth. *Patterns of Culture*. London: Routledge, 1934.

Benlahcene, Badrane. *The Socio-Intellectual Foundations of Malek Bennabi's Approach to Civilization*. London: International Institute of Islamic Thought, 2013.

Berrada, Mohammed. *Like a Summer Never to Be Repeated*. Cairo: The American University in Cairo Press, 2009.

BIBLIOGRAPHY

Bhabha, H. K. *The Location of Culture*. London: Routledge, 1994.

Boskowitz, Alexander Uria. "The Problems of Music in Israel." *Orlogin* 9 (1953): 290. [Hebrew].

Braudel, Fernand. *La Méditerranée: l'Éspace et l'Histoire*. Paris: Flammarion, 1985.

Braudel, Fernand. *The Mediterranean and the Mediterranean World in the Age of Philip II*. Translated by Siân Reynolds. New York: HarperCollins, 1972.

Buber, Martin. *I and Thou*. Translated by Ronald Gregor Smith. New York: Simon and Schuster, 2000.

Bustros, Evelyne. *La main d'Allah*. Paris: Bossard, 1926.

Cahen, Didier. *Edmond Jabès*. Paris: Belfond, 1991.

Calame, Jon, and Charlesworth Esther. *Divided Cities: Belfast, Beirut, Jerusalem, Mostar and Nicosia*. Philadelphia: University of Pennsylvania Press, 2009.

Camus, Albert. "Prèface: Albert Memmi, Prophète de la Dècolonisation." In *La Statue de Sel*, edited by Albert Memmi, 11–12. Paris: Gallimard, 1966.

Chaubey, Ajay Kumar. *An Anthology of 21st Century Criticism*. Edited by V. S. Naipaul. New Delhi: Atlantic, 2015.

Chaudhuri, Nirad C. *The Autobiography of an Unknown Indian*. New York: Macmillan, 1951.

Corm, Charles. *L'Humanisme et la Méditerranée*. Monaco: Cahiers de l'Académie, 1936.

Corm, Charles. *6000 ans de génie pacifique au service de l'humanité*. Beyrouth: Les éditions de la Revue Phénicienne, 1950.

Dizard, Wilson P. *Television: A World View*. New York: Syracuse University Press, 1966.

Dobbs, Stephen Mark. "From Buck Rogers to Buckminster Fuller: On the Future of Art." *Art Education* 29, no. 3 (1976): 8–11.

Efron, Yonit. "In Search of Identity: A Historic Perspective of Hebrew-Writing Israeli Intellectuals from Iraq and Egypt." PhD diss., Tel Aviv University, 2005. [Hebrew].

Eisenstadt, Shmuel N. "Multiple Modernities." *Daedalus* 129, no. 1 (2000): 1–29.

Elbaz, Shlomo. "Israel, les Juifs et la Mediterranée, ou Identité Culturelle à Califourchon." *Journal of Mediterranean Studies* 2 (1994): 170–182.

Eliahu, Eilat. *Return of Zion and Arabia*. Tel Aviv: Dvir, 1974. [Hebrew].

Elial, Mikaél, and Shlomo Elbaz. "De Nouvelles Andalousies." *Levant: Cahiers de l'Espace Méditerranéen* 4, no. 1 (1991).

Ellenblum, Ronnie. *Frankish Rural Settlement in the Latin Kingdom of Jerusalem*. Cambridge: Cambridge University Press, 1998.

Eydar, Dror. "Last Interview with Aharon Amir." *Haaretz*, February 27, 2009. [Hebrew].

Friedlander, Judith. *A Light in Dark Times: The New School for Social Research and Its University in Exile*. New York: Columbia University Press, 2019.

Friedlander, Saul. *When Memory Comes*. Translated by Helen R. Lane. New York: Farrar, Strauss and Giroux, 1979.

Galland, Antoine. *Voyage à Constantinople 1672–1673*. 2 vols. Paris: Maisonneuve et Larose, 2002.

Gamzo, Haim. *Chana Orloff*. Tel Aviv: Masada, 1966. [Hebrew].

Gary, Romain. *Europa*. Paris: Gallimard, 1999.

Gay, Peter. *Weimar Culture: The Outsider as Insider*. New York: W. W. Norton, 2001.

Gendreau, Bernard A. "The Role of Jacques Maritain and Emmanuel Mounier in the Creation of French Personalism." *Personalist Forum* 8, no. 1 (1992): 97–108.

Gerber-Talmon, Yonina. "Time in the Primitive Myth." *Yiun* 2, no. 4 (1952): 201–214.

Godelier, Maurice. *Claude Lévi-Strauss: A Critical Study of His Thought*. Translated by Nora Scott. London: Verso, 2018.

Goitein, Dov Shlomo. *A Mediterranean Society*. 5 vols. Berkeley: University of California Press, 1967–1988.

Goitein, Dov Shlomo. "The Unity of the Mediterranean World in the 'Middle' Middle Ages." *Studia Islamica* 12 (1960): 29–42.

Golan, M. "In the Field of Poetry." *Al Hamishmar*, April 17, 1960. [Hebrew].

Goman, Norbert A. "A Yankee Radical." In *Michael Harrington: Speaking American*, 1–24. New York: Routledge, 1995.

Goodman, Paul. *Growing Up Absurd: Problems of Youth in the Organized Society*. New York: New York Review Books, 1960.

Gordon, Haim. *Naguib Mahfouz's Egypt: Existential Themes in His Writings*. New York: Praeger, 1990.

Goren, Tamir. *Cooperation in the Shadow of Confrontation: Arabs and Jews in Local Government in Haifa during the British Mandate*. Ramat Gan: Bar-Ilhan University Press, 2008. [Hebrew].

Gottman, Jean. *Megalopolis: The Urbanized Northeastern Seaboard of the United States*. Cambridge, MA: MIT Press, 1961.

Gould, Eric, ed. *The Sin of the Book: Edmond Jabès*. Lincoln: University of Nebraska Press, 1985.

BIBLIOGRAPHY

Gouri, Haim. "Wounds of Memory." *Haaretz*, February 22, 2017. [Hebrew].

Graham, Stephen, and Simon Marvin. "Planning Cybercities? Integrating Telecommunications into Urban Planning." *Town Planning Review* 70, no. 1 (1999): 89–114.

Hagenmeyer, H., ed. *Fulcheri Cornotensis Historia Hierosolymitana (1095–1127)*. Lib. 3, c. 37, 748–749. Heidelberg: Carl Winters Universitatsbuchhandlung, 1913.

Harrington, Michael. *The Accidental Century*. New York: Macmillan, 1965.

Harrington, Michael. "Fragments of the Century." *Kirkus Review*, January 1, 1973.

Harrington, Michael. *The Other America: Poverty in the United States*. New York: Scribner, 1962.

Harris, William W. *The Levant: A Fractured Mosaic*. Princeton, NJ: Marcus Weiner, 2005.

Hiddleston, Jane. "Kateb Yacine: Poetry and Revolution." In *Decolonising the Intellectual: Politics, Culture, and Humanism at the End of the French Empire*, edited by Jane Hiddleston, Edmund Smyth, and Charles Forsdick, 205–249. Liverpool: Liverpool University Press, 2014.

Hollinger, David. *Postethnic America: Beyond Multiculturalism*. New York: Basic Books, 2006.

Horden, Peregrine, and Nicholas Purcell. *The Corrupting Sea: A Study of Mediterranean History*. Oxford: Blackwell, 2000.

Huron, Adia. *Eretz Hakedem (The Ancient East)*. Tel Aviv: Hermon, 1970. [Hebrew].

Huron, Adia. *Kedem VeArav: Canaan—The History of the Land of the Hebrews*. Tel Aviv: Dvir, 2000. [Hebrew].

Hussein, Taha. *The Days*. Cairo: The American University in Cairo Press, 2001.

Hussein, Taha. *The Future of Culture in Egypt*. Translated by Sidney Glazer. New York: Hippocrene, 1954.

Hussein, Taha. *Taha Hussein and the Egyptian Revival: Selected Parts from His Writings*. Translated and edited by Immanuel Kopelevich. Jerusalem: Mosad Bialik, 2001. [Hebrew].

Isserman, Maurice. *The Other American: The Life of Michael Harrington*. New York: Public Affairs, 2000.

Jabès, Edmond. *From the Book to the Book: An Edmond Jabès Reader*. Translated by Rosmarie Waldrop. Introductory essay by Richard Stamelman. Middletown, CT: Wesleyan University Press, 1991.

Jabès, Edmond. *Le Livre du Dialogue*. Paris: Gallimard, 1984.

Jabotinsky, Eri. "Israel, Lebanon and the Maronites." *Maariv*, May 30, 1960. [Hebrew].

Jabotinsky, Eri. "Levant Club." Memorandum no. 2: April 1955, File Code: ISA-PMO-Arab AffairsAdvisor-000fi3e, State Archive [Israel].

Jaron, Steven. "French Modernism and the Emergence of Jewish Consciousness in the Writings of Edmond Jabès." PhD diss., Columbia University, 1997.

Jay, Martin. *The Dialectical Imagination: A History of the Frankfurt School and the Institute of Social Research*. Berkeley: University of California Press, 1996.

Jay, Martin. *Downcast Eyes: The Denigration of Vision in Twentieth-Century French Thought*. Berkeley: University of California Press, 1993.

Judt, Tony. *Past Imperfect: French Intellectuals, 1944–1956*. New York: New York University Press, 2011.

Kellner, Vered. "How Lovely the Nights." *Kol Ha'ir*, October 12, 2001. [Hebrew].

Kierkegaard, Søren. *Fear and Trembling*. Translated by Alastair Hannay. London: Penguin, 2005.

Kojève, Alexander. Esquisse d'une doctrine de la politique française. Bibliothèque national de France, August 27, 1945. https://archive.org/details/KOJEVEPOLITIQUE1945/page/n1/mode/2up.

Kramer, Gudrun. *The Jews in Modern Egypt, 1914–1952*. Seattle: University of Washington Press, 1989.

Kritzman, Lawrence D. "A Certain Idea of de Gaulle." *Myth and Modernity* 111 (2007): 158–168.

Landau, Jacob M. *Jews in Nineteenth-Century Egypt*. New York: Routledge, 1969.

Laor, Dan. "I Hear America Singing: On One Aspect of the Canaan Worldview." *New Keshet* 11 (2005): 148–160. [Hebrew].

"Levant." In *Encyclopedia Britannica*. https://www.britannica.com/place/Levant.

Levantine Arabic Verbs: Conjugation Tables and Grammar. London: Lingualism, 2017.

Lévi-Strauss, Claude. *Mythologiques: Le Cru et le Cuit*. Paris: Plon, 1964.

Lévi-Strauss, Claude. *The Savage Mind*. Translated by George Weidenfeld and Nigel Nicolson. London: Weidenfeld & Nicolson, 1966.

Lévinas, Emmanuel. *Quatre Lectures Talmudiques*. Paris: Minuit, 1968.

BIBLIOGRAPHY

Loyer, Emmanuelle. *Lévi-Strauss: A Biography*. Translated by Ninon Vinsonneau and Jonathan Magidoff. Cambridge: Cambridge University Press, 2019.

Maalouf, Amin. "The Challenges of Interculturality in the Mediterranean." *Quaderns de la Mediterrània*, 1. Barcelona: IEMed/Icaria, 2000.

Maalouf, Amin. *Les Échelles du Levant*. Paris: Grasset, 1996.

Maalouf, Amin. *Les identités meurtrières*. Paris: Grasset, 1998.

Maalouf, Amin. "In the Name of Identity: Violence and the Need to Belong." Translated by B. Bray. New York: Time-Warner, 2001.

MacCarthy, Mary. *Memories of a Catholic Girlhood*. New York: Harvest/ HBJ, 1957.

MacNiven, Ian S., and Carol Peirce. "Introduction: Lawrence Durrell: Man and Writer." *Twentieth Century Literature* 33, no. 3 (1987): 255–261.

Mahfouz, Najib. *Palace of Desire*. Translated by William Maynard Hutchins, Lorne M. Kenny, and Olive E. Kenny. New York: Doubleday, 1990.

Mahfouz, Najib. *Palace Walk*. Translated by William Maynard Hutchins and Olive E. Kenny. New York: Doubleday, 1990.

Mahfouz, Najib. *Sugar Street*. Translated by William Maynard Hutchins and Angele Botros Samaan. New York: American University in Cairo Press, 1992.

Malkin, Irad. "Israel: Zionism, Religion and Democracy." *Rive—Review of Mediterranean Politics and Culture* 3 (1997): 29–33.

Malraux, André. *La Condition Humaine*. Paris: Man's Fate, 1934.

Mansel, Philip. *Levant: Splendour and Catastrophe on the Mediterranean*. New Haven, CT: Yale University Press, 2012.

Marcuse, Herbert. *Eros and Civilization*. London: Routledge, 2015.

Marcuse, Herbert. *One-Dimensional Man: Studies in the Ideology of Advanced Industrial Society*. 2nd ed. Boston: Beacon, 1991.

Marmysz, John. "Yukio Mishima and Asian Nihilism." *Laughing at Nothing: Humor as a Response to Nihilism*. Albany: State University of New York Press, 2003.

Masry, Youssef el. *Le drame sexual de la femme dans l'Orient arabe*. Paris: Robert Laffonte, 1962.

Matalon, Ronit. "The Sorrow of Possibilities' End." *Haaretz*, March 4, 1994. [Hebrew].

Matalon, Ronit. "Uprooted from the East." *Haaretz*, August 1, 1986. [Hebrew].

Mendes-Flohr, Paul. *Martin Buber: A Life of Faith and Dissent*. New Haven, CT: Yale University Press, 2019.

BIBLIOGRAPHY

Milson, Menahem. *Naguib Mahfouz: The Novelist-Philosopher of Cairo.* London: Palgrave Macmillan, 1998.

Morris, James McGrath. *The Ambulance Drivers: Hemingway, Dos Passos, and a Friendship Made and Lost in War.* Boston: Da Capo, 2017.

Mosse, George L. *Confronting History: A Memoir.* Madison: University of Wisconsin Press, 2000.

Mounier, Emmanuel. *Le personnalisme.* Translated by Philip Mairet. Notre Dame: University of Notre Dame Press, 1952.

Munthe, Axel. *The Story of San Michele.* New York: E. P. Dutton, 1930.

Nocke, Alexandra. *The Place of the Mediterranean in the Modern Israeli Identity.* Leiden: Brill, 2009.

Ohana, David. "Carl Schmitt's Legal Fascism." *Politics, Religion and Ideology* 20, no. 3 (2019): 273–300.

Ohana, David. *The Dawn of Political Nihilism.* East Sussex: Sussex Academic Press, 2009.

Ohana, David. *The Fascist Temptation: Creating a Political Community of Experiences.* Abingdon: Routledge, 2020.

Ohana, David. "From Rousseau to Tocqueville: Janus Face of Modernity." In *The Intellectual Origins of Modernity,* 29–79. New York: Routledge, 2019.

Ohana, David. "Georges Sorel and the Rise of Political Myth." *History of European Ideas* 13, no. 6 (1991): 733–746.

Ohana, David. *The Intellectual Origins of Modernity.* New York: Routledge, 2019.

Ohana, David. "Mediterranean Humanism." *Mediterranean Historical Review* 18, no. 1 (2003): 59–75.

Ohana, David. *Modernism and Zionism.* New York: Palgrave Macmillan, 2012.

Ohana, David. *Nationalizing Judaism: Zionism as a Theological Ideology.* Lanham, MD: Lexington, 2017.

Ohana, David. *Nietzsche and Jewish Political Theology.* London: Routledge, 2019.

Ohana, David. *The Origins of Israeli Mythology: Neither Canaanites nor Crusaders.* Translated by David Maisel. Cambridge: Cambridge University Press, 2012.

Ohana, David. *Political Theologies in the Holy Land: Israeli Messianism and Its Critics.* London: Routledge, 2009.

Ohana, David. "La politique méditerranéene d'Israël." In *La Méditerranée des Juifs,* edited by Paul Balta, Caherine Dana, and Régine Dhoquois-Cohen, 287–301. Paris: L'Harmattan, 2003.

BIBLIOGRAPHY

Ohana, David. "Reflexions sur léssai d'Albert Memmi." In *Lire Albert Memmi: Déracinement, Exil, Identité,* edited by D. Ohana, C. Sitbon, and D. Mendelson, 29–39. Paris: Decitre, 2002.

Pamuk, Orhan. *Istanbul: Memories and the City.* New York: Faber and Faber, 2006.

Pascal, Laine. *L'irrévolution.* Paris: Gallimard, 1971.

Péguy, Charles. *L'Argent.* Paris: Cahiers De La Quinzaine, 1913.

Péguy, Charles. *Eve.* Paris: Gallimard, 2017.

Péguy, Charles. *Le mystère de la charité de Jeanne d'Arc.* Paris: Gallimard, 1921.

Péguy, Charles. *Notre Jeunesse.* Paris: Gallimard, 2009.

Peled, Mattityahu. *Religion, My Own: The Literary Works of Najib Mahfuz.* New York: Routledge, 1983.

Pizer, Donald. *Toward a Modernist Style: John Dos Passos.* New York: Bloomsbury Academic, 2013.

Plessix Gray, Francine du. *Lovers and Tyrants.* New York: Simon and Schuster, 1976.

Pollio, David M. "Vergil and American Symbolism." *Classical Outlook* 87, no. 4 (2010): 145–146.

Porcel, Baltasar. *Mediterráneo.* Madrid: Planeta, 1996.

Prawer, Joshua. "Confrontation between East and West during the Crusaders Period." In *Lectures in Memory of Moshe Strossta, R.I.P.,* edited by Joseph Geiger. Jerusalem: The Hebrew University, 1994. [Hebrew].

Ramachandra, Guha. *Gandhi: The Years That Changed the World, 1914–1948.* New York: Vintage, 2019.

Saari, Rami. "Duplication and Fusion from inside the Melting Pot." *Haaretz,* October 20, 2006. [Hebrew].

Sachs, Natan. "Of Adonis." *Haaretz,* August 30, 2011. [Hebrew].

Sagan, Françoise. *Des bleus à l'âme.* Paris: Flammarion, 1972.

Said, Edward W. *Orientalism.* New York: Vintage, 1978.

Salameh, Franck. *Charles Corm: An Intellectual Biography of a Twentieth-Century Lebanese "Young Phoenician."* Lanham, MD: Lexington, 2015.

Salameh, Franck. *The Other Middle East: An Anthology of Modern Levantine Literature.* New Haven, CT: Yale University Press, 2018.

Sartre, Jean-Paul. *Black Orpheus.* Translated by S. Allen. New York: Présence African, 1948.

Schiller, Herbert. "Television: A World View." *AV Communication Review* 15, no. 1 (1967): 122–124.

Semprún, Jorge. *Le Grand Voyage.* Paris: Gallimard, 1963.

Semprún, Jorge. *L'écriture ou la vie*. Paris: Gallimard, 1994.

Shamir, Shimon, ed. *The Jews of Egypt: A Mediterranean Society in Modern Times*. London: Routledge, 2019.

Shelleg, Assaf. *Theological Stains: Art Music and the Zionist Project*. New York: Oxford University Press, 2020.

Shiff, Tali. "Between Minor and Major Identity." *Theoria Vebikoret* 37 (2010): 125–149. [Hebrew].

Slouschz, Nahum. *The Book of the Sea: The Conquest of the Seas, an Aspect of the History of Civilization*. Tel Aviv: Hachevel Hayami Le Israel, 1948. [Hebrew].

Snir, Reuven. *Adonis—Mafteach Peulot Haruach*. Tel Aviv: Keshev Leshira, 2012. [Hebrew].

Somekh, Sasson. *The Changing Rhythm: A Study of Naguib Mahfouz's Novels*. Leiden: Brill, 1973.

Sontag, Susan. *Illness as Metaphor*. New York: Farrar, Strauss and Giroux, 1978.

Souder, William. *Mad at the World: A Life of John Steinbeck*. New York: W. W. Norton, 2020.

Ratoush, Yonatan. *Early Days: Hebrew Introductions*. Tel Aviv: Hadar, 1982. [Hebrew].

Tayah, Charbel. "L'Humanisme et la méditerranée dans la pensée de Charles Corm, écrivain libanais de l'entre-deux-guerres." Acts de colloque tenu à le 20–22, Octobre 2001. Lyon: Université Lumìere-Lyon, Université de Chypre, 2003.

Ticotsky, Giddon. *Dahlia Ravikovitch: Her Life and Literature*. Haifa: Haifa University Press, 2016. [Hebrew].

Tocqueville, Alexis de. *Democracy in America*. Translated and edited by Harvey C. Mansfield and Delba Winthrop. Chicago: University of Chicago Press, 2000.

Troen, Ilan. *Imagining Zion: Dreams, Designs, and Realities in a Century of Jewish Settlement*. New Haven, CT: Yale University Press, 2003.

Turner, Frederick Jackson. "The Significance of the Frontier in American History." In *The Frontier in American History*. New York: Henry Holt, 1921. https://www.gutenberg.org/files/22994/22994-h/22994-h.htm.

Vigée, Claude. *Les artistes de la faim*. Paris: Calmann-Lévy, 1960.

Vigée, Claude. *L'été Indien*. Paris: Gallimard, 1957.

Vigée, Claude. *Révolte et louanges*. Paris: J. Corti, 1962.

Villon, François. *Le Grand Testament*. Paris: CreatSpace Independent Publishing Platform, 2015 (1937).

BIBLIOGRAPHY

Wheaton, William L. C. "Jean Gottman, Megalopolis: The Urbanized Northeastern Seaboard of the United States." *Annals of the American Academy of Political and Social Science* 341, no. 1 (1962): 166–167.

Wiener, Norbert. *God & Golem Inc.* Cambridge, MA: MIT Press, 1964.

Wistrich, Robert S. W. *A Lethal Obsession: Anti-Semitism from Antiquity to the Global Jihad.* New York: Random House, 2010.

Yacine, Kateb. "Letter à Albert Camus." In *Éclats de Mémoire*, Documents réunis par Olivier Corpet, Albert Dichy et Mireille Djaider. Paris: Editions de l'IMEC, 1994.

Yacine, Kateb. *Nedjma.* Paris: Seuil, 1956.

Yehoshua, A. B. "Facing the Forests." In *The Continuing Silence of a Poet*, 203–236. New York: Syracuse State University, 1998.

Yehoshua, A. B. "The First Glass of Cognac." *Haaretz*, March 7, 2008. [Hebrew].

Ye'or, Bat. *Les Juifs en Egypt.* Geneva: World Jewish Congress, 1971.

INDEX

Abendanon, J. H., 234
Abishag, 251
Abraham, 94, 119, 193, 194
Abrahams, Peter, 183
Abravanel, 106
Abu-Warda, Yussuf, 288
Académie Française, 56, 182, 288
Academy of the Arabic Language in Cairo, 291
Accidental Century, The, 44, 45
Acre, 4
Adonis, 289
Africa, 77, 138, 178–88, 180–88, 200, 202–3, 208, 233, 253–60. *See also* Egypt; South Africa; Tunisia
"African Path to Socialism, The," 186
African Stories, xxii, 180, 253
African Voices, 184
After Jews and Arabs: Remaking the Levantine Culture, 139
Ahavat tapuah ha-zahav (The Love of an Orange), 163
Aimez-vous Brahms? (Do You Like Brahms?), 195, 218
Aix-en-Provence, 255
Ajar, Emile. *See* Gary, Romain
Alcalay, Ammiel, 139

Alexandria, xi, 29, 140, 203, 214, 260, 265, 291
Alexandria Quartet, The, 103, 147
Algeria, 67–73, 73–74, 79, 146, 147, 148, 149–50, 208, 282, 294
Algerians: in France, 67–73; massacre of Sétif, 79, 294
Algerian War for Independence, 67, 74, 79, 149
Algérie française, 67
Algiers, 74. *See also* Algeria
Al-Hamishmar, 105
Alighieri, Dante, 264
Alinsky, Saul David, 46
Al-Ittahad (The Union), 288
Al-Kahina, 69
Alliance française, 9, 10, 12, 72
Alliance Israélite, 69
al-Qasim, Samih, 288
Alterman, Nathan, 123
Al-yom, 99
"Ambivalent Levantine," 142
America: as Prometheus, 35, 37, 38–39, 40, 42; television, 48–49. *See also* United States
American Civil War, 33
American Indians, 257–58. *See* Native Americans

348 INDEX

American University (Cairo), The, xv, 16
American University in Beirut, The, 291
Am Ha-Sefer, 180
Amir, Aharon, ix, xii, xiv, xvii–xviii, 99–105, 141, 142, 148, 182
Amot, 163
Am Oved, 241
Am Sofer, 241
Amsterdam, 7
Anang, Michael F. Dei, 183
anthropia, 44
anthropological structuralism, viii
Antigone, 168
anti-Semitism, 25, 76, 203
Apadurai, Arjun, 285
Apologies to the Iroquois, 257
Arabism, 286
Arab-Israeli Conflict, 27, 145, 191–94
Aragon, Louis, 87
Araidi, Naim, 138
Arendt, Hannah, 34, 220
Armenians, 258–59
Aron, Raymond, viii, 34, 56
Ashkenazi model, xiii
Ash-Shams, 2
Asia, 234, 257
Asia Minor, 5, 140, 233
Association for Rural Development, 287
At, 279
Ataturk, Mustafa Kemal, 232
Atlantic Monthly (The), viii
Augustine, Saint, 171
Autobiography of an Unknown Indian, The, 252
Awad, Louis, 282, 292
Ayyubids, 3

Baghdad, 7
Bahriyya Mamluks, 4
Bailik, N. H., 209
Baka, 120

Balfour Declaration, 26
Ballata Levantina, 135
Bangladesh, 252
Barbour Youth Center, 115
Baudelaire, Charles, 172, 187
Beauvoir, Simone de, 195, 195–96, 219–20
Beckett, Samuel, 173
Be'er, Haim, 105, 150
Beersheba, xvii, 96–99, 97, 98–99, 112–13
Beirut, xi, 4, 7, 286, 288, 291
Beit Miriam, 273–74
Belfast, 7
Belleville, 64–65
Ben Avi, Itamar, 290
Ben-Bella, Ahmed, 208–9
Benedict, Ruth, 220–21
Ben-Gurion, David, 290
Ben-Gurion University, ix, x
Benhabib, Dolly, 196–97, 232
Benjamin, Walter, 205
Ben-Jelloun, Tahar, xix, 138, 282
Bennabi, Malek, 258
Benvenisti, Meron, 146–47
Ben-Yehuda, Eliezer, 290
Berber tribes, 69, 259, 294
Berrada, Mohammed, 292
Bhabha, Homi K., 200
Bible, 190, 191, 201
Bizert, 72
Black Panthers, 127
Black power movement, 256
Black Power: The Politics of Liberation in America, 256
Blum, Léon, 20, 76
Bombay, 236
Boskowitz, Alexander Uria, 198
Bourguiba, Habib, 208–9, 213, 258
Braudel, Fernand, xii, xiii, xiv, 37, 125, 291
Brazil, 268
Brecht, Bertolt, 79, 294

INDEX

349

Brenner, Y. H., ix

Breton, André, 186

"Bridge towards the 'Olim' of the East, A," 105

Britain. *See* Great Britain

Brit HaKedem (Alliance of Antiquity), 290

Bronowski, Yoram, xi, 148–49

Buber, Martin, xviii, 118, 119–20, 189

Buchenwald, 204

Buddhism, 234, 237, 241–42, 244, 245, 250

Bustros, Evelyne, 287–88

Byzantine Empire, xiii, 125, 140, 146, 293

Cairo, vii, xi, xv, 9–28, 140, 165, 205, 215, 229, 230, 291

Cairo Trilogy, The, 205

Cairo University, 292

"Cairo Wedding," viii

Calderon, Nissim, 147

Calepins bleus (Blue Notebooks), 187

Cambridge University, 292

Camus, Albert, xix, 134, 146, 146–48, 148–49, 170, 182, 189, 200, 242, 247, 282, 283–84, 294–95, 296

Canaanism, 102, 103, 165, 201, 289–90

Canaanite group, ix

cancer, x, xi, xxii, 270, 278–81

Cancer Ward, The, 281

Čapek, Karel, 43

capitalism, 45, 143, 271

Capri, 266

Caribbean, 185, 186, 254

Carlino, Tiziana, 134–35

Catholicism, 167

Cavafy, Constantine P., 103, 150, 282

Cave of the Patriarchs, 94

Céline, Ferdinand, 320n29

Césaire, Aimé, 181, 182, 183

Char, René, 172

Château en Suède (Castle in Sweden), 88

Chaudhuri, Nirad, 252

Chemla, Yvonne, 12

Chicago, 28, 32–34, 93, 165

Chiha, Michel, 287–88

Choucair, Saloua Raouda, 287

Christian humanism, 285

Christianity, xiii, 80, 140, 168, 171, 185, 189, 192, 229, 241–42, 242, 258, 267, 293

Churchill, Winston, 76

Church of the Holy Sepulchre, 4

Cialente, Fausta, 134–35

"Ciaò," 175–76

Circle of Friends of Lebanon, 286

"City in Grey, A," 63

Civil War (American), 185

"Claude Lévi-Strauss, Culture and Cooking," 110

climate, 126–27

Clockwork Orange, A, 222

Cohen, Albert, 203–4, 282, 293

Cold War, 49

colonialism, xix, 1, 10, 12, 20, 21, 69, 77, 135, 137, 141, 151, 171, 179, 180, 181, 186, 187, 193, 194, 196, 199, 200, 215, 227, 252, 255, 256, 258, 259, 260, 292, 294, 295, 296

Columbia University, viii, x, 165, 220

Communist Party, 58, 79, 84, 288, 294

Confessions, 171

Congress Pary, 251

Conquest of the Seas: An Aspect of the History of Civilization, 291

Constantinople, 6

Copts, 15, 27, 103, 128, 137

Corfu, 203, 282, 293

Corm, Charles, xii, 285–88, 291

Corrupting Sea, The, xiv

cows, 257

Crémieux, Adolphe, 69

Crusades, the, 1, 3–4, 6, 78, 145, 161, 164

cultural mutation, 126

Curiel, Henri, 24

Curiel, Raoul, 24
Cyprus, 2, 138
Cyrenaica, 2

d'Amade, Josette, 103–4
d'Amade, Laura, 104
Damascus, 2
Damascus Gate, 229
Darwin, Charles, 20, 141
Darwish, Mahmoud, 288
Dau, Salim, 288
David, King, 251
Days, The, 292
death, 275–77
Decameron, The, 222
de Gaulle, Charles, 51, 73–78, 87, 150, 203, 284
de Lafayette, Madame, 238
Democratic Movement for National Liberation (Egypt), 24
Department of Health, Education, and Welfare (HEW), 47
Des blues á lâme (*Scars on the Soul*), 88
Dialogic genre, 208
Diana (young Jewish woman in Egypt), 216
Diaspora en terre d'Islam: Les communautés Israël du Sud Marocain (*The Diaspora in the Lands of Islam: The Jewish Communities in Southern Morrocco*), 259
Dimona, 98, 112
Diop, David, 181
Dizard, Wilson, 48, 49, 50
Doge's Palace, 265
Dos Passos, John, 31, 56, 56–57
Dostoevsky, Fyoder, 243
Dreyfus, Alfred, xx, 168
Drum, 184
Druze, 122
Druze Mountains, 290
Du Bois, W. E. B., 185, 254
Duhamel, Georges, 56

Durkheim, Emile, 133
Durrell, Lawrence, 103, 147, 150

Eastern Question, the, 3
Ébauches (*Drafts*), 287
École Normale Supérieure, 181
Éditions du Seuil, 79, 80
Effendi, Nahum, 24, 27
Egypt: anti-Semitism, 25; British rule, 103; Gaza Strip, 121; Greek culture, 140; independence, 95, 141; influence on Kahanoff, 133, 134; Israel and, 194; Jewish community in, vii, xiv, xv, 11–12, 24, 25–27, 147, 169, 205–7; Kahanoff's early years in, viii, 9–28, 210, 212, 231; Levantine communities in, 290–91; Levantine minorities in, 21; literature, 205; Mediterranean humanism, 282; modernist renaissance, 292; Ottoman Empire, 5; part of the Levant, xiii; peace with Israel, 90; society, 142; women in, 195, 212–21; writers, xx
Egyptian Gazette, The, 247
Egypt nouvelle, 17
Eid al-Adha, 194
Eilat, Eliahu, 291
Einstein, Albert, 201
Eisenstadt, Shmuel, 133
El Alamein, 216
Elbaz, Shlomo, 138
elephants, 257
Elial, Mikaél, 138
el Masry, Youssef, 213
Enciclopedia del Mediterraneo, 284
England, 179, 203, 249
Enlightenment, 282–83, 296
Erasmus of Rotterdam, 285
Erdogan, Recep Tayyip, 232
Eretz-Israel Museum, ix
Esau, 86, 88, 192
Esber, Ali Ahmed Said, 289
ethnography, 66

INDEX

Etzel, 113

Europa, 88

Europe: Arab-Israeli Conflict, 193; colonialism, 256; cultural formation, 146; Enlightenment, 283; fascism, 204; Hitler, 93; immigrants in, 296; immigration of Africans to, 254–55; Israel and, 162; Japan and, 243; Kahanoff and, 260–69; Mediterranean humanism, 282; nationalism, 95; postwar writers, 242; Prometheus, 283; relationship with the Levant, 5–6; theater, 239; Turkey and, 293

"Europe from Afar," 140, 141

Eurovision, 50

"Eve," 75, 167

Évian Accords, 68

evil, 320n29

Evocations, 287

existentialism, xvi, xx, 50, 76, 166, 167, 171, 178, 187

"False Mediterranean Harbor," 146

Farouk, King, 24, 216

Faulkner, William, 31, 295

Fellini, Federico, 222, 261

feminism, ix, 20, 134, 135, 142, 194–97, 212, 215, 217, 219, 224–27, 235, 287, 288

"Femme noire" ("Black Women," 186

Fifth Republic, 73

First World War, 288

Fitzgerald, F. Scott, 31

Flamand, Pierre, 259

Flint, Ralph, 47

FLN. *See* National Liberation Front

Florence, 262, 262–63, 264

food (culture of), 84–86

"Forbidden Fruit," 177–78

Forester, E. M., 235, 251

Forum for Mediterranean Cultures, 101, 105, 146, 147

Foucault, Michel, 283

Fourastié, Jean, 275

Fourth Republic, 73

France: Algeria, 67–73; Algerian problem, 77, 149–50; alliance with the Ottoman Empire, 6; Charles Péguy and, xx, 166–68, 168; colonialism, xiii, 10, 69, 77, 181, 183, 185–86, 187; commedia dell'arte, 242; diversity in, 66; Jewish community in, 65, 71, 73, 200, 201; Kahanoff's impressions of, 52–53; National Front for the Liberation of Algeria, 24; national society, 210; racial tolerance, 64, 254–55; relationship with Israel, 78; resistance, 75; Second World War, 76–77. *See also* Paris

"France Chronicles," 161

Francis, Saint, 166

Franco, Francisco, 284

Françoise (French Christian acquaintance of Kahanoff's), 214

Frankfurt school, 271

French Guinea, 181, 185

French Resistance, 204

French Revolution, 15, 52, 183, 275

Freud, Sigmund, 201

From East the Sun, ix, 101, 105, 131, 149

Fromm, Erich, 34

From the Poems of the Great Island Madagascar, 187

Fuad, King, 205

Fuller, Buckminster, 41, 42

Future of Culture in Egypt, The, 292

Gabon, 253

Galilee, 111, 112

Gandhi, Indira, 249

Gandhi, Mahatma, 247–51

Garden City, 12

Gary, Romain, 65, 88, 257

Gauls, 19

Gaza Strip, xviii, 120–22, 232

Gelblum, Aryeah, 143

Genesis, 171

Geneva, 203
Genoa, 6, 260
Germany, 95, 128, 210, 242
Gezira, 12
Gide, André, 169, 182, 206
Gifts of Passage, 180
Ginossar, Yaira, 150
Giva't Haviva, 118, 120
Gleizes, Albert, 56
Gnazim Archives of the Hebrew Writers' Association, ix, 173
God & Golem, 43
Goddard, Jean-Luc, 87
Goethe, 43
Gogol, Nikolai, 243
Golan Heights, xviii, 122–23
Golden Gate Bridge, 267
Golem syndrome, 43
Goodman, Paul, 36
Gottmann, Jean, 37, 38, 39, 40, 41
Grand Guignol, 242
Grapes of Wrath, The, 30, 31
Gray, Francine du Plessix, 217–18
Great Britain: colonialism, xiii, 10, 12, 14, 91, 141, 183, 215, 247–48; Jewish community in, 9; libraries in, 39
"Great Couple in French Literature," 195
Great Depression, 30, 33
Greece, 2, 138, 140, 148, 189, 201, 203, 204, 282, 289
"Greetings to the Little Woman," 142
Growing Up Absurd, 36
Guadeloupe, 185
Guillén, Jorge, 172
Gulf War, the, 284

Haaretz, 143
Hafsid dynasty, 4
Haifa, 127, 288
Haiti, 185
ha-merhav, 105
Hamilton, Charles V., 256

Hannibal, 164
hara-kiri, 243, 243–44
Harat al-yahud, 20, 93
Harrington, Michael, 44, 45, 46
hashish, 195, 212
Hatikvah, 113, 114–16
Hebrew Immigrant Aid Society (HIAS), 97
Hebrews, The, ix
Hebrew University, 94–95, 96
Hebron, 94
Hegel, Georg Wilhelm Friedrich, 294
Heidegger, Martin, 244
Heksherim Institute, ix
Hemingway, Ernest, 31
Henein, Georges, 24
Hentoff, Nat, 46
Hever, Hannan, 139
Hinduism, 250, 252
Hiroshima, 243
Histadrut, 99
History of the Hebrew People, A, 289–90
Hitler, Adolf, 25, 93, 259, 320n29
Hochberg, Gil Z., 136–37, 138, 139
Ho Chi Minh, 294
Holocaust, 131
Holy Land, 3, 4, 119
Horden, Peregrine, xii, xiv
Horon, A. G., 289–90
Human Use of Human Beings: Cybernetics and Society, The, 43
"Hunger Artist, The," 171
Hussein, Taha, xii, 282, 291–92

I, General de Gaulle, 74
"Idiot, The," 247
Ihud, 119
Illness as a Metaphor, 270
India, 39, 95, 106, 236, 247–52, 257
Indian Ocean, 4
Indochina, 63
Indonesia, 234
Industrial Revolution, 256, 276

INDEX 353

"In Gilat 'All Problems Are Solved,'" 105
Inquisition, 193
Institute of Contemporary
  Jewry, 208
Institut Europeu de la Mediterràneo, 284
Iran, 138
Iraq, 2, 9, 138
Isaac, 193–94, 194
Ishmael, 193–94
Iskandar, George, 288
Islam, 5, 6, 26, 100, 108, 146, 192, 194,
  195, 212, 213, 228–29, 230, 231, 232,
  258, 259, 286, 293
Islamic Empire, xiii
Iso, Einosuki, 246–47
Israel: Americanization of, 131; Ameri-
  can megapolis and, 40; Arabs in, 119,
  144, 227; Ashkenazi Jews in, 65, 109;
  Diaspora, 143; formation of, 90; Gaza
  Strip, 120–22; Golan Heights, 122–23;
  Greater, 102, 190; Hebrews and, 290;
  immigrants in, 296; as an immigrant
  society, 48, 143, 147, 210; immigration of the Jews to, 4–5, 143; Israeli
  identity, 164, 165; Israelis and Jews, 93;
  Israeli society, 105–16, 196–97; Japanese literature and, 241; Jewish identity, 200; Jews and Arabs in, 118–23;
  Judaism, 106, 189–94; Kahanoff and,
  vii–xiii, xv–xx, 89, 105–16; Levant, 125;
  the Levant and, xiii, xviii, 2–5, 131, 134;
  Levantine option, 132–43; Levantism,
  66, 124–51; literature, 201–2; Mediterranean, 143–51, 146; Mediterranean,
  the, 163; music, 197–98; Occupied
  Territories, 230; peace with Egypt, 90;
  relationship with France, 78; republic
  of letters, 144; Sadat visit, 194; state
  of, 71, 72–73, 93, 106, 126, 129, 164, 192,
  258; War of Independence, 112; West
  Bank, 102; women in, 195–97, 225–27;
  Zionism, 25, 131. See also Haifa;
  Tel Aviv

Israeli-Arab dispute. See Arab-Israeli
  Conflict
"Israel's Levantinization," 129
Issa, Norman, 288
Istanbul, xi
Istanbul—Memories and the City, 293
Italy, 242, 260–67
Ithaca, 297

Jabés, Edmond, xii, xix, xx, 165, 169–71,
  206–7, 282
Jabotinsky, Eri, 290
Jabotinsky, Ze'ev, 290
Jacob, 86, 88, 192
Jacobs, W., 43
Jacob's Ladder, viii
Jakobson, Roman, 34
Jamaica, 179
Japan, 237–47; theater, 239–40
Jason and the Argonauts, 164
Java, 234, 235
Je bâtis ma demeure (I'm Building My
  Home), 169
Jerusalem, xviii, 3, 7, 164
Jerusalem, East, xviii, 196, 227, 230, 232
Jesuits, xv, 16, 24, 217
Jesus, 148, 205, 285
Jeune Afrique, 288
Jewish-Arab conflict, 118–23. See also
  Arab-Israeli Conflict
Jewish Frontier, 99
Jews: Algerian, 69, 70, 71, 72, 73; among
  Berber tribes, 259; Ashkenazi, 26, 103,
  109, 125, 131, 137, 139, 143, 150, 215; Bene
  Israel, 106; climate and, 126; culture,
  201; Diaspora, 107, 143; Egyptian,
  70, 107, 130, 147; European, 71, 107,
  108, 111, 128; German, 95; Hebrews
  and, 289; identity, 200, 201, 202; Iraq,
  100, 113; Iraqi, 210; Italian, 206–7; in
  Italy, 266; Kurdish, 106; leaving Arab
  countries, 70–71; Levantine, 139;
  Mediterranean, 291; Mizrahi, 71, 72,

Jews: Algerian (*Cont.*)
92, 93, 100, 107–11, 113, 114, 127, 128,
129, 130, 137, 139, 142, 143, 144, 150,
164, 165, 194, 195–97, 196–97, 232, 265;
Moroccan, 72, 111–12, 130; Oriental,
26; Romanian, 98; Sephardic, 26, 70,
93, 96, 143, 203–4; Tunisian, 112, 130,
202, 210; Yeminite, 106, 111–12, 113, 115
"Jews, Christians, and Muslims in the
Mediterranean Basin," 145
Jihad, 5, 6
Joan of Arc, 75, 77, 166, 167, 168
Johnson, Lyndon, 44, 47
Jonas, Hans, 34
Joséphine (Kahanoff's dressmaker and
friend), 53–55
Jubran, Salam, 288
Judaism, xiii, 170, 171, 189–94, 258
Judt, Tony, 80
"Jules Romains, on His Seventy-fifth
Birthday," 56

Kabbalah, 170, 208
Kafka, Franz, 139, 171, 201
Kahanoff, Alexander, 96, 97
Kahanoff, Jacqueline Shohet: Abie
Nathan, 120; Africa, 253–60; African
poetry and literature, 178–88; *African
Stories*, 180, 253; African Zionism,
185; aging, 270, 270–73, 276–78, 277;
agriculture in the United States,
47; Aharon Amir, 99–105; Albert
Camus, 146–47; on Albert Cohen,
203–4; on Albert Memmi, 201–2,
295–96; Algerian problem, 68, 70;
"Ambivalent Levantine," 142; *Amot*,
163; anthropological structuralism,
viii; anthropology, 35, 107, 111, 221,
258, 263; anti-facism, 24; Anwar
Sadat's visit to Israel, 194; Arabs of
Palestine, 91–92; Beersheba, 96–99,
112–13; "On Being a Tourist," 268;
Black literature, 179; "Bridge towards

the 'Olim" of the East, A," 105;
Cairo, 50, 133, 154; "Cairo Wedding,"
viii; in California, 29; Canaanism,
201; cancer, xxii–xxiii, 90, 278–81;
capitalism and, 44, 46, 116, 271; on
Charles Darwin, 20, 141; Charles
Péguy, 75, 166–69; Chicago, 28,
32–34, 93; Christianity, 42; "Ciaò,"
175–76; "Claude Lévi-Strauss,
Culture and Cooking," 110; Claude
Lévi-Strauss and, viii, 35, 84–86;
Claude Vigée, 171–73, 296; climate,
126–27; colonialism, 255–56, 256, 259,
260; communism, 24; consumer-
ism, 36–37; cultural mutation, 126;
cultural theory, 179; culture of food,
84–86; Dahlia Ravikovitch, 123;
Dahlia Ravikovitch, Dahlia, 161–65;
death, 90, 275–78; death of, 279–81;
on de Gaulle, 76–77, 78; dialogic
genre and, 208–11; Diana (young
Jewish woman in Egypt), 216; "To
Die a Modern Death," xxii, 271;
Dimona, 98; divorce from Alexander
Kahanoff, 278; divorce from Izzy
Margoliash, viii, 279; *From East the
Sun*, ix, 101, 105, 131, 149; Egypt, vii,
xv, 9–28, 91, 134, 194, 205–7, 208, 231;
environmental concerns, 31; Europe
and, 260–69; "Europe from Afar,"
140, 141; existentialism, 187; family,
154; family history, 9–10; father's
illness and death, 270–75, 273–75;
feminism, ix, x, xxi, 92, 134, 135, 142,
165, 192, 194–97, 209, 212, 213–14,
215–16, 217, 221, 223–27, 233; "Forbidden Fruit," 177–78; Forum for Mediterranean Culture, 146–47; France
and, 75; "France Chronicles," 161;
on Francine du Plessix Gray, 217–18;
on Françoise Sagan, 218; freelance
writing, 105; French culture, 87–89;
friendship with Madame Joséphine,

53–55; funeral of Saad Zaghoul, 24; Gaza Strip, 120–22; "In Gilat 'All Problems Are Solved,'" 105; God, 141, 167; Golan Heights, 122–23; grandfather, 271–72; "The Great Couple in French Literature," 195; "Greetings to the Little Woman," 142; Haifa, 288; Hatikvah, 114–16; Hebrew Immigrant Aid Society (HIAS), 97; Hebron, 94; immigrants in Israel, 105–23, 130; immigration to France, 134; immigration to Israel, 67, 90, 165; immigration to the United States, viii, xv, 28, 134; impressions of Paris, 55–56, 58–65; impressions of the United States, 29–30, 33–34, 35, 36, 39–41; India, 247–52; inequality, 251; influence of, ix; integral humanism, 182; interest in Israeli films, xi; interest in television, xi; interests in art and architecture, xi; introductions to *From the Poems of the Great Island of Madagascar*, 187; Israel, viii, ix, xi, 37, 42–43, 48, 73, 89–96, 96–99, 105–16, 170, 206–7, 208, 264, 266, 268; Israeli cuisine, 110–11; Israeli society, 105–16, 116–17, 127, 130–31, 144, 151, 189–90; "Israel's Levantinization," 129; Italy, 260–67; Jabés, Edmond, 169–70, 206–7, 296; "On Jacob," 191; *Jacob's Ladder*, viii; Japan, 237–47; Japanese literature, 241; on Jean-Paul Sarte, 83–84; Jewish-Arab conflict, 118–23; Jewish culture and, ix, 259–60; Jewish identity, 165, 201, 207, 209; Joséphine (dressmaker and friend), 53–55; Josette d'Amade, 103–4; Judaism, 93–94, 106, 165, 173, 189–94, 194; "Jules Romains, on His Seventy-fifth Birthday," 56; on Kateb Yacine, 79; kibbutzim, 92–93; "To Kiss the Light," 174–75; and the Langstrom family, 33; languages

spoken, vii; the Levant and, xv, 30; "The Levantine Generation," 132, 161; Levantine identity, 15–16, 21–22, 27–28, 100, 102, 104, 105, 117, 131, 134, 135–36, 140–41, 142, 211, 214, 297; Levantine option in Israel, 132–43; Levantinization, 66; Levantism, xiii, xiv, xviii, 1, 8, 20, 124–51, 198, 236, 290–91; libraries in the United States, 47; "Life Was," 173–74; *L'irrévolution*, 88–89; literary influences on, x; "The Literature of Social Mutation," 198–99, 202, 209–10; literature of social mutation, 179, 180, 184, 198–205; on Mahatma Gandhi, 247–51; marriage to Alexander Kahanoff, viii, 96–97, 99; marriage to Izzy Margoliash, xv, 28, 32; Martin Buber, 119–20; on Mary McCarthy, 220; Mediterranean, the, 163; Mediterranean culture, 145; Mediterranean humanism, 282, 297; Mediterranean idea, xix, xxiii, 151; Mediterranean option, 144–45, 145, 189, 209; "The Migration of Peoples in the West," 40; Mizrahi Jews in Israel, 107–11; "Mizrahi Music in Israel," 197; modernity, 133, 197, 230–31, 232, 268; mother, 279; on Mounier, 80; Musée de la Homme, 66–67; "My America," 30; "My Brother Ishmael," 193; "My Brother the Rebel," 208; nationalism (Israeli), xviii, 24; nature, 85, 276–77; Negev, 96, 98–99; network and, xii; new journalism and, x; New School for Social Research in Greenwich Village, 34; New York, x, 28, 29, 51, 89; niece Laura, 104; Nietzsche, 141; "The Nobel Prize 1962—Why John Steinbeck?" 30–31; "Nothing Sweet Comes out of Gaza," 120–21; "Nothing to Wear," 176–77; *One Thousand and One Nights*, 228–30;

INDEX

Kahanoff, Jacqueline Shohet: Abie Nathan (*Cont.*)

otherness, 208–9; Paris, viii, x, 50–67, 61; poems, 173–78; poetry, xix, 161–88; in Portugal, 267–69; poverty in the United States, 47; prejudice, 251, 252; princess of the Levant, ix; prize from *The Atlantic Monthly*, viii; progress and, 17–18; Prometheus and America, 37, 38–39, 40, 41, 43, 48, 50; Rachel, 94; racial segregation, 30; racism, 255–56; *Ramat-Hadassah-Szold: Youth Aliyah Screening and Classification Centre*, 116–18; recognition of, vii; "Reflections of a Levantine," 99; Regina (immigrant to Israel from Tunisia), 109–10; religion, 13–14, 21–24, 166–73, 230, 251; "With the Return to the East," 227, 229, 232; "The Revolution in Education," 47; "Ritornello," 177; on Ruth Benedict, 221; on Santha Rama Rau, 236; science and, 44; secularism, 141; sexual freedom and, 221–24; on Simone de Beauvoir, 219–20; "The Sound of the Horn," 178; status of women and, xi–xii; "Stiches," 177; student at Columbia University, viii; "Such Is Rachel," viii; "Summer in Portugal," 267; surgery, 280; Susan Sontag and, x; Sylvie (friend), 90, 92, 94–95, 95, 215; teaching French in Israel, 97–98; technology and, xxii, 29–30, 36, 42–43, 44, 46, 47, 48, 50, 126, 127, 129, 270–71, 275–76, 281; Tel Aviv, 96–97, 113–14; television and, 48–50; "Television as a Springboard: To Swim or to Sink," 48; "They Do Not Absorb Children," 105; "They Need an Attentive Ear," 105; time and, 18–19, 124, 131, 140; Touchy family, 53–55; "The Tragedy of the Eastern Woman," 195; treatment of animals, 30, 86, 276; United States, x, 48; US aid, 48; on Ved Mehta, 249–50; visit to a working class home, 58–59; volunteer work, 19–20, 215, 226–27; "Wake of the Waves," 163; "Where Does One Get the Color of One's Skin," 253; "Why They Did Not Understand Regina," 105; *WIZO-Hadassah*, xi; women in society, 18, 33, 212–36, 223, 224–36; "Women with a Pen of Their Own," 219; writings about the Levantine, xi; Yad Eliyahu, 104; YMCA, 32; Yoram Bronowski and, xi; on Yukio Mishima, 243, 244, 244–46; Zionism, 24, 26, 37, 91–92, 95, 96, 97, 111, 112, 116, 118, 123, 131, 190, 191, 201, 260

Karavan, Dani, 205
"Karnei Hattin," 164
Kartini, Princess Adjeng, 234–35
Kartini Foundation, 234
Kashua, Sayed, 138
Kennedy, John F., 44
Kenya, 183
Kenyatta, Jomo, 183
Keshet, viii, xviii, xxii, 99, 100, 105, 132, 161, 163, 165, 182, 271
Kfar Shalem, 115
Khoury, Makram, 288
kibbutzim, 92–93, 110, 118, 165
Kierkegaard, Søren, 217
Kish-Kish Bey Theater, 16
Kojève, Alexandre, 284
Kook, Rabbi Zvi Yehuda, 102
Kubrick, Christiane, 223
Kubrick, Stanley, 222–23, 320n29
Kyoto, 238

La condition humaine, 88
La Fontaine, 187
L'âge de raison (*The Age of Reason*), 84
La libération du juif (*The Liberation of the Jew*), 200–201, 202

INDEX

La main d'Allah (*The Hand of Allah*), 287
L'Amérique insolite, 35
La Revue Phénicienne (*The Phoenician Review*), 286, 287
L'Argent (*Money*), 167
La statue de sel (*The Pillar of Salt*), 202
Latin Quarter, 64
Latrun, 231
La Vie devant soi, 58–65
Laye, Camara, 181
Lean, David, 235
Lebanese Arab Women's Union (Lebanese Women's Council), 287
Lebanese Civil War, 288, 289
Lebanon, xiii, 2, 78, 285–89, 290, 291
Le cru et le cuit (*The Raw and the Cooked*), 84
Le drama sexual de la femme dans l'Orient arabe (*The Sexual Drama of Women in the Arab Orient*), 213
Le fil de l'épée, 75
Légitime défense (*Legitimate Defense*), 186
Lehi, 113
Le livre des questions (The Book of Questions), 170, 206–8
Le Monde, 87
Le mystère de la charité de Jeanne d'Arc, 75
L'Enfant noir (*The Dark Child*), 181
Le premier homme (*The First Man*), 149
Les 40 000 heures (*The 40,000 Heures*), 275
Les artistes de la faim (*The Artists of Hunger*), 171
Les chemins de la liberté (The Roads to Freedom), 84
Les Croisades vues par les Arabes (*The Crusades through Arab Eyes*), 288
Les échelles du Levant (*The Ports of the Levant*), 288
Les hommes de bonne volonté (Men of Goodwill), 57
Les hommes de bonne volonté (*Men of Goodwill*), 56

Les identités meurtrières (*Deadly Identities*), 289
L'Esprit, 80
Les racines du ciel (*The Roots of Heaven*), 257
"Letter Found in a Cement Barrel, A," 247
Letters of a Javanese Princess, 234
"L'etudiant noir" ("The Black Student"), 181
Levant (journal), 138
Levant, the: Aharon Amir, 103; Brit HaKedem (Alliance of Antiquity), 290; culture, 132, 140; definition, 1–2, 134, 137–39; as a distinct cultural space, xiv, xv, 6, 6–7, 124–25, 284, 286; effect of the Crusades on, 3–4, 5–6; effect of the Ottoman Empire on, 4–5, 6–8; Europe and North Africa, 285; feminism, 142; Fernand Braudel and, 37; France and, 78; Greek, 140; Hebrews, 289–90; history of, 1–8; intellectual, 164; Jewish community in, 9; Latin, 4; literature of social mutation, 199; Mediterranean, 291, 291–92; Ottoman, 4–5; Romans, 126. *See also* Levantism
Levantine Generation, The, xviii, 132, 163
Levantine identity. *See* Levantism
Levantine network, xii
Levantine option, 125, 132–43
Levantinization, 236
Levantism, xiii, xiv, xviii, 1–8, 5–6, 7, 20, 64, 101, 103, 124–51, 141, 179. *See also* Levantine identity
Levant: Splendour and Catastrophe on the Mediterranean, 1
Lévinas, Emmanuel, 189–91
Lévi-Strauss, Claude, viii, 34–35, 37, 66, 84–85, 134, 279
L'Express, 87

"L'Humanisme et la Mediterranée"
("Humanism and the Mediterra-
nean"), 286
Libya, 2, 138
"Life Was," 173–74
Light in August, 295
Liguria, 263
Lincoln, Abraham, 33
L'irrévolution (Non-revolution), 88–89
Lisbon, 267
literature of social mutation, xx, xxi,
179, 180, 184, 198–205
"Literature of Social Mutation, The,"
198–99, 202, 209–10
Livni, Yitzhak, 105
Livorno, 266–67
London, 75, 76
longue durée, xiii
Lorraine, 75
Louis IX, 3–4
Louis XIV, 240
Louis XV, 238
Lovers and Tyrants, 217–18
Lvinas, Emmanuel, xii, xxi
lycée, 72, 88, 90, 140

Maalouf, Amin, xii, 285, 288–89
Maalouf, Rushdi, 288
Machiavelli, Nicolo, 73, 78
"Machine," 247
Madagascar, 182, 187
Maghreb, 71, 171, 284
Maginot Line, 75
Mahfouz, Najib, xix, 203, 205, 282
Malkin, Irad, xii
Mallarmé, Stéphane, 172
Malraux, André, 87, 169, 206
Mameluke-Ottoman War, 5
Mandela, Nelson, 79, 294
Mannoni, Eugene, 74
Mansel, Phillip, 1
Mansour, Atalha, 138
Mansoura, 291

Man'yōshū (Collection of Ten Thou-
sand Leaves), 237
Marcuse, Herbert, 36, 244
Margery (friend of Kahanoff's), 263
Margoliash, Izzy: divorce from Jac-
queline Kahanoff, xvi; marriage to
Jacqueline Kahanoff, xv, 28
Maronite Christians, 290, 291
Marseille, 7, 203, 255, 260
Martinique, 181, 182, 185
Marx, Karl, 133, 166, 201
Mashrak, 2, 138, 171
Massalha, Salman, 138
Matalon, Ronit, 196
McCarthy, Mary, 220
McLuhan, Marshall, 49
Mecca, 5, 6, 16, 258
Medina, 5, 6
Mediterranean, the, xii, xiii, xiv, xx, 1, 2,
4, 5, 103, 124–25, 134, 138, 142, 143–51,
145, 163, 165, 171, 193, 204–5, 284–87,
285, 291
Mediterranean Academy, 286
Mediterranean enlightenment,
202–3
Mediterranean humanism, xix, 282,
282–97, 296, 297. *See also* Mediter-
ranean idea
Mediterranean idea, xix, xxiii, 151, 285.
See also Mediterranean humanism
Mediterraneanism, 137
Mediterranean option, the, 143,
144–45, 146, 149, 189, 209
"Mediterranean Option: On the
Politics of Regional Affiliation in the
Current Israeli Cultural Imagina-
tion, The," 136
Mediterranean Sea, 78, 163, 205, 285,
287
*Megalopolis: The Urbanized Northeast-
ern Seaboard of the United States*, 37
megapolis, 39–40
Mehta, Ved, 180, 248–49

INDEX

Mehta, Zubin, 180
Mein Kampf, 25
Meir, Golda, 224
Memmi, Albert, xii, xix, xxi, 135, 180, 200–201, 202, 282, 295–96
Memoirs of a Dutiful Daughter, 220
Memories of a Catholic Girlhood, 220
Mercure de France, 56
Mesopotamia, xiii
Michael, Sami, 148, 288
"Migration of Peoples in the West, The," 40
Milan, 263–64
Miriam (Kahanoff's cousin), 262
Mishima, Yukio, xxii, 237, 242–46
Mizrahi Democratic Coalition, 196
Mizrahim, ix
"Mizrahi Music in Israel," 197
modernism, 283–84
Mohammad, 148
Mohammad Ali clinic, 19
Mongrels or Marvels: The Levantine Writings of Jacqueline Kahanoff, vii, 150
Montaigne, x
Monterescu, Daniel, 135, 136
Montesquieu, 126
Montherlant, Henry de, 87
Montpellier, 71
Montreal, 41
Moraes, Dom, 180
Moravia, Alberto, 222
Morocco, 259, 282, 292
Morocco Writers Union, 292
Moses, 148, 205
Moshav Gila, 112
Mosseri, Albert, 24
Mounier, Emmanuel, 80
Muhammad, 205
Muhammad Ali, Taha, 288
Munthe, Axel, 266
Murasaki, Shikibu, 238
Musée de la Homme, 67

music, 197–98
Muslim Brotherhood, 25, 128
Mussolini, Benito, 284
Mutsuhito, Emperor, 240–41
"My America," 30
"My Brother Ishmael," 193
"My Brother the Rebel," 208

Naipaul, V. S., xxii, 179, 248–49
Najjar, Anissa Rawda, 287
Naples, 260, 262
Napoleon, 103
Nasi, Don Joseph, 106
Nasser, Abdel, 120, 213, 291
Nathan, Abie, xviii, 120
National Front for the Liberation of Algeria, 24
National Liberation Front, 67, 68, 70, 84. *See also* National Front for the Liberation of Algeria
Native Americans, 39
Natour, Salman, 288
nature, 256–57, 258, 268, 283
Nazareth, 120
Nazis, 76, 141, 193, 222, 242, 259
Nedjma, 294
Negev, 96, 98, 99, 109, 112
Négritude, 181, 182, 186
Netherlands, 234
network, definition, xii
Neve Shalem, 115
new journalism (movement), x
new novel, 50
new radicals, 46
New School for Social Research in Greenwich Village, viii, 34, 165
New York (State), 257
New York City, 34–50, 51, 89, 104
Nice, 71
Nietzsche, Friedrich, 100, 141, 170, 189, 251, 283–84
"Nightingale," 246–47
Nobel Prize, 30, 182, 294

360 INDEX

"Nobel Prize 1962, The—Why John Steinbeck?" 30
Nocke, Alexandra, 139–40
"Nothing Sweet Comes out of Gaza," 120–21
"Nothing to Wear," 176–77
Notre Jeunesse, 169

Occupied Territories, 197
Oedipus, 168
Ohana, David, 139
Okara, Gabriel, 186
Olivero, Betty, 198
"On Being a Tourist," 268
One-Dimensional Man, 244
One Thousand and One Nights, 43, 227–30, 232
"On Jacob," 191
Open University, ix
Opoku, Amankwa Andrew, 184
Organisation armée secrète (OAS), 67, 68, 70
Organization of Sephardic Women, 226–27
Orient, 1–2
Orientalization, 3
Orléans, 168
Orloff, Chana, 291
Orpheus, 218
Other America: Poverty in the United States, The, 44
otherness, 208–9, 219, 297
Ottoman Empire, 1, 2, 5, 6–8, 261, 293
"Our Fifty Million Poor," 45
Over the Wild River, 184
Oz, Amos, 138

Pakistan, 248
Palestine, ix, 5, 10, 16, 17, 19, 26, 29, 90, 91, 92, 95, 96, 107, 140, 141–42, 190–91, 201, 225, 270, 290
Palestinian Authority, 232
Palm-wine Drinkard, The, 184

Pamuk, Orhan, 282, 292–93
pan-Arabism, xiii, 125, 128
Paris, viii, xii, 6, 7, 50–67, 74, 165
Pasolini, Piero, 261
Passage to India, A, 235, 251–52
Pasternak, Boris, 243
Patterns of Culture, 221
Péguy, Charles, xix, xx, 73, 74, 75, 78, 80, 166–69
PEN, 56
"Permanent Immigration: Jacqueline Kahanoff, Ronit Matalon, and the Impetus of Levantinism," 137
Persia, xiii
personalism, 80–82
Phoenicians, 286–87, 289–90, 291
"Piano and Drums," 186
pieds noirs, 68–69
Pillow Book of Sei Shōnagon, The, 240, 240–41
Place de la Concorde, 51, 61
Place of the Mediterranean in Modern Israeli Identity, The, 139
Plato, 293
Poe, Edgar Alan, 187
poetry, 161–88
polygamy, 195, 212, 213, 228, 229, 233
Pompidou, Georges, 87
Portrait d'un juif (Portrait of a Jew), 200
Portugal, 267–69
Positano, 264
poverty, 47
Prague, 204
Prawar, Joshua, 3, 145
Présence africaine, 182
Prévert, Jacques, 53
Prince, The, 74
Princeton University, 292
Prometheus, 16, 41, 43, 283, 284, 293, 293–94
"Promised Land or the Permitted Land, The," 190
Proust, Marcel, 12, 17, 55

INDEX

Purcell, Nicholas, xii, xiv
Pyrenees, 268

Quaderns de la Mediterrània, 284
Quatre lectures talmudiques, 189

Rabearivelo, Jean-Joseph, 187–88
Rabin, Yitzhak, 149
Rachel, 94
racism, 184, 296, 297
Ramadan, 258
"Rama Kam," 181
Rama Rau, Santha, xxii, 179–80,
    235–36, 251–52
*Ramat-Hadassah-Szold: Youth Aliyah
    Screening and Classification Centre*,
    xviii, 116–18
Ratosh, Yonatan, 102, 289, 290
Ravenna, 261, 264
Ravikovitch, Dahlia, xix, 123, 161–65,
    171, 178, 180
"Reflections of a Levantine," 99
Regina (immigrant to Israel from
    Tunisia), 109–10
Reichenbach, François, 35, 36
Rejwan, Nissim, 99–100
Remember the House, 236
Renaissance, 283, 285–86
Renoir, Jean, 87
*Representations of the Mediterranean
    Spirit*, 284
*Révolte et louanges (Revolt and
    Praise)*, 172
"Revolution in Education, The," 47
Revue juive, 203
Rimbaud, Arthur, 172, 187
Rippin, Sarah, 279, 280
"Ritornello," 177
River Magra, 263
Romains, Jules, 55, 56, 57, 58, 88
Roman Empire, xiii, 140
Romans, 148
Rome, 260–61

Roosevelt, Franklin D., 33, 76
Rousseau, Jean-Jacques, 283
R.U.R. (Rossum's Universal
    Robots), 43
Russia, 291
Rustin, Bayard, 46

Saari, Rami, 292–93
Sabra, 136, 164, 165, 190
Sadako, Empress, 240
Sadat, Anwar, xvii, xviii, 90, 193, 194
Sagan, Françoise, 88, 195, 218–19
Said, Edward, 138, 138–39
Sakaguchi, Ango, 247
Saladin, 3, 164
Salazar Bridge, 267
San Francisco Bay, 267
Sarte, Jean-Paul, 56, 79, 87, 182, 195,
    219–20, 242, 244, 247, 253, 294
Scheherazade, 227–28
Schiller, Herbert, 49
Schmitt, Carl, 146
Second Sex, The, 219
Second World War, viii, xvi, 2, 28, 34,
    48, 67, 80, 89, 172, 182, 193, 203, 216,
    222, 237, 242, 284
Sei Shōnagon, 240–41
Selim the First, Sultan, 5
Semprún, Jorge, xix, 203, 204–5, 282,
    293–94
Senegal, 182
Senghor, Léopold, 181–82, 183, 186
seppuku, 243
September 11, 2001, 285
Seter, Mordecai, 198
Sétif, 79
Sévigné, Marquise, 240
sexual freedom, 221–24
Sham-el-nessim, 16
Shammas, Anton, 138
Shelleg, Assaf, 198
Shemer, Naomi, 63
Shikibu, Murasaki, 238

362 INDEX

Shohet, Jacob, 9
Shohet, Joseph, 10, 12
Shohet, Yvonne Chemla, 10–11
Shukri, Hassan Bey, 288
Silicon Valley, 40
Simmel, Georg, 135
Simon, Akiva Ernst, 119
Sinai Campaign, 129
Sinai Desert, 2
Six-Day War, xviii, 27, 102, 120, 150, 190, 191, 192, 229
Slouschz, Nahum, 291
socialism, 46
Solal, 203–4, 293
Soliman, Lotfallah, 24
Solzhenitsyn, Aleksandr, 243, 281
Somekh, Sasson, 100, 105, 150
Sontag, Susan, x–xi, 270
Sorbonne, 80, 169, 215
Sotah, 190
Souls of Black Folk, The, 185
"Sound of the Horn, The," 178
South Africa, 180, 183, 247, 249
Soviets, 78
Soviet Union, 79, 115
Spain, 204, 282, 293
"Spirit of the East and Judaism, The," 119
Stalinism, 24, 80
Starr, Deborah Anne, 139, 150
Steinbeck, John, 30–31
Steiner, Rudolf, 32
"Stiches," 177
Stokeley Carmichael, 256
Story of San Michele, The, 266
Strauss, Leo, 34
structuralism, 50, 66
"Such Is Rachel," viii
Suez campaign, 78
Suez Canal, 9, 27, 169
"Summer in Portugal," 267
surrealism, 170, 186
Suyin, Han, 257

Sweid, Yousef, 288
Sylvie (friend of Kahanoff's), 90, 92, 94, 95, 215
Syria, 2, 5, 289, 290
Szold, Henrietta, xviii, 116, 117

Tagus River, 267
Tale of the Genji, The, 238
Talmud, 190
Tammuz, 289
technology, 283
Tel Aviv, ix, xii, xvii, 66, 89–96, 99, 104, 113–14, 173, 280. *See also* Israel
"Television as a Springboard: To Swim or to Sink," 48
Television: A World View, 48–49
Temple of the Golden Pavilion, The, 244–45
Ten Commandments, 26
Themba, Can, 184
"The Sparrow Shall Fall," 257
The Story of the Lady Ochikubo (The Lady in the Basement), 239
"They Do Not Absorb Children," 105
"They Need an Attentive Ear," 105
This Is India, 252
Thomas, H. Carey, 254
Tobruk, 216
"To Die a Modern Death," xxii, 271
"To Kiss the Light," 174–75
Tolstoy, Leo, 243
Tocqueville, Alexis de, 40, 41
Toscanini, Arturo, 16
Touchy family, 53–55
Toulouse, 71
"Tragedy of the Eastern Woman, The," 195
Trieste, 203
"Trip in the Mediterranean, A," 147
Troen, Ilan, 37
Trotskyism, 24
Tsalka, Dan, 148
Tsohar Publishing House, 148

INDEX

Tunis, 202
Tunisia, 10, 72, 208, 213, 258, 267, 282
Turin, 264
Turkey, 2, 10, 138, 232, 266, 282
Tuscany, 263
Tutuola, Amos, 184
Twin Towers, 285
"Two Sisters," 104

unanism, 58
United Jewish Appeal, 71–72, 73
United Nations, 212
United States: Black Americans, 254; capitalism in, 45–46; discrimination in, 32–33; education, 39; Great Seal of, 39; history of Black Americans, 185, 295; immigrant culture, 210; Israel and, 291; Japan and, 246; Kahanoff's impressions of, 29; "land of opportunity," 40; libraries, 39; poverty and, 47; poverty in, 45; racial segregation, 30; Rama Rau, Santha, 180; Second World War, 33; Vietnam, 78, 220; women's liberation movement, 225. *See also* America; New York City
United States Information Agency, 49
University of Alexandria, 291
University of Algiers, 69
University of Paris, 53

Valéry, Paul, 172, 187
Van Leer Jerusalem Institute, 101, 146
Vatican, 261
Venice, 264–65
Véronique, French friend of Kahanoff's, 233
Vers l'armée du metier, 75
Vie Nouvelle, 80–81
Vietnam, 79
Vietnam War, 217
Vigée, Claude, viii, xii, xix, xx, xxi, 171–73

Vigney, Alfred de, 172
Villon, François, 53–54
Virgil, 39
Virgin Mary, 222
Visconti, Luchiano, 222, 261

Wadi Salib, 127
Wafd Party, 12
Wailing Wall, 93
"Wake of the Waves," 163
Walzer, Michael, 297
War of Independence (Israel), 112, 115, 225
Watad, Muhammad, 138
Weber, Max, 33, 38, 133
Weintraub, Eva, 280
Weizmann, Chaim, 203
West Bank, 102, 121
western culture, xiii
West Indies, 182
"Where Does One Get the Color of One's Skin," 253
"Why They Did Not Understand Regina," 105
Wiener, Norbert, 43, 44
Wilson, Edmund, 257–58
Windsor, Duchess of, 216
"With the Return to the East," 227, 229, 232
women: Islam and, 213; Japan, 238; Judaism and, 212; liberation movement, 225; in society, 212–36; writing and, 217–21. *See also* feminism
Women's International Zionist Organization (WIZO), xi, 20
"Women with a Pen of Their Own," 219
World's Fair, 41
World War I. *See* First World War
World War II. *See* Second World War

Yacine, Kateb, 294–95
Yad Eliyahu, 104, 115
Yale University Press, ix

INDEX

Yacine, Kateb, 79, 282
Yehoshua, A. B., 100, 101, 150, 164, 288
Yemen, 138
Yishuv, 90, 108, 126, 225
YMCA, 34
Yokomitsu, Riichi, 247
Yom Kippur War, xviii, 279
Yoshiki, Hayama, 247
Young Turks, 259
Youth Aliyah, 118

Zach, Natan, 288, 289
Zaghloul, Saad, 12, 24–25, 205
Ziad, Tawfiq, 288
Zionism, xiii, 25, 26, 37, 72, 91–92, 95, 96, 102, 104, 107, 108, 109, 111, 112, 116, 118, 120, 123, 125, 130, 131, 136, 150, 161, 190, 191, 198, 201, 260, 290
Zionist establishment. *See* Zionism
Zohar, Ezra, 105
Zulu, 184

DAVID OHANA is Professor (emeritus) of Modern European History, Mediterranean and Israeli Studies at Ben-Gurion University of the Negev, Israel, a senior Fellow at the Jerusalem Van Leer Institute, and Life Member at the Clare Hall, University of Cambridge. His many books include *Political Theologies in the Holly Land* (Routledge, 2009), *Israel and Its Mediterranean Identity* (Palgrave Macmillan, 2011), *Modernism and Zionism* (Palgrave Macmillan, 2012), *The Origins of Israeli Mythology* (Cambridge University Press, 2014), *The Nihilist Order: The Intellectual Roots of Totalitarianism* (Sussex Academic Press, 2016), *Nationalizing Judaism* (Lexington Books, 2017), *Albert Camus and the Critique of Violence* (Sussex Academic Press, 2017), *Nietzsche and Jewish Political Theology* (Routledge, 2019), *The Intellectual Origins of Modernity* (Routledge, 2019), *Birth-Throes of the Israeli Homeland* (Routledge, 2020), *and The Fascist Temptation* (Routledge, 2021).

For Indiana University Press

Emily Baugh, Editorial Assistant
Lesley Bolton, Project Manager/Editor
Brian Carroll, Rights Manager
Gary Dunham, Acquisitions Editor and Director
Anna Francis, Assistant Acquisitions Editor
Brenna Hosman, Production Coordinator
Katie Huggins, Production Manager
Dan Pyle, Online Publishing Manager
Stephen Williams, Marketing and Publicity Manager
Jennifer L. Witzke, Senior Artist and Book Designer